THE SAD CASE

Script: John Wagner
Art: Carlos Ezquerra
Letters: Tom Frame

Originally published in *2000 AD* Prog 2001

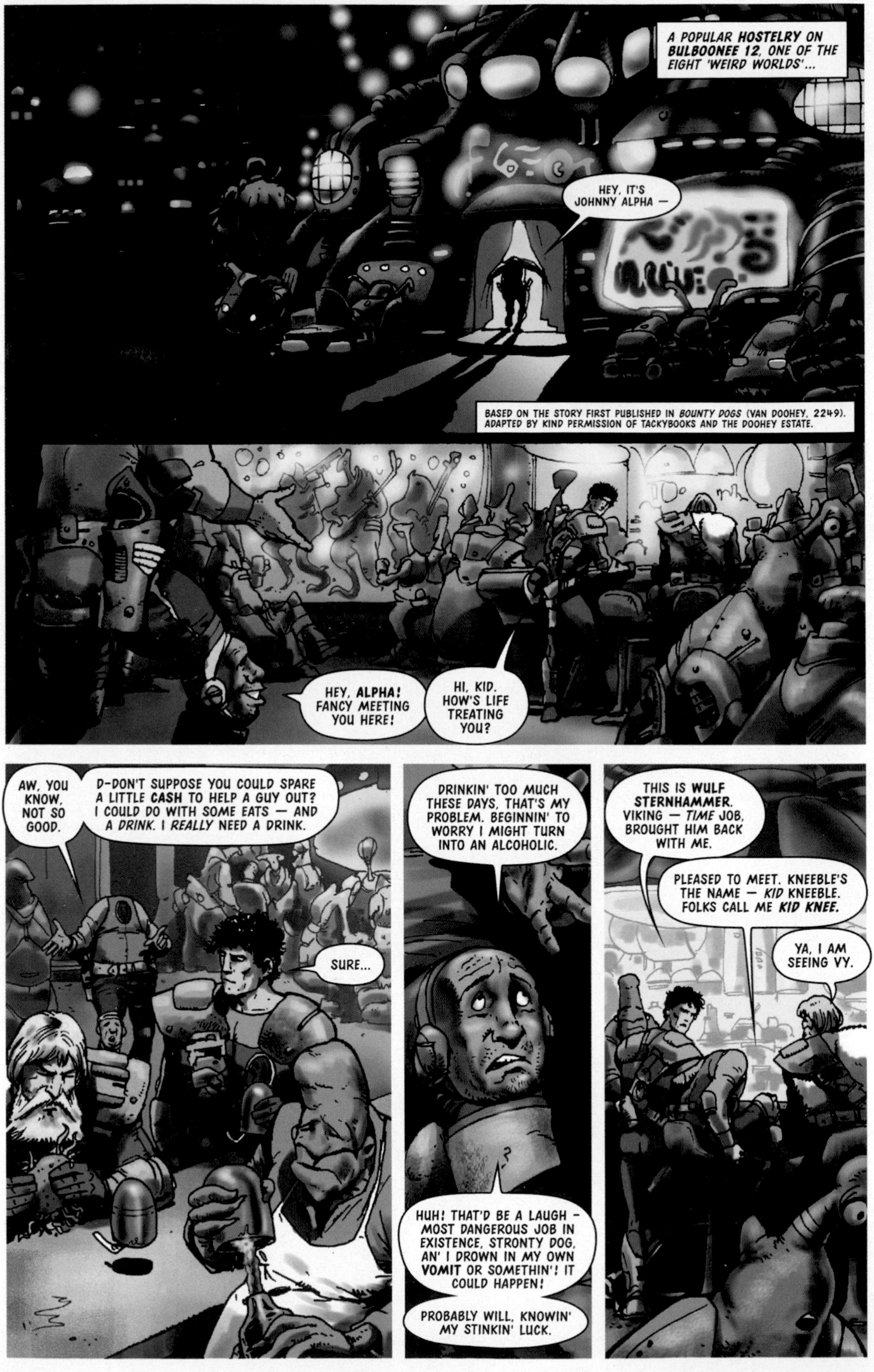
A POPULAR HOSTELRY ON BULBOONEE 12, ONE OF THE EIGHT 'WEIRD WORLDS'...
HEY, IT'S JOHNNY ALPHA —
BASED ON THE STORY FIRST PUBLISHED IN BOUNTY DOGS (VAN DOOHEY, 2249). ADAPTED BY KIND PERMISSION OF TACKYBOOKS AND THE DOOHEY ESTATE.
HEY, ALPHA! FANCY MEETING YOU HERE!
HI, KID. HOW'S LIFE TREATING YOU?
AW, YOU KNOW, NOT SO GOOD.
D-DON'T SUPPOSE YOU COULD SPARE A LITTLE CASH TO HELP A GUY OUT? I COULD DO WITH SOME EATS — AND A DRINK. I REALLY NEED A DRINK.
SURE...
DRINKIN' TOO MUCH THESE DAYS, THAT'S MY PROBLEM. BEGINNIN' TO WORRY I MIGHT TURN INTO AN ALCOHOLIC.
HUH! THAT'D BE A LAUGH - MOST DANGEROUS JOB IN EXISTENCE, STRONTY DOG, AN' I DROWN IN MY OWN VOMIT OR SOMETHIN'! IT COULD HAPPEN!
PROBABLY WILL, KNOWIN' MY STINKIN' LUCK.
THIS IS WULF STERNHAMMER. VIKING — TIME JOB, BROUGHT HIM BACK WITH ME.
PLEASED TO MEET. KNEEBLE'S THE NAME — KID KNEEBLE. FOLKS CALL ME KID KNEE.
YA, I AM SEEING VY.

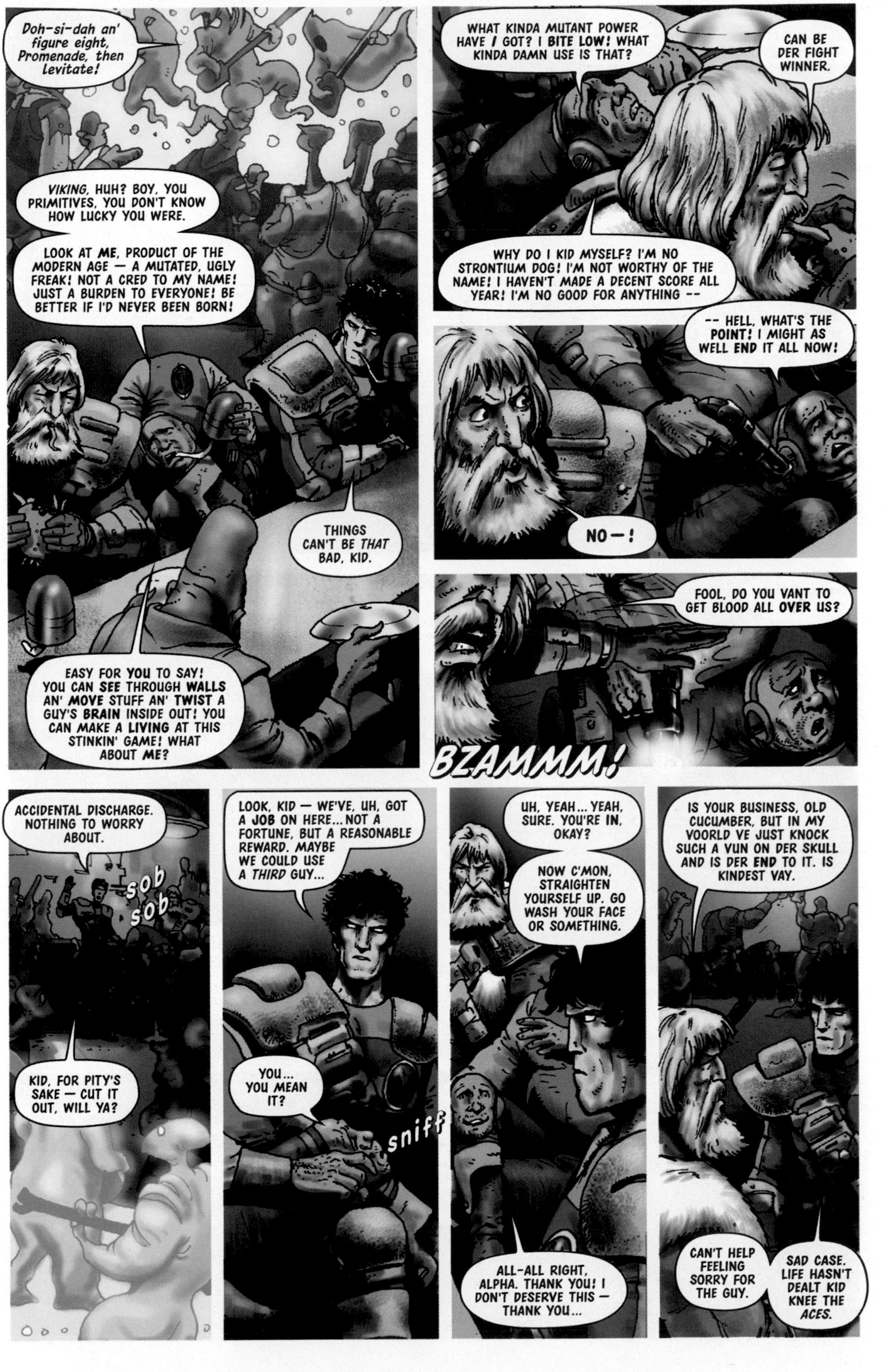
Doh-si-dah an' figure eight, Promenade, then levitate!
VIKING, HUH? BOY, YOU PRIMITIVES, YOU DON'T KNOW HOW LUCKY YOU WERE.
LOOK AT ME, PRODUCT OF THE MODERN AGE — A MUTATED, UGLY FREAK! NOT A CRED TO MY NAME! JUST A BURDEN TO EVERYONE! BE BETTER IF I'D NEVER BEEN BORN!
THINGS CAN'T BE THAT BAD, KID.
EASY FOR YOU TO SAY! YOU CAN SEE THROUGH WALLS AN' MOVE STUFF AN' TWIST A GUY'S BRAIN INSIDE OUT! YOU CAN MAKE A LIVING AT THIS STINKIN' GAME! WHAT ABOUT ME?
WHAT KINDA MUTANT POWER HAVE I GOT? I BITE LOW! WHAT KINDA DAMN USE IS THAT?
CAN BE DER FIGHT WINNER.
WHY DO I KID MYSELF? I'M NO STRONTIUM DOG! I'M NOT WORTHY OF THE NAME! I HAVEN'T MADE A DECENT SCORE ALL YEAR! I'M NO GOOD FOR ANYTHING --
-- HELL, WHAT'S THE POINT! I MIGHT AS WELL END IT ALL NOW!
NO—!
FOOL, DO YOU VANT TO GET BLOOD ALL OVER US?
BZAMMM!
ACCIDENTAL DISCHARGE. NOTHING TO WORRY ABOUT.
sob sob
KID, FOR PITY'S SAKE — CUT IT OUT, WILL YA?
LOOK, KID — WE'VE, UH, GOT A JOB ON HERE... NOT A FORTUNE, BUT A REASONABLE REWARD. MAYBE WE COULD USE A THIRD GUY...
YOU... YOU MEAN IT?
sniff
UH, YEAH... YEAH, SURE. YOU'RE IN, OKAY?
NOW C'MON, STRAIGHTEN YOURSELF UP. GO WASH YOUR FACE OR SOMETHING.
ALL-ALL RIGHT, ALPHA. THANK YOU! I DON'T DESERVE THIS — THANK YOU...
IS YOUR BUSINESS, OLD CUCUMBER, BUT IN MY VOORLD VE JUST KNOCK SUCH A VUN ON DER SKULL AND IS DER END TO IT. IS KINDEST VAY.
CAN'T HELP FEELING SORRY FOR THE GUY.
SAD CASE. LIFE HASN'T DEALT KID KNEE THE ACES.

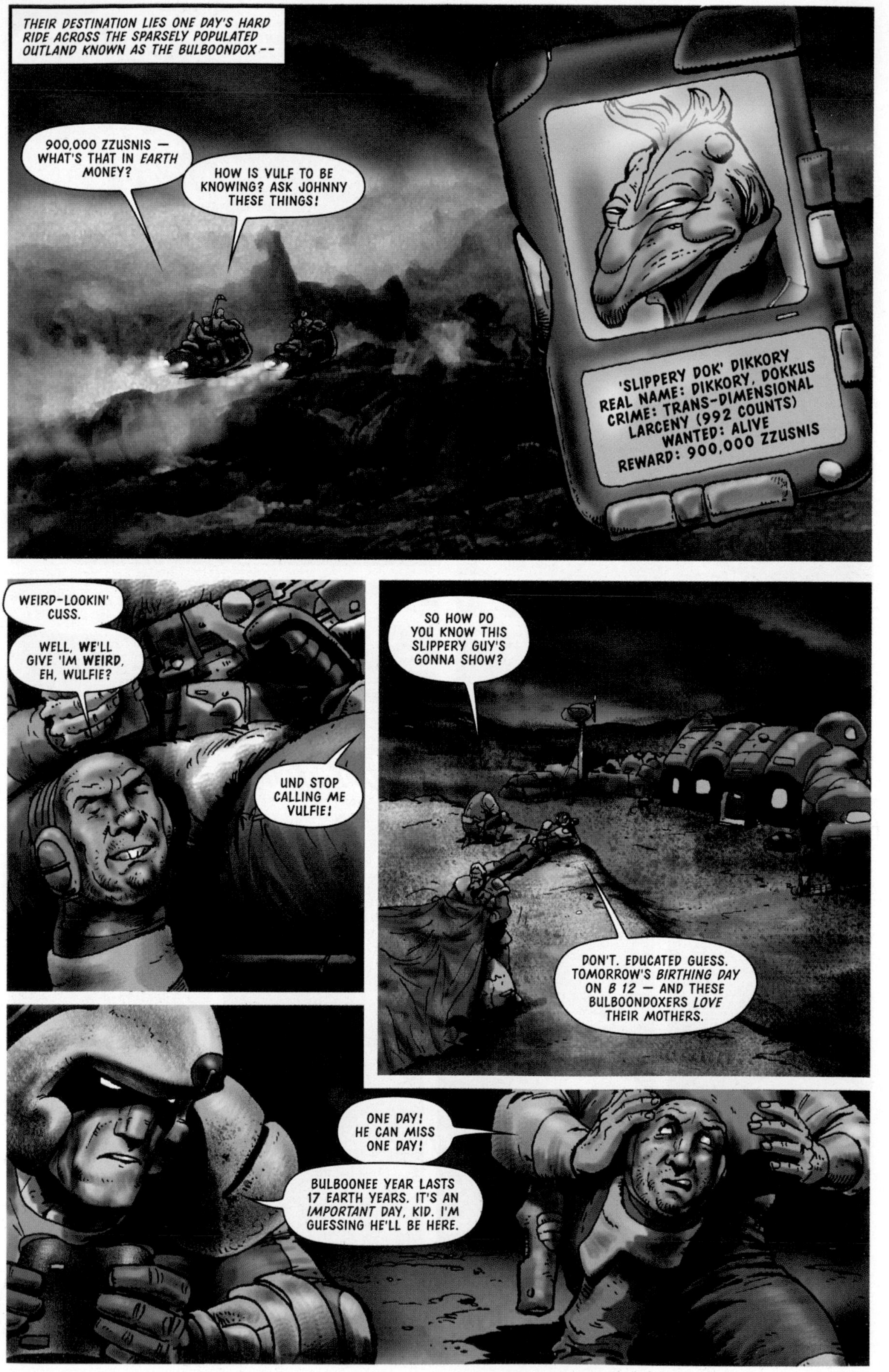
THEIR DESTINATION LIES ONE DAY'S HARD RIDE ACROSS THE SPARSELY POPULATED OUTLAND KNOWN AS THE BULBOONDOX --
900,000 ZZUSNIS — WHAT'S THAT IN EARTH MONEY?
HOW IS VULF TO BE KNOWING? ASK JOHNNY THESE THINGS!
'SLIPPERY DOK' DIKKORY
REAL NAME: DIKKORY, DOKKUS
CRIME: TRANS-DIMENSIONAL LARCENY (992 COUNTS)
WANTED: ALIVE
REWARD: 900,000 ZZUSNIS
WEIRD-LOOKIN' CUSS.
WELL, WE'LL GIVE 'IM WEIRD, EH, WULFIE?
UND STOP CALLING ME VULFIE!
SO HOW DO YOU KNOW THIS SLIPPERY GUY'S GONNA SHOW?
DON'T. EDUCATED GUESS. TOMORROW'S BIRTHING DAY ON B 12 — AND THESE BULBOONDOXERS LOVE THEIR MOTHERS.
ONE DAY! HE CAN MISS ONE DAY!
BULBOONEE YEAR LASTS 17 EARTH YEARS. IT'S AN IMPORTANT DAY, KID. I'M GUESSING HE'LL BE HERE.

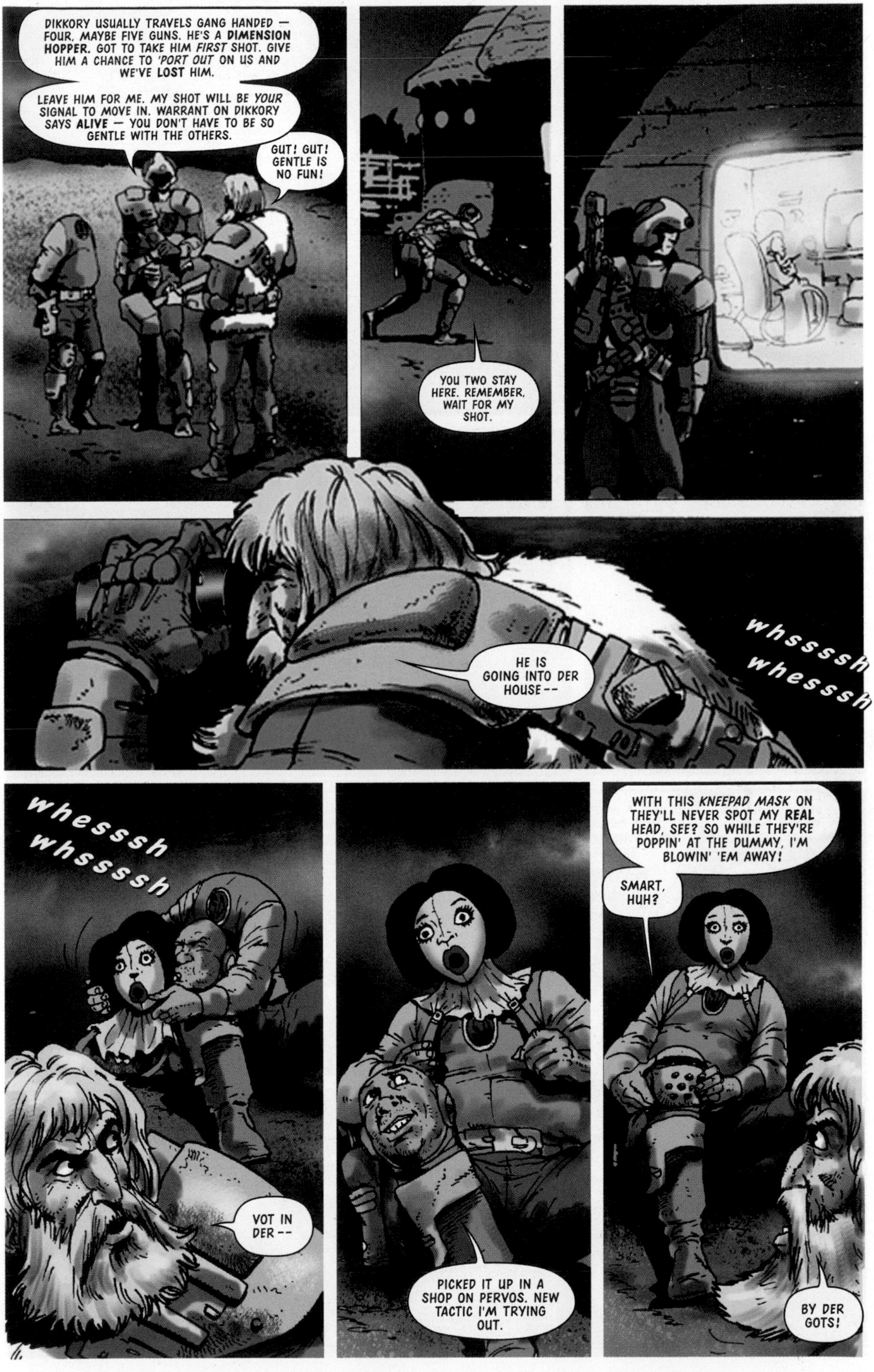
DIKKORY USUALLY TRAVELS GANG HANDED — FOUR, MAYBE FIVE GUNS. HE'S A DIMENSION HOPPER. GOT TO TAKE HIM FIRST SHOT. GIVE HIM A CHANCE TO 'PORT OUT ON US AND WE'VE LOST HIM.
LEAVE HIM FOR ME. MY SHOT WILL BE YOUR SIGNAL TO MOVE IN. WARRANT ON DIKKORY SAYS ALIVE — YOU DON'T HAVE TO BE SO GENTLE WITH THE OTHERS.
GUT! GUT! GENTLE IS NO FUN!
YOU TWO STAY HERE. REMEMBER, WAIT FOR MY SHOT.
HE IS GOING INTO DER HOUSE--
whsssssh
whessssh
whesssh
whssssh
VOT IN DER--
PICKED IT UP IN A SHOP ON PERVOS. NEW TACTIC I'M TRYING OUT.
WITH THIS KNEEPAD MASK ON THEY'LL NEVER SPOT MY REAL HEAD, SEE? SO WHILE THEY'RE POPPIN' AT THE DUMMY, I'M BLOWIN' 'EM AWAY!
SMART, HUH?
BY DER GOTS!

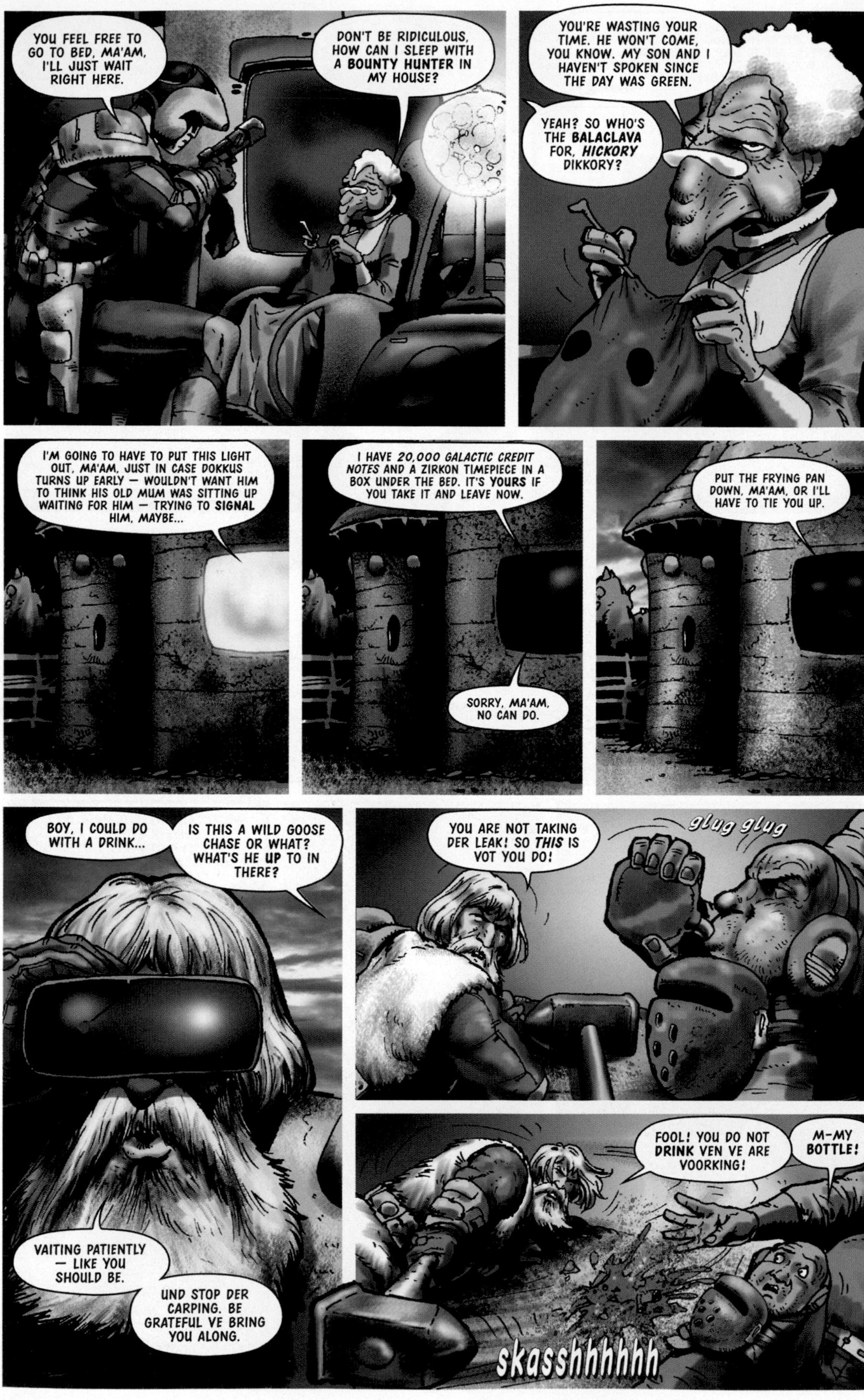
YOU FEEL FREE TO GO TO BED, MA'AM, I'LL JUST WAIT RIGHT HERE.
DON'T BE RIDICULOUS, HOW CAN I SLEEP WITH A **BOUNTY HUNTER** IN MY HOUSE?
YOU'RE WASTING YOUR TIME. HE WON'T COME, YOU KNOW. MY SON AND I HAVEN'T SPOKEN SINCE THE DAY WAS GREEN.
YEAH? SO WHO'S THE **BALACLAVA** FOR, ***HICKORY*** DIKKORY?
I'M GOING TO HAVE TO PUT THIS LIGHT OUT, *MA'AM*, JUST IN CASE DOKKUS TURNS UP EARLY — WOULDN'T WANT HIM TO THINK HIS OLD **MUM** WAS SITTING UP WAITING FOR HIM — TRYING TO **SIGNAL** HIM, MAYBE...
I HAVE *20,000 GALACTIC CREDIT NOTES* AND A ZIRKON TIMEPIECE IN A BOX UNDER THE BED. IT'S **YOURS** IF YOU TAKE IT AND LEAVE NOW.
SORRY, MA'AM, NO CAN DO.
PUT THE FRYING PAN DOWN, MA'AM, OR I'LL HAVE TO TIE YOU UP.
BOY, I COULD DO WITH A DRINK...
IS THIS A WILD GOOSE CHASE OR WHAT? WHAT'S HE **UP** TO IN THERE?
VAITING PATIENTLY — LIKE YOU SHOULD BE.
UND STOP DER CARPING. BE GRATEFUL VE BRING YOU ALONG.
YOU ARE NOT TAKING DER LEAK! SO ***THIS*** IS VOT YOU DO!
glug glug
FOOL! YOU DO NOT **DRINK** VEN VE ARE VOORKING!
M-MY **BOTTLE!**
skasshhhhhh

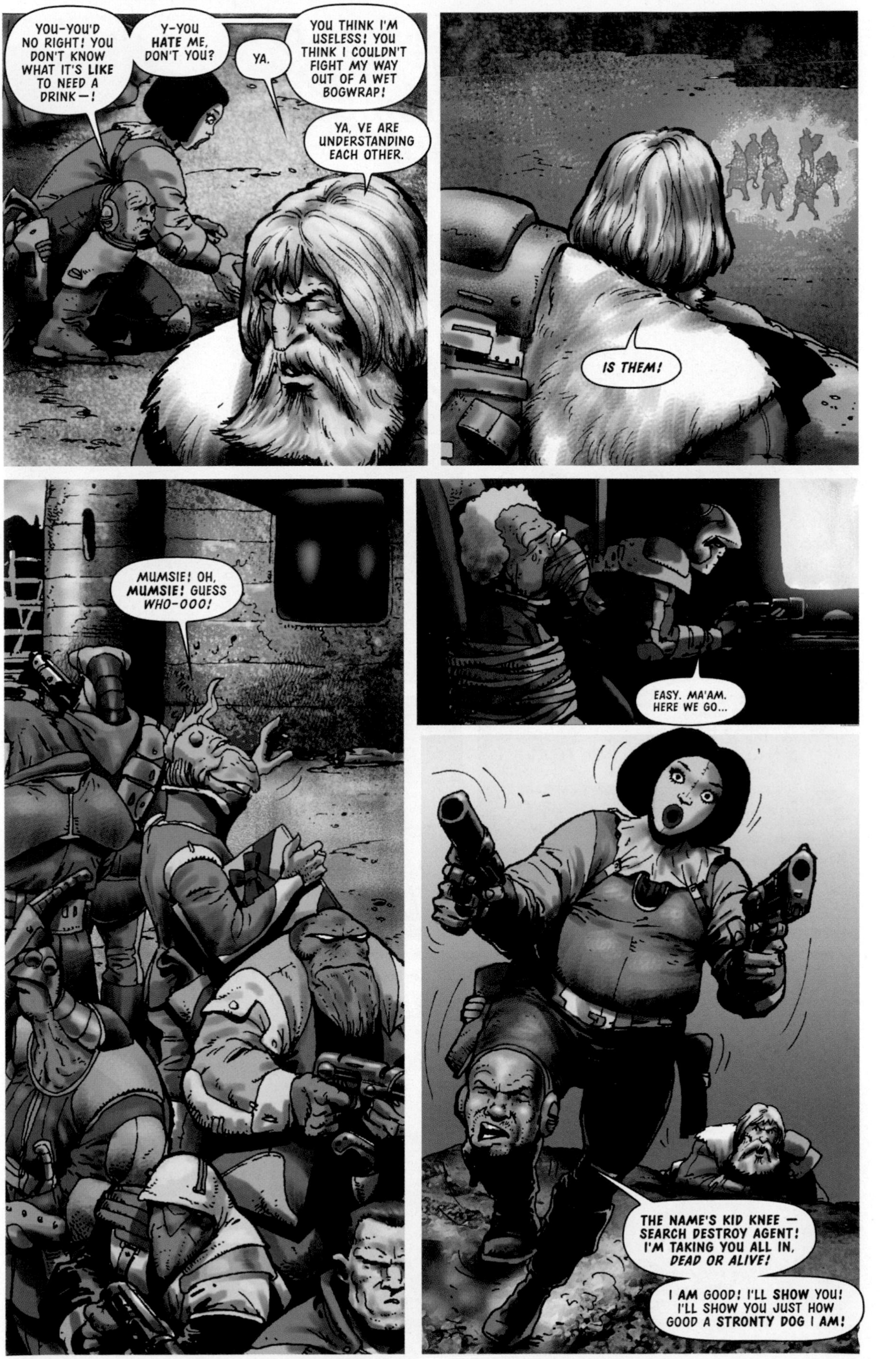
YOU-YOU'D NO RIGHT! YOU DON'T KNOW WHAT IT'S LIKE TO NEED A DRINK—!
Y-YOU HATE ME, DON'T YOU?
YA.
YOU THINK I'M USELESS! YOU THINK I COULDN'T FIGHT MY WAY OUT OF A WET BOGWRAP!
YA, VE ARE UNDERSTANDING EACH OTHER.
IS THEM!
MUMSIE! OH, MUMSIE! GUESS WHO-OOO!
EASY. MA'AM. HERE WE GO...
THE NAME'S KID KNEE — SEARCH DESTROY AGENT! I'M TAKING YOU ALL IN, DEAD OR ALIVE!
I AM GOOD! I'LL SHOW YOU! I'LL SHOW YOU JUST HOW GOOD A STRONTY DOG I AM!

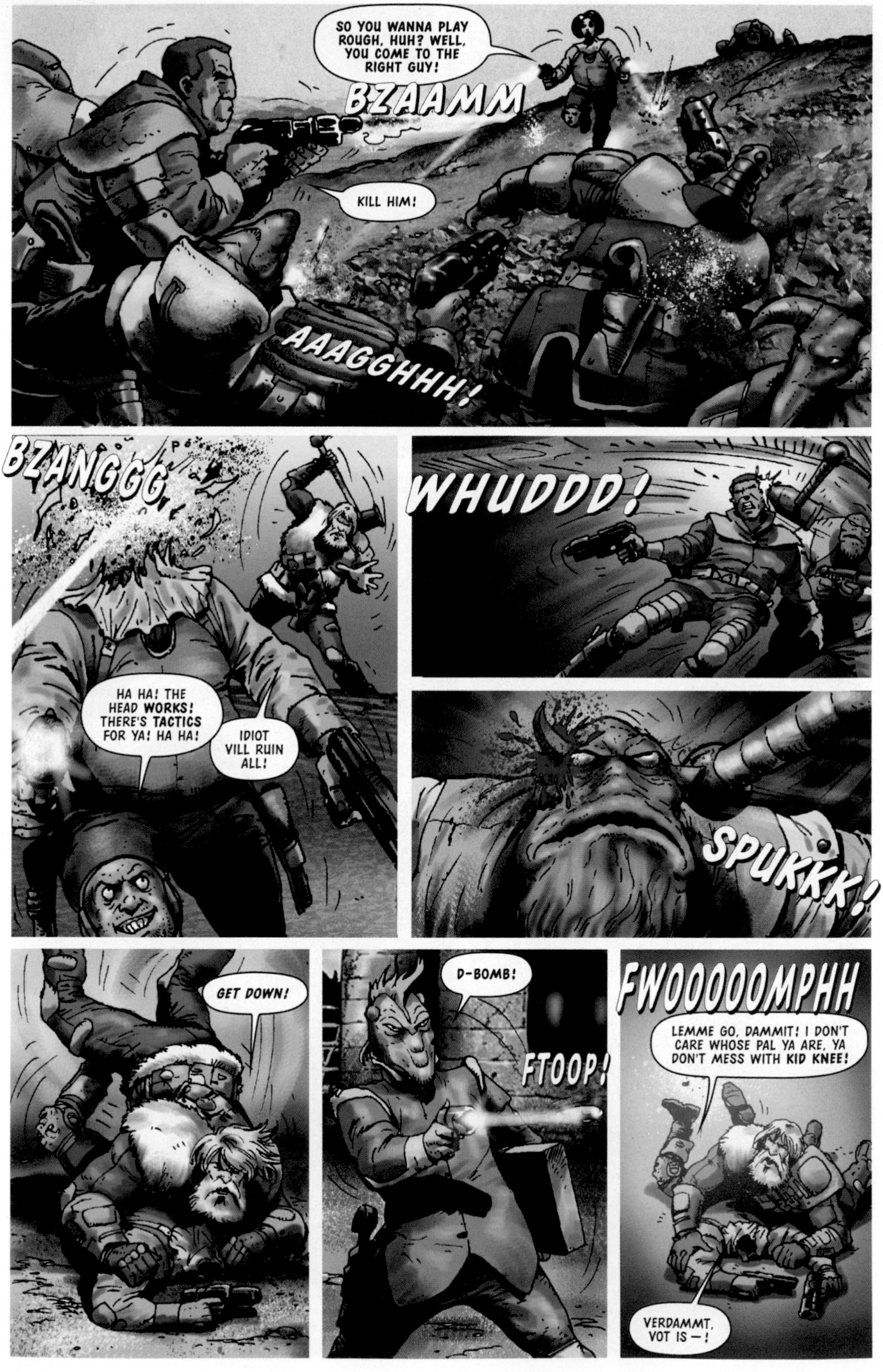

SO YOU WANNA PLAY ROUGH, HUH? WELL, YOU COME TO THE RIGHT GUY!
BZAAMM
KILL HIM!
AAAGGHHH!
BZANGGG
HA HA! THE HEAD WORKS! THERE'S TACTICS FOR YA! HA HA!
IDIOT VILL RUIN ALL!
WHUDDD!
SPUKKK!
GET DOWN!
D-BOMB!
FTOOP!
FWOOOOOMPHH
LEMME GO, DAMMIT! I DON'T CARE WHOSE PAL YA ARE, YA DON'T MESS WITH KID KNEE!
VERDAMMT, VOT IS —!

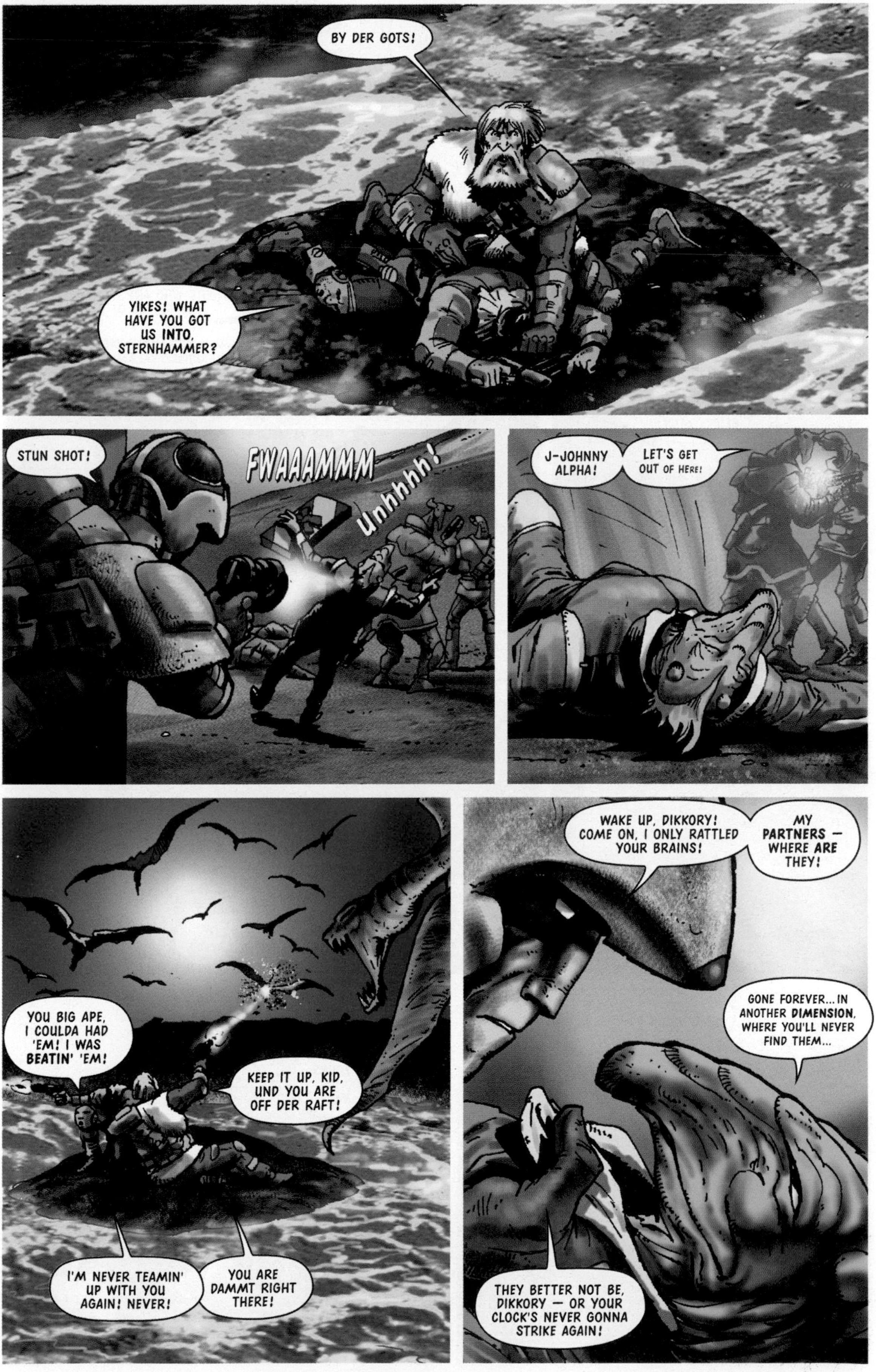
BY DER GOTS!
YIKES! WHAT HAVE YOU GOT US INTO, STERNHAMMER?
STUN SHOT!
FWAAAMMM
Unnhhh!
J-JOHNNY ALPHA!
LET'S GET OUT OF HERE!
YOU BIG APE, I COULDA HAD 'EM! I WAS BEATIN' 'EM!
KEEP IT UP, KID, UND YOU ARE OFF DER RAFT!
I'M NEVER TEAMIN' UP WITH YOU AGAIN! NEVER!
YOU ARE DAMMT RIGHT THERE!
WAKE UP, DIKKORY! COME ON, I ONLY RATTLED YOUR BRAINS!
MY PARTNERS — WHERE ARE THEY!
GONE FOREVER... IN ANOTHER DIMENSION, WHERE YOU'LL NEVER FIND THEM...
THEY BETTER NOT BE, DIKKORY — OR YOUR CLOCK'S NEVER GONNA STRIKE AGAIN!

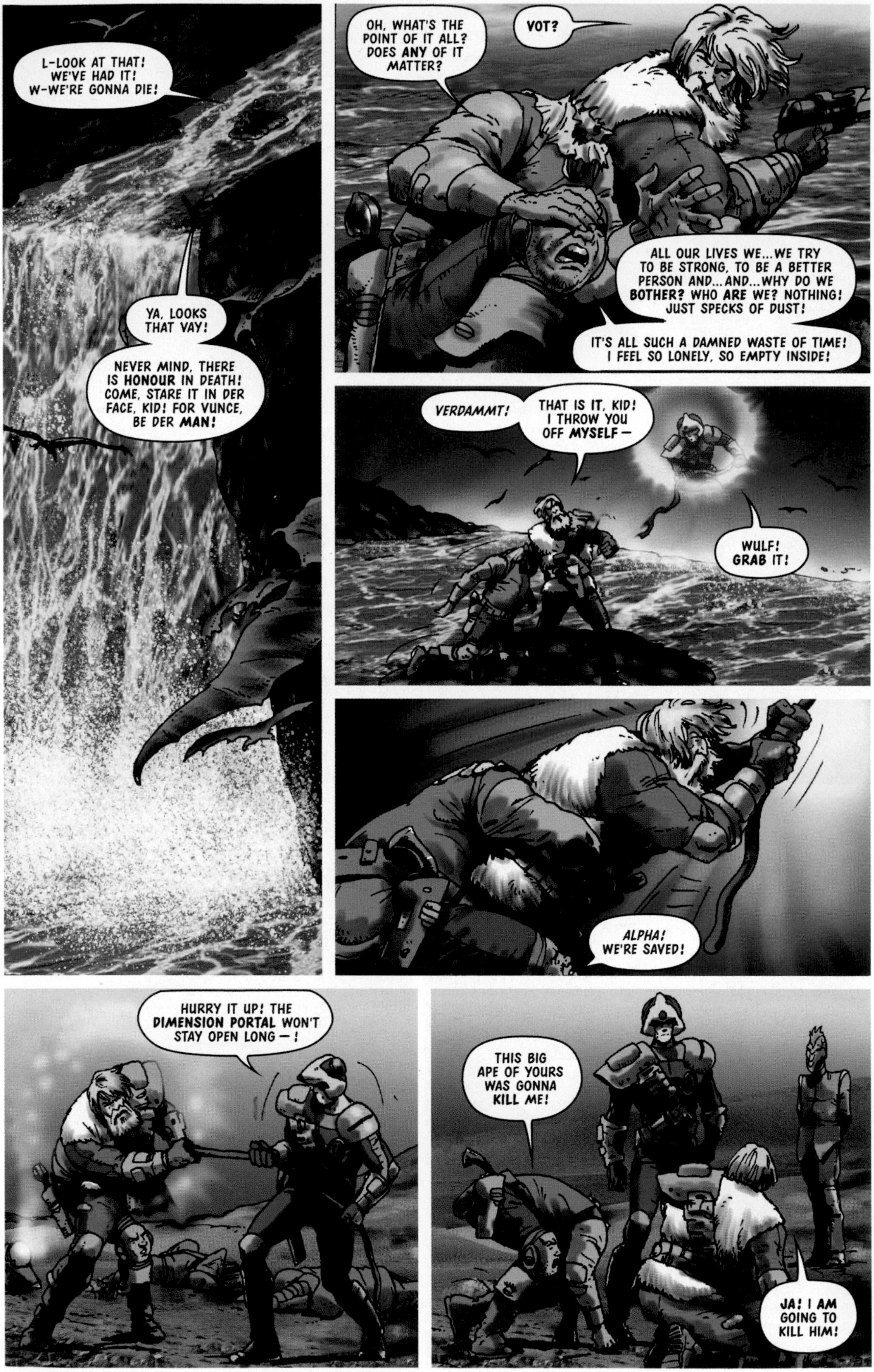
L-LOOK AT THAT! WE'VE HAD IT! W-WE'RE GONNA DIE!
YA, LOOKS THAT VAY!
NEVER MIND, THERE IS HONOUR IN DEATH! COME, STARE IT IN DER FACE, KID! FOR VUNCE, BE DER MAN!
OH, WHAT'S THE POINT OF IT ALL? DOES ANY OF IT MATTER?
VOT?
ALL OUR LIVES WE... WE TRY TO BE STRONG, TO BE A BETTER PERSON AND... AND... WHY DO WE BOTHER? WHO ARE WE? NOTHING! JUST SPECKS OF DUST!
IT'S ALL SUCH A DAMNED WASTE OF TIME! I FEEL SO LONELY, SO EMPTY INSIDE!
VERDAMMT!
THAT IS IT, KID! I THROW YOU OFF MYSELF —
WULF! GRAB IT!
ALPHA! WE'RE SAVED!
HURRY IT UP! THE DIMENSION PORTAL WON'T STAY OPEN LONG —!
THIS BIG APE OF YOURS WAS GONNA KILL ME!
JA! I AM GOING TO KILL HIM!

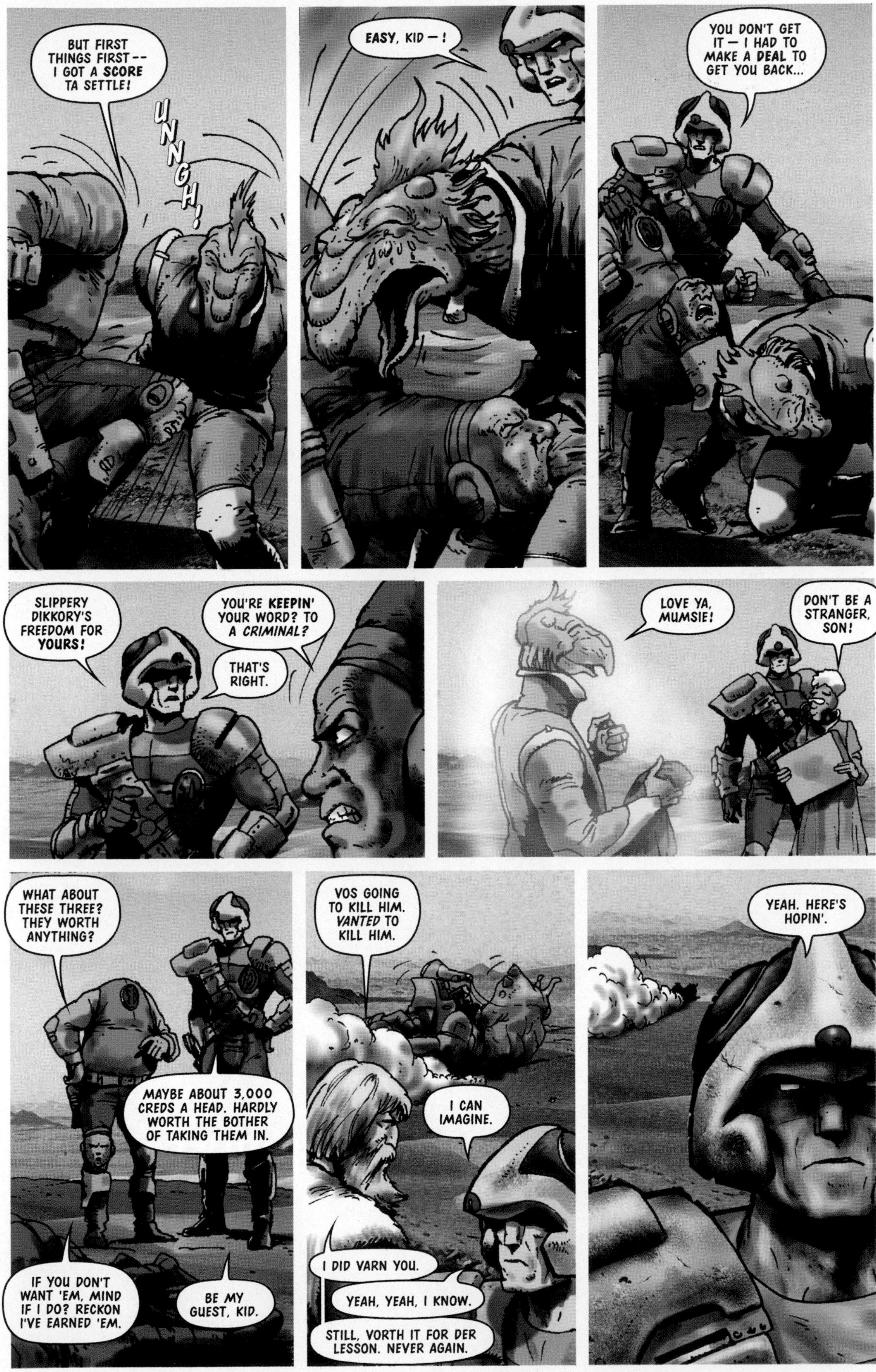
BUT FIRST THINGS FIRST-- I GOT A SCORE TA SETTLE!
UNNGH!
EASY, KID — !
YOU DON'T GET IT — I HAD TO MAKE A DEAL TO GET YOU BACK...
SLIPPERY DIKKORY'S FREEDOM FOR YOURS!
YOU'RE KEEPIN' YOUR WORD? TO A CRIMINAL?
THAT'S RIGHT.
LOVE YA, MUMSIE!
DON'T BE A STRANGER, SON!
WHAT ABOUT THESE THREE? THEY WORTH ANYTHING?
MAYBE ABOUT 3,000 CREDS A HEAD. HARDLY WORTH THE BOTHER OF TAKING THEM IN.
IF YOU DON'T WANT 'EM, MIND IF I DO? RECKON I'VE EARNED 'EM.
BE MY GUEST, KID.
VOS GOING TO KILL HIM. VANTED TO KILL HIM.
I CAN IMAGINE.
I DID VARN YOU.
YEAH, YEAH, I KNOW.
STILL, VORTH IT FOR DER LESSON. NEVER AGAIN.
YEAH. HERE'S HOPIN'.

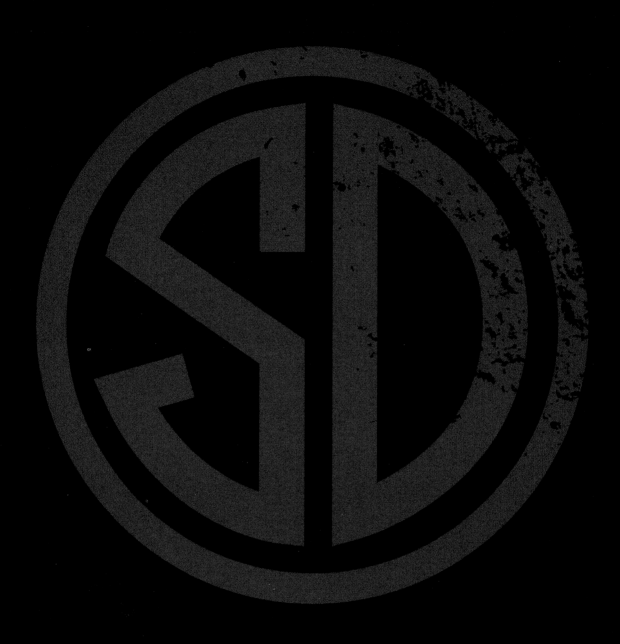

THE HEADLY FOOT JOB

Script: John Wagner
Art: Carlos Ezquerra
Letters: Annie Parkhouse

Originally published in *2000 AD* Prog 1400-1403

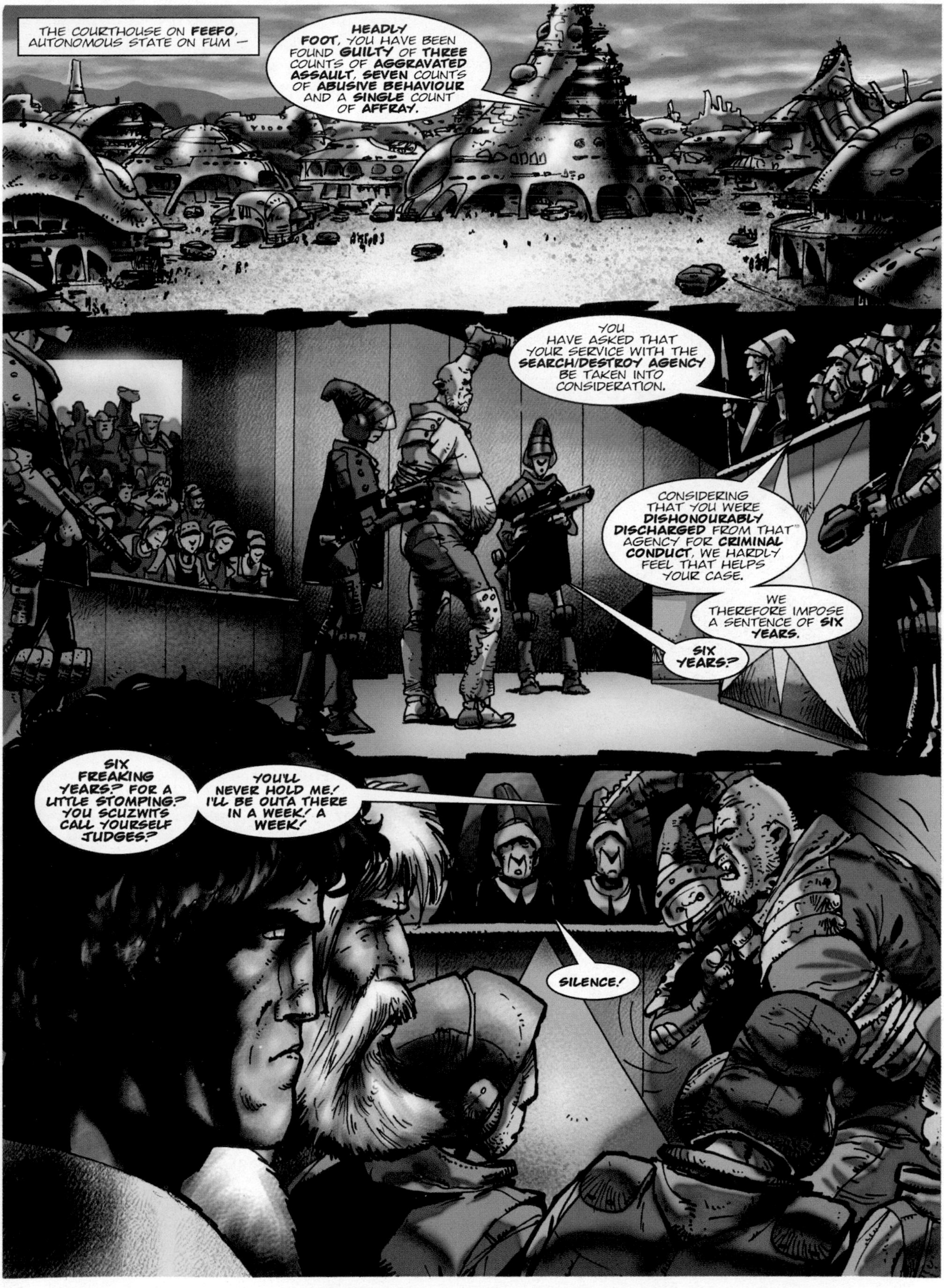
THE COURTHOUSE ON FEEFO, AUTONOMOUS STATE ON FUM —
HEADLY FOOT, YOU HAVE BEEN FOUND GUILTY OF THREE COUNTS OF AGGRAVATED ASSAULT, SEVEN COUNTS OF ABUSIVE BEHAVIOUR AND A SINGLE COUNT OF AFFRAY.
YOU HAVE ASKED THAT YOUR SERVICE WITH THE SEARCH/DESTROY AGENCY BE TAKEN INTO CONSIDERATION.
CONSIDERING THAT YOU WERE DISHONOURABLY DISCHARGED FROM THAT AGENCY FOR CRIMINAL CONDUCT, WE HARDLY FEEL THAT HELPS YOUR CASE.
WE THEREFORE IMPOSE A SENTENCE OF SIX YEARS.
SIX YEARS?
SIX FREAKING YEARS? FOR A LITTLE STOMPING? YOU SCUZWITS CALL YOURSELF JUDGES?
YOU'LL NEVER HOLD ME! I'LL BE OUTA THERE IN A WEEK! A WEEK!
SILENCE!

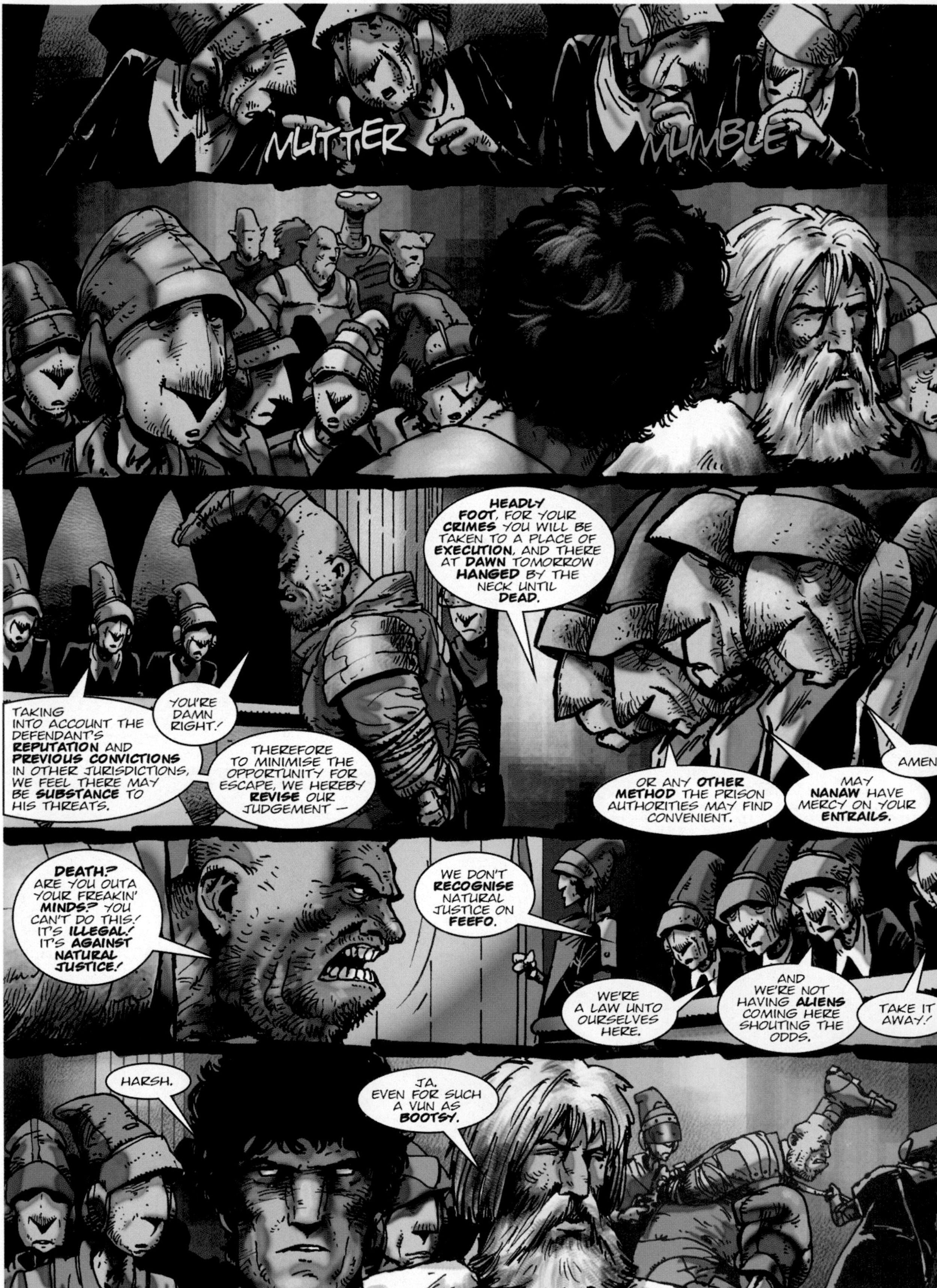
MUTTER
MUMBLE
TAKING INTO ACCOUNT THE DEFENDANT'S REPUTATION AND PREVIOUS CONVICTIONS IN OTHER JURISDICTIONS, WE FEEL THERE MAY BE SUBSTANCE TO HIS THREATS.
YOU'RE DAMN RIGHT!
THEREFORE TO MINIMISE THE OPPORTUNITY FOR ESCAPE, WE HEREBY REVISE OUR JUDGEMENT —
HEADLY FOOT, FOR YOUR CRIMES YOU WILL BE TAKEN TO A PLACE OF EXECUTION, AND THERE AT DAWN TOMORROW HANGED BY THE NECK UNTIL DEAD.
OR ANY OTHER METHOD THE PRISON AUTHORITIES MAY FIND CONVENIENT.
MAY NANAW HAVE MERCY ON YOUR ENTRAILS.
AMEN.
DEATH? ARE YOU OUTA YOUR FREAKIN' MINDS? YOU CAN'T DO THIS! IT'S ILLEGAL! IT'S AGAINST NATURAL JUSTICE!
WE DON'T RECOGNISE NATURAL JUSTICE ON FEEFO.
WE'RE A LAW UNTO OURSELVES HERE.
AND WE'RE NOT HAVING ALIENS COMING HERE SHOUTING THE ODDS.
TAKE IT AWAY!
HARSH.
JA. EVEN FOR SUCH A VUN AS BOOTSY.

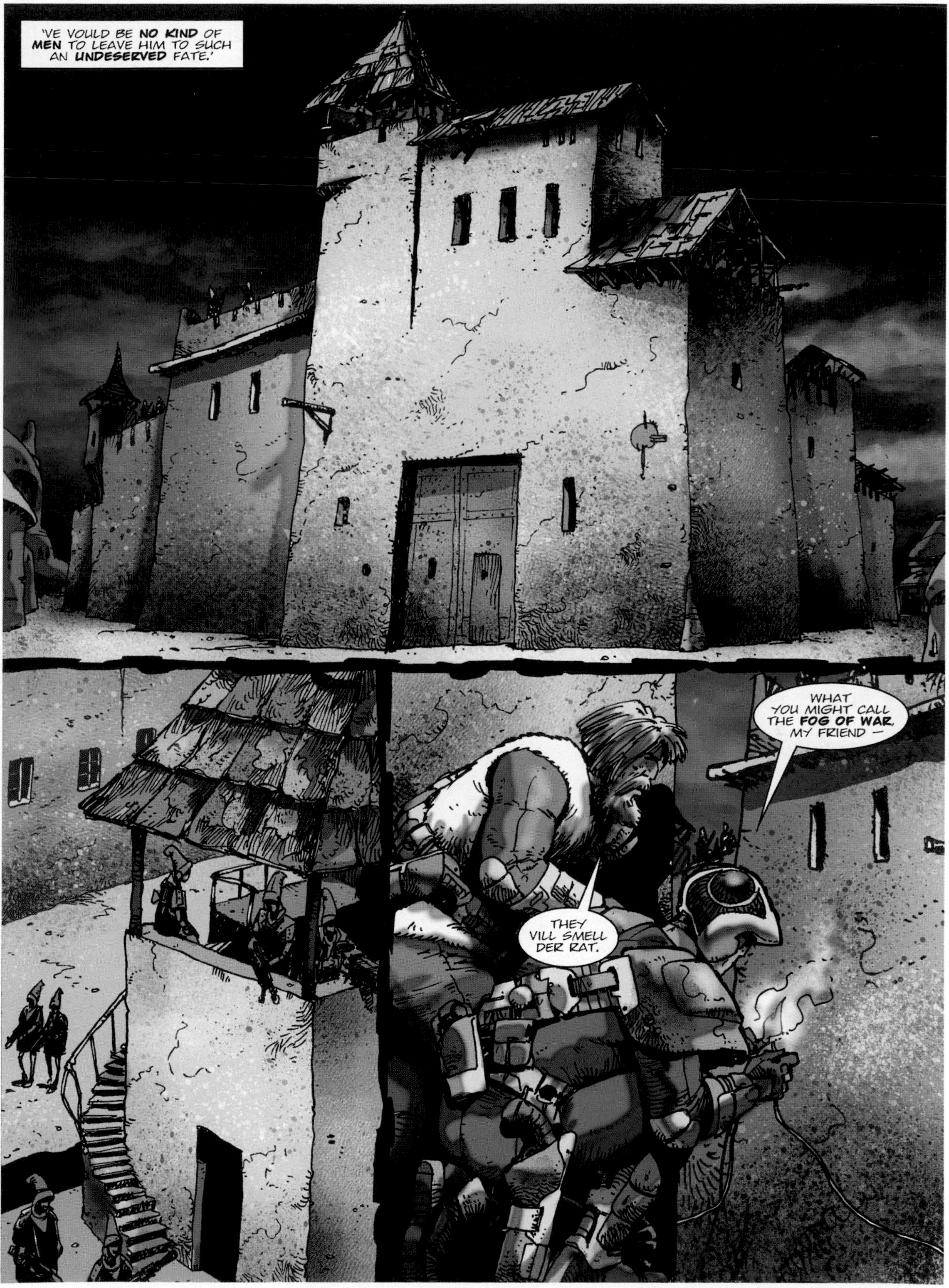
'VE VOULD BE **NO KIND** OF **MEN** TO LEAVE HIM TO SUCH AN **UNDESERVED** FATE.'
WHAT YOU MIGHT CALL THE **FOG OF WAR**, MY FRIEND —
THEY VILL SMELL DER RAT.

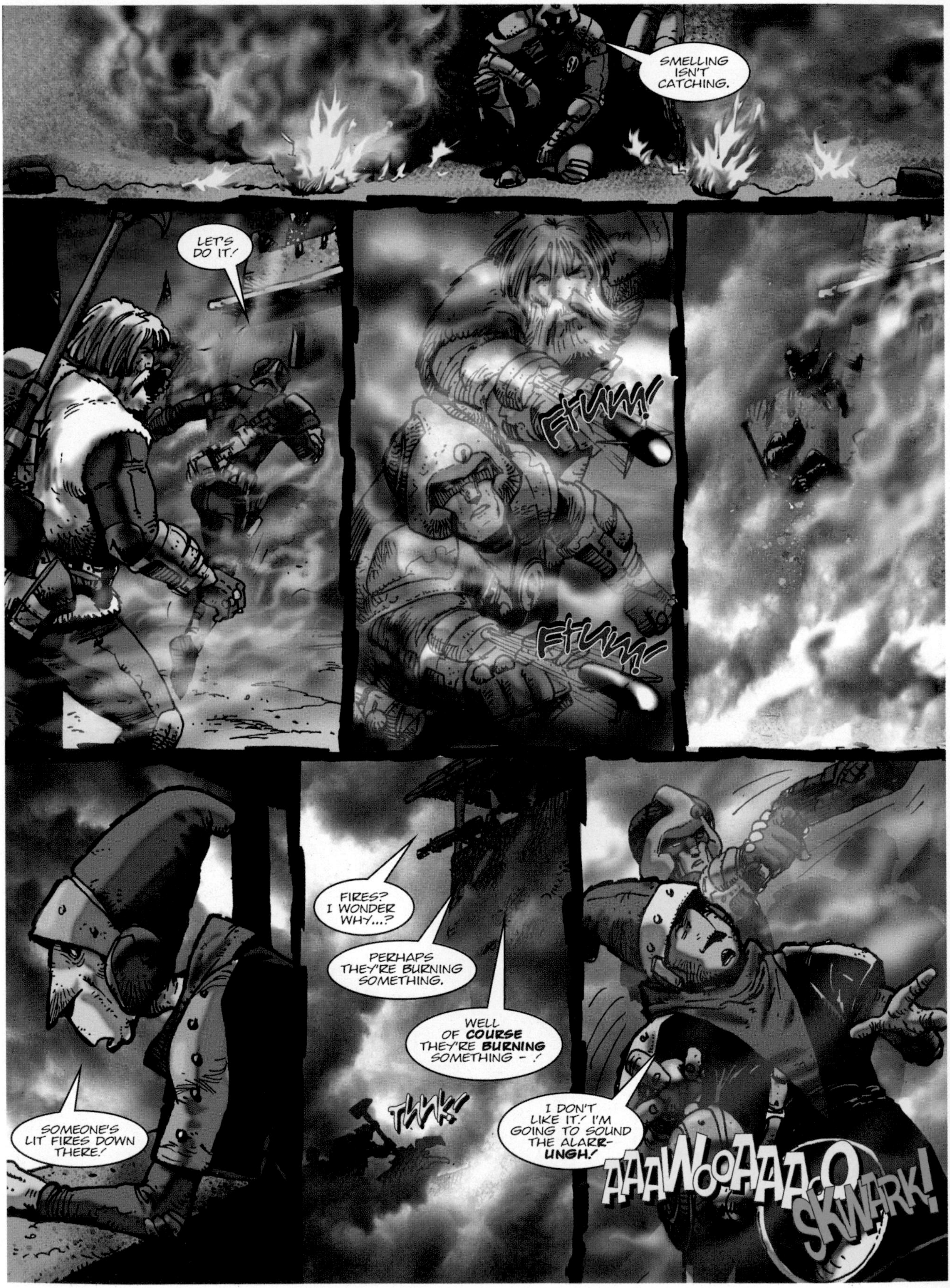
SMELLING ISN'T CATCHING.
LET'S DO IT!
FTUMM!
FTUMM!
SOMEONE'S LIT FIRES DOWN THERE!
FIRES? I WONDER WHY...?
PERHAPS THEY'RE BURNING SOMETHING.
WELL OF COURSE THEY'RE BURNING SOMETHING -!
THNK!
I DON'T LIKE IT! I'M GOING TO SOUND THE ALARR-UNGH!
AAAWOOAAAOO
SKWARK!

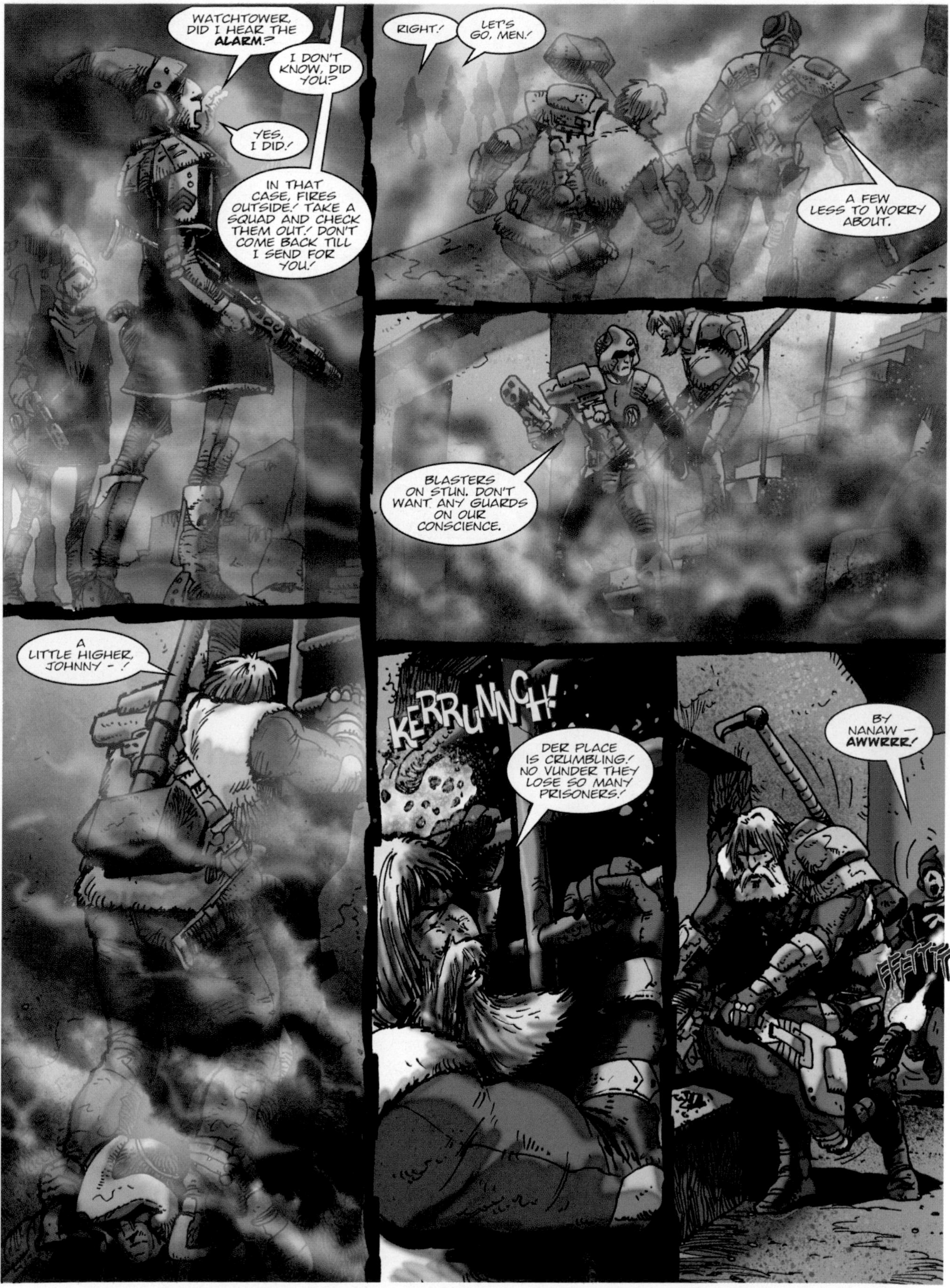
WATCHTOWER, DID I HEAR THE ALARM?
I DON'T KNOW, DID YOU?
YES, I DID!
IN THAT CASE, FIRES OUTSIDE! TAKE A SQUAD AND CHECK THEM OUT! DON'T COME BACK TILL I SEND FOR YOU!
RIGHT!
LET'S GO, MEN!
A FEW LESS TO WORRY ABOUT.
BLASTERS ON STUN. DON'T WANT ANY GUARDS ON OUR CONSCIENCE.
A LITTLE HIGHER, JOHNNY -!
KERRUNNCH!
DER PLACE IS CRUMBLING! NO VUNDER THEY LOSE SO MANY PRISONERS!
BY NANAW — AWWRRR!

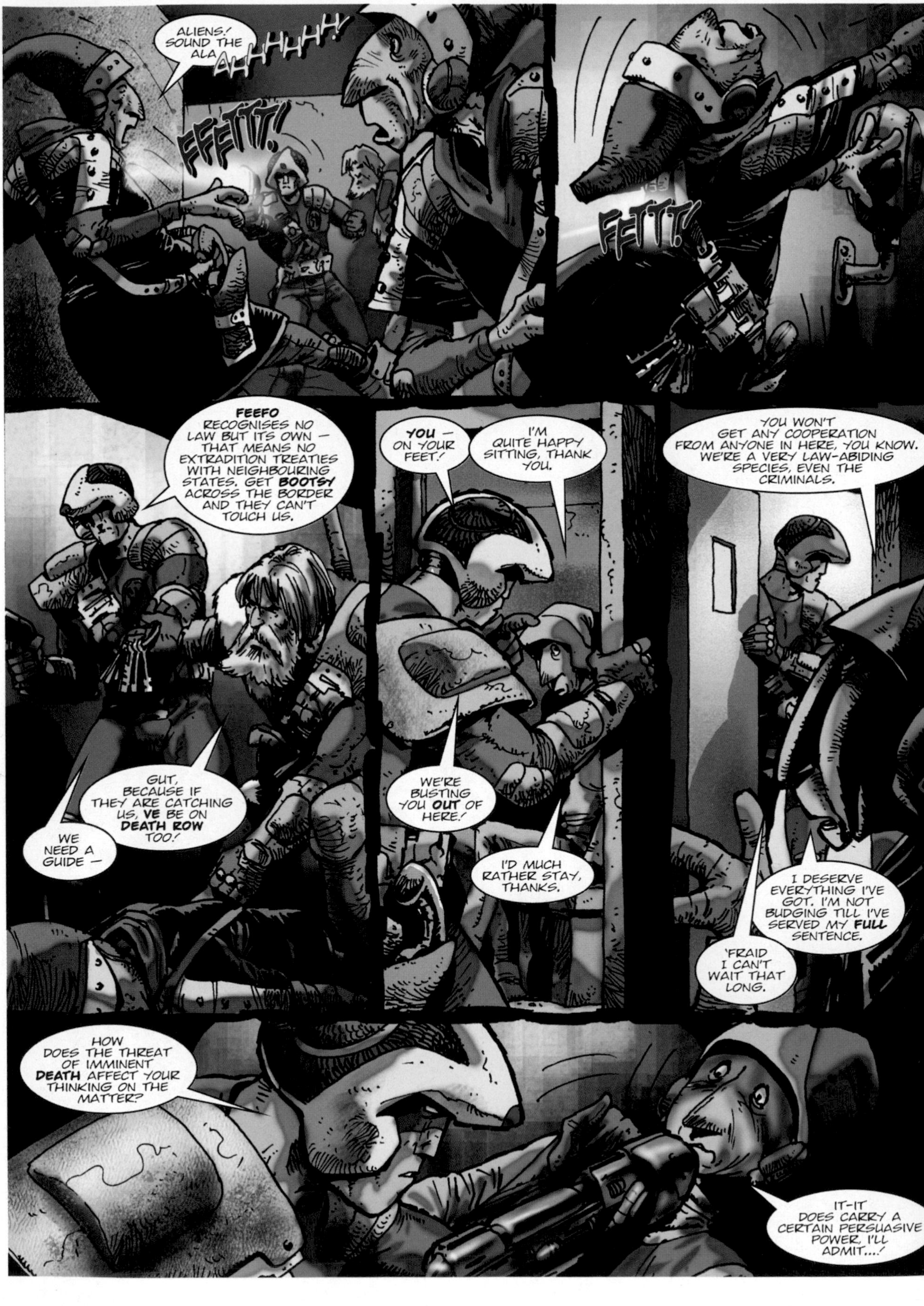

ALIENS! SOUND THE ALA AHHHHHH!
FFFTTT!
FFTTT!
FEEFO RECOGNISES NO LAW BUT ITS OWN — THAT MEANS NO EXTRADITION TREATIES WITH NEIGHBOURING STATES. GET BOOTSY ACROSS THE BORDER AND THEY CAN'T TOUCH US.
WE NEED A GUIDE —
GUT, BECAUSE IF THEY ARE CATCHING US, VE BE ON DEATH ROW TOO!
YOU — ON YOUR FEET!
I'M QUITE HAPPY SITTING, THANK YOU.
WE'RE BUSTING YOU OUT OF HERE!
I'D MUCH RATHER STAY, THANKS.
YOU WON'T GET ANY COOPERATION FROM ANYONE IN HERE, YOU KNOW. WE'RE A VERY LAW-ABIDING SPECIES, EVEN THE CRIMINALS.
I DESERVE EVERYTHING I'VE GOT. I'M NOT BUDGING TILL I'VE SERVED MY FULL SENTENCE.
'FRAID I CAN'T WAIT THAT LONG.
HOW DOES THE THREAT OF IMMINENT DEATH AFFECT YOUR THINKING ON THE MATTER?
IT-IT DOES CARRY A CERTAIN PERSUASIVE POWER, I'LL ADMIT...!

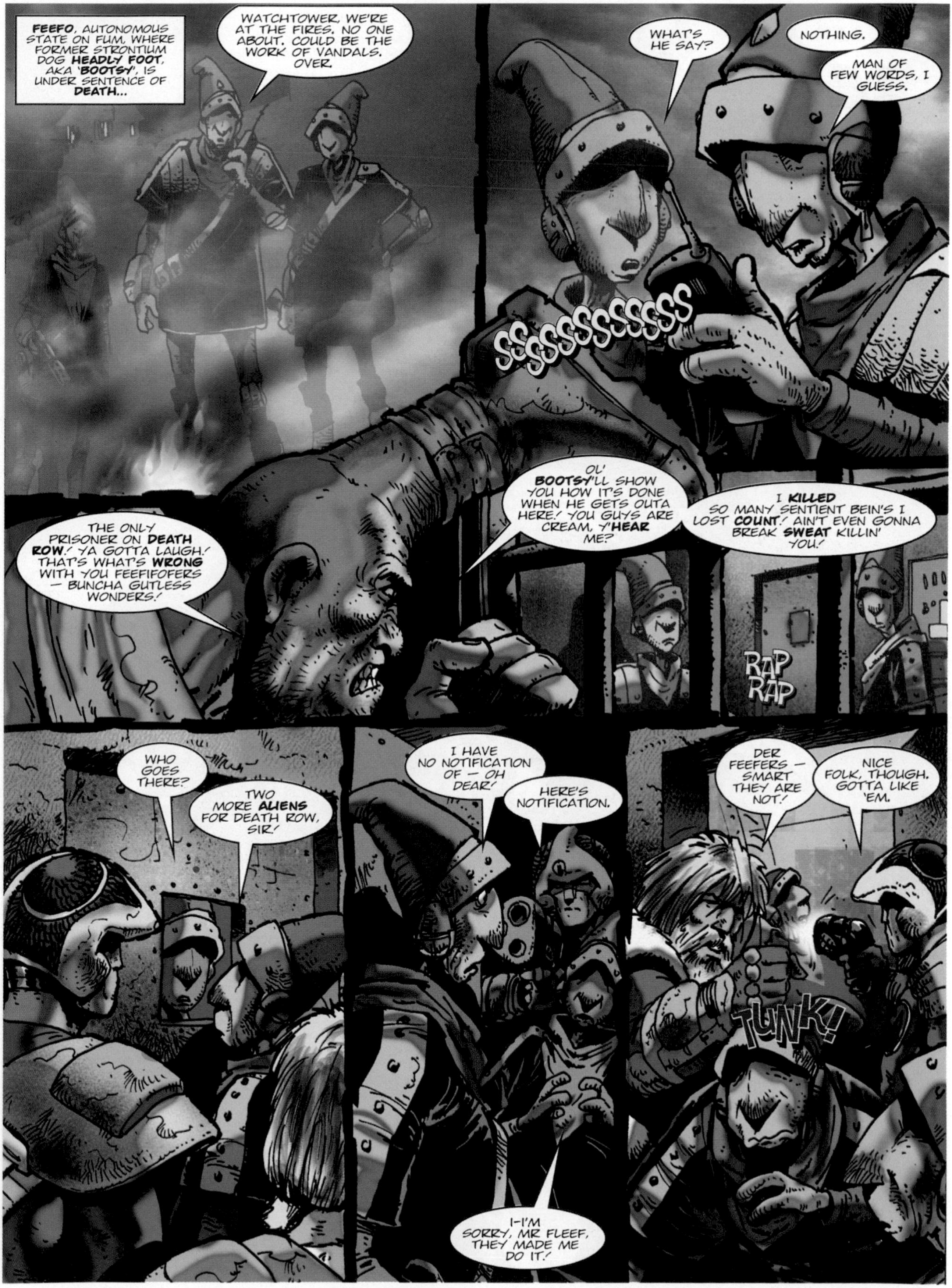
FEEFO, AUTONOMOUS STATE ON FUM, WHERE FORMER STRONTIUM DOG HEADLY FOOT, AKA 'BOOTSY', IS UNDER SENTENCE OF DEATH...
WATCHTOWER, WE'RE AT THE FIRES. NO ONE ABOUT. COULD BE THE WORK OF VANDALS. OVER.
WHAT'S HE SAY?
NOTHING.
MAN OF FEW WORDS, I GUESS.
SSSSSSSSSSSS
THE ONLY PRISONER ON DEATH ROW! YA GOTTA LAUGH! THAT'S WHAT'S WRONG WITH YOU FEEFIFOFERS — BUNCHA GUTLESS WONDERS!
OL' BOOTSY'LL SHOW YOU HOW IT'S DONE WHEN HE GETS OUTA HERE! YOU GUYS ARE CREAM, Y'HEAR ME?
I KILLED SO MANY SENTIENT BEIN'S I LOST COUNT! AIN'T EVEN GONNA BREAK SWEAT KILLIN' YOU!
RAP RAP
WHO GOES THERE?
TWO MORE ALIENS FOR DEATH ROW, SIR!
I HAVE NO NOTIFICATION OF — OH DEAR!
HERE'S NOTIFICATION.
I-I'M SORRY, MR FLEEF, THEY MADE ME DO IT!
DER FEEFERS — SMART THEY ARE NOT!
NICE FOLK, THOUGH. GOTTA LIKE 'EM.
TUNK!

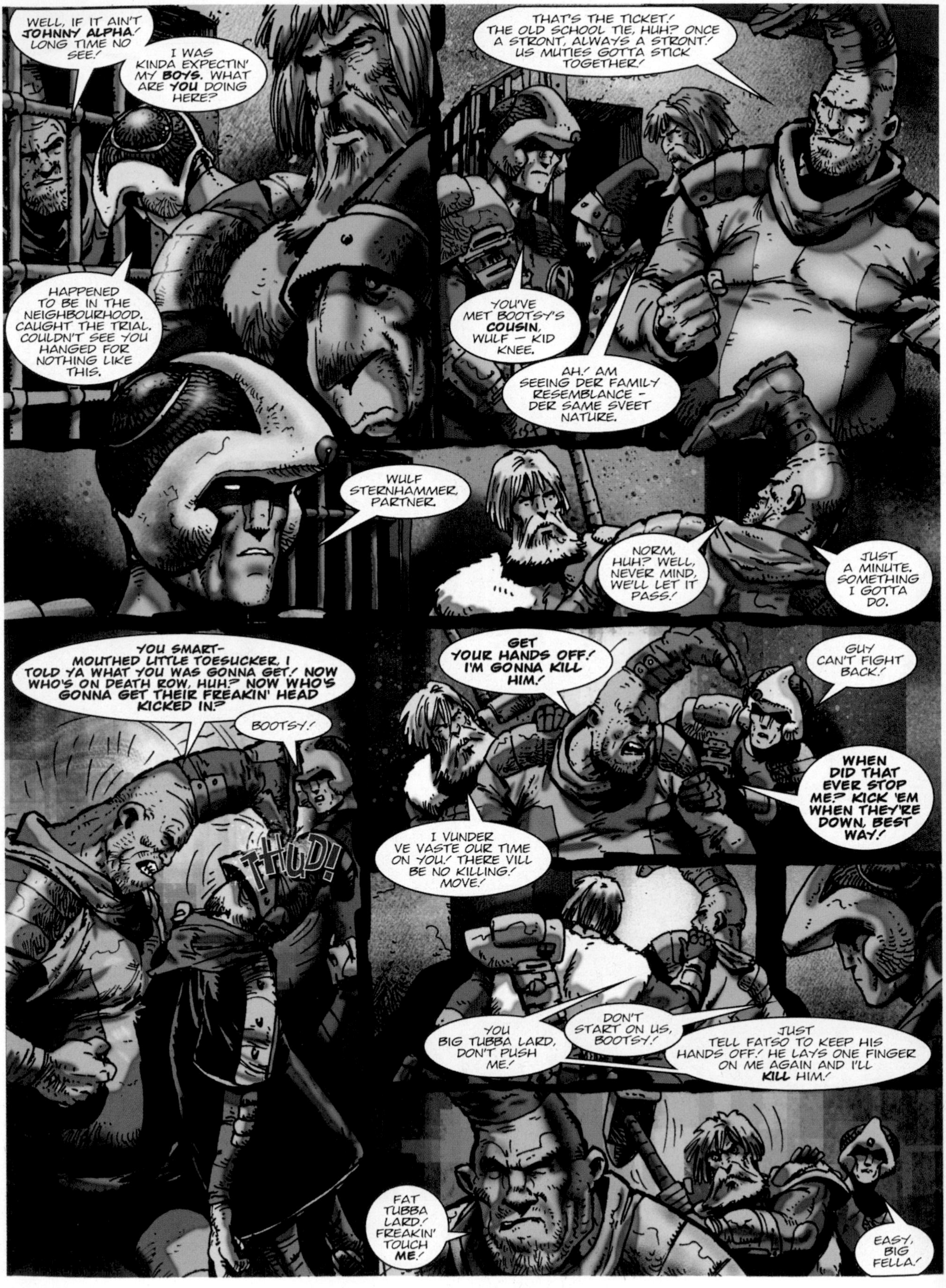

WELL, IF IT AIN'T **JOHNNY ALPHA**! LONG TIME NO SEE!
I WAS KINDA EXPECTIN' MY **BOYS**. WHAT ARE **YOU** DOING HERE?
HAPPENED TO BE IN THE NEIGHBOURHOOD. CAUGHT THE TRIAL. COULDN'T SEE YOU HANGED FOR NOTHING LIKE THIS.
THAT'S THE TICKET! THE OLD SCHOOL TIE, HUH? ONCE A STRONT, ALWAYS A STRONT! US MUTIES GOTTA STICK TOGETHER!
YOU'VE MET BOOTSY'S **COUSIN**, WULF — KID KNEE.
AH! AM SEEING DER FAMILY RESEMBLANCE - DER SAME SVEET NATURE.
WULF STERNHAMMER, PARTNER.
NORM, HUH? WELL, NEVER MIND, WE'LL LET IT PASS!
JUST A MINUTE. SOMETHING I GOTTA DO.
YOU SMART-MOUTHED LITTLE TOESUCKER. I TOLD YA WHAT YOU WAS GONNA GET! NOW WHO'S ON DEATH ROW, HUH? NOW WHO'S GONNA GET THEIR FREAKIN' HEAD KICKED IN?
BOOTSY!
THUD!
GET YOUR HANDS OFF! I'M GONNA KILL HIM!
GUY CAN'T FIGHT BACK!
WHEN DID THAT EVER STOP ME? KICK 'EM WHEN THEY'RE DOWN, BEST WAY!
I VUNDER VE VASTE OUR TIME ON YOU! THERE VILL BE NO KILLING! MOVE!
YOU BIG TUBBA LARD, DON'T PUSH ME!
DON'T START ON US, BOOTSY!
JUST TELL FATSO TO KEEP HIS HANDS OFF! HE LAYS ONE FINGER ON ME AGAIN AND I'LL **KILL** HIM!
FAT TUBBA LARD! FREAKIN' TOUCH **ME**!
EASY, BIG FELLA!

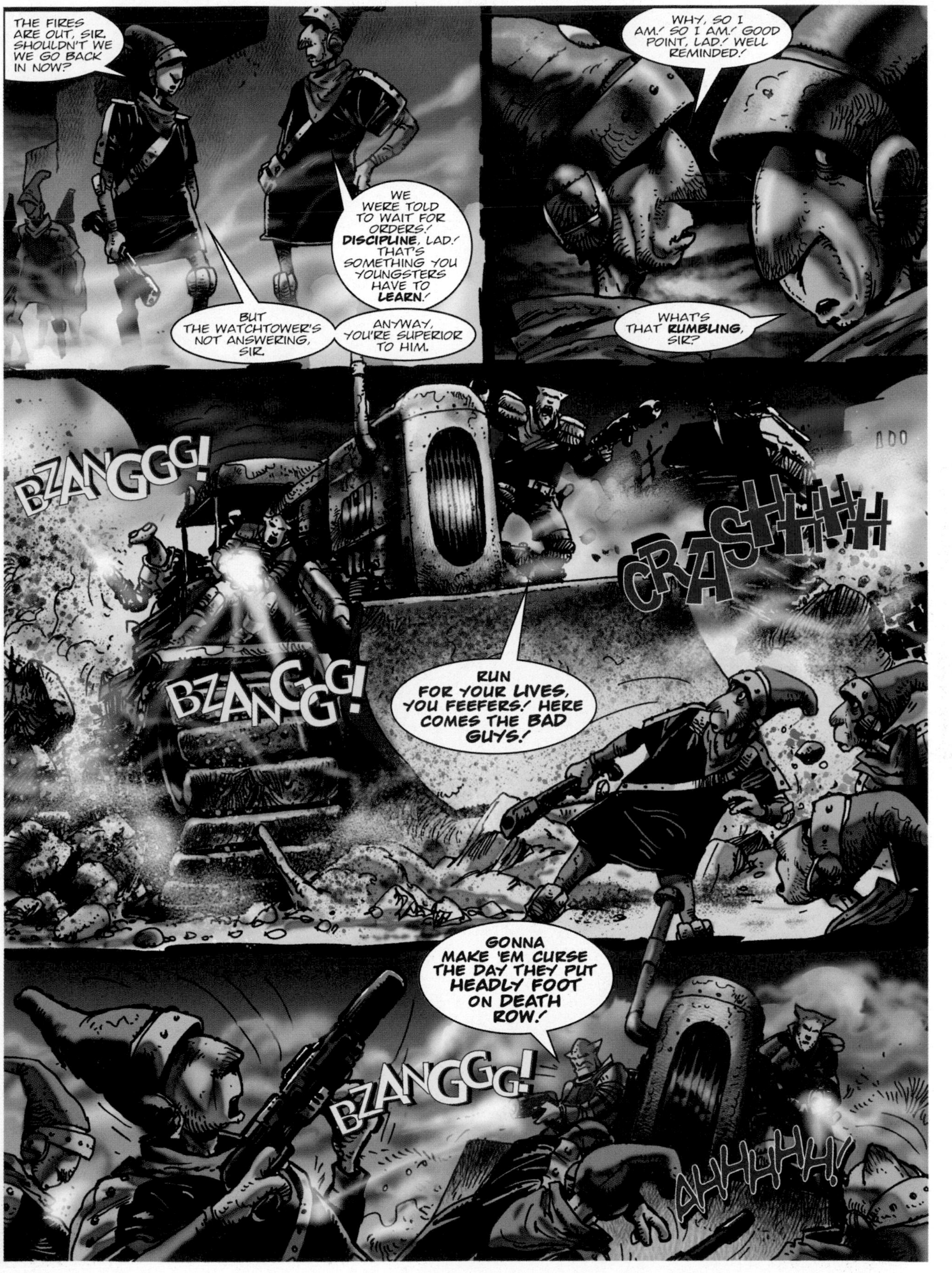
THE FIRES ARE OUT, SIR. SHOULDN'T WE WE GO BACK IN NOW?
WE WERE TOLD TO WAIT FOR ORDERS! DISCIPLINE, LAD! THAT'S SOMETHING YOU YOUNGSTERS HAVE TO LEARN!
BUT THE WATCHTOWER'S NOT ANSWERING, SIR.
ANYWAY, YOU'RE SUPERIOR TO HIM.
WHY, SO I AM! SO I AM! GOOD POINT, LAD! WELL REMINDED!
WHAT'S THAT RUMBLING, SIR?
BZANGGG!
CRASHHHHH
BZANGGG!
RUN FOR YOUR LIVES, YOU FEEFERS! HERE COMES THE BAD GUYS!
GONNA MAKE 'EM CURSE THE DAY THEY PUT HEADLY FOOT ON DEATH ROW!
BZANGGG!
AHHHHH!

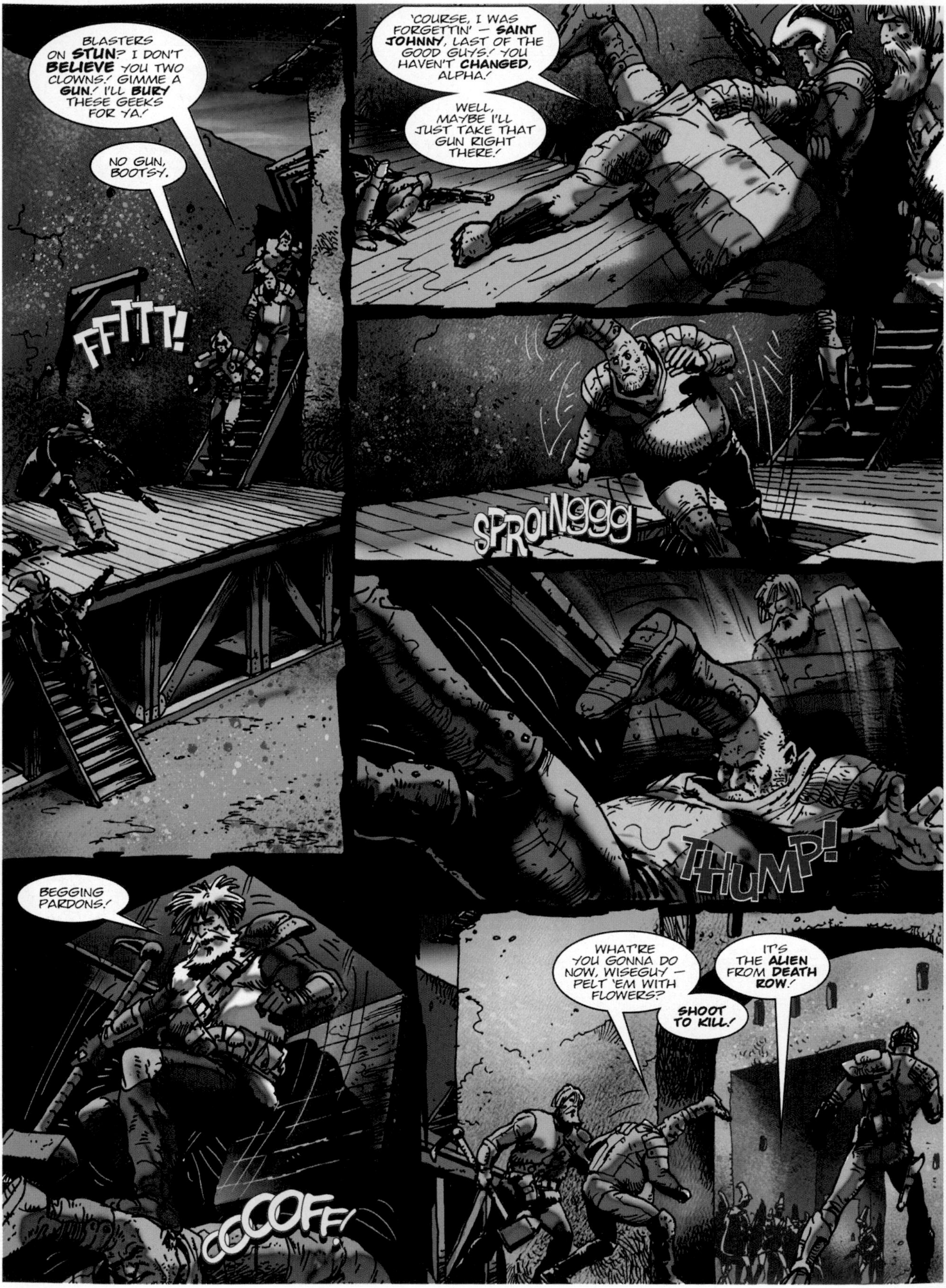

BLASTERS ON STUN? I DON'T BELIEVE YOU TWO CLOWNS! GIMME A GUN! I'LL BURY THESE GEEKS FOR YA!
NO GUN, BOOTSY.
FFTTT!
'COURSE, I WAS FORGETTIN' — SAINT JOHNNY, LAST OF THE GOOD GUYS! YOU HAVEN'T CHANGED, ALPHA!
WELL, MAYBE I'LL JUST TAKE THAT GUN RIGHT THERE!
SPROINGGG
THUMP!
BEGGING PARDONS!
COCCOFF!
WHAT'RE YOU GONNA DO NOW, WISEGUY — PELT 'EM WITH FLOWERS?
SHOOT TO KILL!
IT'S THE ALIEN FROM DEATH ROW!

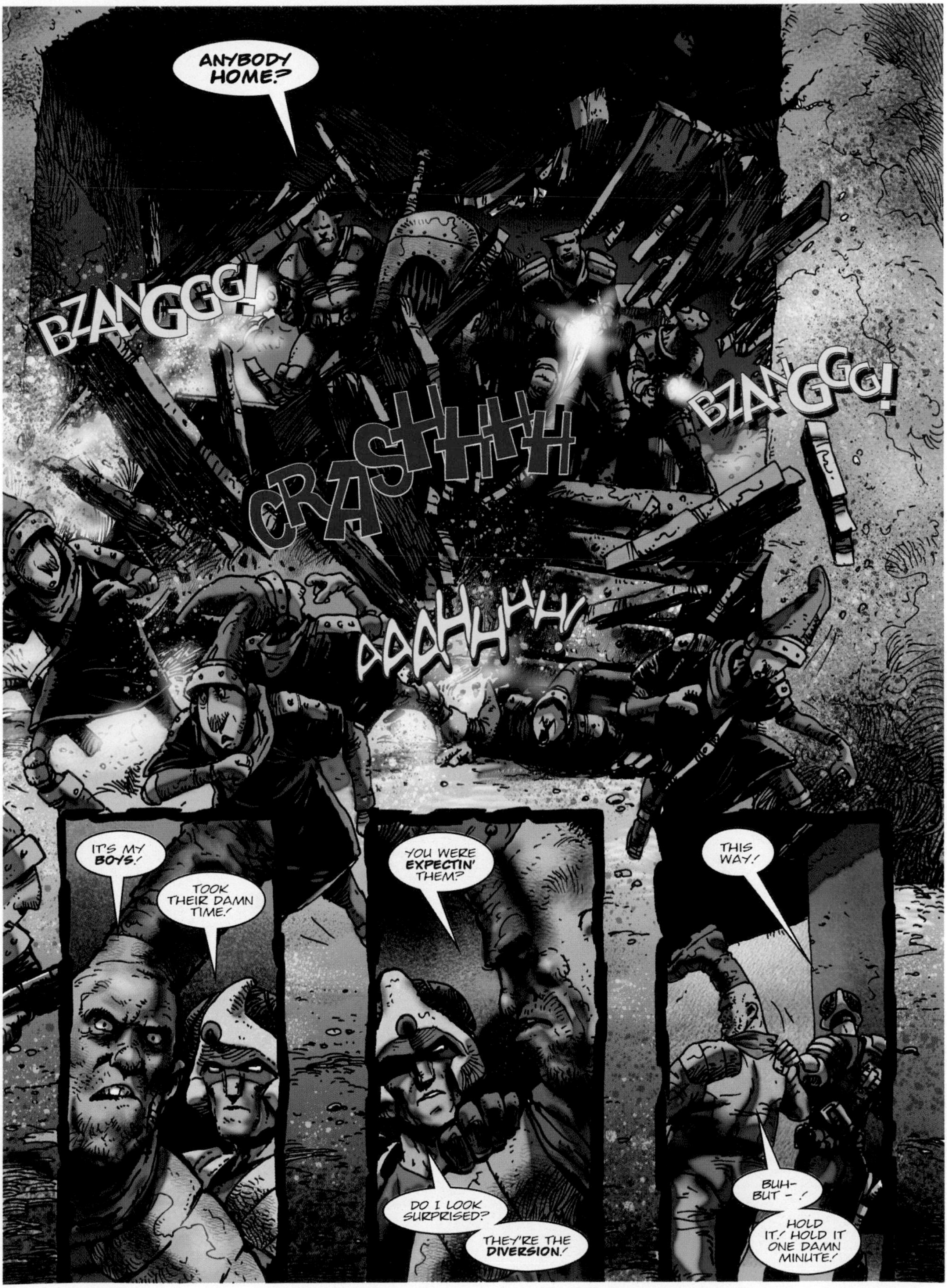

ANYBODY HOME?
BZANGGG!
BZANGGG!
CRASHHHH
AAAGHHHH!
IT'S MY BOYS!
TOOK THEIR DAMN TIME!
YOU WERE EXPECTIN' THEM?
DO I LOOK SURPRISED?
THEY'RE THE DIVERSION!
THIS WAY!
BUH-BUT -!
HOLD IT! HOLD IT ONE DAMN MINUTE!

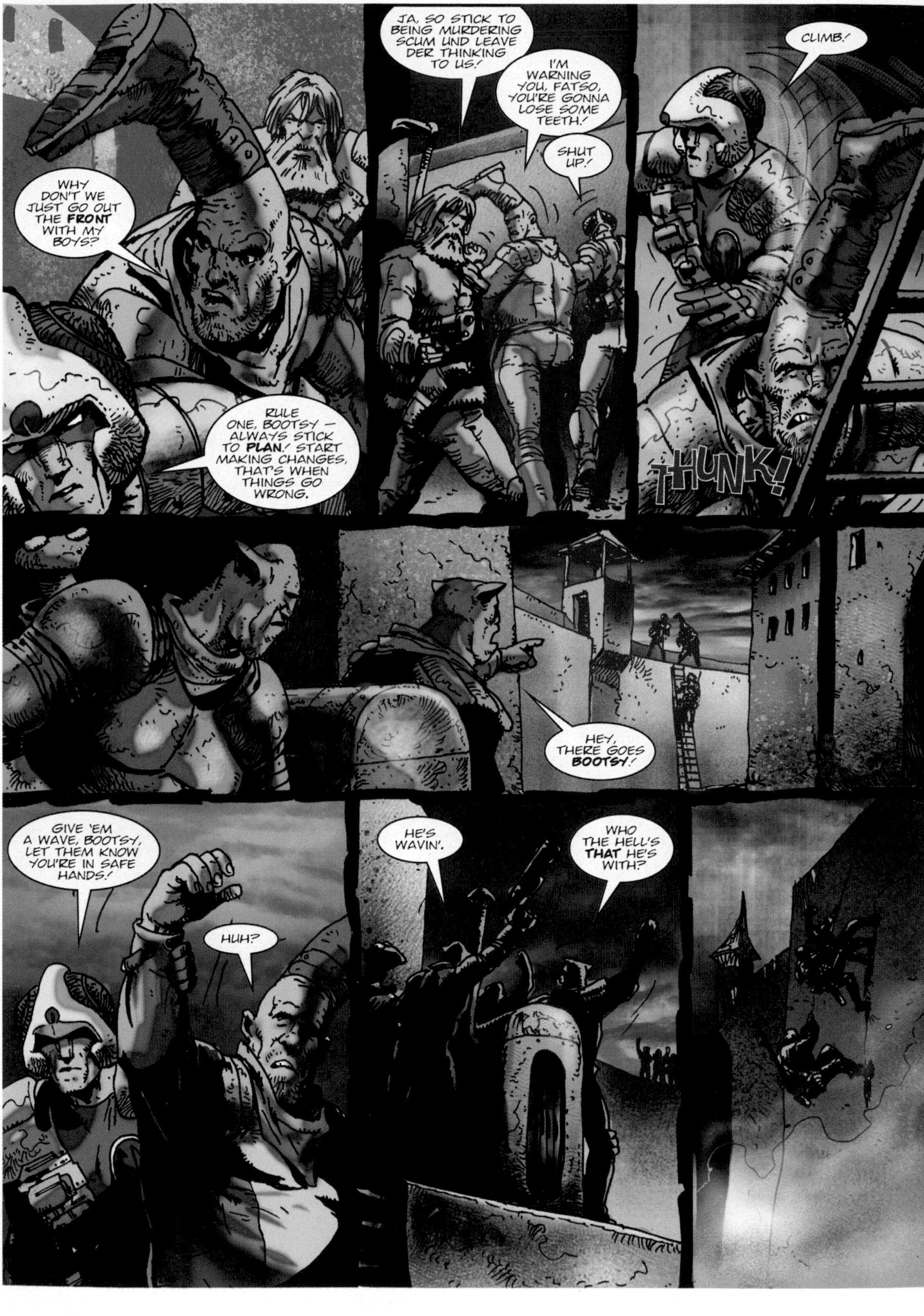

WHY DON'T WE JUST GO OUT THE **FRONT** WITH MY BOYS?
RULE ONE, BOOTSY — ALWAYS STICK TO **PLAN**! START MAKING CHANGES, THAT'S WHEN THINGS GO WRONG.
JA, SO STICK TO BEING MURDERING SCUM UND LEAVE DER THINKING TO US!
I'M WARNING YOU, FATSO, YOU'RE GONNA LOSE SOME TEETH!
SHUT UP!
CLIMB!
THUNK!
HEY, THERE GOES **BOOTSY**!
GIVE 'EM A WAVE, BOOTSY, LET THEM KNOW YOU'RE IN SAFE HANDS!
HUH?
HE'S WAVIN'.
WHO THE HELL'S **THAT** HE'S WITH?

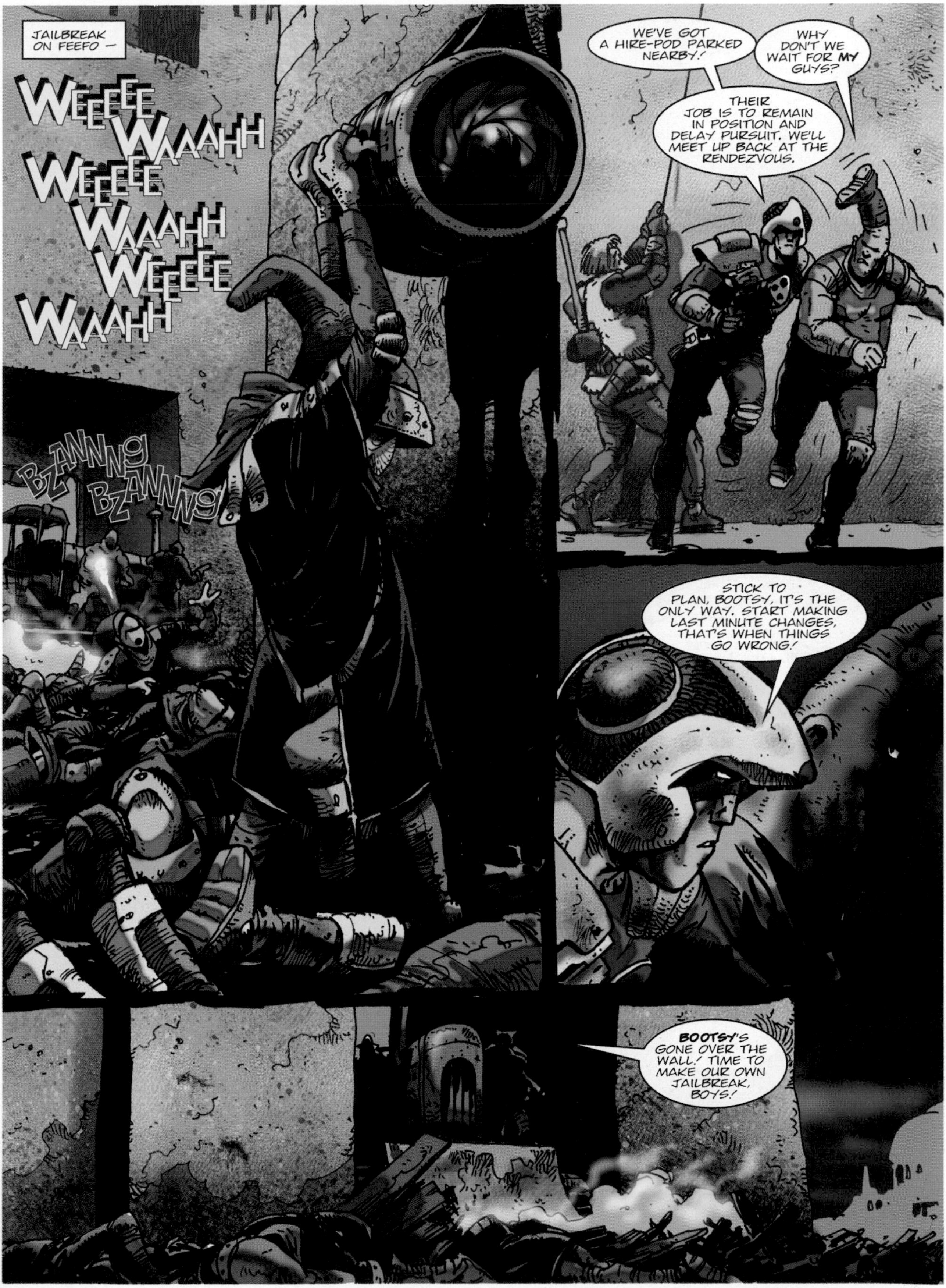
JAILBREAK ON FEEFO —
WEEEEE WAAAHH WEEEEE WAAAHH WEEEEE WAAAHH
BZANNNG BZANNNG
WE'VE GOT A HIRE-POD PARKED NEARBY!
WHY DON'T WE WAIT FOR MY GUYS?
THEIR JOB IS TO REMAIN IN POSITION AND DELAY PURSUIT. WE'LL MEET UP BACK AT THE RENDEZVOUS.
STICK TO PLAN, BOOTSY, IT'S THE ONLY WAY. START MAKING LAST MINUTE CHANGES, THAT'S WHEN THINGS GO WRONG!
BOOTSY'S GONE OVER THE WALL! TIME TO MAKE OUR OWN JAILBREAK, BOYS!

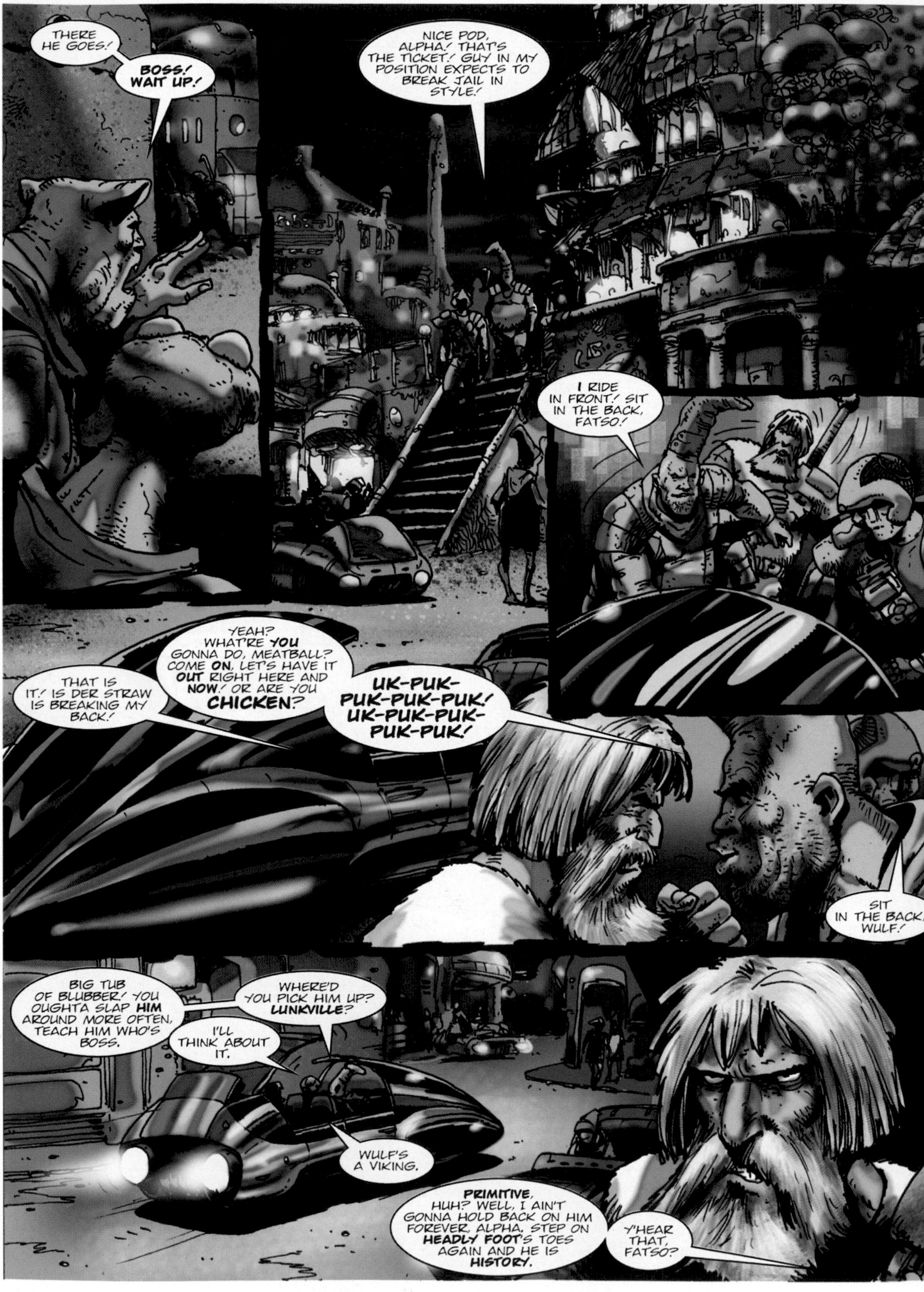
THERE HE GOES!
BOSS! WAIT UP!
NICE POD, ALPHA! THAT'S THE TICKET! GUY IN MY POSITION EXPECTS TO BREAK JAIL IN STYLE!
I RIDE IN FRONT! SIT IN THE BACK, FATSO!
THAT IS IT! IS DER STRAW IS BREAKING MY BACK!
YEAH? WHAT'RE YOU GONNA DO, MEATBALL? COME ON, LET'S HAVE IT OUT RIGHT HERE AND NOW! OR ARE YOU CHICKEN?
UK-PUK-PUK-PUK-PUK! UK-PUK-PUK-PUK-PUK-PUK!
SIT IN THE BACK, WULF!
BIG TUB OF BLUBBER! YOU OUGHTA SLAP HIM AROUND MORE OFTEN, TEACH HIM WHO'S BOSS.
WHERE'D YOU PICK HIM UP? LUNKVILLE?
I'LL THINK ABOUT IT.
WULF'S A VIKING.
PRIMITIVE, HUH? WELL, I AIN'T GONNA HOLD BACK ON HIM FOREVER, ALPHA. STEP ON HEADLY FOOT'S TOES AGAIN AND HE IS HISTORY.
Y'HEAR THAT, FATSO?

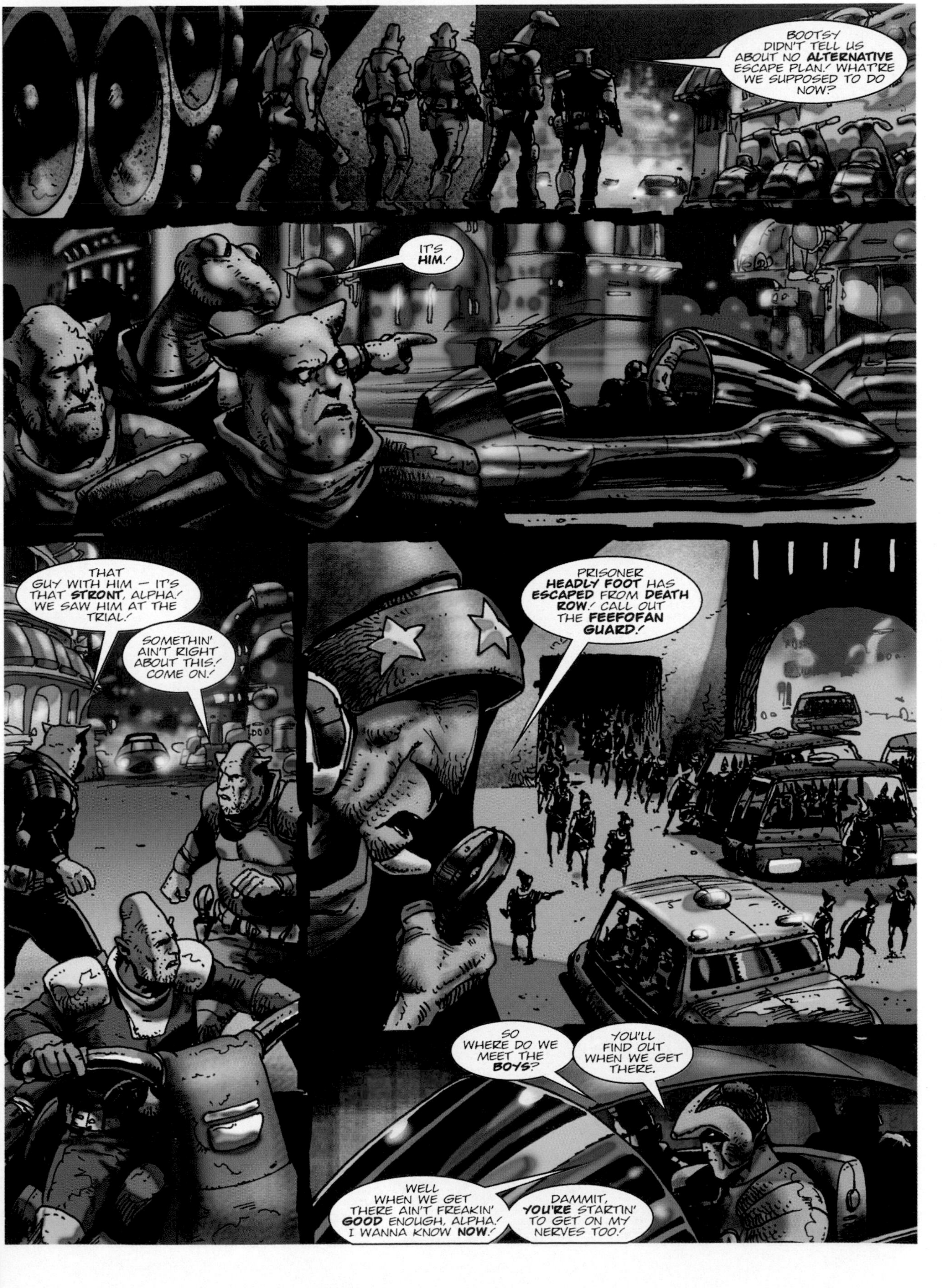
BOOTSY DIDN'T TELL US ABOUT NO ALTERNATIVE ESCAPE PLAN! WHAT'RE WE SUPPOSED TO DO NOW?
IT'S HIM!
THAT GUY WITH HIM — IT'S THAT STRONT, ALPHA! WE SAW HIM AT THE TRIAL!
SOMETHIN' AIN'T RIGHT ABOUT THIS! COME ON!
PRISONER HEADLY FOOT HAS ESCAPED FROM DEATH ROW! CALL OUT THE FEEFOFAN GUARD!
SO WHERE DO WE MEET THE BOYS?
YOU'LL FIND OUT WHEN WE GET THERE.
WELL WHEN WE GET THERE AIN'T FREAKIN' GOOD ENOUGH, ALPHA! I WANNA KNOW NOW!
DAMMIT, YOU'RE STARTIN' TO GET ON MY NERVES TOO!

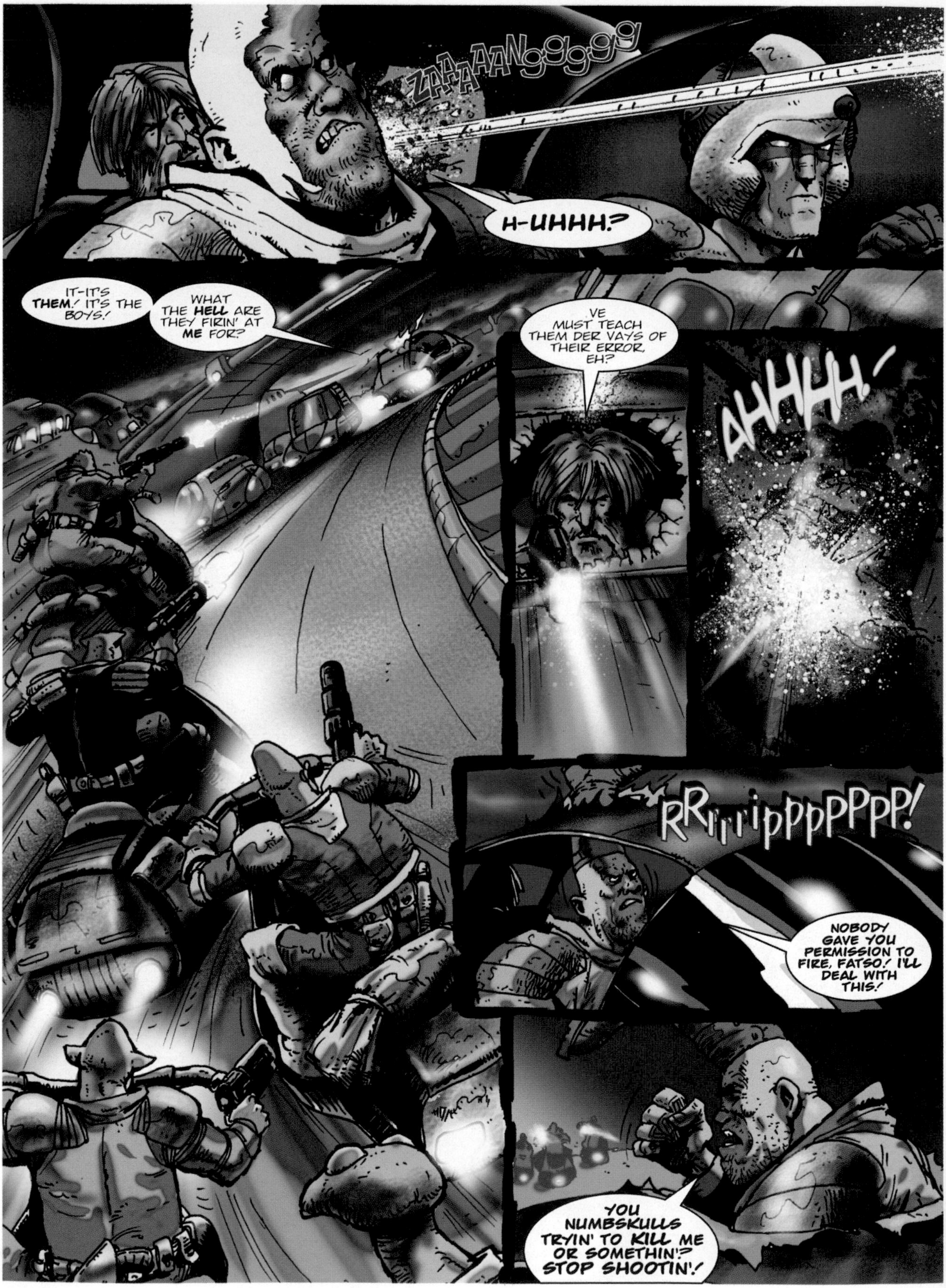
ZAAAAANGGGGGG
H-UHHH?
IT-IT'S THEM! IT'S THE BOYS!
WHAT THE HELL ARE THEY FIRIN' AT ME FOR?
VE MUST TEACH THEM DER VAYS OF THEIR ERROR, EH?
AHHHH!
RRrrrripPPPPPP!
NOBODY GAVE YOU PERMISSION TO FIRE, FATSO! I'LL DEAL WITH THIS!
YOU NUMBSKULLS TRYIN' TO KILL ME OR SOMETHIN'? STOP SHOOTIN'!

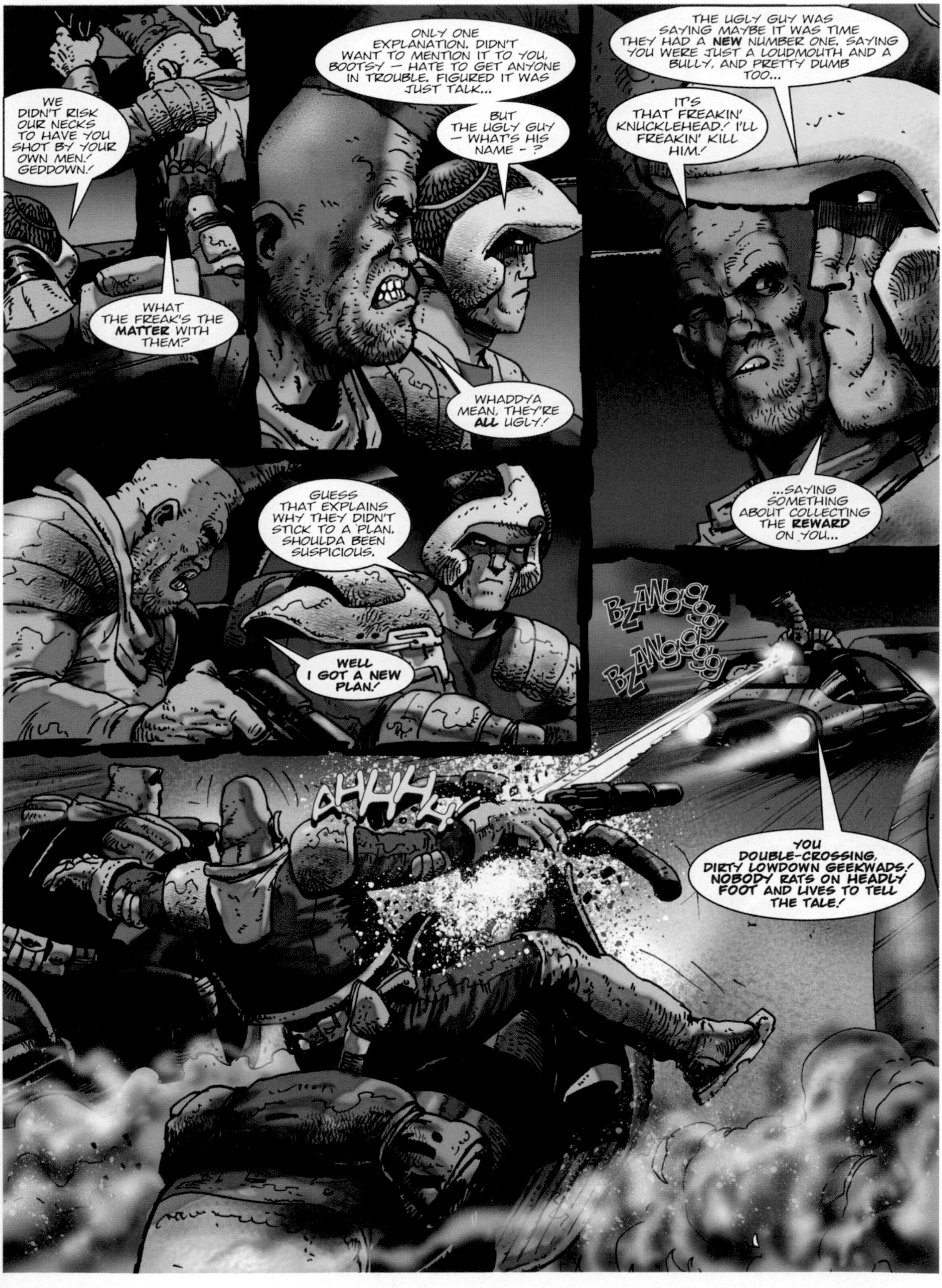
WE DIDN'T RISK OUR NECKS TO HAVE YOU SHOT BY YOUR OWN MEN! GEDDOWN!
WHAT THE FREAK'S THE MATTER WITH THEM?
ONLY ONE EXPLANATION. DIDN'T WANT TO MENTION IT TO YOU, BOOTSY — HATE TO GET ANYONE IN TROUBLE. FIGURED IT WAS JUST TALK...
BUT THE UGLY GUY — WHAT'S HIS NAME - ?
WHADDYA MEAN, THEY'RE ALL UGLY!
THE UGLY GUY WAS SAYING MAYBE IT WAS TIME THEY HAD A NEW NUMBER ONE. SAYING YOU WERE JUST A LOUDMOUTH AND A BULLY, AND PRETTY DUMB TOO...
IT'S THAT FREAKIN' KNUCKLEHEAD! I'LL FREAKIN' KILL HIM!
...SAYING SOMETHING ABOUT COLLECTING THE REWARD ON YOU...
GUESS THAT EXPLAINS WHY THEY DIDN'T STICK TO A PLAN. SHOULDA BEEN SUSPICIOUS.
WELL I GOT A NEW PLAN!
BZANGGGG
BZANGGGG
AHHHH
YOU DOUBLE-CROSSING, DIRTY LOWDOWN GEEKWADS! NOBODY RATS ON HEADLY FOOT AND LIVES TO TELL THE TALE!

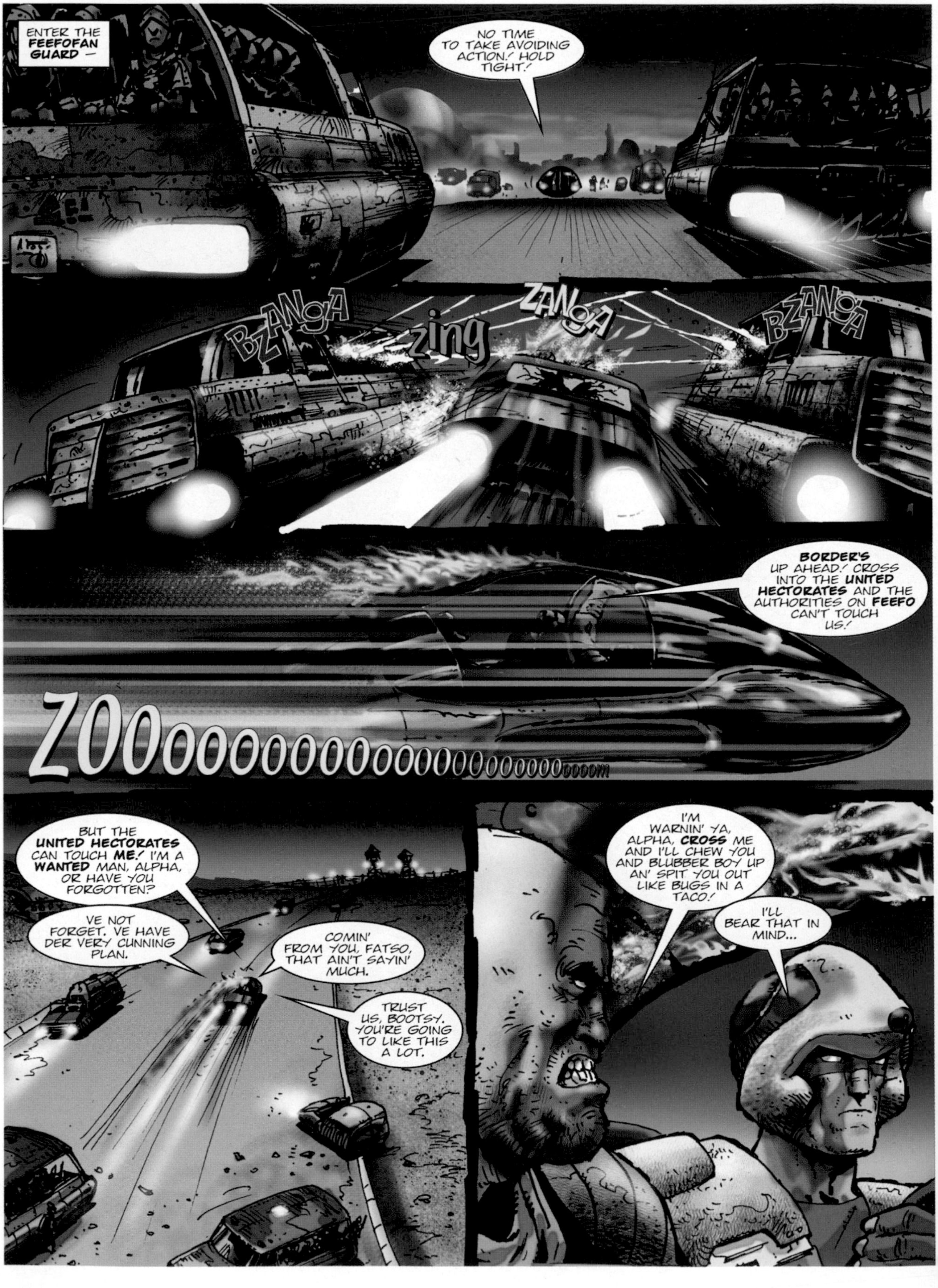

ENTER THE **FEEFOFAN GUARD** —
NO TIME TO TAKE AVOIDING ACTION! HOLD TIGHT!
BZANGA
ZANGA
zing
BZANGA
BORDER'S UP AHEAD! CROSS INTO THE **UNITED HECTORATES** AND THE AUTHORITIES ON **FEEFO** CAN'T TOUCH US!
ZOOoooooooooooooooooooooom
BUT THE **UNITED HECTORATES** CAN TOUCH **ME!** I'M A **WANTED** MAN, ALPHA, OR HAVE YOU FORGOTTEN?
VE NOT FORGET. VE HAVE DER VERY CUNNING PLAN.
COMIN' FROM YOU, FATSO, THAT AIN'T SAYIN' MUCH.
TRUST US, BOOTSY. YOU'RE GOING TO LIKE THIS A LOT.
I'M WARNIN' YA, ALPHA, **CROSS** ME AND I'LL CHEW YOU AND BLUBBER BOY UP AN' SPIT YOU OUT LIKE BUGS IN A TACO!
I'LL BEAR THAT IN MIND...

TRAITOR TO HIS KIND

Script: John Wagner
Art: Carlos Ezquerra
Letters: Annie Parkhouse

Originally published in *2000 AD* Prog 1406-1415

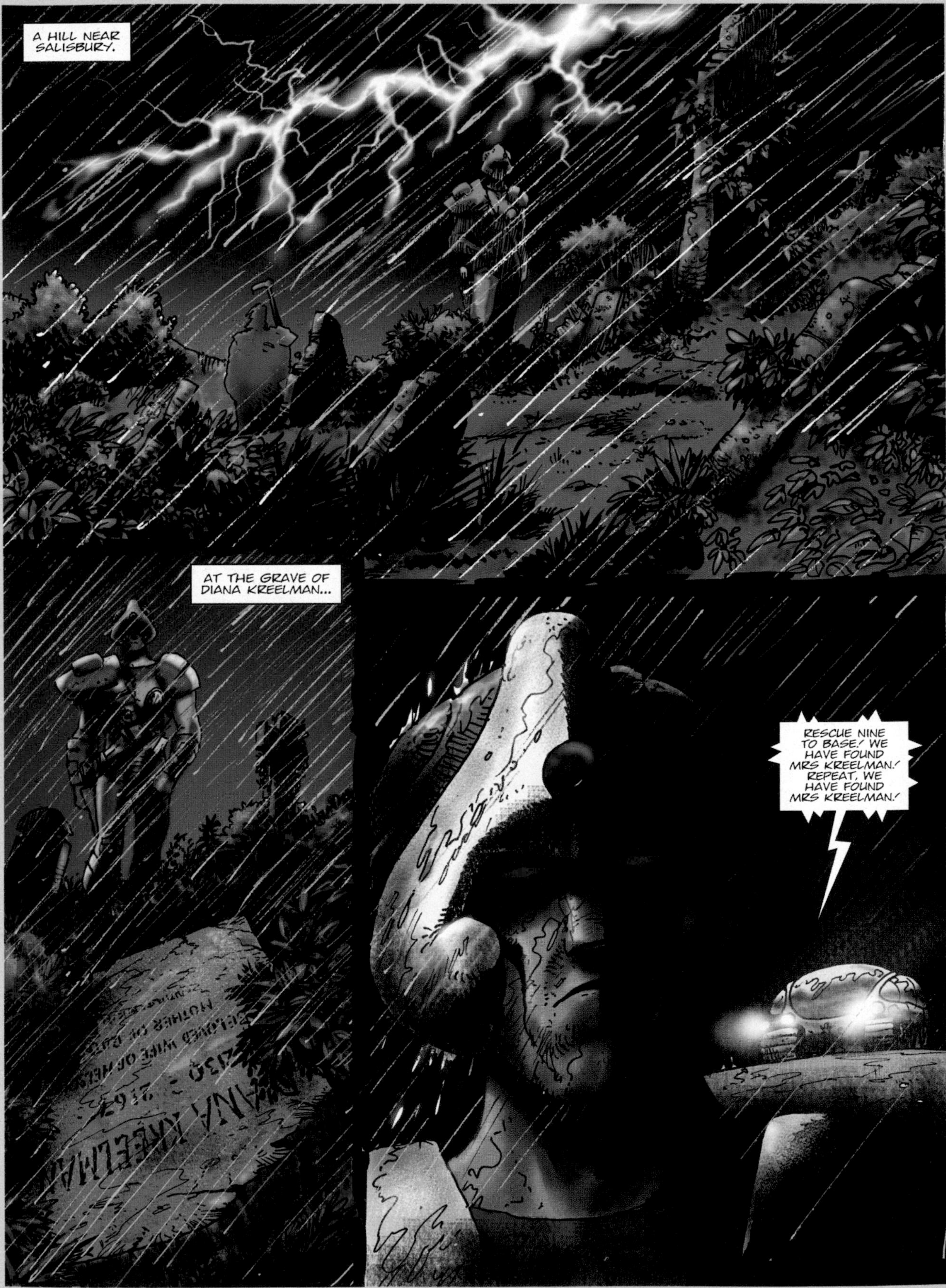
A HILL NEAR SALISBURY.
AT THE GRAVE OF DIANA KREELMAN...
RESCUE NINE TO BASE! WE HAVE FOUND MRS KREELMAN! REPEAT, WE HAVE FOUND MRS KREELMAN!

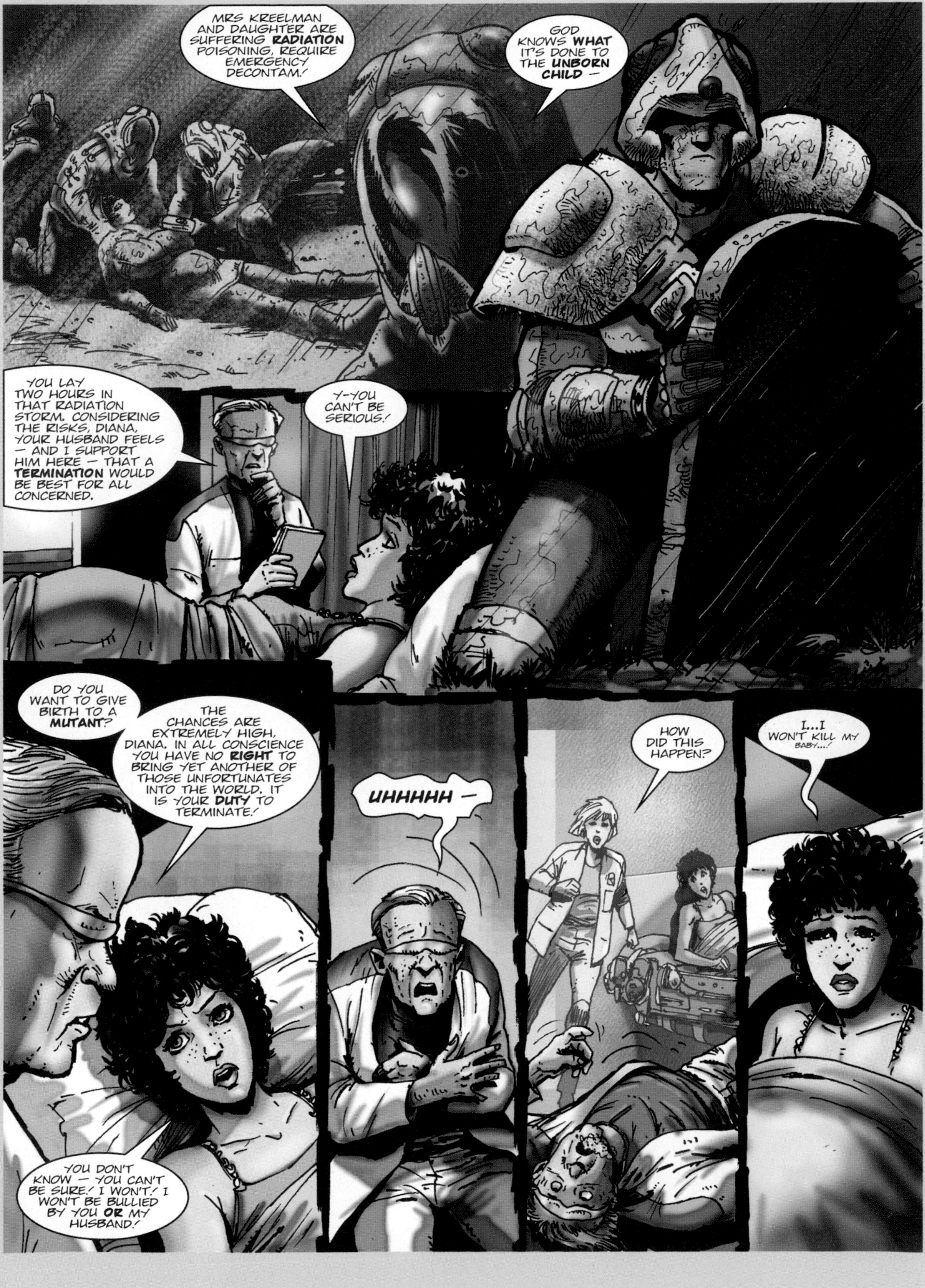
MRS KREELMAN AND DAUGHTER ARE SUFFERING RADIATION POISONING, REQUIRE EMERGENCY DECONTAM!
GOD KNOWS WHAT IT'S DONE TO THE UNBORN CHILD —
YOU LAY TWO HOURS IN THAT RADIATION STORM. CONSIDERING THE RISKS, DIANA, YOUR HUSBAND FEELS — AND I SUPPORT HIM HERE — THAT A TERMINATION WOULD BE BEST FOR ALL CONCERNED.
Y-YOU CAN'T BE SERIOUS!
DO YOU WANT TO GIVE BIRTH TO A MUTANT?
THE CHANCES ARE EXTREMELY HIGH, DIANA. IN ALL CONSCIENCE YOU HAVE NO RIGHT TO BRING YET ANOTHER OF THOSE UNFORTUNATES INTO THE WORLD. IT IS YOUR DUTY TO TERMINATE!
YOU DON'T KNOW — YOU CAN'T BE SURE! I WON'T! I WON'T BE BULLIED BY YOU OR MY HUSBAND!
UHHHHH —
HOW DID THIS HAPPEN?
I...I WON'T KILL MY BABY...!

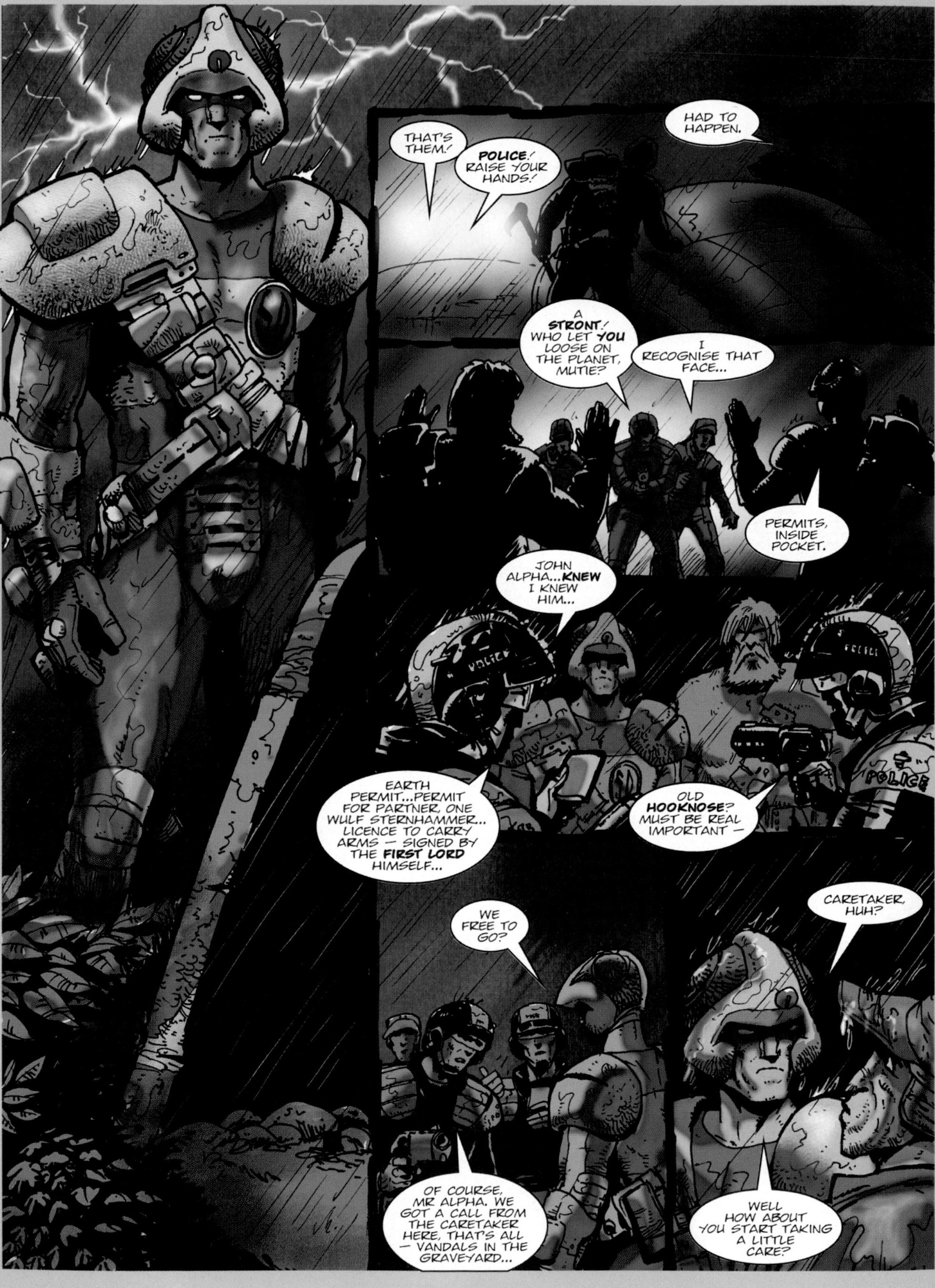
THAT'S THEM!
POLICE! RAISE YOUR HANDS!
HAD TO HAPPEN.
A STRONT! WHO LET YOU LOOSE ON THE PLANET, MUTIE?
I RECOGNISE THAT FACE...
PERMITS, INSIDE POCKET.
JOHN ALPHA...KNEW I KNEW HIM...
EARTH PERMIT...PERMIT FOR PARTNER, ONE WULF STERNHAMMER... LICENCE TO CARRY ARMS — SIGNED BY THE FIRST LORD HIMSELF...
OLD HOOKNOSE? MUST BE REAL IMPORTANT —
WE FREE TO GO?
OF COURSE, MR ALPHA. WE GOT A CALL FROM THE CARETAKER HERE, THAT'S ALL — VANDALS IN THE GRAVEYARD...
CARETAKER, HUH?
WELL HOW ABOUT YOU START TAKING A LITTLE CARE?

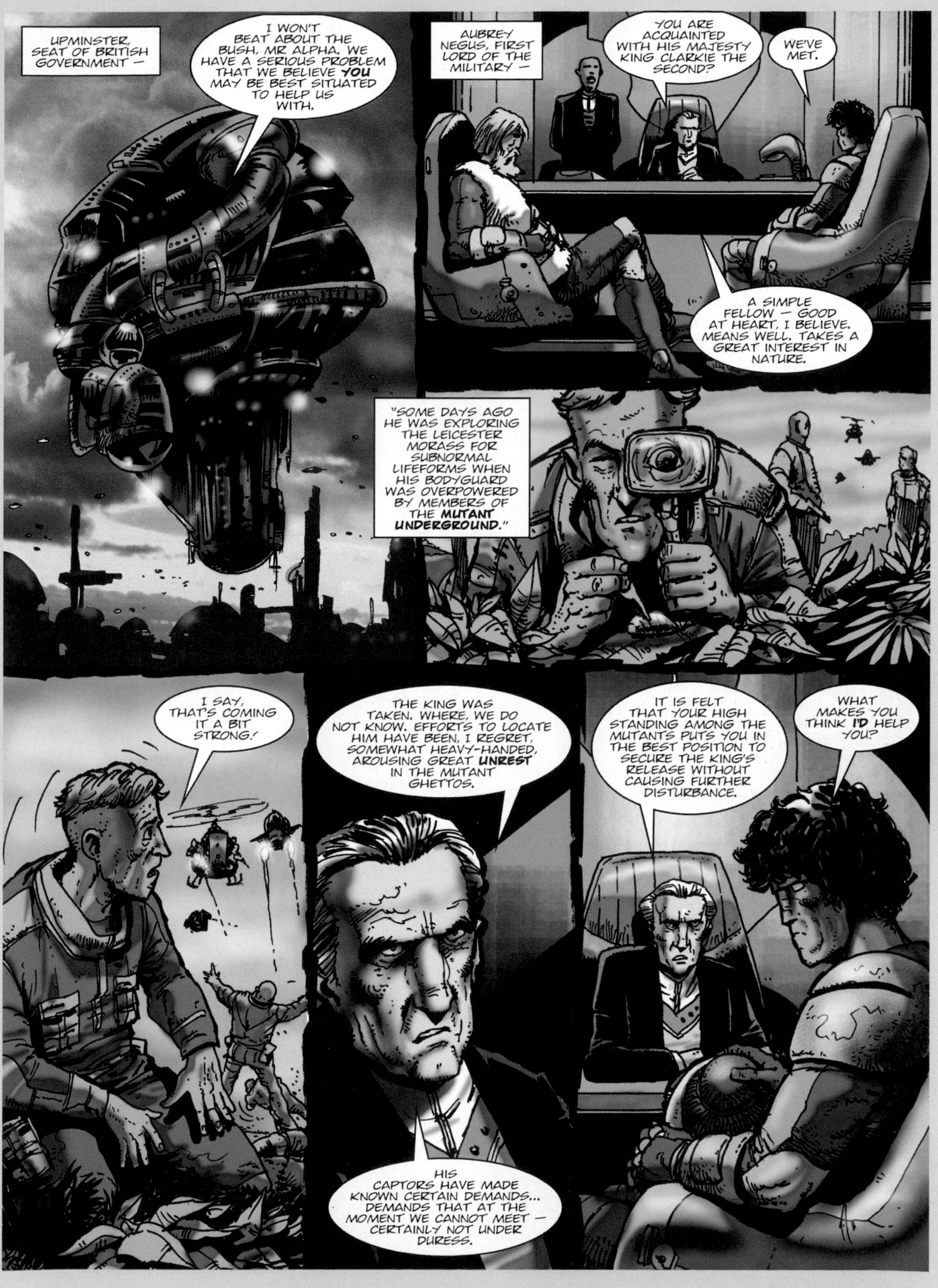
UPMINSTER, SEAT OF BRITISH GOVERNMENT —
I WON'T BEAT ABOUT THE BUSH, MR ALPHA. WE HAVE A SERIOUS PROBLEM THAT WE BELIEVE **YOU** MAY BE BEST SITUATED TO HELP US WITH.
AUBREY NEGUS, FIRST LORD OF THE MILITARY —
YOU ARE ACQUAINTED WITH HIS MAJESTY KING CLARKIE THE SECOND?
WE'VE MET.
A SIMPLE FELLOW — GOOD AT HEART, I BELIEVE. MEANS WELL. TAKES A GREAT INTEREST IN NATURE.
"SOME DAYS AGO HE WAS EXPLORING THE LEICESTER MORASS FOR SUBNORMAL LIFEFORMS WHEN HIS BODYGUARD WAS OVERPOWERED BY MEMBERS OF THE **MUTANT UNDERGROUND**."
I SAY, THAT'S COMING IT A BIT STRONG!
THE KING WAS TAKEN. WHERE, WE DO NOT KNOW. EFFORTS TO LOCATE HIM HAVE BEEN, I REGRET, SOMEWHAT HEAVY-HANDED, AROUSING GREAT **UNREST** IN THE MUTANT GHETTOS.
HIS CAPTORS HAVE MADE KNOWN CERTAIN DEMANDS... DEMANDS THAT AT THE MOMENT WE CANNOT MEET — CERTAINLY NOT UNDER DURESS.
IT IS FELT THAT YOUR HIGH STANDING AMONG THE MUTANTS PUTS YOU IN THE BEST POSITION TO SECURE THE KING'S RELEASE WITHOUT CAUSING FURTHER DISTURBANCE.
WHAT MAKES YOU THINK **I'D** HELP YOU?

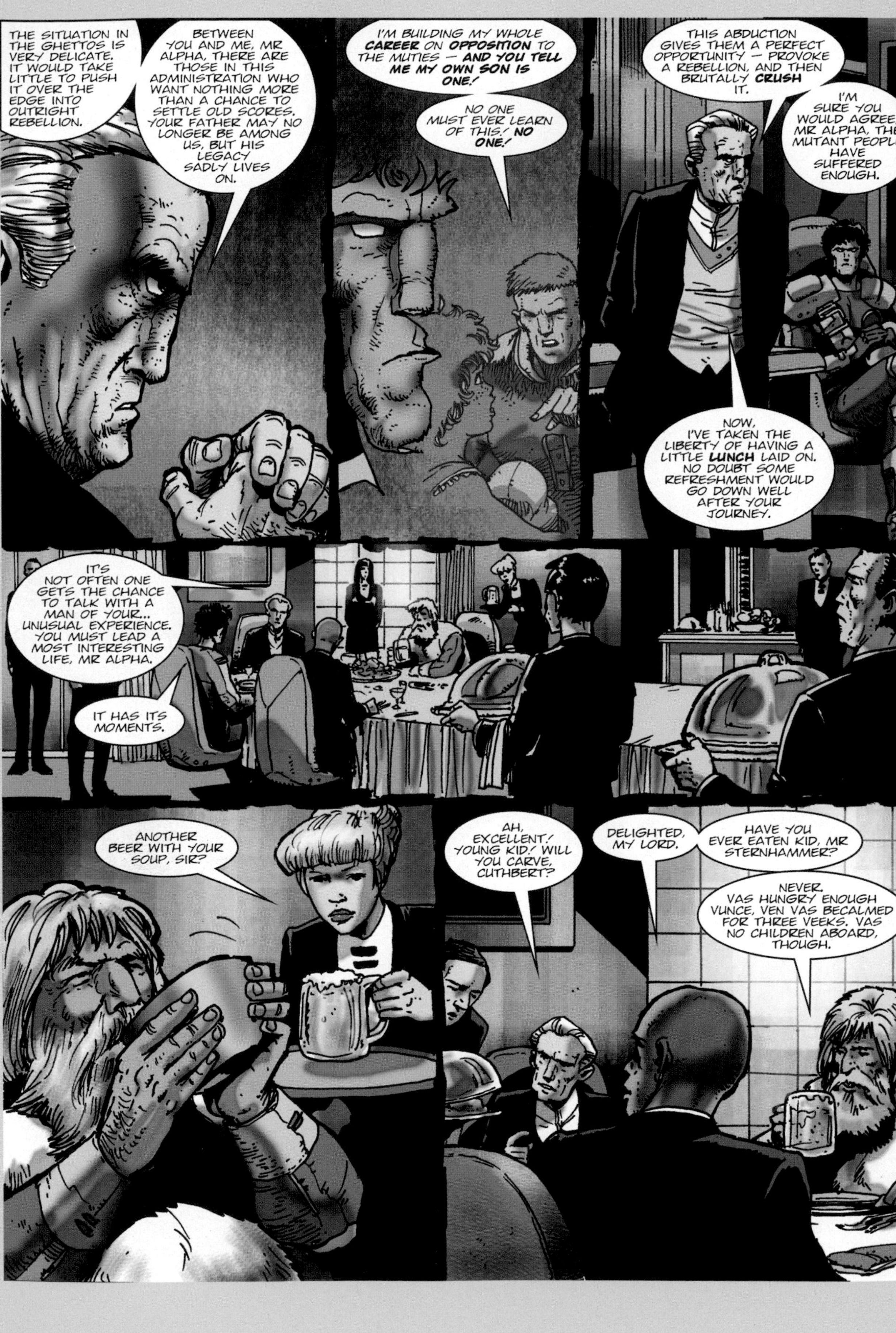

THE SITUATION IN THE GHETTOS IS VERY DELICATE. IT WOULD TAKE LITTLE TO PUSH IT OVER THE EDGE INTO OUTRIGHT REBELLION.
BETWEEN YOU AND ME, MR ALPHA, THERE ARE THOSE IN THIS ADMINISTRATION WHO WANT NOTHING MORE THAN A CHANCE TO SETTLE OLD SCORES. YOUR FATHER MAY NO LONGER BE AMONG US, BUT HIS LEGACY SADLY LIVES ON.
I'M BUILDING MY WHOLE **CAREER** ON **OPPOSITION** TO THE MUTIES — **AND YOU TELL ME MY OWN SON IS ONE!**
NO ONE MUST EVER LEARN OF THIS! **NO ONE!**
THIS ABDUCTION GIVES THEM A PERFECT OPPORTUNITY — PROVOKE A REBELLION, AND THEN BRUTALLY **CRUSH** IT.
I'M SURE YOU WOULD AGREE, MR ALPHA, THE MUTANT PEOPLE HAVE SUFFERED ENOUGH.
NOW, I'VE TAKEN THE LIBERTY OF HAVING A LITTLE **LUNCH** LAID ON. NO DOUBT SOME REFRESHMENT WOULD GO DOWN WELL AFTER YOUR JOURNEY.
IT'S NOT OFTEN ONE GETS THE CHANCE TO TALK WITH A MAN OF YOUR... UNUSUAL EXPERIENCE. YOU MUST LEAD A MOST INTERESTING LIFE, MR ALPHA.
IT HAS ITS MOMENTS.
ANOTHER BEER WITH YOUR SOUP, SIR?
AH, EXCELLENT! YOUNG KID! WILL YOU CARVE, CUTHBERT?
DELIGHTED, MY LORD.
HAVE YOU EVER EATEN KID, MR STERNHAMMER?
NEVER. VAS HUNGRY ENOUGH VUNCE, VEN VAS BECALMED FOR THREE VEEKS. VAS NO CHILDREN ABOARD, THOUGH.

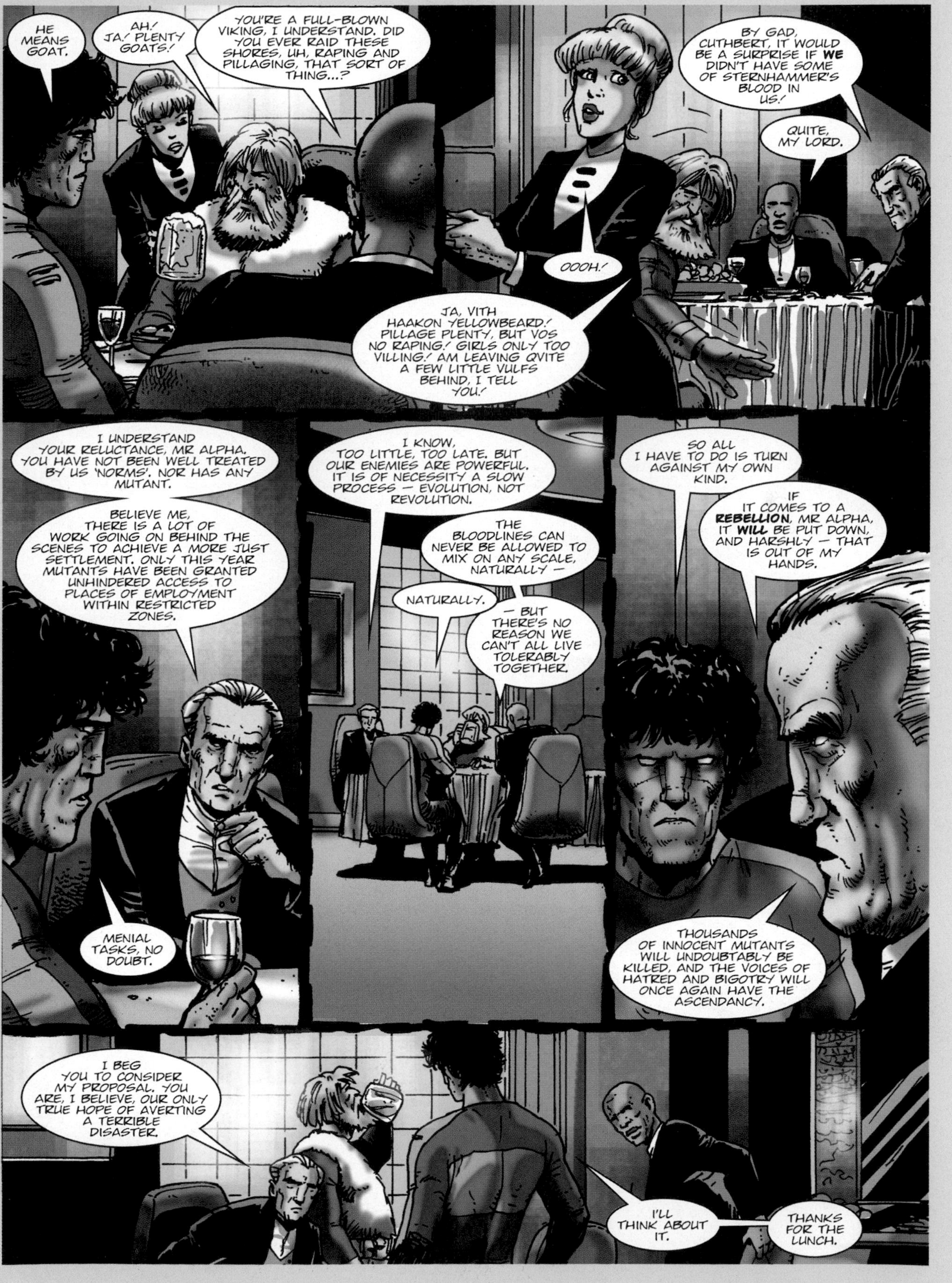

HE MEANS GOAT.
AH! JA! PLENTY GOATS!
YOU'RE A FULL-BLOWN VIKING, I UNDERSTAND. DID YOU EVER RAID THESE SHORES, UH, RAPING AND PILLAGING, THAT SORT OF THING...?
OOOH!
JA, VITH HAAKON YELLOWBEARD! PILLAGE PLENTY, BUT VOS NO RAPING! GIRLS ONLY TOO VILLING! AM LEAVING QVITE A FEW LITTLE VULFS BEHIND, I TELL YOU!
BY GAD, CUTHBERT, IT WOULD BE A SURPRISE IF **WE** DIDN'T HAVE SOME OF STERNHAMMER'S BLOOD IN US!
QUITE, MY LORD.
I UNDERSTAND YOUR RELUCTANCE, MR ALPHA. YOU HAVE NOT BEEN WELL TREATED BY US 'NORMS', NOR HAS ANY MUTANT.
BELIEVE ME, THERE IS A LOT OF WORK GOING ON BEHIND THE SCENES TO ACHIEVE A MORE JUST SETTLEMENT. ONLY THIS YEAR MUTANTS HAVE BEEN GRANTED UNHINDERED ACCESS TO PLACES OF EMPLOYMENT WITHIN RESTRICTED ZONES.
MENIAL TASKS, NO DOUBT.
I KNOW, TOO LITTLE, TOO LATE. BUT OUR ENEMIES ARE POWERFUL. IT IS OF NECESSITY A SLOW PROCESS — EVOLUTION, NOT REVOLUTION.
THE BLOODLINES CAN NEVER BE ALLOWED TO MIX ON ANY SCALE, NATURALLY —
NATURALLY.
— BUT THERE'S NO REASON WE CAN'T ALL LIVE TOLERABLY TOGETHER.
SO ALL I HAVE TO DO IS TURN AGAINST MY OWN KIND.
IF IT COMES TO A **REBELLION**, MR ALPHA, IT **WILL** BE PUT DOWN, AND HARSHLY — THAT IS OUT OF MY HANDS.
THOUSANDS OF INNOCENT MUTANTS WILL UNDOUBTABLY BE KILLED, AND THE VOICES OF HATRED AND BIGOTRY WILL ONCE AGAIN HAVE THE ASCENDANCY.
I BEG YOU TO CONSIDER MY PROPOSAL. YOU ARE, I BELIEVE, OUR ONLY TRUE HOPE OF AVERTING A TERRIBLE DISASTER.
I'LL THINK ABOUT IT.
THANKS FOR THE LUNCH.

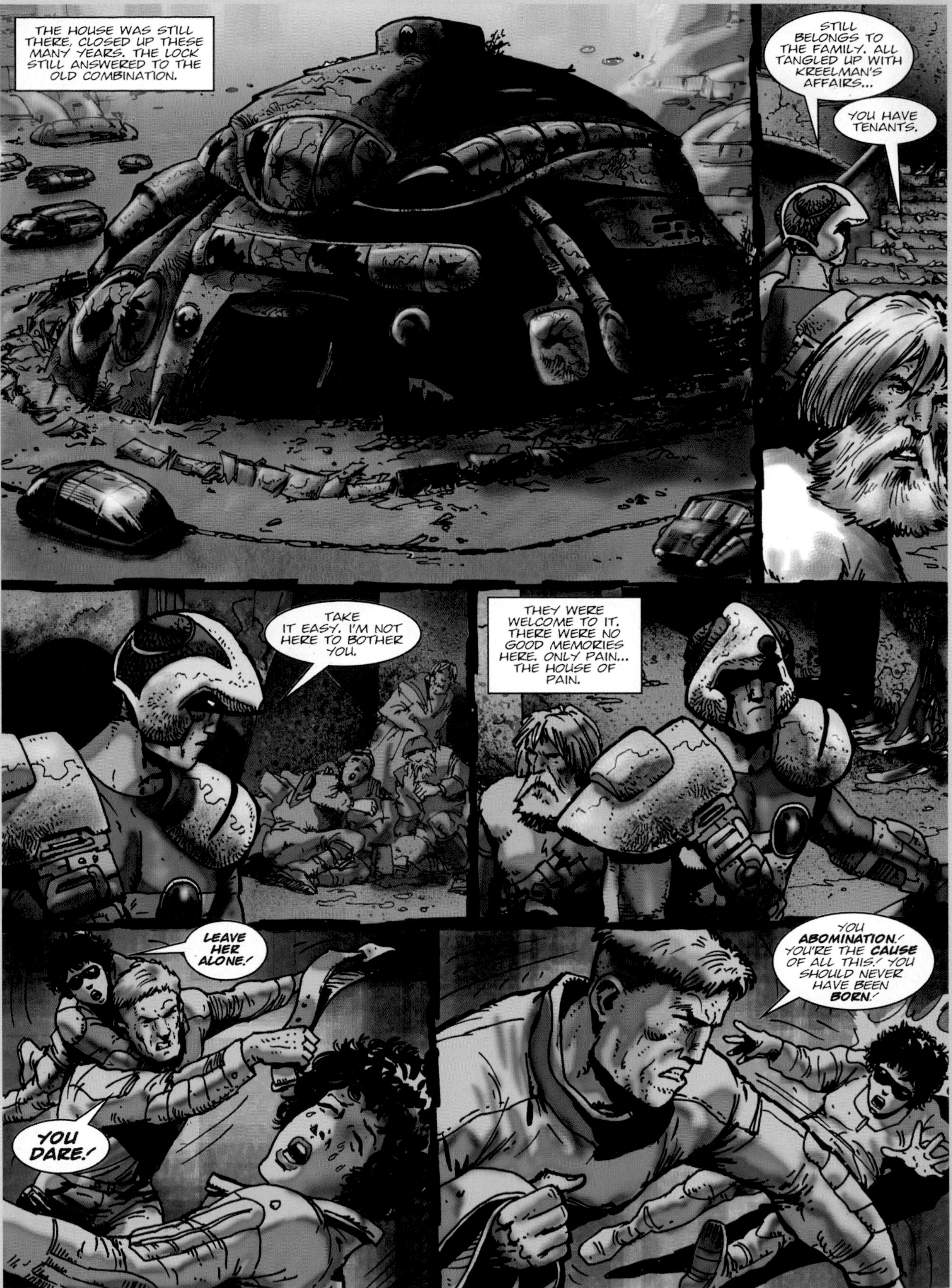

THE HOUSE WAS STILL THERE, CLOSED UP THESE MANY YEARS. THE LOCK STILL ANSWERED TO THE OLD COMBINATION.
STILL BELONGS TO THE FAMILY. ALL TANGLED UP WITH KREELMAN'S AFFAIRS...
YOU HAVE TENANTS.
TAKE IT EASY. I'M NOT HERE TO BOTHER YOU.
THEY WERE WELCOME TO IT. THERE WERE NO GOOD MEMORIES HERE. ONLY PAIN... THE HOUSE OF PAIN.
LEAVE HER ALONE!
YOU DARE!
YOU ABOMINATION! YOU'RE THE CAUSE OF ALL THIS! YOU SHOULD NEVER HAVE BEEN BORN!

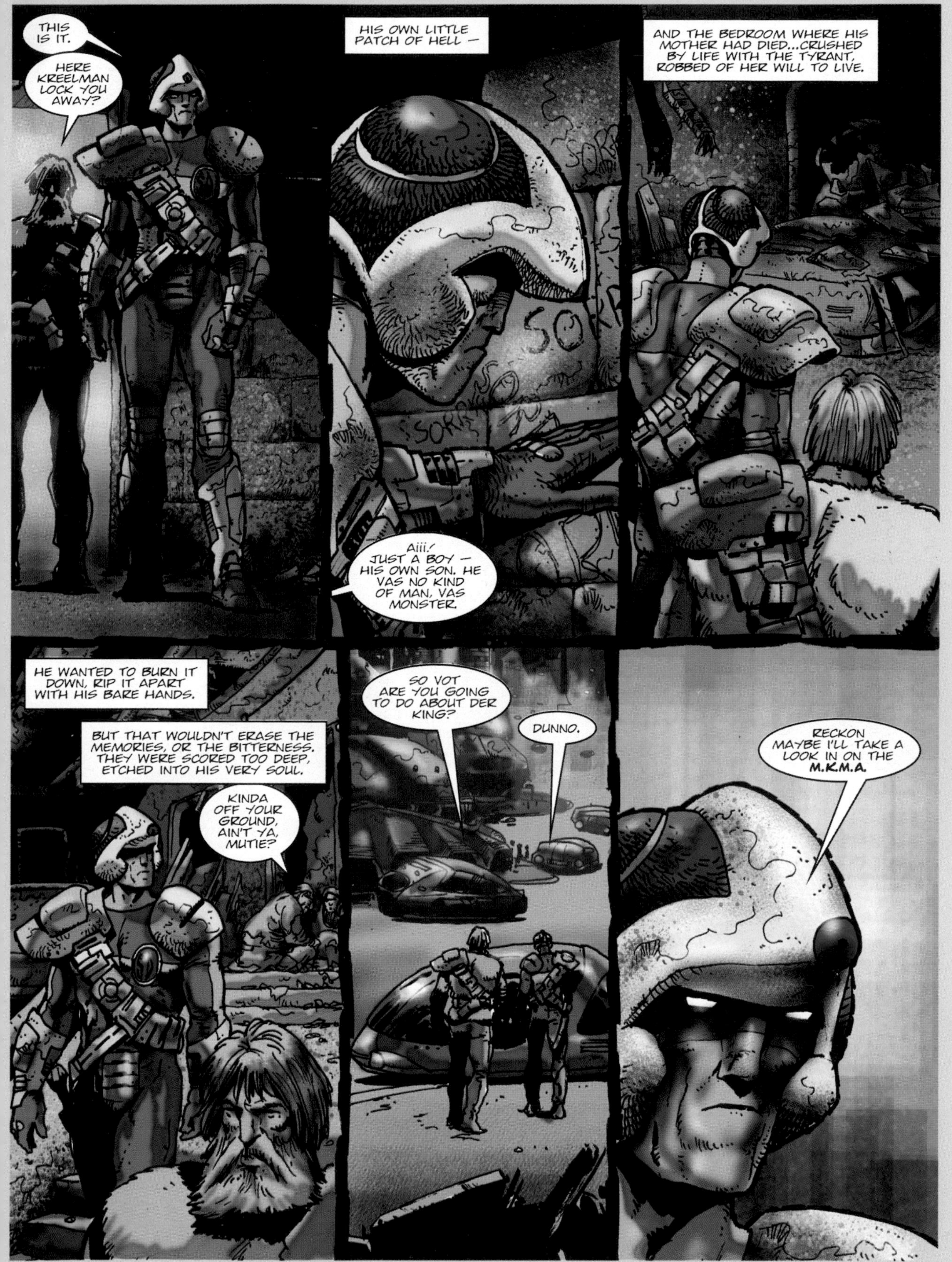
THIS IS IT.
HERE KREELMAN LOCK YOU AWAY?
HIS OWN LITTLE PATCH OF HELL —
Aiii! JUST A BOY — HIS OWN SON. HE VAS NO KIND OF MAN, VAS MONSTER.
AND THE BEDROOM WHERE HIS MOTHER HAD DIED...CRUSHED BY LIFE WITH THE TYRANT, ROBBED OF HER WILL TO LIVE.
HE WANTED TO BURN IT DOWN, RIP IT APART WITH HIS BARE HANDS.
BUT THAT WOULDN'T ERASE THE MEMORIES, OR THE BITTERNESS. THEY WERE SCORED TOO DEEP, ETCHED INTO HIS VERY SOUL.
KINDA OFF YOUR GROUND, AIN'T YA, MUTIE?
SO VOT ARE YOU GOING TO DO ABOUT DER KING?
DUNNO.
RECKON MAYBE I'LL TAKE A LOOK IN ON THE **M.K.M.A.**

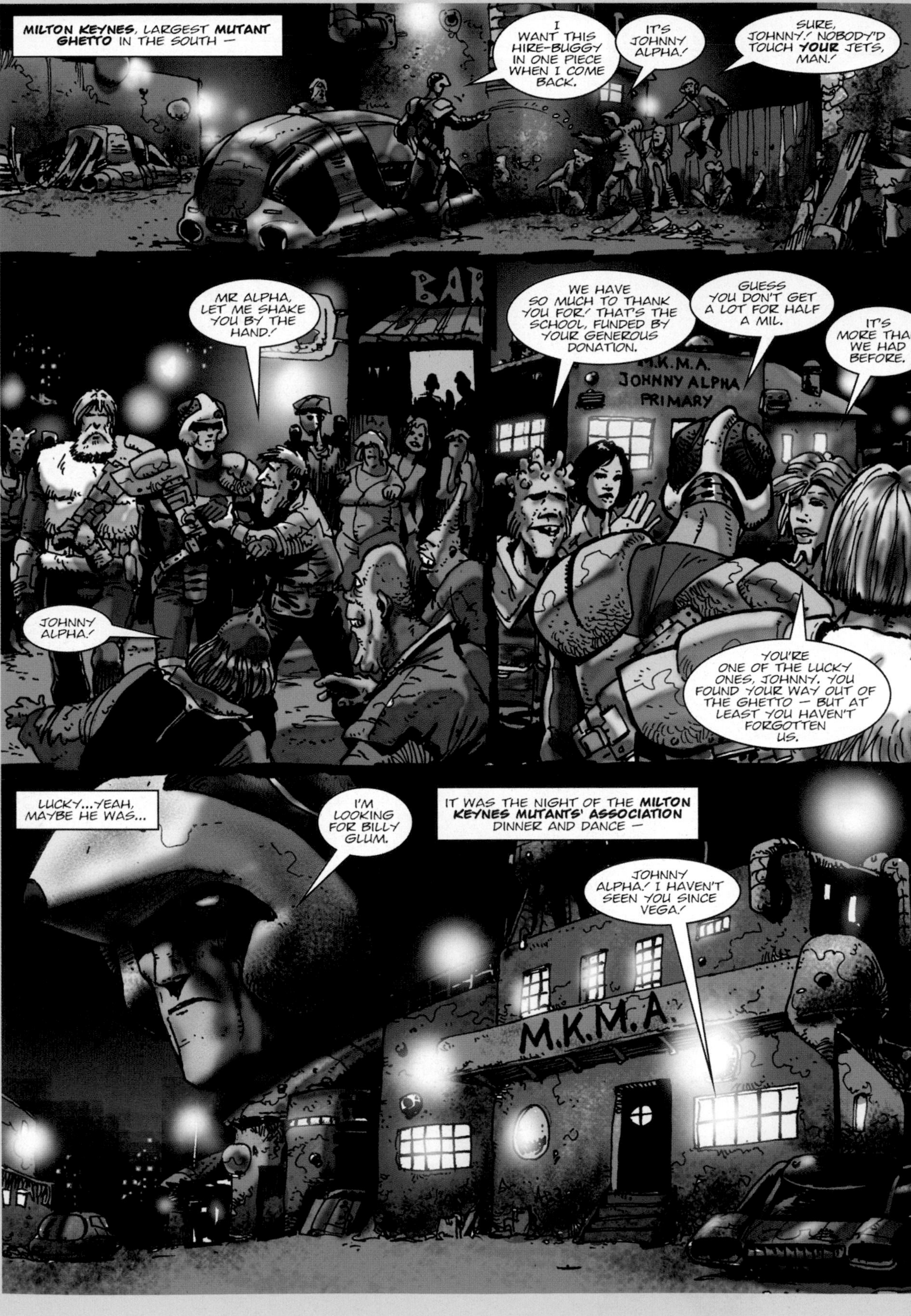
MILTON KEYNES, LARGEST MUTANT GHETTO IN THE SOUTH —
I WANT THIS HIRE-BUGGY IN ONE PIECE WHEN I COME BACK.
IT'S JOHNNY ALPHA!
SURE, JOHNNY! NOBODY'D TOUCH YOUR JETS, MAN!
BAR
MR ALPHA, LET ME SHAKE YOU BY THE HAND!
JOHNNY ALPHA!
WE HAVE SO MUCH TO THANK YOU FOR! THAT'S THE SCHOOL, FUNDED BY YOUR GENEROUS DONATION.
M.K.M.A. JOHNNY ALPHA PRIMARY
GUESS YOU DON'T GET A LOT FOR HALF A MIL.
IT'S MORE THAN WE HAD BEFORE.
YOU'RE ONE OF THE LUCKY ONES, JOHNNY. YOU FOUND YOUR WAY OUT OF THE GHETTO — BUT AT LEAST YOU HAVEN'T FORGOTTEN US.
LUCKY...YEAH, MAYBE HE WAS...
I'M LOOKING FOR BILLY GLUM.
IT WAS THE NIGHT OF THE MILTON KEYNES MUTANTS' ASSOCIATION DINNER AND DANCE —
JOHNNY ALPHA! I HAVEN'T SEEN YOU SINCE VEGA!
M.K.M.A.

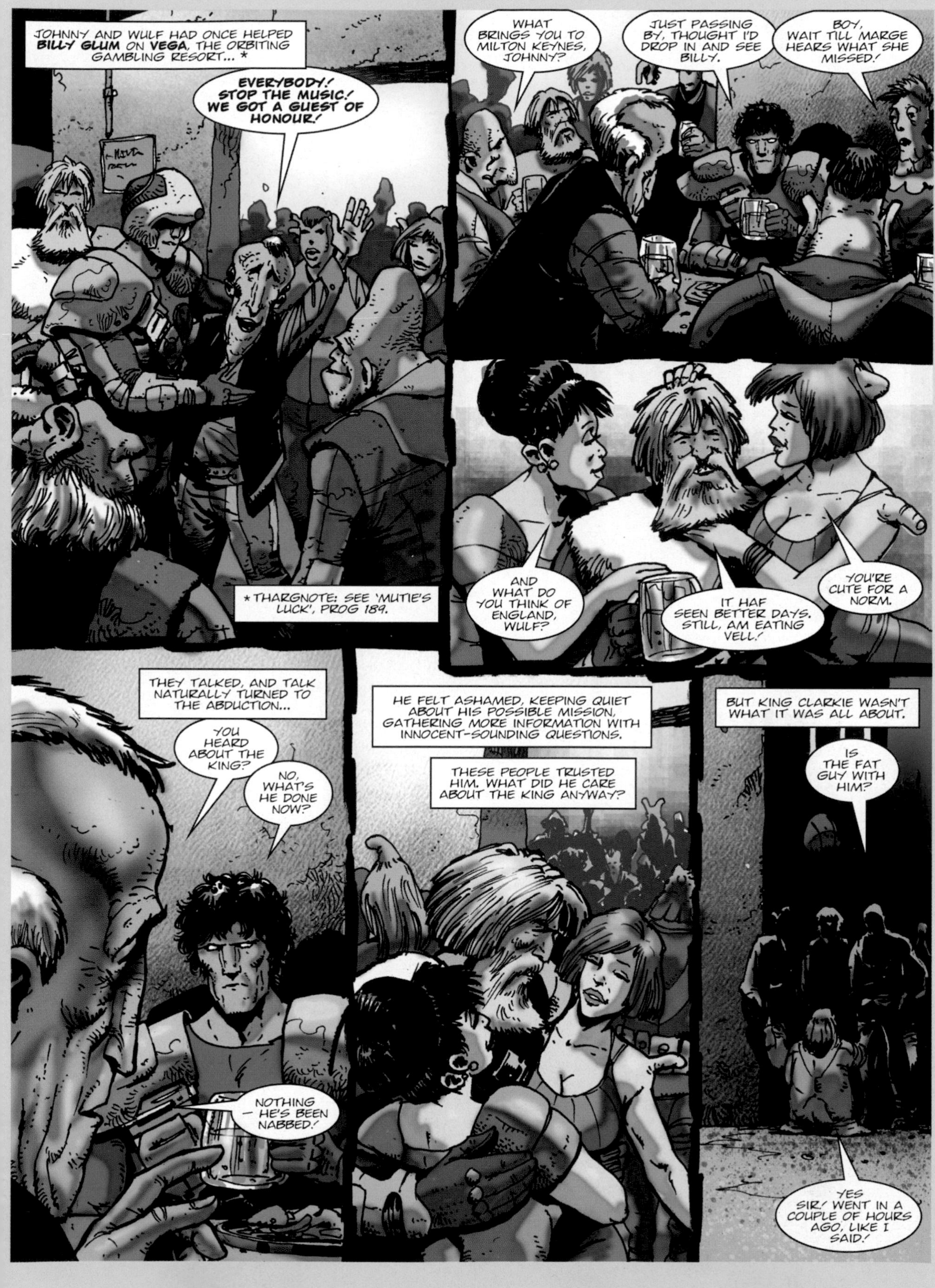
JOHNNY AND WULF HAD ONCE HELPED BILLY GLUM ON VEGA, THE ORBITING GAMBLING RESORT... *
EVERYBODY! STOP THE MUSIC! WE GOT A GUEST OF HONOUR!
* THARGNOTE: SEE 'MUTIE'S LUCK', PROG 189.
WHAT BRINGS YOU TO MILTON KEYNES, JOHNNY?
JUST PASSING BY, THOUGHT I'D DROP IN AND SEE BILLY.
BOY, WAIT TILL MARGE HEARS WHAT SHE MISSED!
AND WHAT DO YOU THINK OF ENGLAND, WULF?
IT HAF SEEN BETTER DAYS. STILL, AM EATING VELL!
YOU'RE CUTE FOR A NORM.
THEY TALKED, AND TALK NATURALLY TURNED TO THE ABDUCTION...
YOU HEARD ABOUT THE KING?
NO, WHAT'S HE DONE NOW?
NOTHING — HE'S BEEN NABBED!
HE FELT ASHAMED, KEEPING QUIET ABOUT HIS POSSIBLE MISSION, GATHERING MORE INFORMATION WITH INNOCENT-SOUNDING QUESTIONS.
THESE PEOPLE TRUSTED HIM. WHAT DID HE CARE ABOUT THE KING ANYWAY?
BUT KING CLARKIE WASN'T WHAT IT WAS ALL ABOUT.
IS THE FAT GUY WITH HIM?
YES SIR! WENT IN A COUPLE OF HOURS AGO, LIKE I SAID!

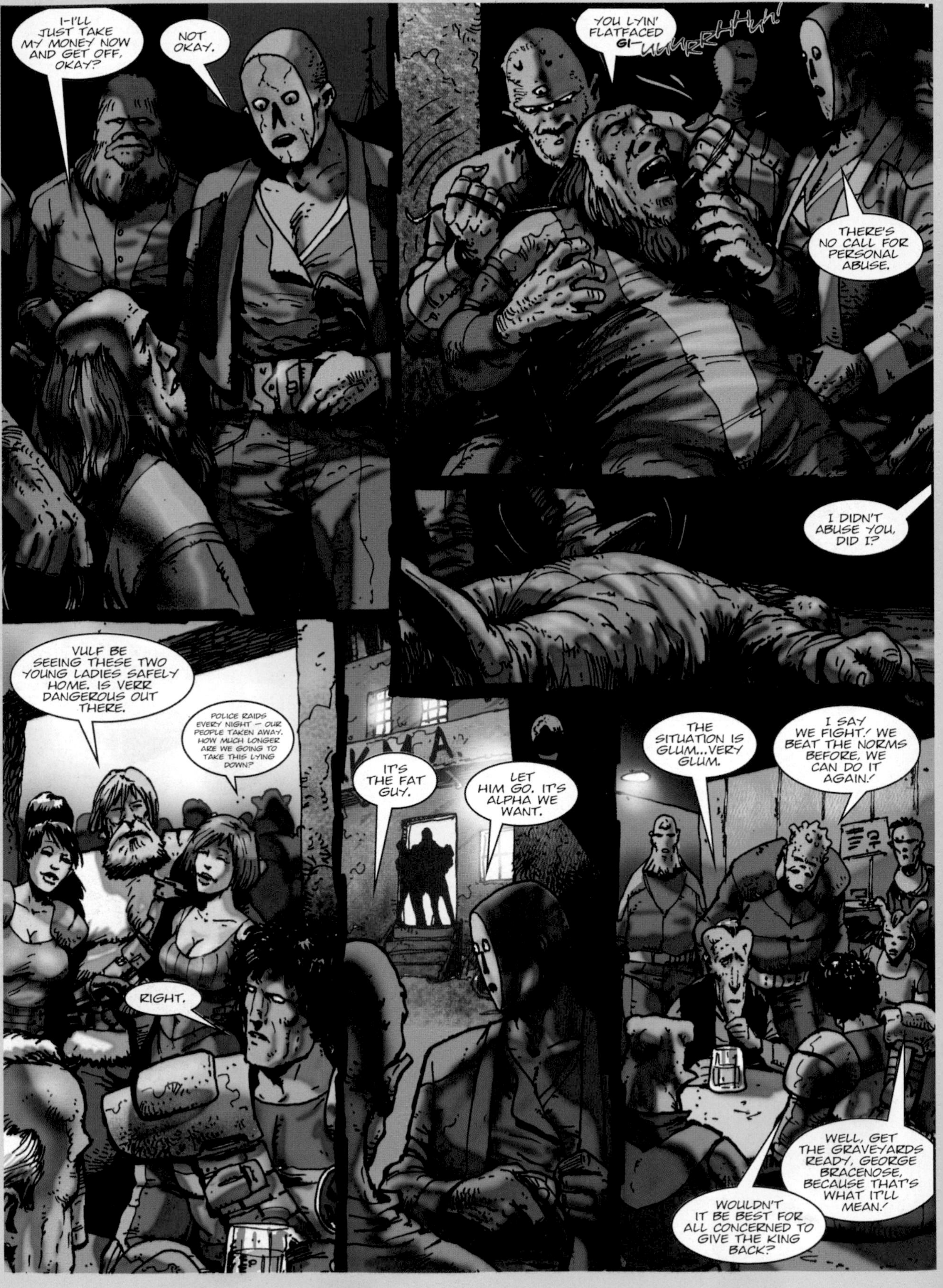
I-I'LL JUST TAKE MY MONEY NOW AND GET OFF, OKAY?
NOT OKAY.
YOU LYIN' FLATFACED GI-
UUURRHHHUH!
THERE'S NO CALL FOR PERSONAL ABUSE.
I DIDN'T ABUSE YOU, DID I?
VULF BE SEEING THESE TWO YOUNG LADIES SAFELY HOME. IS VERR DANGEROUS OUT THERE.
POLICE RAIDS EVERY NIGHT — OUR PEOPLE TAKEN AWAY. HOW MUCH LONGER ARE WE GOING TO TAKE THIS LYING DOWN?
RIGHT.
IT'S THE FAT GUY.
LET HIM GO. IT'S ALPHA WE WANT.
THE SITUATION IS GLUM...VERY GLUM.
I SAY WE FIGHT! WE BEAT THE NORMS BEFORE, WE CAN DO IT AGAIN!
WOULDN'T IT BE BEST FOR ALL CONCERNED TO GIVE THE KING BACK?
WELL, GET THE GRAVEYARDS READY, GEORGE BRACENOSE, BECAUSE THAT'S WHAT IT'LL MEAN!

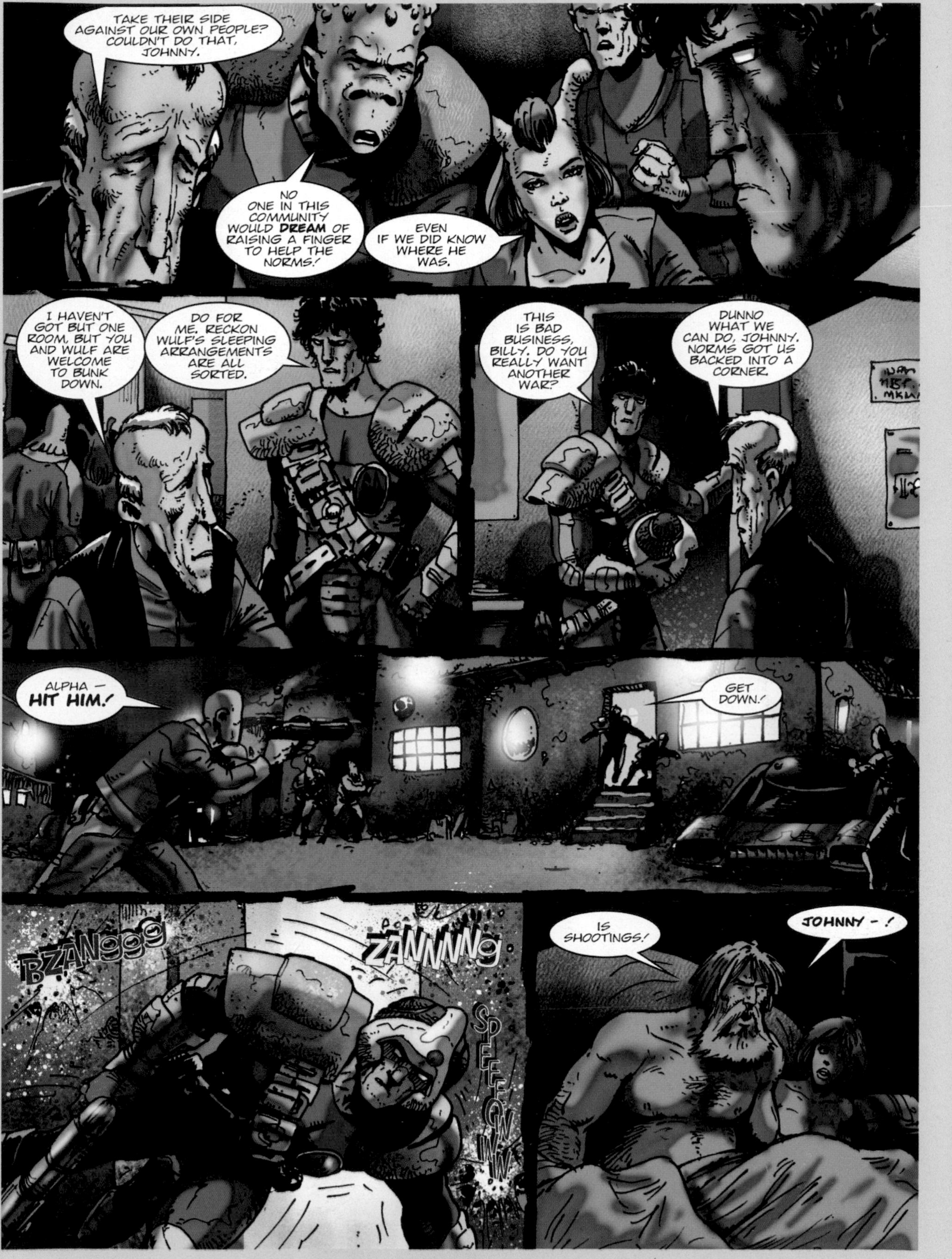
TAKE THEIR SIDE AGAINST OUR OWN PEOPLE? COULDN'T DO THAT, JOHNNY.
NO ONE IN THIS COMMUNITY WOULD **DREAM** OF RAISING A FINGER TO HELP THE NORMS.!
EVEN IF WE DID KNOW WHERE HE WAS.
I HAVEN'T GOT BUT ONE ROOM, BUT YOU AND WULF ARE WELCOME TO BUNK DOWN.
DO FOR ME. RECKON WULF'S SLEEPING ARRANGEMENTS ARE ALL SORTED.
THIS IS BAD BUSINESS, BILLY. DO YOU REALLY WANT ANOTHER WAR?
DUNNO WHAT WE CAN DO, JOHNNY. NORMS GOT US BACKED INTO A CORNER.
ALPHA — **HIT HIM.!**
GET DOWN.!
BZANggg
ZANNNNg
IS SHOOTINGS.!
JOHNNY - !

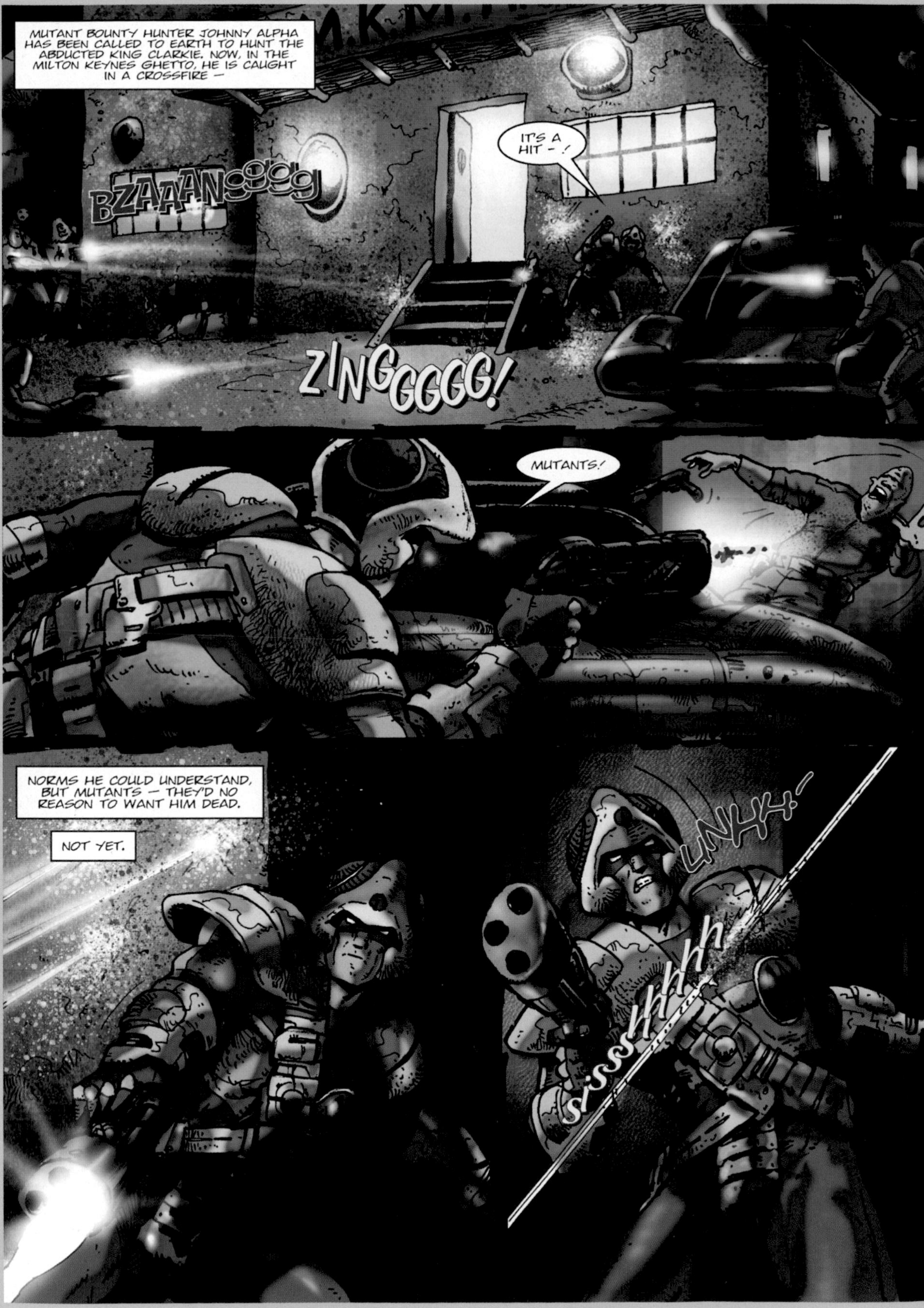
MUTANT BOUNTY HUNTER JOHNNY ALPHA HAS BEEN CALLED TO EARTH TO HUNT THE ABDUCTED KING CLARKIE. NOW, IN THE MILTON KEYNES GHETTO, HE IS CAUGHT IN A CROSSFIRE —
BZAAANGGGG
IT'S A HIT – !
ZINGGGGG!
MUTANTS!
NORMS HE COULD UNDERSTAND, BUT MUTANTS — THEY'D NO REASON TO WANT HIM DEAD.
NOT YET.
UNKK!
SSSSHHHHH

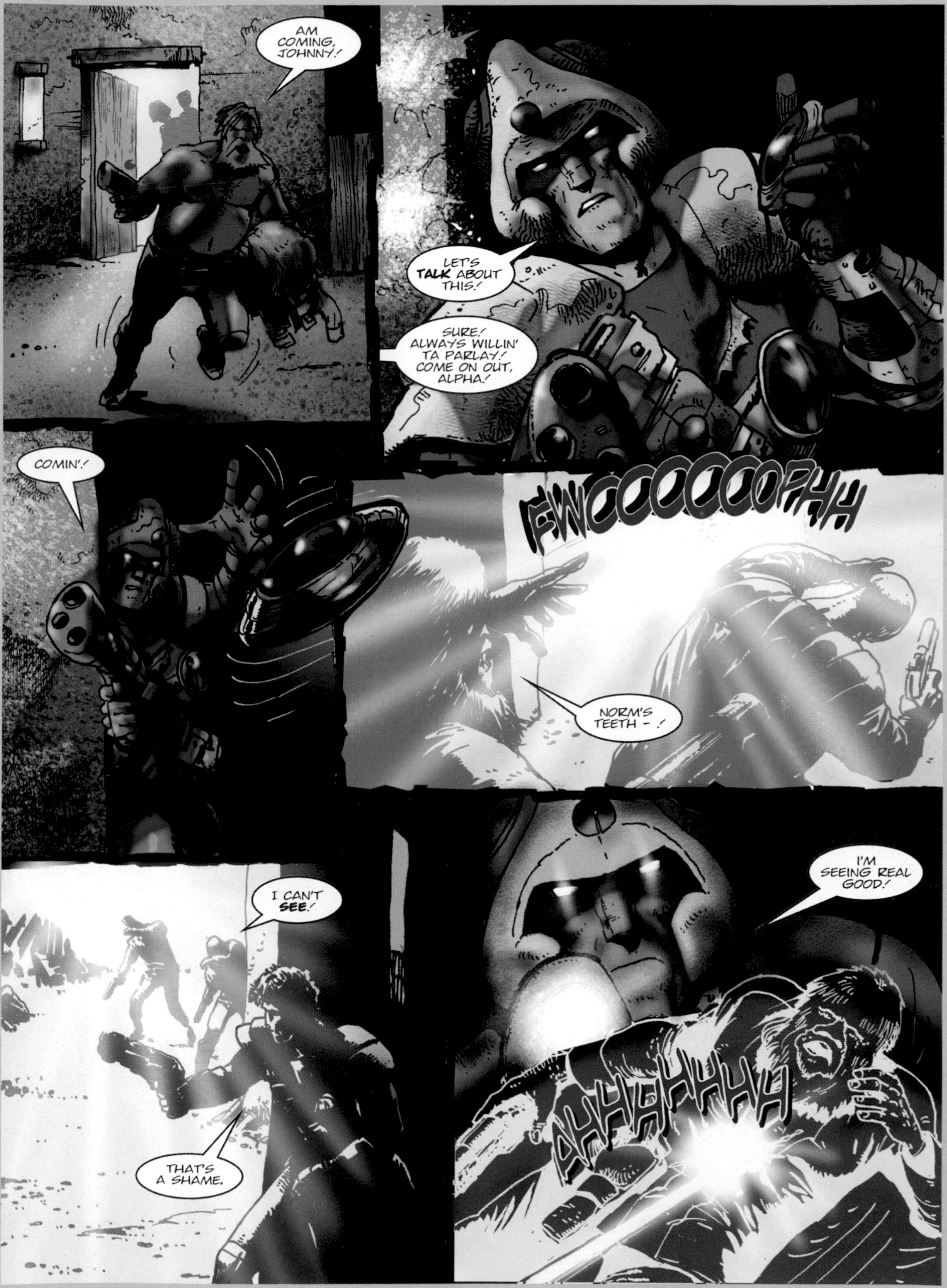
AM COMING, JOHNNY!
LET'S TALK ABOUT THIS!
SURE! ALWAYS WILLIN' TA PARLAY! COME ON OUT, ALPHA!
COMIN'!
FWOOOOOOOOPHH
NORM'S TEETH -!
I CAN'T SEE!
THAT'S A SHAME.
I'M SEEING REAL GOOD!
AHHHHHHH

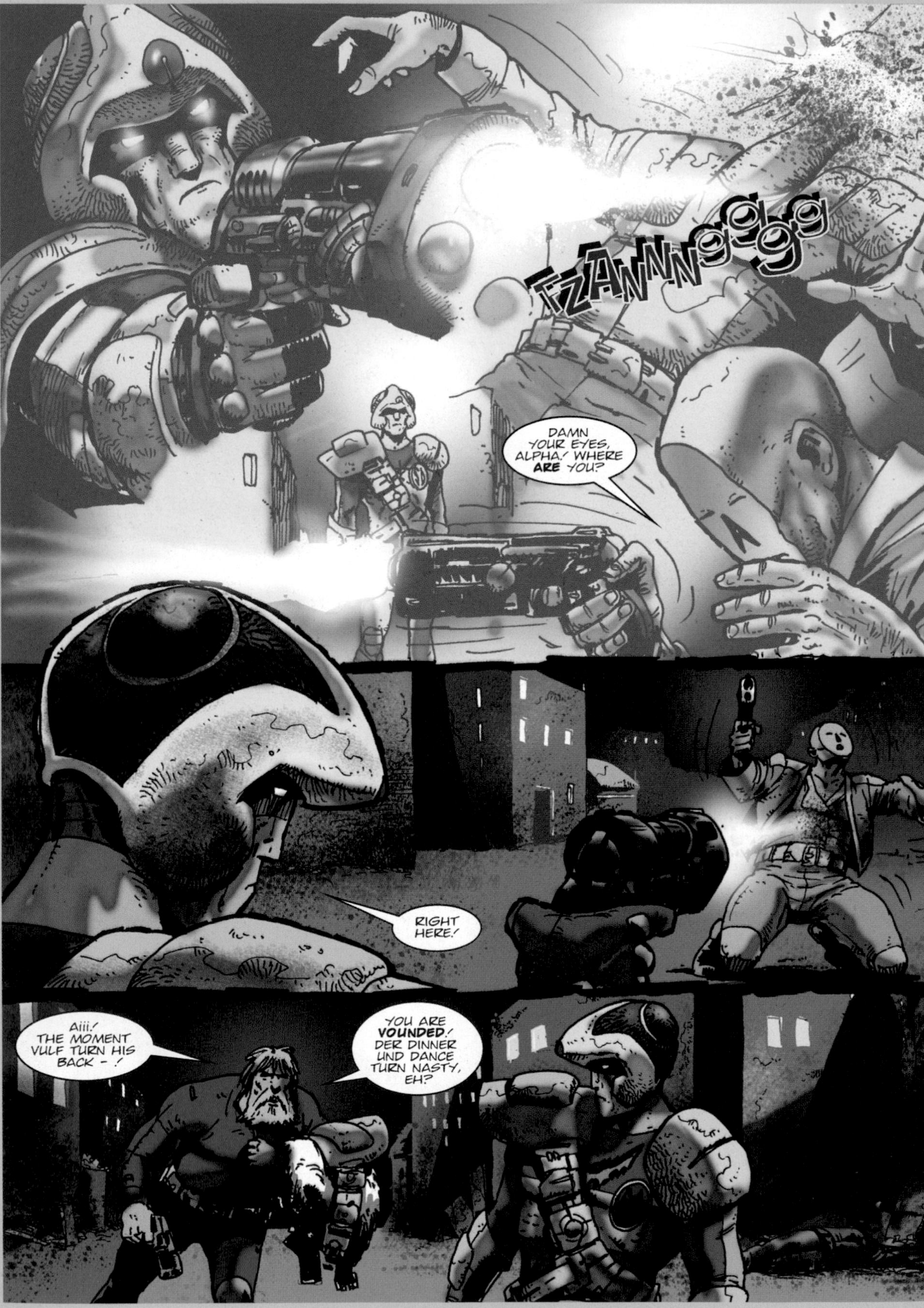
FZANNNggggg
DAMN YOUR EYES, ALPHA! WHERE ARE YOU?
RIGHT HERE!
Aiii! THE MOMENT VULF TURN HIS BACK -!
YOU ARE VOUNDED! DER DINNER UND DANCE TURN NASTY, EH?

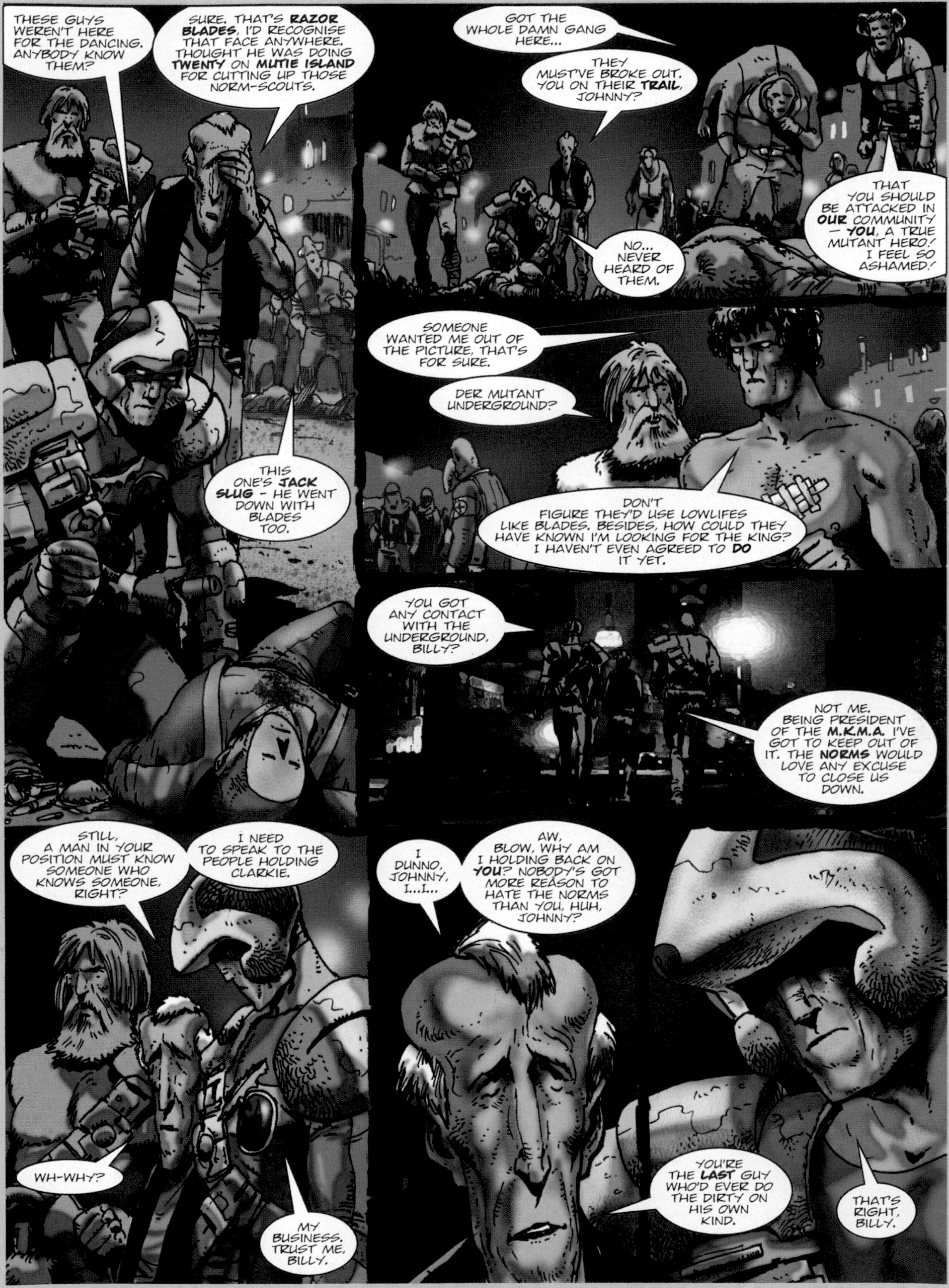
THESE GUYS WEREN'T HERE FOR THE DANCING. ANYBODY KNOW THEM?
SURE. THAT'S **RAZOR BLADES**, I'D RECOGNISE THAT FACE ANYWHERE. THOUGHT HE WAS DOING **TWENTY** ON **MUTIE ISLAND** FOR CUTTING UP THOSE NORM-SCOUTS.
THIS ONE'S **JACK SLUG** - HE WENT DOWN WITH BLADES TOO.
GOT THE WHOLE DAMN GANG HERE...
THEY MUST'VE BROKE OUT. YOU ON THEIR **TRAIL**, JOHNNY?
NO... NEVER HEARD OF THEM.
THAT YOU SHOULD BE ATTACKED IN **OUR** COMMUNITY — **YOU**, A TRUE MUTANT HERO! I FEEL SO ASHAMED!
SOMEONE WANTED ME OUT OF THE PICTURE, THAT'S FOR SURE.
DER MUTANT UNDERGROUND?
DON'T FIGURE THEY'D USE LOWLIFES LIKE BLADES. BESIDES, HOW COULD THEY HAVE KNOWN I'M LOOKING FOR THE KING? I HAVEN'T EVEN AGREED TO **DO** IT YET.
YOU GOT ANY CONTACT WITH THE UNDERGROUND, BILLY?
NOT ME. BEING PRESIDENT OF THE **M.K.M.A.** I'VE GOT TO KEEP OUT OF IT. THE **NORMS** WOULD LOVE ANY EXCUSE TO CLOSE US DOWN.
STILL, A MAN IN YOUR POSITION MUST KNOW SOMEONE WHO KNOWS SOMEONE, RIGHT?
I NEED TO SPEAK TO THE PEOPLE HOLDING CLARKIE.
WH-WHY?
MY BUSINESS. TRUST ME, BILLY.
I DUNNO, JOHNNY, I...I...
AW, BLOW, WHY AM I HOLDING BACK ON **YOU**? NOBODY'S GOT MORE REASON TO HATE THE NORMS THAN YOU, HUH, JOHNNY?
YOU'RE THE **LAST** GUY WHO'D EVER DO THE DIRTY ON HIS OWN KIND.
THAT'S RIGHT, BILLY.

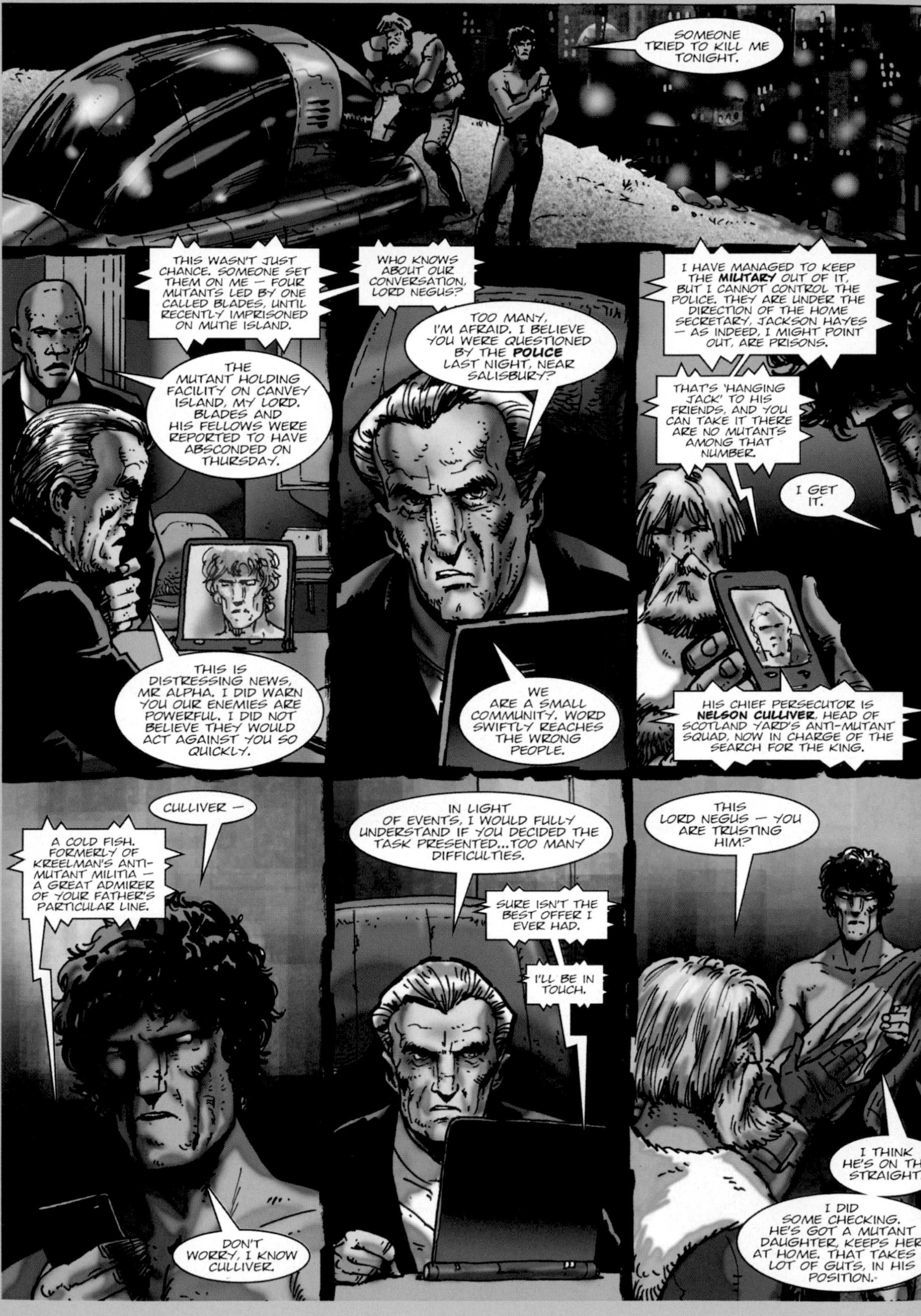

SOMEONE TRIED TO KILL ME TONIGHT.
THIS WASN'T JUST CHANCE. SOMEONE SET THEM ON ME — FOUR MUTANTS LED BY ONE CALLED BLADES, UNTIL RECENTLY IMPRISONED ON MUTIE ISLAND.
THE MUTANT HOLDING FACILITY ON CANVEY ISLAND, MY LORD. BLADES AND HIS FELLOWS WERE REPORTED TO HAVE ABSCONDED ON THURSDAY.
THIS IS DISTRESSING NEWS, MR ALPHA. I DID WARN YOU OUR ENEMIES ARE POWERFUL. I DID NOT BELIEVE THEY WOULD ACT AGAINST YOU SO QUICKLY.
WHO KNOWS ABOUT OUR CONVERSATION, LORD NEGUS?
TOO MANY, I'M AFRAID. I BELIEVE YOU WERE QUESTIONED BY THE POLICE LAST NIGHT, NEAR SALISBURY?
WE ARE A SMALL COMMUNITY. WORD SWIFTLY REACHES THE WRONG PEOPLE.
I HAVE MANAGED TO KEEP THE MILITARY OUT OF IT, BUT I CANNOT CONTROL THE POLICE. THEY ARE UNDER THE DIRECTION OF THE HOME SECRETARY, JACKSON HAYES — AS INDEED, I MIGHT POINT OUT, ARE PRISONS.
THAT'S 'HANGING JACK' TO HIS FRIENDS, AND YOU CAN TAKE IT THERE ARE NO MUTANTS AMONG THAT NUMBER.
I GET IT.
HIS CHIEF PERSECUTOR IS NELSON CULLIVER, HEAD OF SCOTLAND YARD'S ANTI-MUTANT SQUAD, NOW IN CHARGE OF THE SEARCH FOR THE KING.
CULLIVER —
A COLD FISH. FORMERLY OF KREELMAN'S ANTI-MUTANT MILITIA — A GREAT ADMIRER OF YOUR FATHER'S PARTICULAR LINE.
DON'T WORRY, I KNOW CULLIVER.
IN LIGHT OF EVENTS, I WOULD FULLY UNDERSTAND IF YOU DECIDED THE TASK PRESENTED...TOO MANY DIFFICULTIES.
SURE ISN'T THE BEST OFFER I EVER HAD.
I'LL BE IN TOUCH.
THIS LORD NEGUS — YOU ARE TRUSTING HIM?
I THINK HE'S ON THE STRAIGHT.
I DID SOME CHECKING. HE'S GOT A MUTANT DAUGHTER, KEEPS HER AT HOME. THAT TAKES A LOT OF GUTS, IN HIS POSITION.

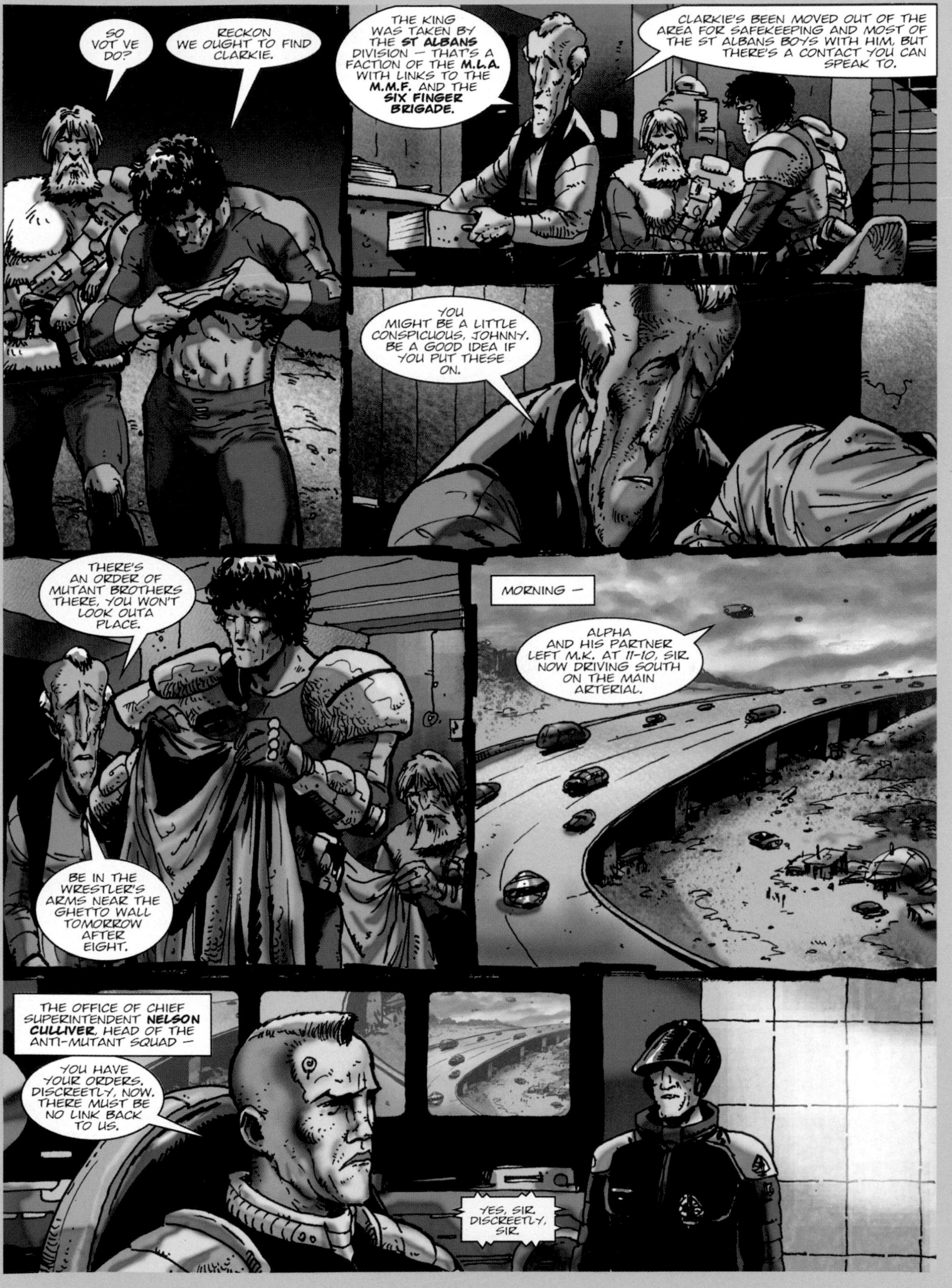

SO VOT VE DO?
RECKON WE OUGHT TO FIND CLARKIE.
THE KING WAS TAKEN BY THE ST ALBANS DIVISION — THAT'S A FACTION OF THE M.L.A. WITH LINKS TO THE M.M.F. AND THE SIX FINGER BRIGADE.
CLARKIE'S BEEN MOVED OUT OF THE AREA FOR SAFEKEEPING AND MOST OF THE ST ALBANS BOYS WITH HIM, BUT THERE'S A CONTACT YOU CAN SPEAK TO.
YOU MIGHT BE A LITTLE CONSPICUOUS, JOHNNY. BE A GOOD IDEA IF YOU PUT THESE ON.
THERE'S AN ORDER OF MUTANT BROTHERS THERE, YOU WON'T LOOK OUTA PLACE.
BE IN THE WRESTLER'S ARMS NEAR THE GHETTO WALL TOMORROW AFTER EIGHT.
MORNING —
ALPHA AND HIS PARTNER LEFT M.K. AT 11-10, SIR. NOW DRIVING SOUTH ON THE MAIN ARTERIAL.
THE OFFICE OF CHIEF SUPERINTENDENT NELSON CULLIVER, HEAD OF THE ANTI-MUTANT SQUAD —
YOU HAVE YOUR ORDERS. DISCREETLY, NOW. THERE MUST BE NO LINK BACK TO US.
YES, SIR. DISCREETLY, SIR.

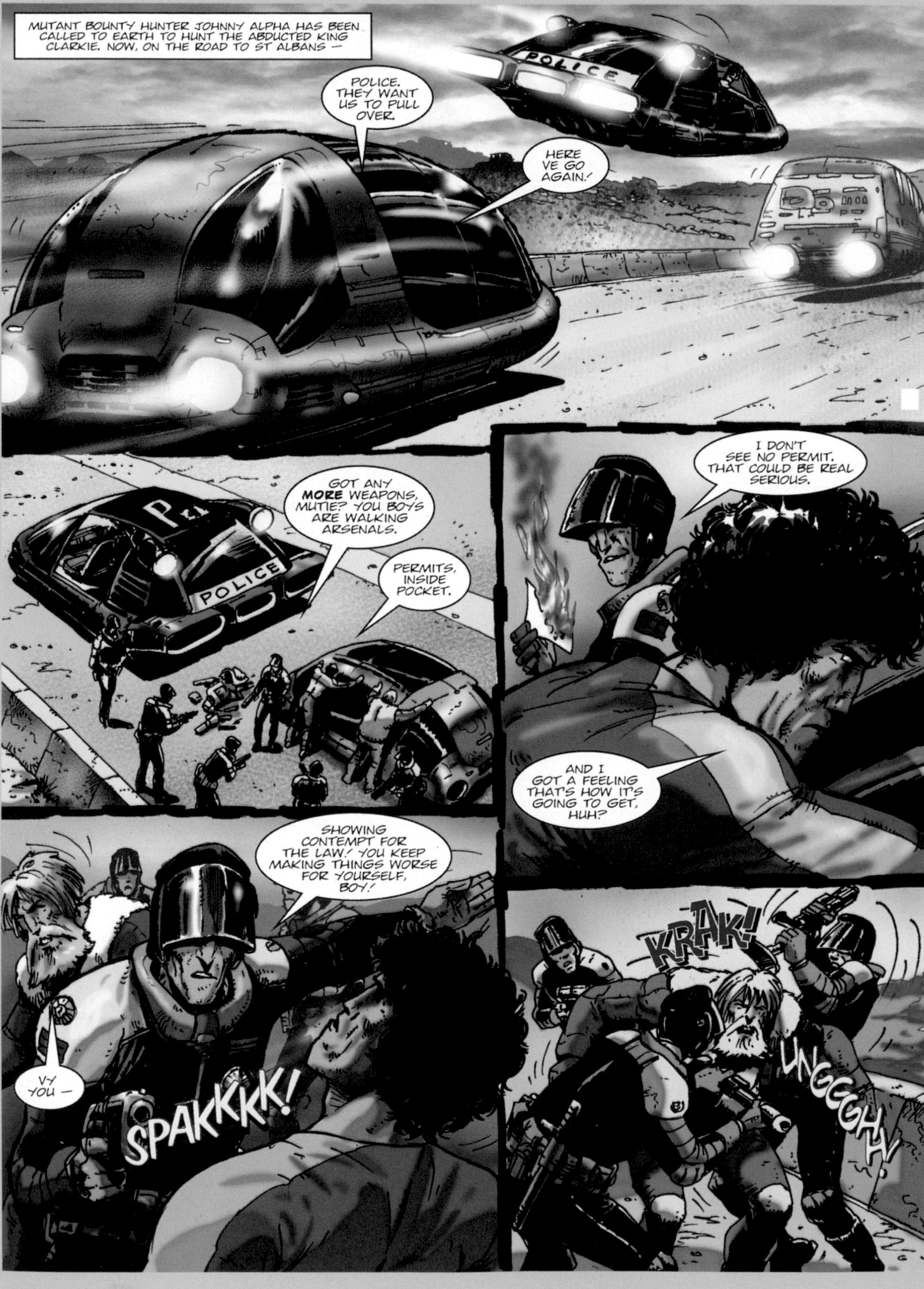
MUTANT BOUNTY HUNTER JOHNNY ALPHA HAS BEEN CALLED TO EARTH TO HUNT THE ABDUCTED KING CLARKIE. NOW, ON THE ROAD TO ST ALBANS —
POLICE
POLICE. THEY WANT US TO PULL OVER.
HERE VE GO AGAIN.!
GOT ANY MORE WEAPONS, MUTIE? YOU BOYS ARE WALKING ARSENALS.
POLICE
PERMITS, INSIDE POCKET.
I DON'T SEE NO PERMIT. THAT COULD BE REAL SERIOUS.
AND I GOT A FEELING THAT'S HOW IT'S GOING TO GET, HUH?
SHOWING CONTEMPT FOR THE LAW.! YOU KEEP MAKING THINGS WORSE FOR YOURSELF, BOY.!
VY YOU —
SPAKKKK!
KRAK!
UNGGGHH!

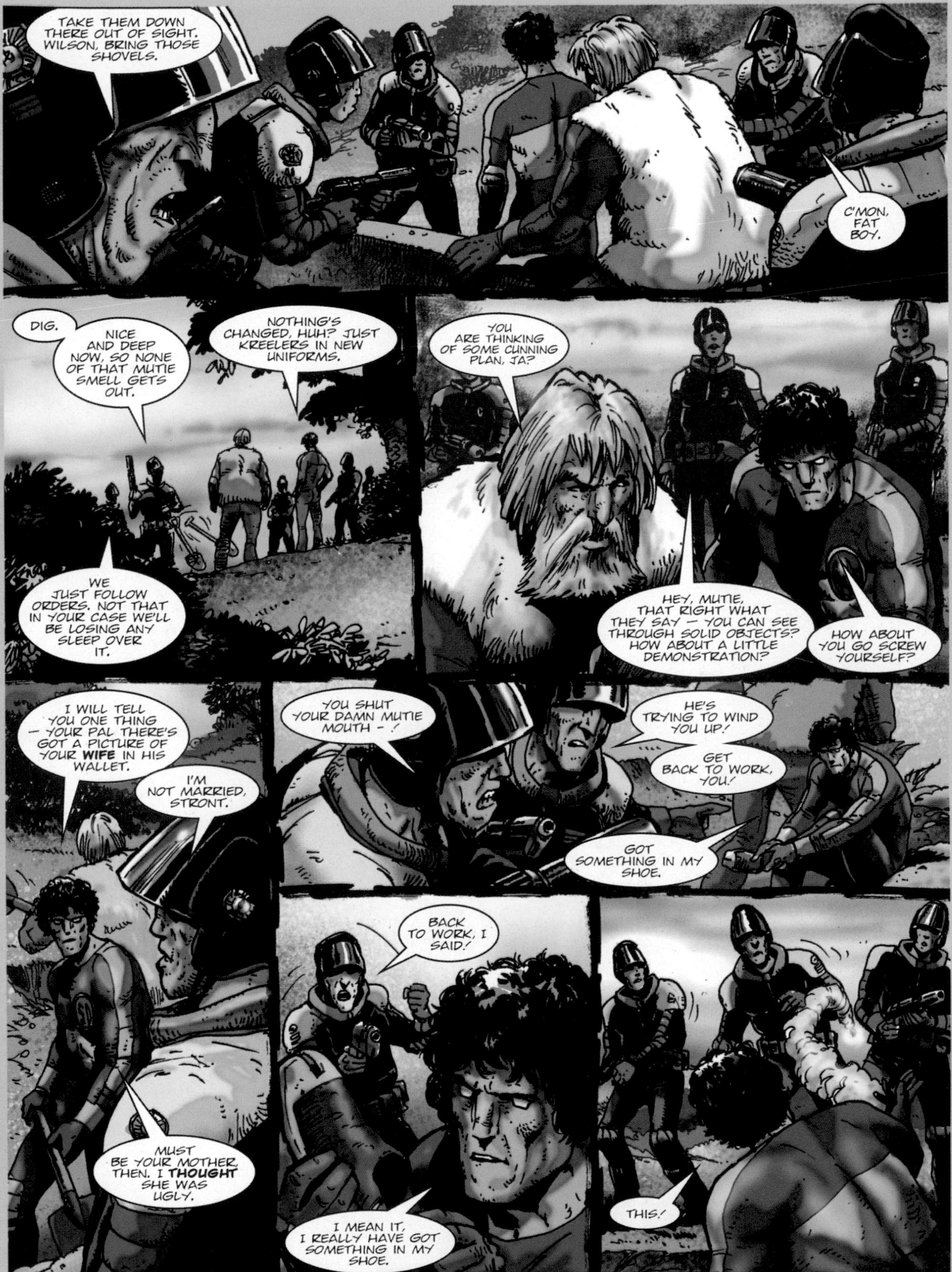
TAKE THEM DOWN THERE OUT OF SIGHT. WILSON, BRING THOSE SHOVELS.
C'MON, FAT BOY.
DIG.
NICE AND DEEP NOW, SO NONE OF THAT MUTIE SMELL GETS OUT.
NOTHING'S CHANGED, HUH? JUST KREELERS IN NEW UNIFORMS.
WE JUST FOLLOW ORDERS. NOT THAT IN YOUR CASE WE'LL BE LOSING ANY SLEEP OVER IT.
YOU ARE THINKING OF SOME CUNNING PLAN, JA?
HEY, MUTIE, THAT RIGHT WHAT THEY SAY — YOU CAN SEE THROUGH SOLID OBJECTS? HOW ABOUT A LITTLE DEMONSTRATION?
HOW ABOUT YOU GO SCREW YOURSELF?
I WILL TELL YOU ONE THING — YOUR PAL THERE'S GOT A PICTURE OF YOUR **WIFE** IN HIS WALLET.
I'M NOT MARRIED, STRONT.
MUST BE YOUR MOTHER, THEN. I **THOUGHT** SHE WAS UGLY.
YOU SHUT YOUR DAMN MUTIE MOUTH — !
HE'S TRYING TO WIND YOU UP!
GET BACK TO WORK, YOU!
GOT SOMETHING IN MY SHOE.
BACK TO WORK, I SAID!
I MEAN IT, I REALLY HAVE GOT SOMETHING IN MY SHOE.
THIS!

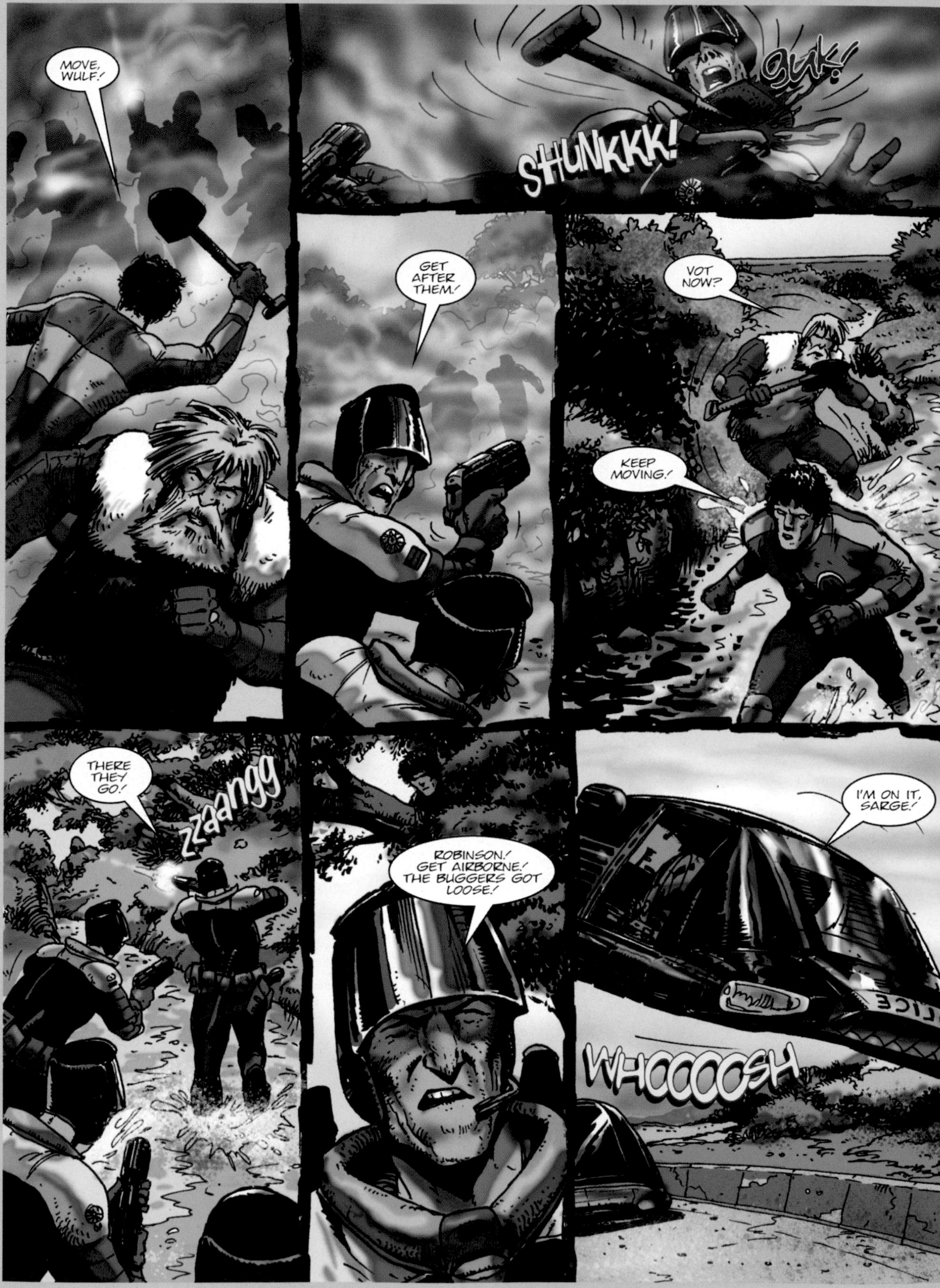
MOVE, WULF!
SHUNKKK!
GUK!
GET AFTER THEM!
VOT NOW?
KEEP MOVING!
THERE THEY GO!
ZZAANGG
ROBINSON! GET AIRBORNE! THE BUGGERS GOT LOOSE!
I'M ON IT, SARGE!
WHOOOOSH

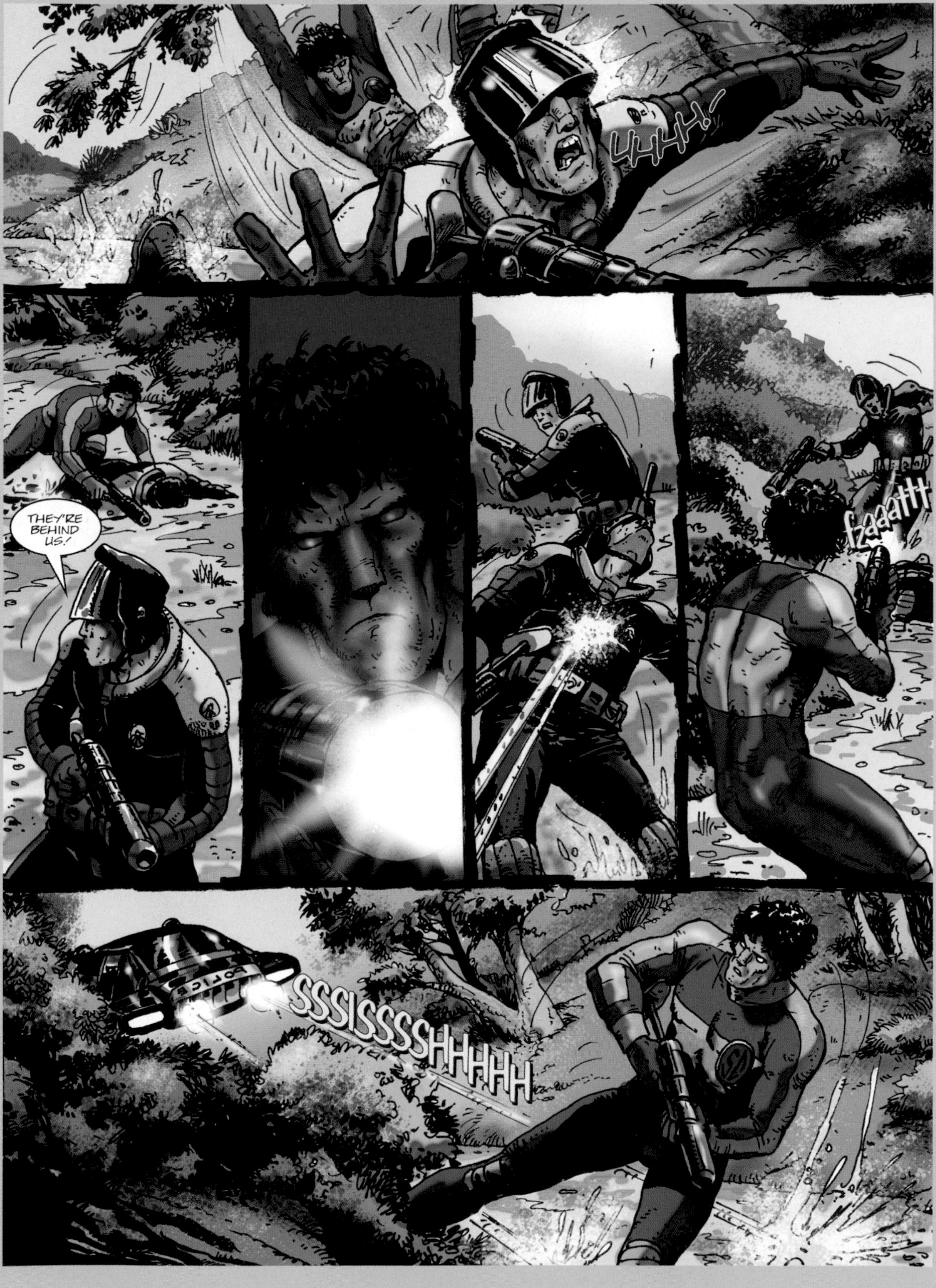
UHHH!
THEY'RE BEHIND US!
fzaaattt
POLICE
SSSISSSSSHHHHHH

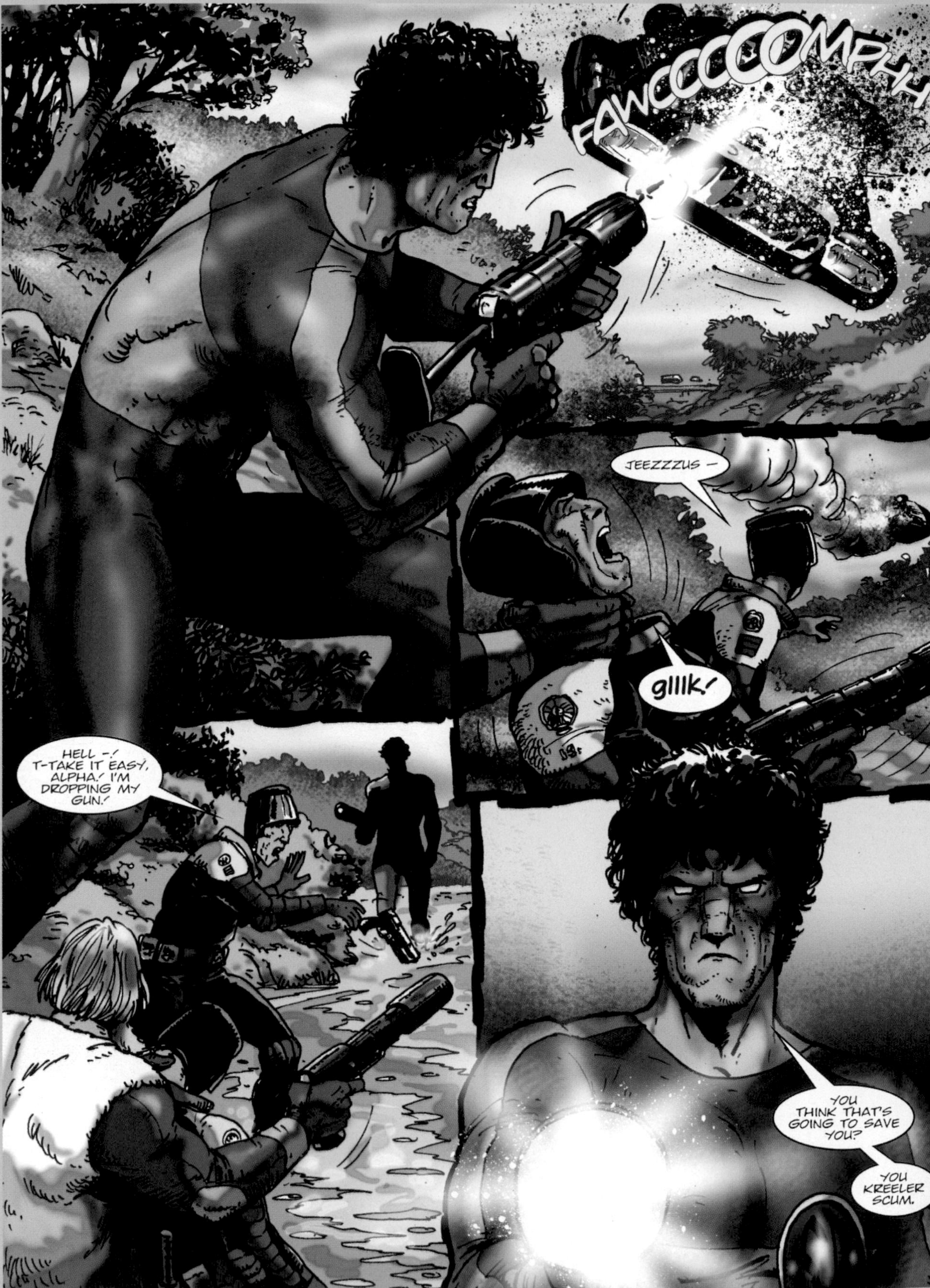
FAWCCCCOMPHH
JEEZZZUS –
gllIk!
HELL –! T-TAKE IT EASY, ALPHA! I'M DROPPING MY GUN!
YOU THINK THAT'S GOING TO SAVE YOU?
YOU KREELER SCUM.

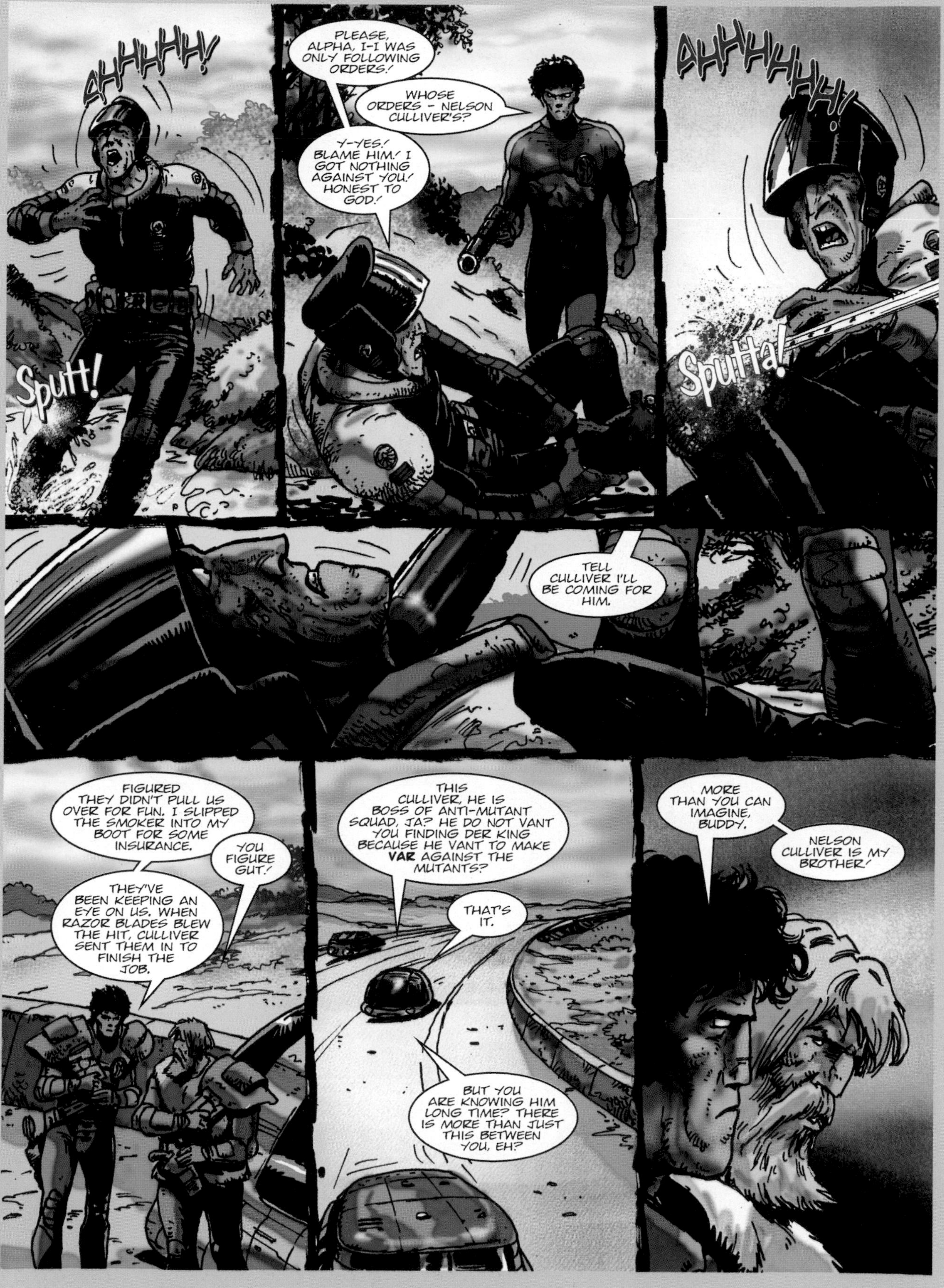
AHHHHH!
SPUTT!
PLEASE, ALPHA, I-I WAS ONLY FOLLOWING ORDERS!
WHOSE ORDERS - NELSON CULLIVER'S?
Y-YES! BLAME HIM! I GOT NOTHING AGAINST YOU! HONEST TO GOD!
AHHHHHHH!
SPUTTA!
TELL CULLIVER I'LL BE COMING FOR HIM.
FIGURED THEY DIDN'T PULL US OVER FOR FUN. I SLIPPED THE SMOKER INTO MY BOOT FOR SOME INSURANCE.
YOU FIGURE GUT!
THEY'VE BEEN KEEPING AN EYE ON US. WHEN RAZOR BLADES BLEW THE HIT, CULLIVER SENT THEM IN TO FINISH THE JOB.
THIS CULLIVER, HE IS BOSS OF ANTI-MUTANT SQUAD, JA? HE DO NOT VANT YOU FINDING DER KING BECAUSE HE VANT TO MAKE VAR AGAINST THE MUTANTS?
THAT'S IT.
BUT YOU ARE KNOWING HIM LONG TIME? THERE IS MORE THAN JUST THIS BETWEEN YOU, EH?
MORE THAN YOU CAN IMAGINE, BUDDY.
NELSON CULLIVER IS MY BROTHER!

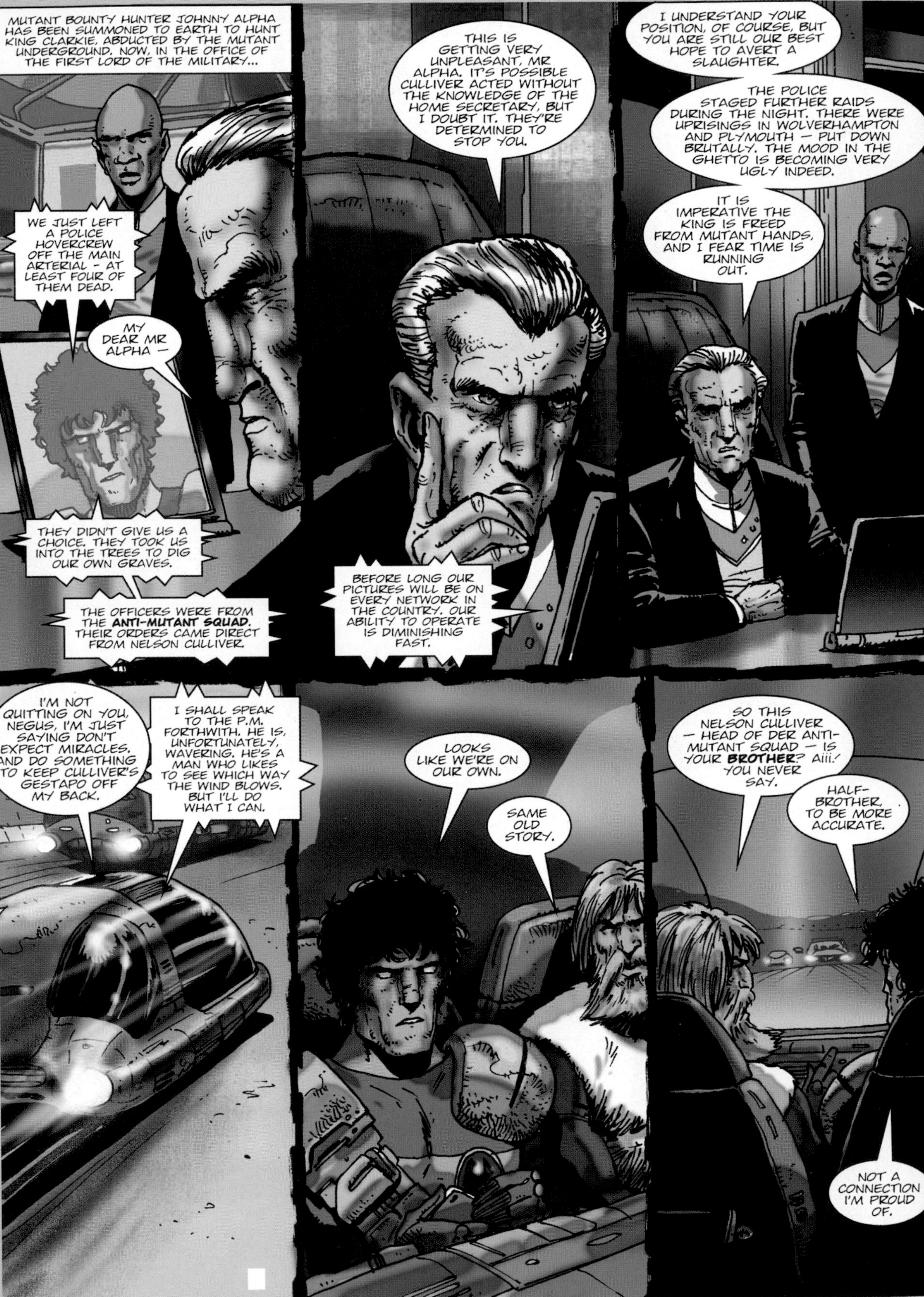
MUTANT BOUNTY HUNTER JOHNNY ALPHA HAS BEEN SUMMONED TO EARTH TO HUNT KING CLARKIE, ABDUCTED BY THE MUTANT UNDERGROUND. NOW, IN THE OFFICE OF THE FIRST LORD OF THE MILITARY...
WE JUST LEFT A POLICE HOVERCREW OFF THE MAIN ARTERIAL - AT LEAST FOUR OF THEM DEAD.
MY DEAR MR ALPHA —
THEY DIDN'T GIVE US A CHOICE. THEY TOOK US INTO THE TREES TO DIG OUR OWN GRAVES.
THE OFFICERS WERE FROM THE **ANTI-MUTANT SQUAD**. THEIR ORDERS CAME DIRECT FROM NELSON CULLIVER.
THIS IS GETTING VERY UNPLEASANT, MR ALPHA. IT'S POSSIBLE CULLIVER ACTED WITHOUT THE KNOWLEDGE OF THE HOME SECRETARY, BUT I DOUBT IT. THEY'RE DETERMINED TO STOP YOU.
BEFORE LONG OUR PICTURES WILL BE ON EVERY NETWORK IN THE COUNTRY. OUR ABILITY TO OPERATE IS DIMINISHING FAST.
I UNDERSTAND YOUR POSITION, OF COURSE, BUT YOU ARE STILL OUR BEST HOPE TO AVERT A SLAUGHTER.
THE POLICE STAGED FURTHER RAIDS DURING THE NIGHT. THERE WERE UPRISINGS IN WOLVERHAMPTON AND PLYMOUTH — PUT DOWN BRUTALLY. THE MOOD IN THE GHETTO IS BECOMING VERY UGLY INDEED.
IT IS IMPERATIVE THE KING IS FREED FROM MUTANT HANDS, AND I FEAR TIME IS RUNNING OUT.
I'M NOT QUITTING ON YOU, NEGUS, I'M JUST SAYING DON'T EXPECT MIRACLES. AND DO SOMETHING TO KEEP CULLIVER'S GESTAPO OFF MY BACK.
I SHALL SPEAK TO THE P.M. FORTHWITH. HE IS, UNFORTUNATELY, WAVERING. HE'S A MAN WHO LIKES TO SEE WHICH WAY THE WIND BLOWS. BUT I'LL DO WHAT I CAN.
LOOKS LIKE WE'RE ON OUR OWN.
SAME OLD STORY.
SO THIS NELSON CULLIVER — HEAD OF DER ANTI-MUTANT SQUAD — IS YOUR **BROTHER**? Aiii! YOU NEVER SAY.
HALF-BROTHER, TO BE MORE ACCURATE.
NOT A CONNECTION I'M PROUD OF.

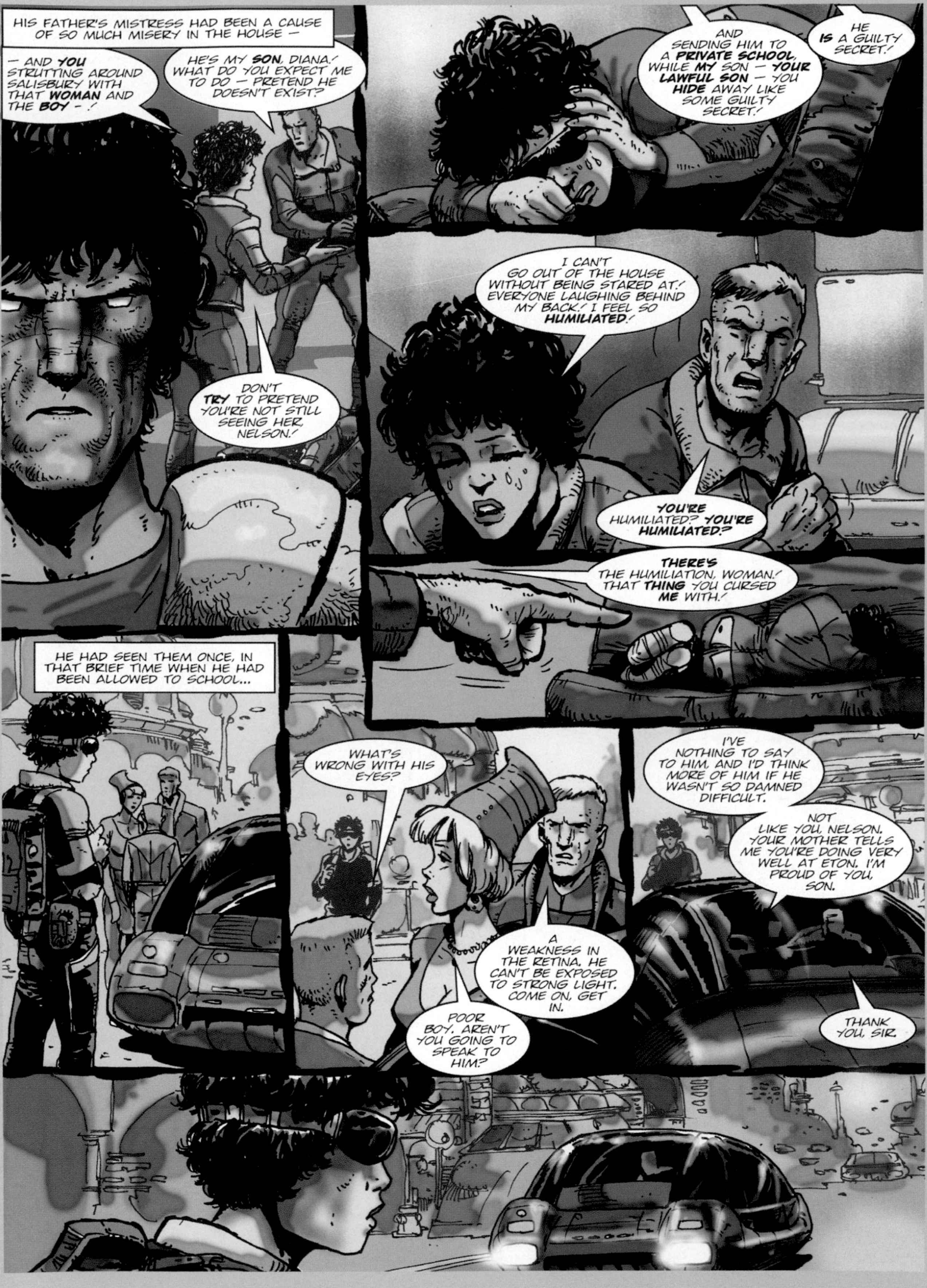
HIS FATHER'S MISTRESS HAD BEEN A CAUSE OF SO MUCH MISERY IN THE HOUSE —
— AND YOU STRUTTING AROUND SALISBURY WITH THAT WOMAN AND THE BOY —!
HE'S MY SON, DIANA! WHAT DO YOU EXPECT ME TO DO — PRETEND HE DOESN'T EXIST?
DON'T TRY TO PRETEND YOU'RE NOT STILL SEEING HER, NELSON!
AND SENDING HIM TO A PRIVATE SCHOOL, WHILE MY SON — YOUR LAWFUL SON — YOU HIDE AWAY LIKE SOME GUILTY SECRET!
HE IS A GUILTY SECRET!
I CAN'T GO OUT OF THE HOUSE WITHOUT BEING STARED AT! EVERYONE LAUGHING BEHIND MY BACK! I FEEL SO HUMILIATED!
YOU'RE HUMILIATED? YOU'RE HUMILIATED?
THERE'S THE HUMILIATION, WOMAN! THAT THING YOU CURSED ME WITH!
HE HAD SEEN THEM ONCE, IN THAT BRIEF TIME WHEN HE HAD BEEN ALLOWED TO SCHOOL...
WHAT'S WRONG WITH HIS EYES?
A WEAKNESS IN THE RETINA. HE CAN'T BE EXPOSED TO STRONG LIGHT. COME ON, GET IN.
POOR BOY. AREN'T YOU GOING TO SPEAK TO HIM?
I'VE NOTHING TO SAY TO HIM, AND I'D THINK MORE OF HIM IF HE WASN'T SO DAMNED DIFFICULT.
NOT LIKE YOU, NELSON. YOUR MOTHER TELLS ME YOU'RE DOING VERY WELL AT ETON. I'M PROUD OF YOU, SON.
THANK YOU, SIR.

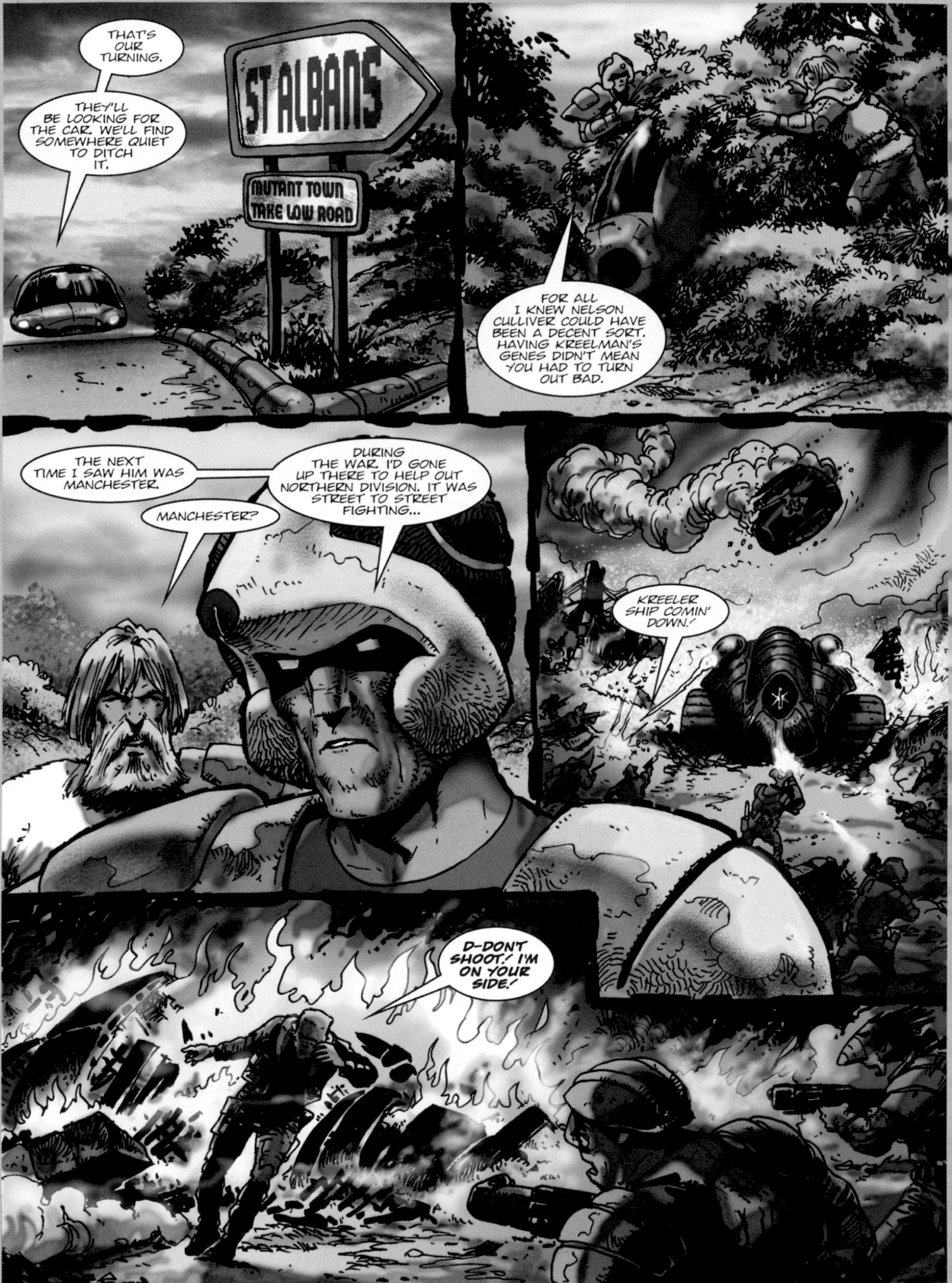
THAT'S OUR TURNING.
THEY'LL BE LOOKING FOR THE CAR. WE'LL FIND SOMEWHERE QUIET TO DITCH IT.
ST ALBANS
MUTANT TOWN
TAKE LOW ROAD
FOR ALL I KNEW NELSON CULLIVER COULD HAVE BEEN A DECENT SORT. HAVING KREELMAN'S GENES DIDN'T MEAN YOU HAD TO TURN OUT BAD.
THE NEXT TIME I SAW HIM WAS MANCHESTER.
MANCHESTER?
DURING THE WAR, I'D GONE UP THERE TO HELP OUT NORTHERN DIVISION. IT WAS STREET TO STREET FIGHTING...
KREELER SHIP COMIN' DOWN!
D-DON'T SHOOT! I'M ON YOUR SIDE!

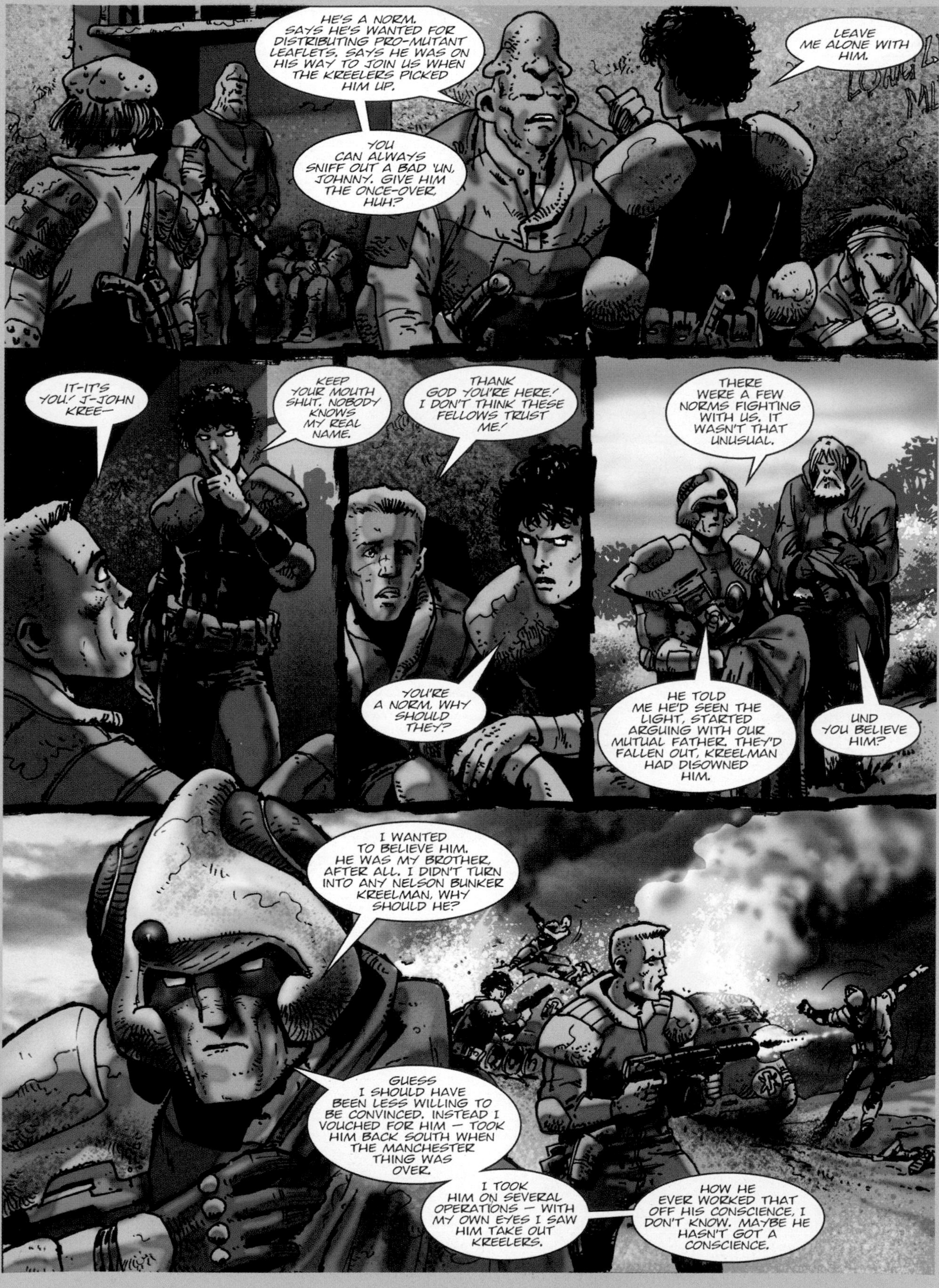
HE'S A NORM. SAYS HE'S WANTED FOR DISTRIBUTING PRO-MUTANT LEAFLETS. SAYS HE WAS ON HIS WAY TO JOIN US WHEN THE KREELERS PICKED HIM UP.
YOU CAN ALWAYS SNIFF OUT A BAD 'UN, JOHNNY. GIVE HIM THE ONCE-OVER, HUH?
LEAVE ME ALONE WITH HIM.
IT-IT'S YOU! J-JOHN KREE—
KEEP YOUR MOUTH SHUT. NOBODY KNOWS MY REAL NAME.
THANK GOD YOU'RE HERE! I DON'T THINK THESE FELLOWS TRUST ME!
YOU'RE A NORM, WHY SHOULD THEY?
THERE WERE A FEW NORMS FIGHTING WITH US. IT WASN'T THAT UNUSUAL.
HE TOLD ME HE'D SEEN THE LIGHT, STARTED ARGUING WITH OUR MUTUAL FATHER. THEY'D FALLEN OUT. KREELMAN HAD DISOWNED HIM.
UND YOU BELIEVE HIM?
I WANTED TO BELIEVE HIM. HE WAS MY BROTHER, AFTER ALL. I DIDN'T TURN INTO ANY NELSON BUNKER KREELMAN, WHY SHOULD HE?
GUESS I SHOULD HAVE BEEN LESS WILLING TO BE CONVINCED. INSTEAD I VOUCHED FOR HIM — TOOK HIM BACK SOUTH WHEN THE MANCHESTER THING WAS OVER.
I TOOK HIM ON SEVERAL OPERATIONS — WITH MY OWN EYES I SAW HIM TAKE OUT KREELERS.
HOW HE EVER WORKED THAT OFF HIS CONSCIENCE, I DON'T KNOW. MAYBE HE HASN'T GOT A CONSCIENCE.

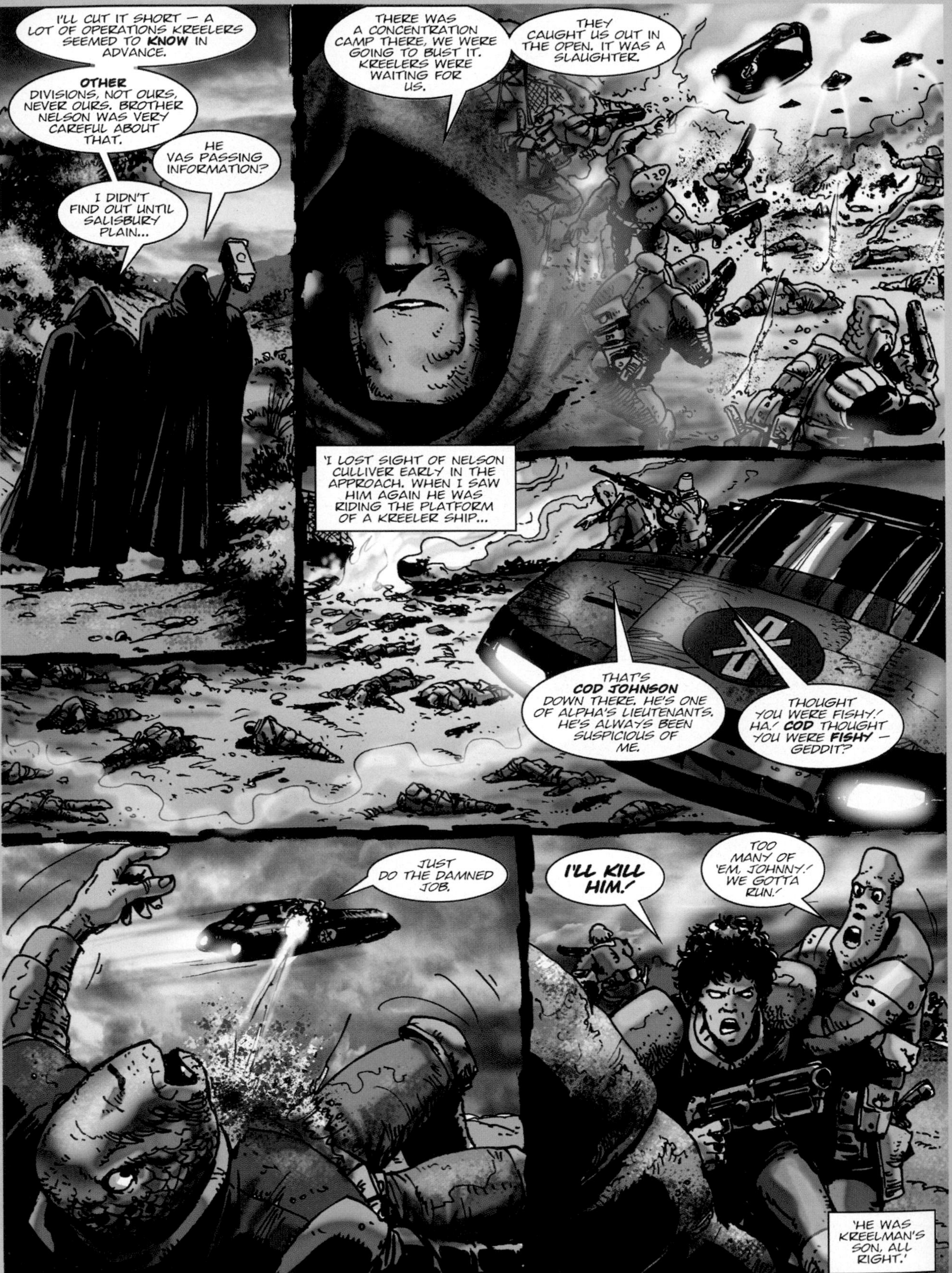
I'LL CUT IT SHORT — A LOT OF OPERATIONS KREELERS SEEMED TO KNOW IN ADVANCE.
OTHER DIVISIONS, NOT OURS, NEVER OURS. BROTHER NELSON WAS VERY CAREFUL ABOUT THAT.
HE VAS PASSING INFORMATION?
I DIDN'T FIND OUT UNTIL SALISBURY PLAIN...
THERE WAS A CONCENTRATION CAMP THERE, WE WERE GOING TO BUST IT. KREELERS WERE WAITING FOR US.
THEY CAUGHT US OUT IN THE OPEN. IT WAS A SLAUGHTER.
'I LOST SIGHT OF NELSON CULLIVER EARLY IN THE APPROACH. WHEN I SAW HIM AGAIN HE WAS RIDING THE PLATFORM OF A KREELER SHIP...
THAT'S COD JOHNSON DOWN THERE. HE'S ONE OF ALPHA'S LIEUTENANTS. HE'S ALWAYS BEEN SUSPICIOUS OF ME.
THOUGHT YOU WERE FISHY! HA! COD THOUGHT YOU WERE FISHY — GEDDIT?
JUST DO THE DAMNED JOB.
I'LL KILL HIM!
TOO MANY OF 'EM, JOHNNY! WE GOTTA RUN.
'HE WAS KREELMAN'S SON, ALL RIGHT.'

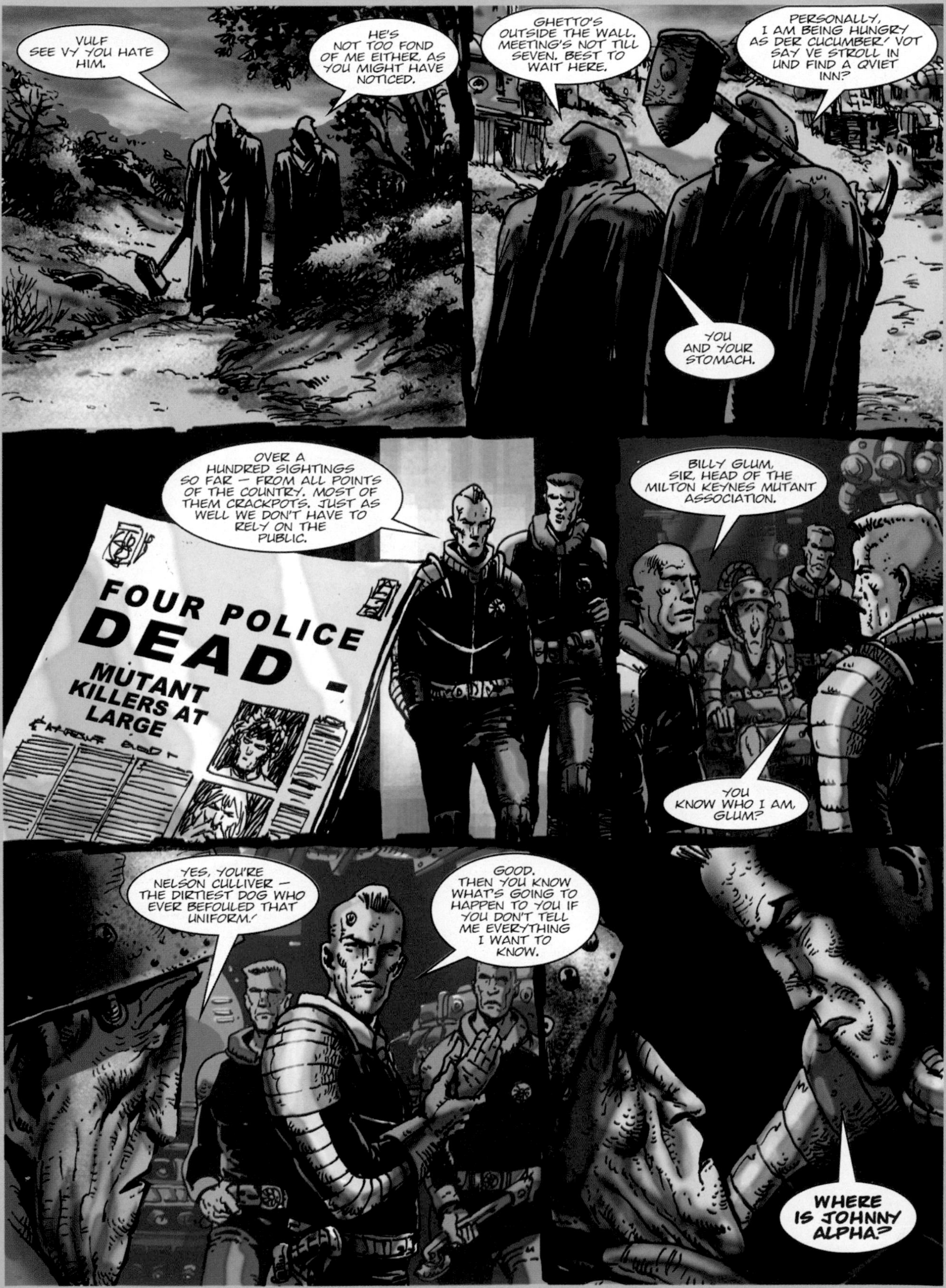
VULF SEE VY YOU HATE HIM.
HE'S NOT TOO FOND OF ME EITHER, AS YOU MIGHT HAVE NOTICED.
GHETTO'S OUTSIDE THE WALL. MEETING'S NOT TILL SEVEN. BEST TO WAIT HERE.
PERSONALLY, I AM BEING HUNGRY AS DER CUCUMBER! VOT SAY VE STROLL IN UND FIND A QVIET INN?
YOU AND YOUR STOMACH.
OVER A HUNDRED SIGHTINGS SO FAR — FROM ALL POINTS OF THE COUNTRY. MOST OF THEM CRACKPOTS. JUST AS WELL WE DON'T HAVE TO RELY ON THE PUBLIC.
FOUR POLICE DEAD - MUTANT KILLERS AT LARGE
BILLY GLUM, SIR, HEAD OF THE MILTON KEYNES MUTANT ASSOCIATION.
YOU KNOW WHO I AM, GLUM?
YES, YOU'RE NELSON CULLIVER — THE DIRTIEST DOG WHO EVER BEFOULED THAT UNIFORM!
GOOD. THEN YOU KNOW WHAT'S GOING TO HAPPEN TO YOU IF YOU DON'T TELL ME EVERYTHING I WANT TO KNOW.
WHERE IS JOHNNY ALPHA?

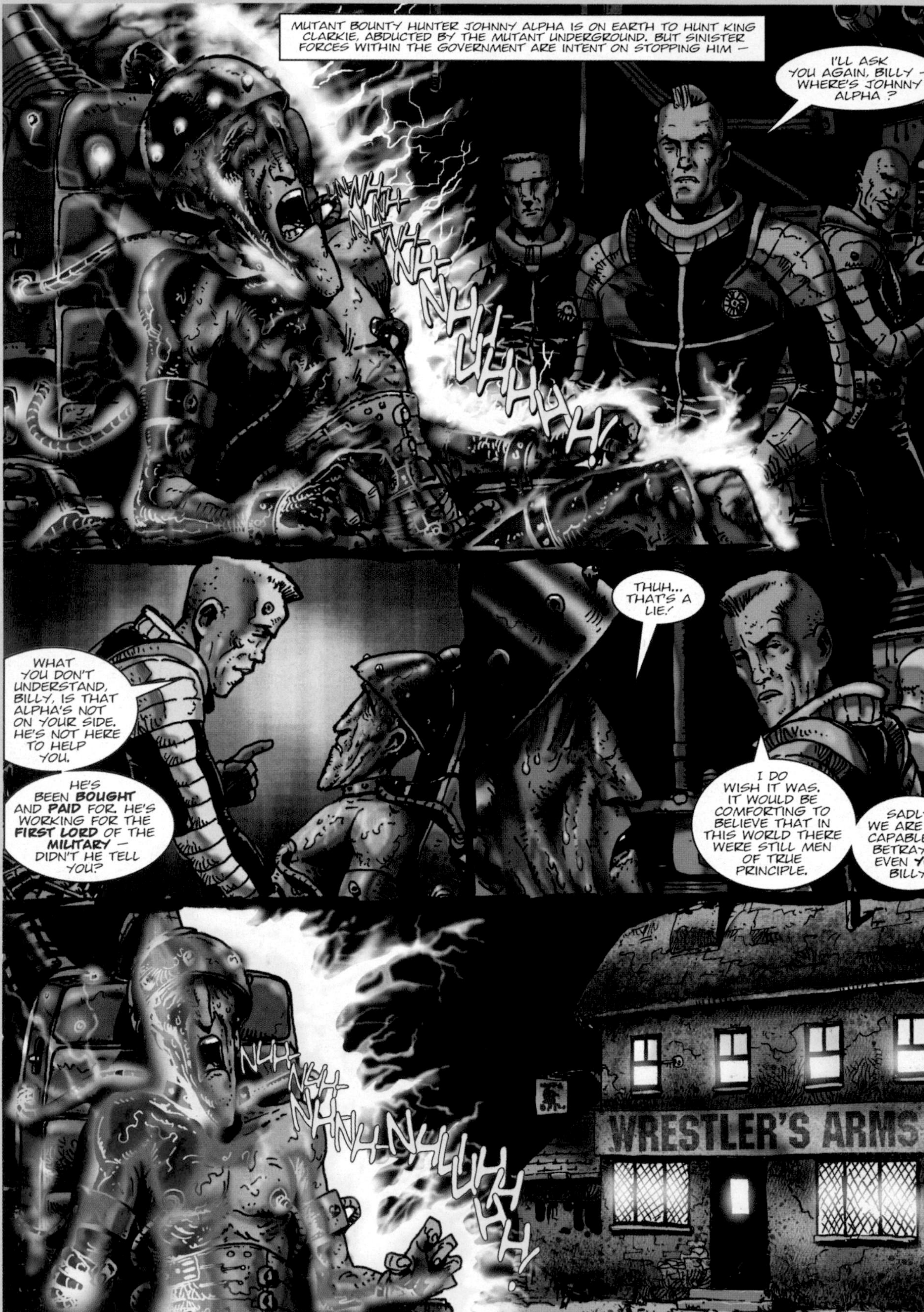
MUTANT BOUNTY HUNTER JOHNNY ALPHA IS ON EARTH TO HUNT KING CLARKIE, ABDUCTED BY THE MUTANT UNDERGROUND. BUT SINISTER FORCES WITHIN THE GOVERNMENT ARE INTENT ON STOPPING HIM —
I'LL ASK YOU AGAIN, BILLY — WHERE'S JOHNNY ALPHA ?
UNNH NHH NHNH NH-NHHUHHHHH!
WHAT YOU DON'T UNDERSTAND, BILLY, IS THAT ALPHA'S NOT ON YOUR SIDE. HE'S NOT HERE TO HELP YOU.
HE'S BEEN **BOUGHT** AND **PAID** FOR. HE'S WORKING FOR THE **FIRST LORD** OF THE **MILITARY** — DIDN'T HE TELL YOU?
THUH... THAT'S A LIE.'
I DO WISH IT WAS. IT WOULD BE COMFORTING TO BELIEVE THAT IN THIS WORLD THERE WERE STILL MEN OF TRUE PRINCIPLE.
SADLY, WE ARE ALL CAPABLE OF BETRAYAL. EVEN **YOU**, BILLY.
NUH-NUH-NUHNUH-NUUUHHHH!
WRESTLER'S ARMS

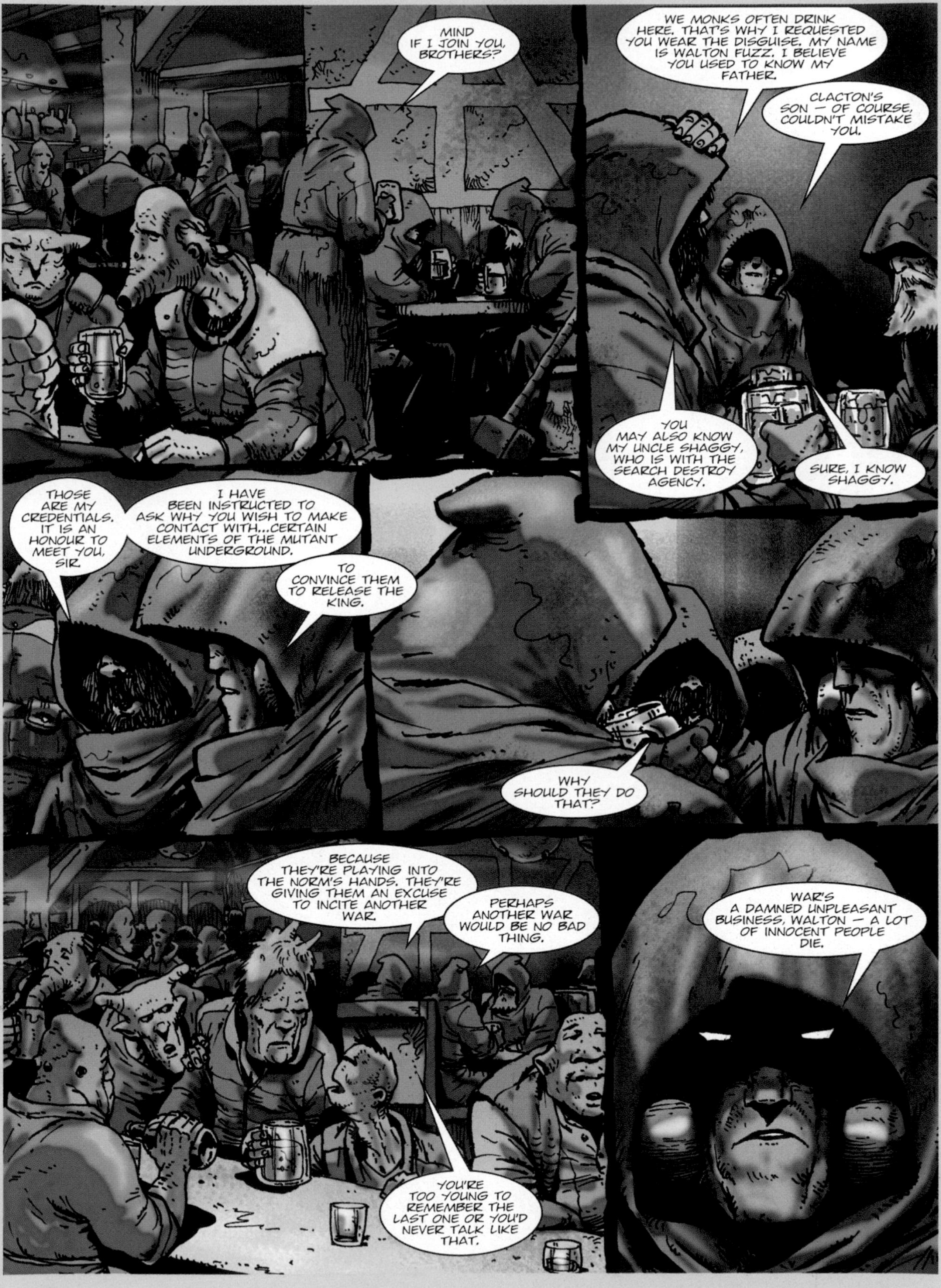
MIND IF I JOIN YOU, BROTHERS?
WE MONKS OFTEN DRINK HERE. THAT'S WHY I REQUESTED YOU WEAR THE DISGUISE. MY NAME IS WALTON FUZZ. I BELIEVE YOU USED TO KNOW MY FATHER.
CLACTON'S SON — OF COURSE, COULDN'T MISTAKE YOU.
YOU MAY ALSO KNOW MY UNCLE SHAGGY, WHO IS WITH THE SEARCH DESTROY AGENCY.
SURE, I KNOW SHAGGY.
THOSE ARE MY CREDENTIALS. IT IS AN HONOUR TO MEET YOU, SIR.
I HAVE BEEN INSTRUCTED TO ASK WHY YOU WISH TO MAKE CONTACT WITH...CERTAIN ELEMENTS OF THE MUTANT UNDERGROUND.
TO CONVINCE THEM TO RELEASE THE KING.
WHY SHOULD THEY DO THAT?
BECAUSE THEY'RE PLAYING INTO THE NORM'S HANDS. THEY'RE GIVING THEM AN EXCUSE TO INCITE ANOTHER WAR.
PERHAPS ANOTHER WAR WOULD BE NO BAD THING.
YOU'RE TOO YOUNG TO REMEMBER THE LAST ONE OR YOU'D NEVER TALK LIKE THAT.
WAR'S A DAMNED UNPLEASANT BUSINESS, WALTON — A LOT OF INNOCENT PEOPLE DIE.

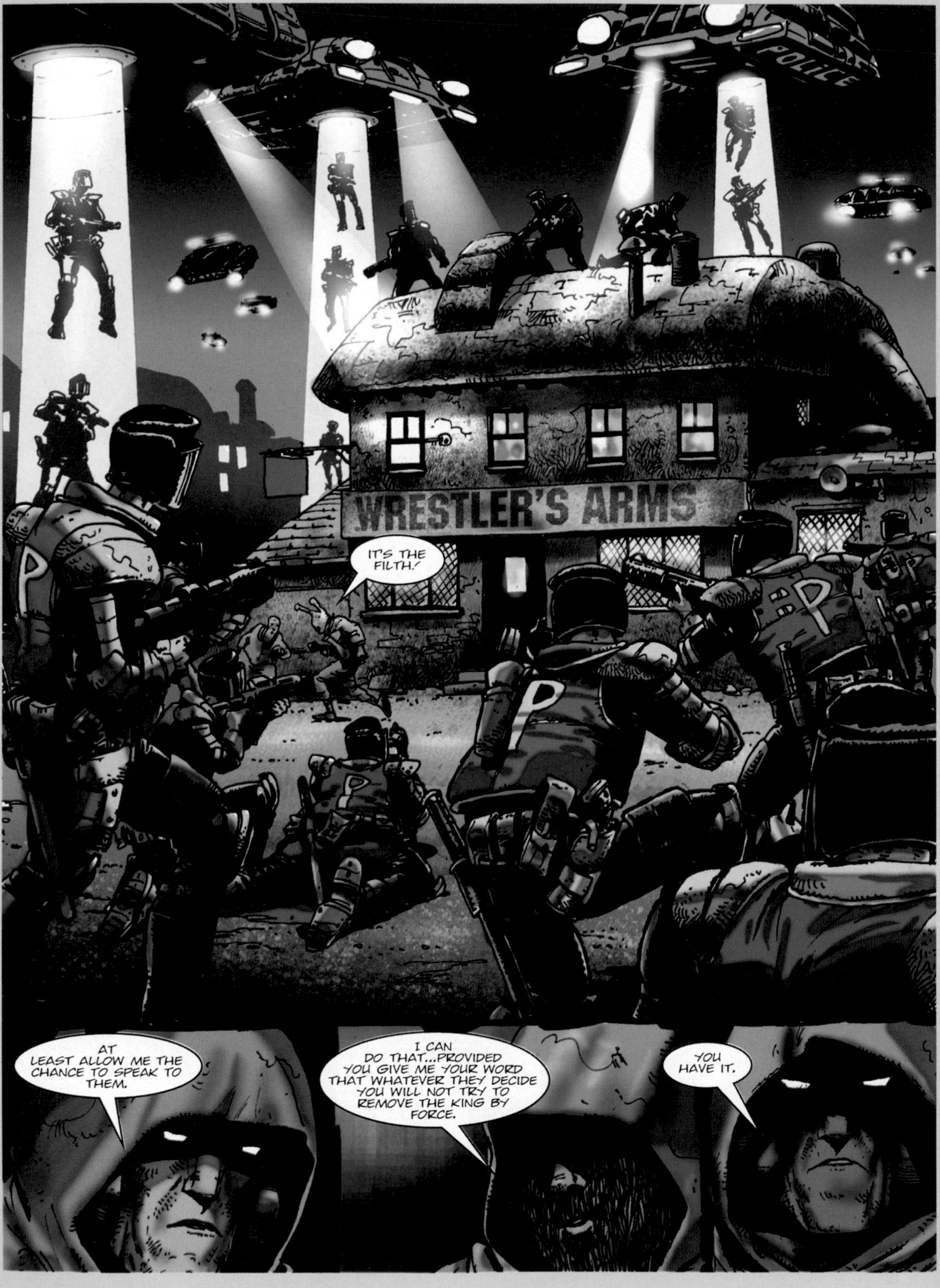
POLICE
WRESTLER'S ARMS
IT'S THE FILTH!
AT LEAST ALLOW ME THE CHANCE TO SPEAK TO THEM.
I CAN DO THAT...PROVIDED YOU GIVE ME YOUR WORD THAT WHATEVER THEY DECIDE YOU WILL NOT TRY TO REMOVE THE KING BY FORCE.
YOU HAVE IT.

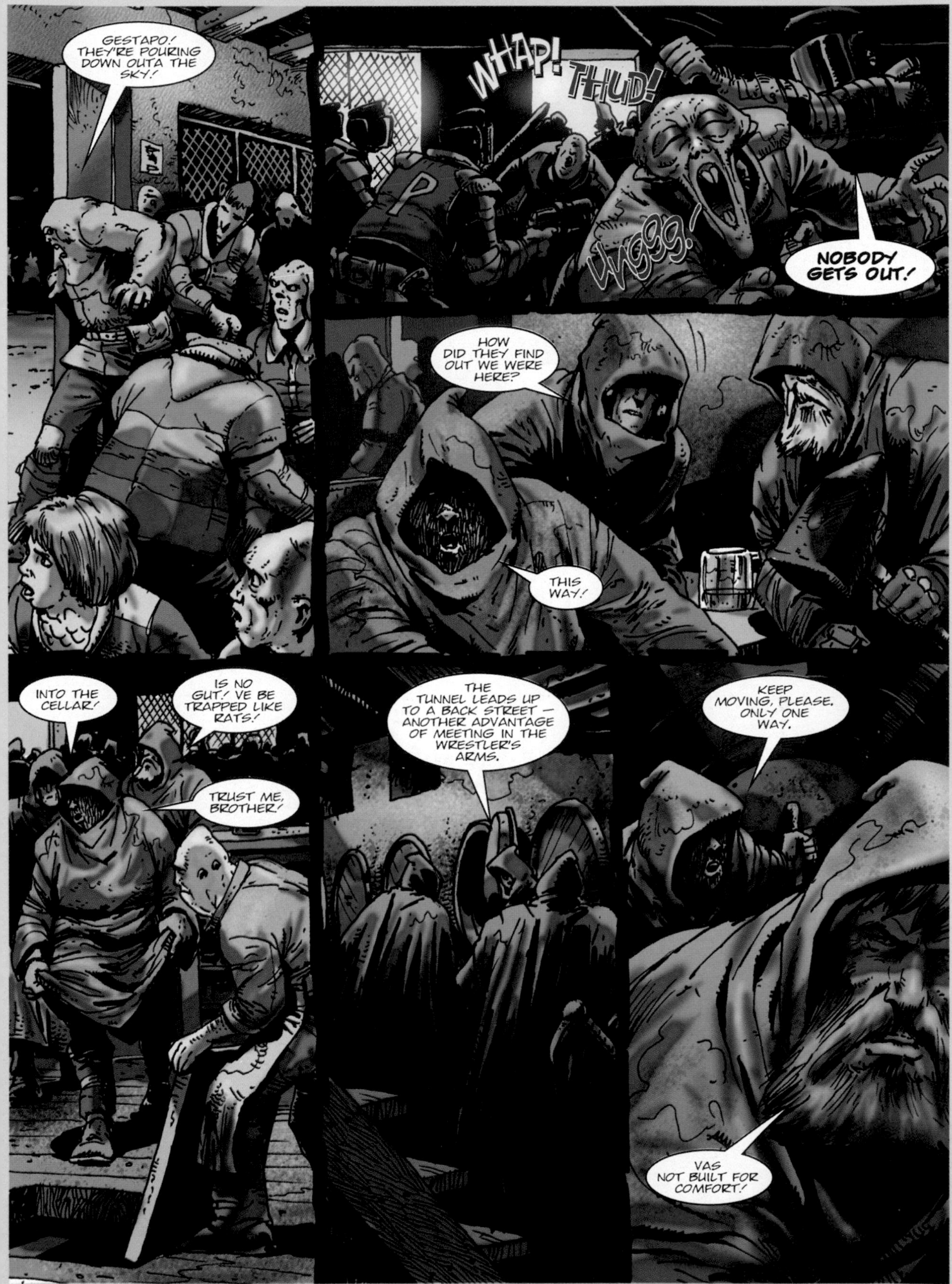
GESTAPO! THEY'RE POURING DOWN OUTA THE SKY!
WHAP!
THUD!
UNGGG!
NOBODY GETS OUT!
HOW DID THEY FIND OUT WE WERE HERE?
THIS WAY!
INTO THE CELLAR!
IS NO GUT! VE BE TRAPPED LIKE RATS!
TRUST ME, BROTHER!
THE TUNNEL LEADS UP TO A BACK STREET — ANOTHER ADVANTAGE OF MEETING IN THE WRESTLER'S ARMS.
KEEP MOVING, PLEASE. ONLY ONE WAY.
VAS NOT BUILT FOR COMFORT!

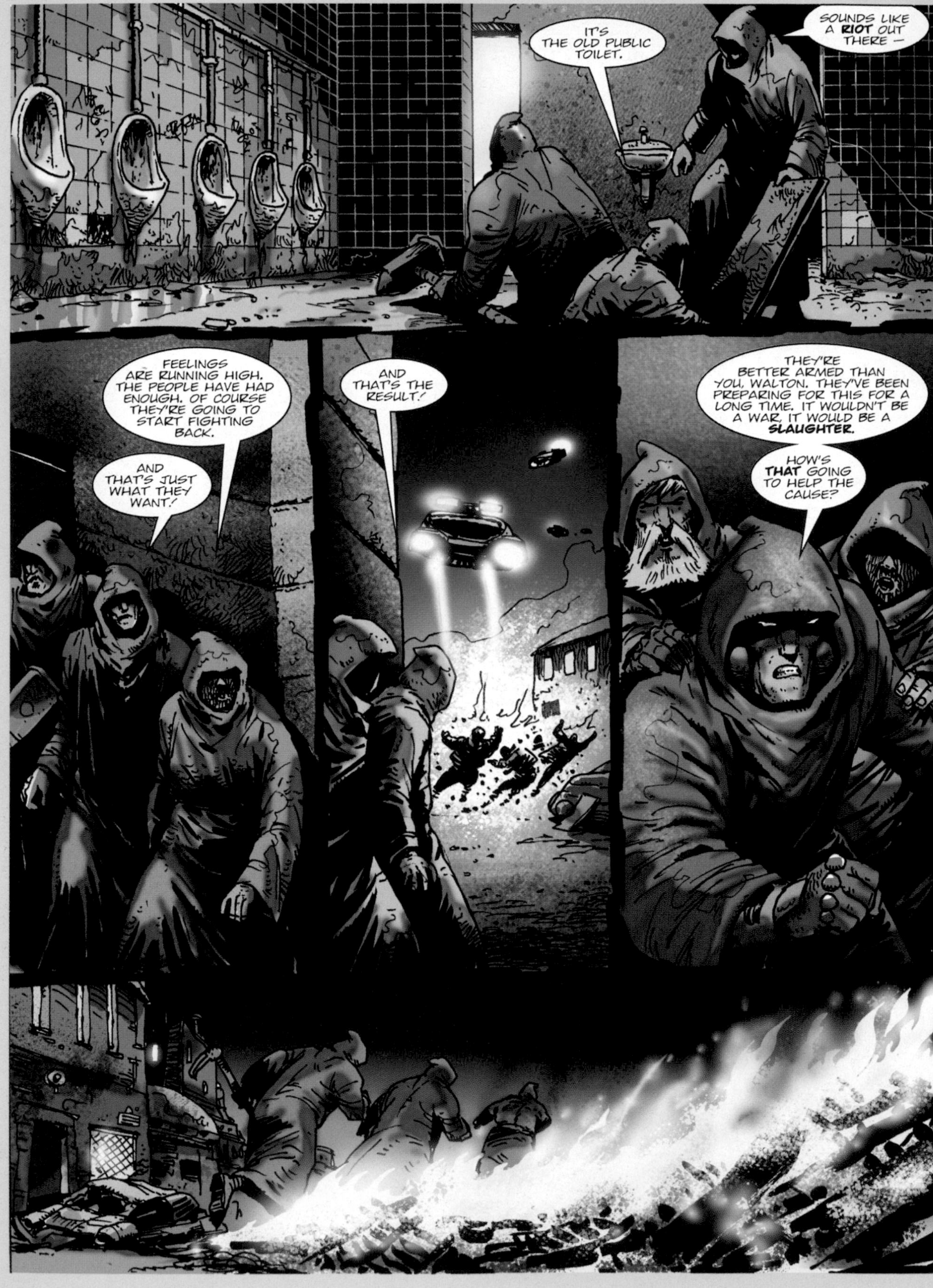

IT'S THE OLD PUBLIC TOILET.
SOUNDS LIKE A **RIOT** OUT THERE —
FEELINGS ARE RUNNING HIGH. THE PEOPLE HAVE HAD ENOUGH. OF COURSE THEY'RE GOING TO START FIGHTING BACK.
AND THAT'S JUST WHAT THEY WANT!
AND THAT'S THE RESULT!
THEY'RE BETTER ARMED THAN YOU, WALTON. THEY'VE BEEN PREPARING FOR THIS FOR A LONG TIME. IT WOULDN'T BE A WAR, IT WOULD BE A **SLAUGHTER**.
HOW'S **THAT** GOING TO HELP THE CAUSE?

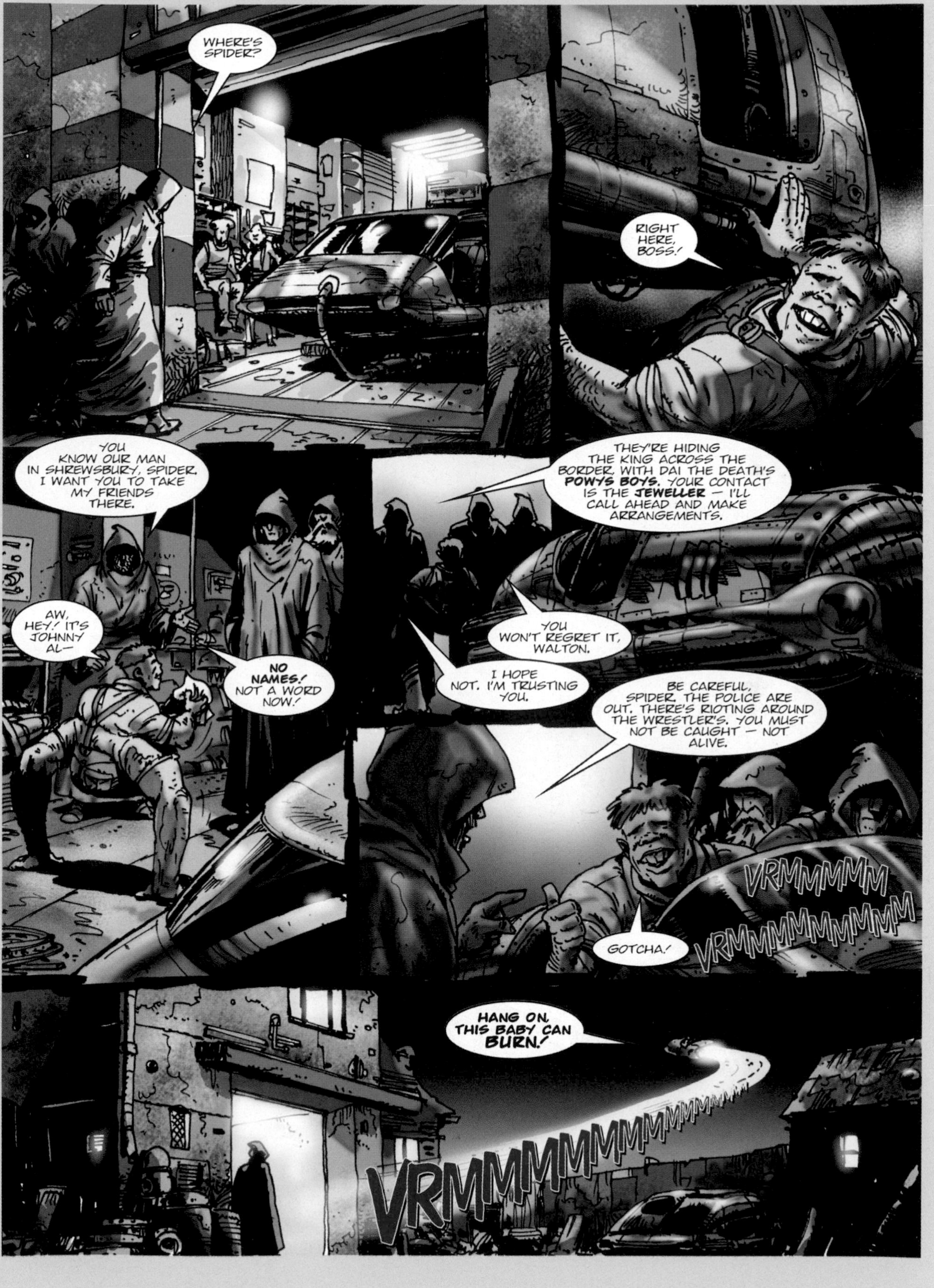
WHERE'S SPIDER?
RIGHT HERE, BOSS!
YOU KNOW OUR MAN IN SHREWSBURY, SPIDER. I WANT YOU TO TAKE MY FRIENDS THERE.
AW, HEY! IT'S JOHNNY AL—
NO NAMES! NOT A WORD NOW!
THEY'RE HIDING THE KING ACROSS THE BORDER, WITH DAI THE DEATH'S **POWYS BOYS**. YOUR CONTACT IS THE **JEWELLER** — I'LL CALL AHEAD AND MAKE ARRANGEMENTS.
YOU WON'T REGRET IT, WALTON.
I HOPE NOT. I'M TRUSTING YOU.
BE CAREFUL, SPIDER. THE POLICE ARE OUT. THERE'S RIOTING AROUND THE WRESTLER'S. YOU MUST NOT BE CAUGHT — NOT ALIVE.
GOTCHA!
VRMMMMMM
VRMMMMMMMMMMMM
HANG ON, THIS BABY CAN **BURN!**
VRMMMMMMMMMMMMMM

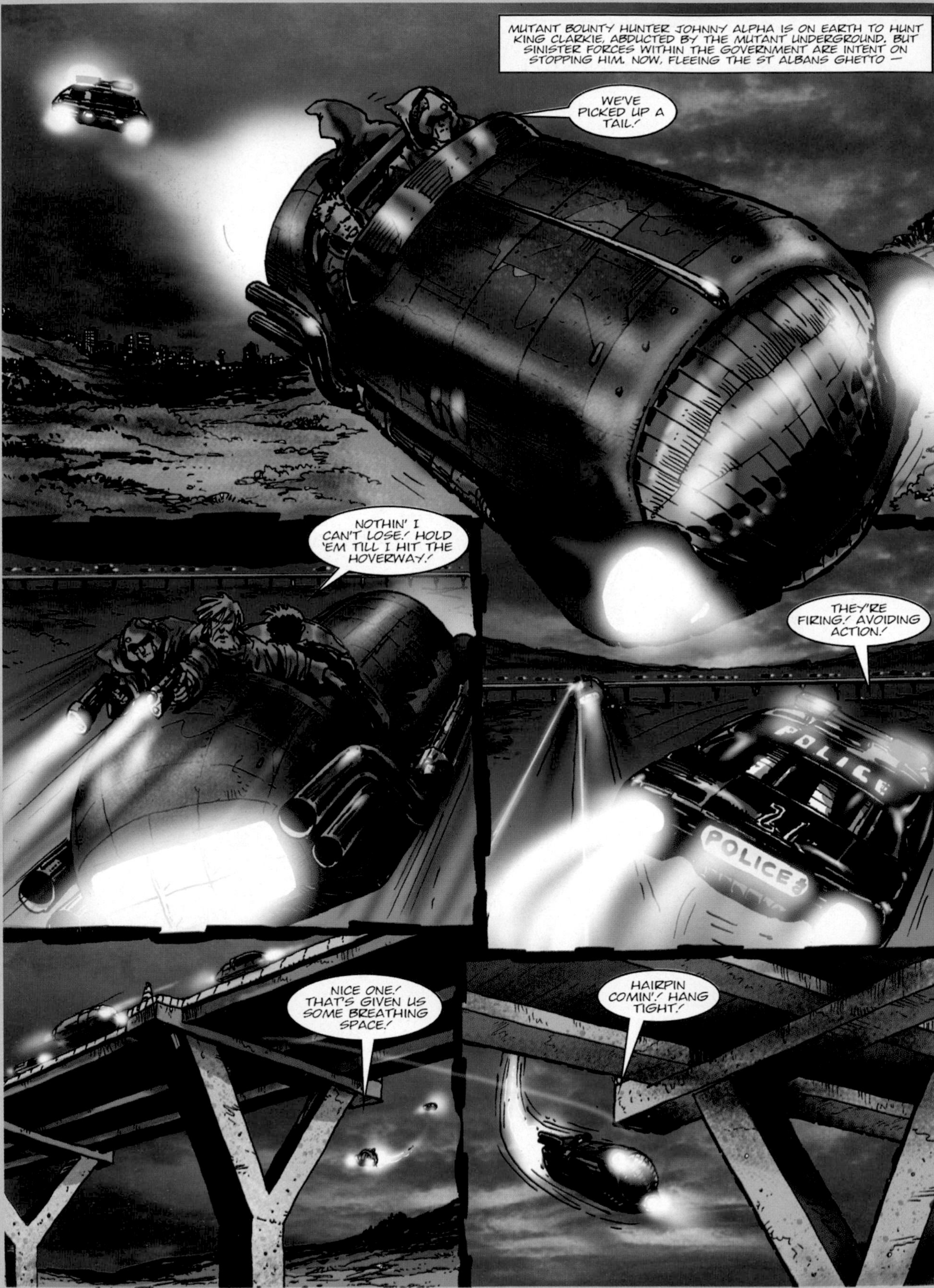
MUTANT BOUNTY HUNTER JOHNNY ALPHA IS ON EARTH TO HUNT KING CLARKIE, ABDUCTED BY THE MUTANT UNDERGROUND. BUT SINISTER FORCES WITHIN THE GOVERNMENT ARE INTENT ON STOPPING HIM. NOW, FLEEING THE ST ALBANS GHETTO —
WE'VE PICKED UP A TAIL!
NOTHIN' I CAN'T LOSE! HOLD 'EM TILL I HIT THE HOVERWAY!
THEY'RE FIRING! AVOIDING ACTION!
POLICE
POLICE
NICE ONE! THAT'S GIVEN US SOME BREATHING SPACE!
HAIRPIN COMIN'! HANG TIGHT!

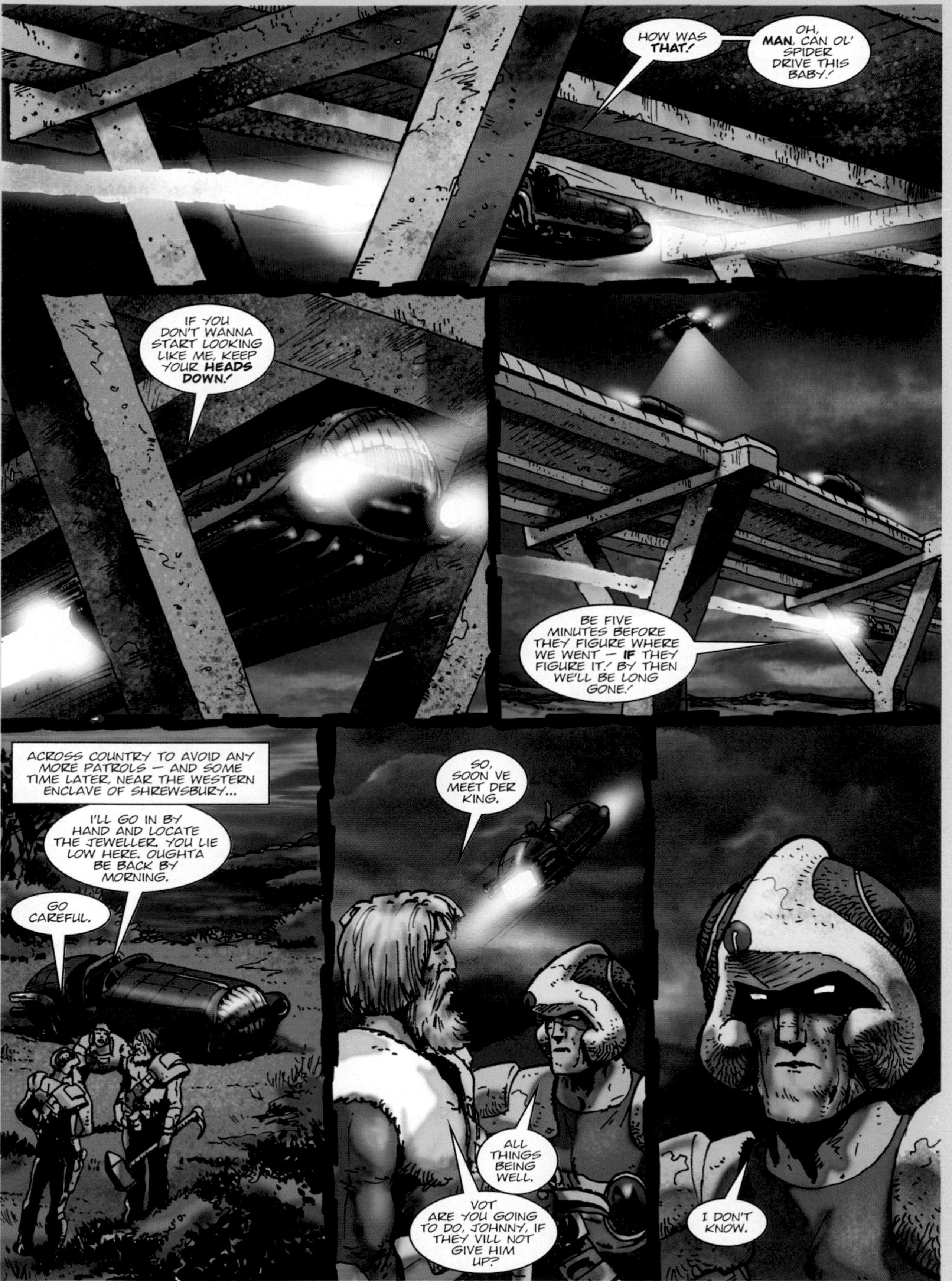
HOW WAS THAT!
OH, MAN, CAN OL' SPIDER DRIVE THIS BABY!
IF YOU DON'T WANNA START LOOKING LIKE ME, KEEP YOUR HEADS DOWN!
BE FIVE MINUTES BEFORE THEY FIGURE WHERE WE WENT — IF THEY FIGURE IT! BY THEN WE'LL BE LONG GONE!
ACROSS COUNTRY TO AVOID ANY MORE PATROLS — AND SOME TIME LATER, NEAR THE WESTERN ENCLAVE OF SHREWSBURY...
I'LL GO IN BY HAND AND LOCATE THE JEWELLER. YOU LIE LOW HERE. OUGHTA BE BACK BY MORNING.
GO CAREFUL.
SO, SOON VE MEET DER KING.
ALL THINGS BEING WELL.
VOT ARE YOU GOING TO DO, JOHNNY, IF THEY VILL NOT GIVE HIM UP?
I DON'T KNOW.

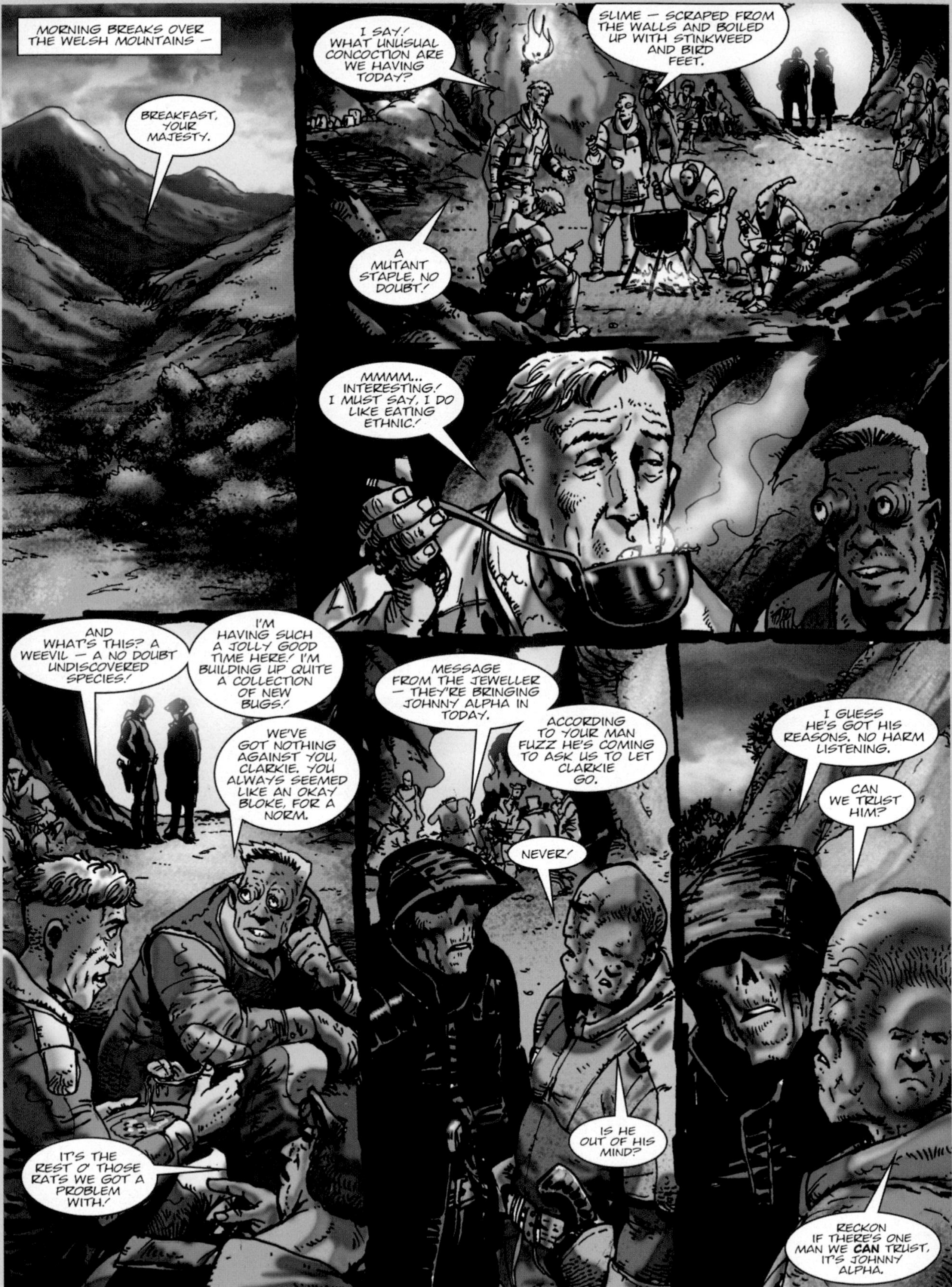

MORNING BREAKS OVER THE WELSH MOUNTAINS —
BREAKFAST, YOUR MAJESTY.
I SAY! WHAT UNUSUAL CONCOCTION ARE WE HAVING TODAY?
SLIME — SCRAPED FROM THE WALLS AND BOILED UP WITH STINKWEED AND BIRD FEET.
A MUTANT STAPLE, NO DOUBT!
MMMM... INTERESTING! I MUST SAY, I DO LIKE EATING ETHNIC!
AND WHAT'S THIS? A WEEVIL — A NO DOUBT UNDISCOVERED SPECIES!
I'M HAVING SUCH A JOLLY GOOD TIME HERE! I'M BUILDING UP QUITE A COLLECTION OF NEW BUGS!
WE'VE GOT NOTHING AGAINST YOU, CLARKIE. YOU ALWAYS SEEMED LIKE AN OKAY BLOKE, FOR A NORM.
IT'S THE REST O' THOSE RATS WE GOT A PROBLEM WITH!
MESSAGE FROM THE JEWELLER — THEY'RE BRINGING JOHNNY ALPHA IN TODAY.
ACCORDING TO YOUR MAN FUZZ HE'S COMING TO ASK US TO LET CLARKIE GO.
NEVER!
IS HE OUT OF HIS MIND?
I GUESS HE'S GOT HIS REASONS. NO HARM LISTENING.
CAN WE TRUST HIM?
RECKON IF THERE'S ONE MAN WE **CAN** TRUST, IT'S JOHNNY ALPHA.

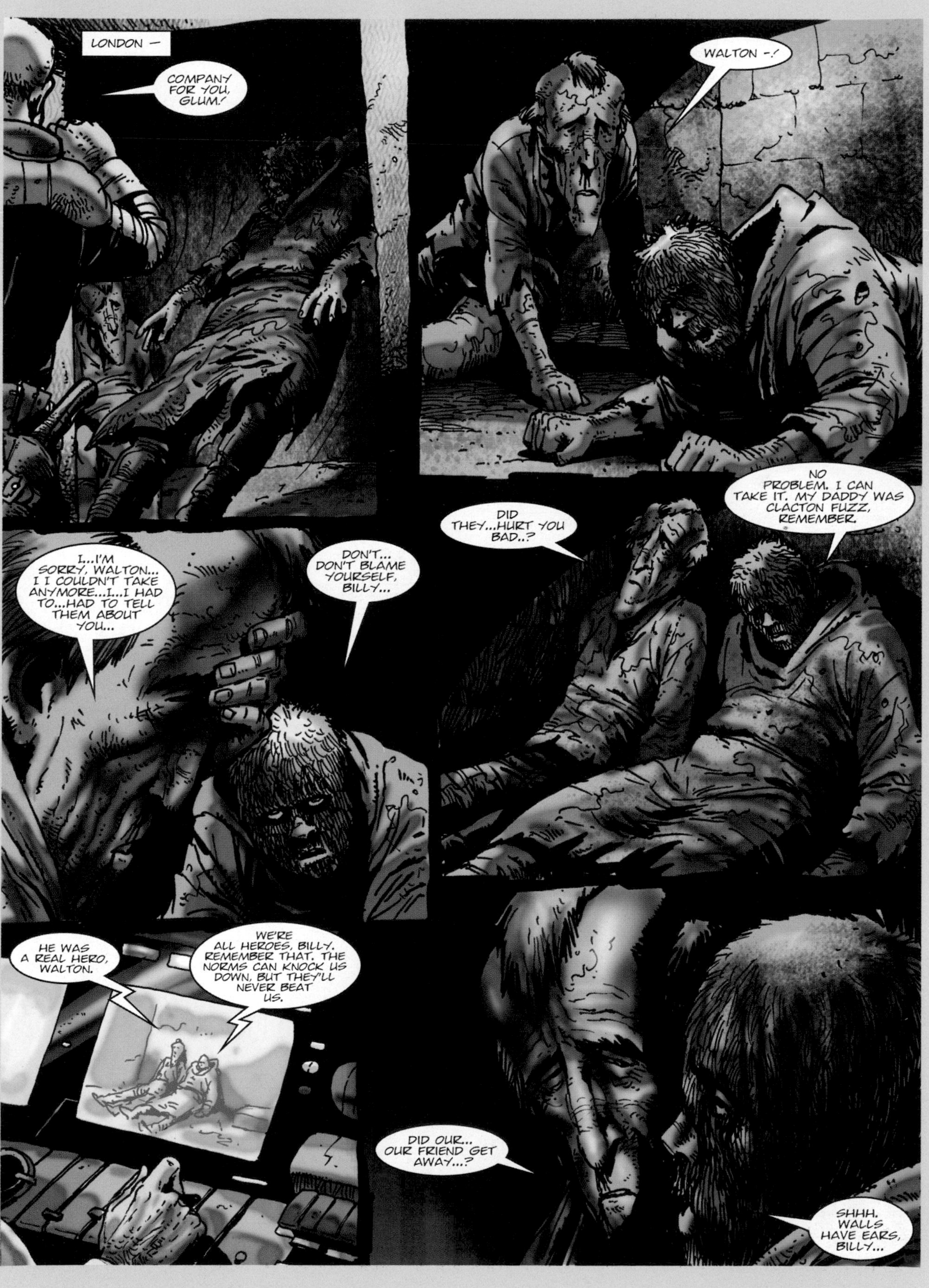
LONDON —
COMPANY FOR YOU, GLUM!
WALTON -!
I...I'M SORRY, WALTON... I I COULDN'T TAKE ANYMORE...I...I HAD TO...HAD TO TELL THEM ABOUT YOU...
DON'T... DON'T BLAME YOURSELF, BILLY...
DID THEY...HURT YOU BAD..?
NO PROBLEM. I CAN TAKE IT. MY DADDY WAS CLACTON FUZZ, REMEMBER.
HE WAS A REAL HERO, WALTON.
WE'RE ALL HEROES, BILLY. REMEMBER THAT. THE NORMS CAN KNOCK US DOWN, BUT THEY'LL NEVER BEAT US.
DID OUR... OUR FRIEND GET AWAY...?
SHHH. WALLS HAVE EARS, BILLY...

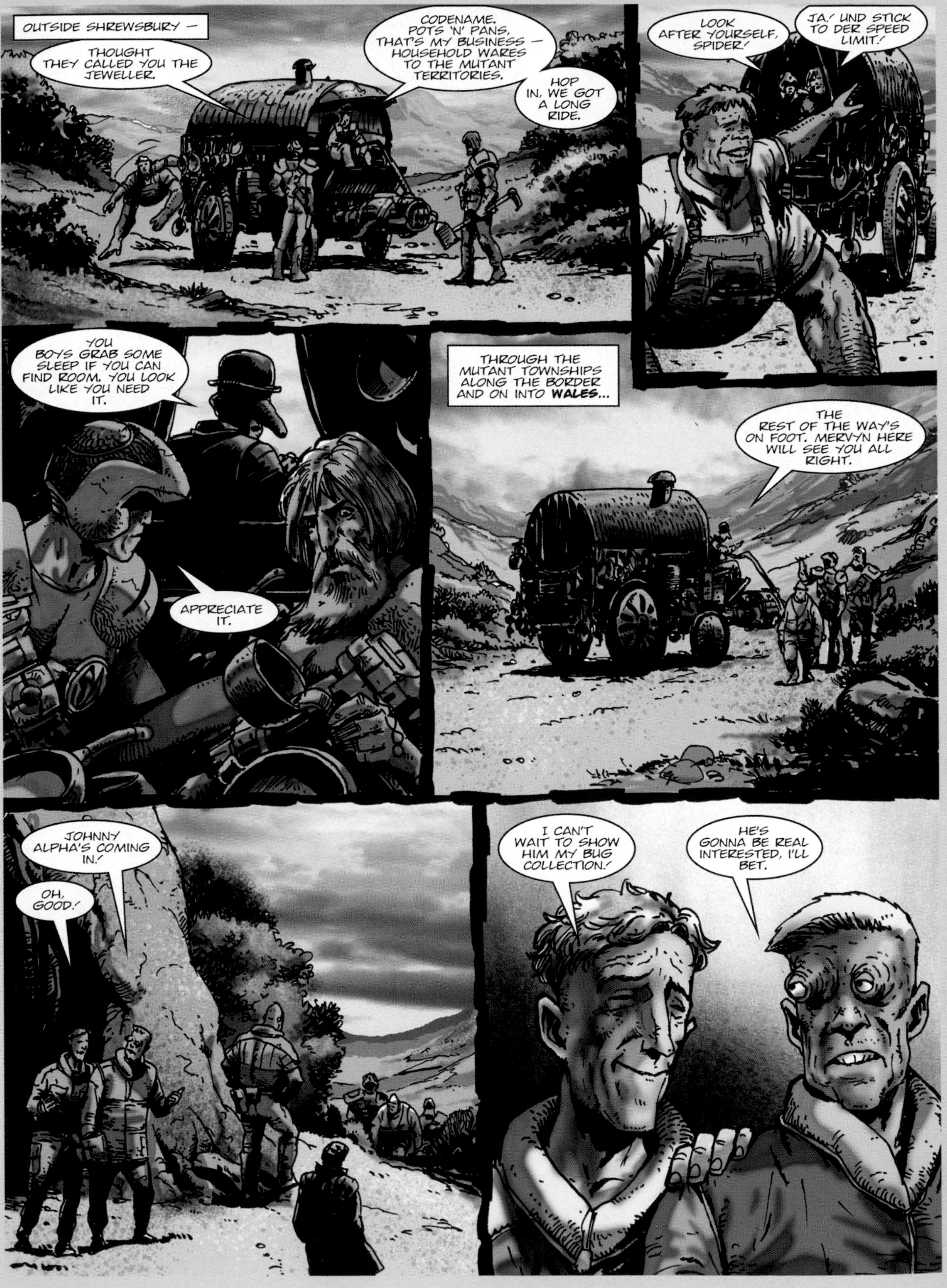
OUTSIDE SHREWSBURY —
THOUGHT THEY CALLED YOU THE JEWELLER.
CODENAME. POTS 'N' PANS, THAT'S MY BUSINESS — HOUSEHOLD WARES TO THE MUTANT TERRITORIES.
HOP IN, WE GOT A LONG RIDE.
LOOK AFTER YOURSELF, SPIDER!
JA! UND STICK TO DER SPEED LIMIT!
YOU BOYS GRAB SOME SLEEP IF YOU CAN FIND ROOM. YOU LOOK LIKE YOU NEED IT.
APPRECIATE IT.
THROUGH THE MUTANT TOWNSHIPS ALONG THE BORDER AND ON INTO **WALES**...
THE REST OF THE WAY'S ON FOOT. MERVYN HERE WILL SEE YOU ALL RIGHT.
JOHNNY ALPHA'S COMING IN!
OH, GOOD!
I CAN'T WAIT TO SHOW HIM MY BUG COLLECTION!
HE'S GONNA BE REAL INTERESTED, I'LL BET.

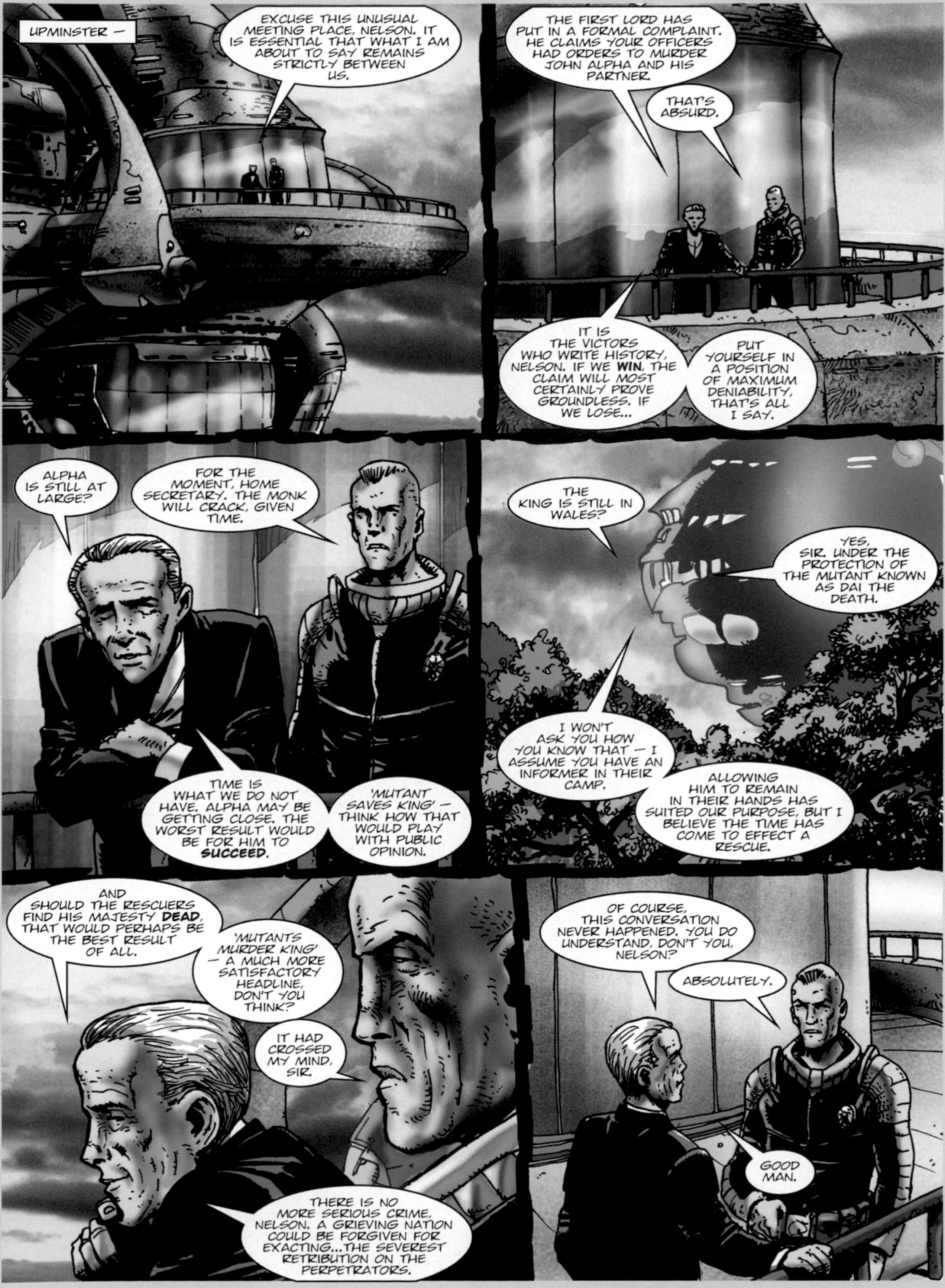
UPMINSTER —
EXCUSE THIS UNUSUAL MEETING PLACE, NELSON. IT IS ESSENTIAL THAT WHAT I AM ABOUT TO SAY REMAINS STRICTLY BETWEEN US.
THE FIRST LORD HAS PUT IN A FORMAL COMPLAINT. HE CLAIMS YOUR OFFICERS HAD ORDERS TO MURDER JOHN ALPHA AND HIS PARTNER.
THAT'S ABSURD.
IT IS THE VICTORS WHO WRITE HISTORY, NELSON. IF WE **WIN**, THE CLAIM WILL MOST CERTAINLY PROVE GROUNDLESS. IF WE LOSE...
PUT YOURSELF IN A POSITION OF MAXIMUM DENIABILITY, THAT'S ALL I SAY.
ALPHA IS STILL AT LARGE?
FOR THE MOMENT, HOME SECRETARY. THE MONK WILL CRACK, GIVEN TIME.
TIME IS WHAT WE DO NOT HAVE. ALPHA MAY BE GETTING CLOSE. THE WORST RESULT WOULD BE FOR HIM TO **SUCCEED**.
'MUTANT SAVES KING' — THINK HOW THAT WOULD PLAY WITH PUBLIC OPINION.
THE KING IS STILL IN WALES?
YES, SIR. UNDER THE PROTECTION OF THE MUTANT KNOWN AS DAI THE DEATH.
I WON'T ASK YOU HOW YOU KNOW THAT — I ASSUME YOU HAVE AN INFORMER IN THEIR CAMP.
ALLOWING HIM TO REMAIN IN THEIR HANDS HAS SUITED OUR PURPOSE, BUT I BELIEVE THE TIME HAS COME TO EFFECT A RESCUE.
AND SHOULD THE RESCUERS FIND HIS MAJESTY **DEAD**, THAT WOULD PERHAPS BE THE BEST RESULT OF ALL.
'MUTANTS MURDER KING' — A MUCH MORE SATISFACTORY HEADLINE, DON'T YOU THINK?
IT HAD CROSSED MY MIND, SIR.
THERE IS NO MORE SERIOUS CRIME, NELSON. A GRIEVING NATION COULD BE FORGIVEN FOR EXACTING...THE SEVEREST RETRIBUTION ON THE PERPETRATORS.
OF COURSE, THIS CONVERSATION NEVER HAPPENED. YOU DO UNDERSTAND, DON'T YOU, NELSON?
ABSOLUTELY.
GOOD MAN.

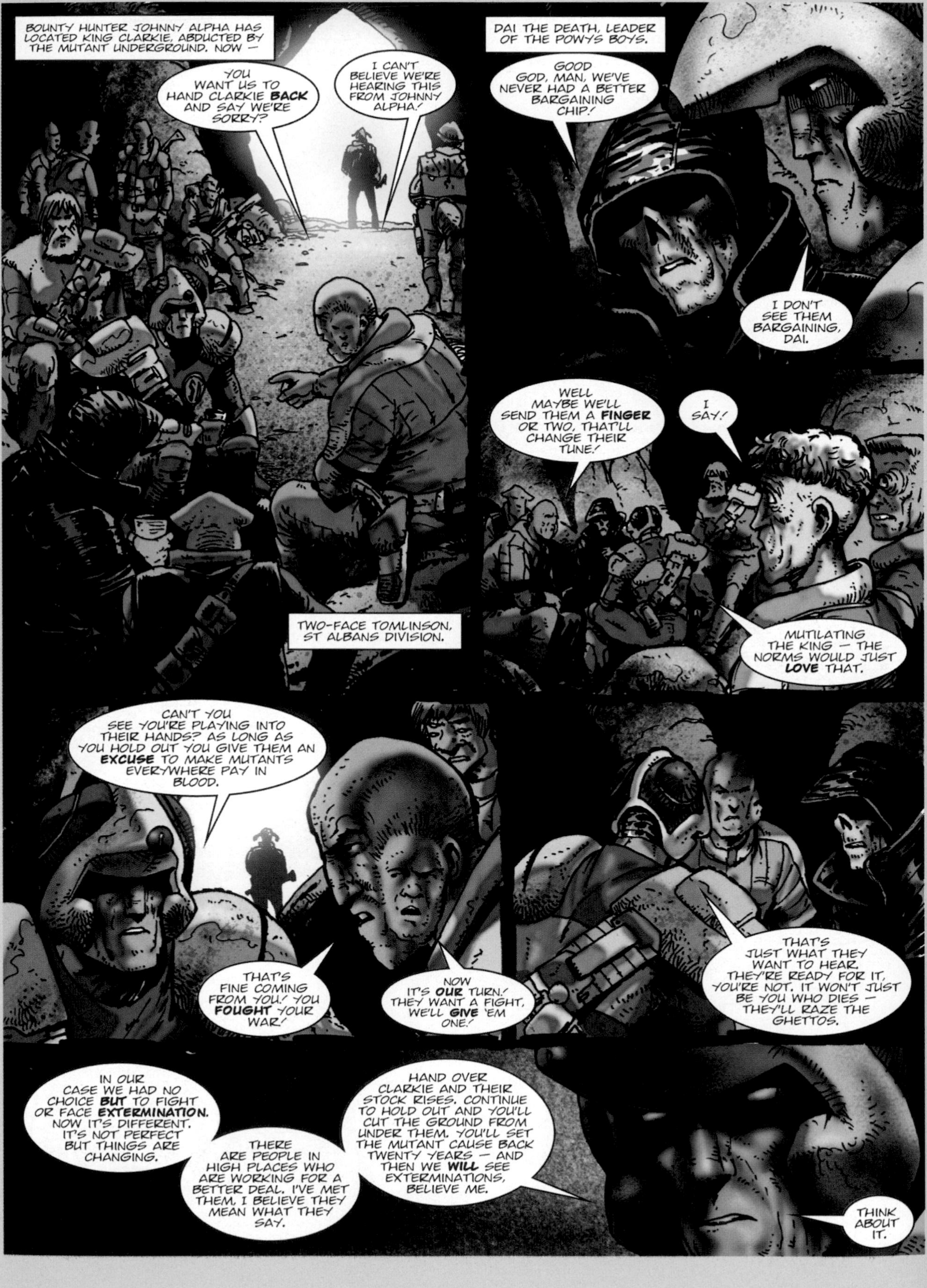

BOUNTY HUNTER JOHNNY ALPHA HAS LOCATED KING CLARKIE, ABDUCTED BY THE MUTANT UNDERGROUND. NOW —
YOU WANT US TO HAND CLARKIE **BACK** AND SAY WE'RE SORRY?
I CAN'T BELIEVE WE'RE HEARING THIS FROM JOHNNY ALPHA!
TWO-FACE TOMLINSON, ST ALBANS DIVISION.
DAI THE DEATH, LEADER OF THE POWYS BOYS.
GOOD GOD, MAN, WE'VE NEVER HAD A BETTER BARGAINING CHIP!
I DON'T SEE THEM BARGAINING, DAI.
WELL MAYBE WE'LL SEND THEM A **FINGER** OR TWO, THAT'LL CHANGE THEIR TUNE!
I SAY!
MUTILATING THE KING — THE NORMS WOULD JUST **LOVE** THAT.
CAN'T YOU SEE YOU'RE PLAYING INTO THEIR HANDS? AS LONG AS YOU HOLD OUT YOU GIVE THEM AN **EXCUSE** TO MAKE MUTANTS EVERYWHERE PAY IN BLOOD.
THAT'S FINE COMING FROM YOU! YOU **FOUGHT** YOUR WAR!
NOW IT'S **OUR** TURN! THEY WANT A FIGHT, WE'LL **GIVE** 'EM ONE!
THAT'S JUST WHAT THEY WANT TO HEAR. THEY'RE READY FOR IT, YOU'RE NOT. IT WON'T JUST BE YOU WHO DIES — THEY'LL RAZE THE GHETTOS.
IN OUR CASE WE HAD NO CHOICE **BUT** TO FIGHT OR FACE **EXTERMINATION**. NOW IT'S DIFFERENT. IT'S NOT PERFECT BUT THINGS ARE CHANGING.
THERE ARE PEOPLE IN HIGH PLACES WHO ARE WORKING FOR A BETTER DEAL. I'VE MET THEM. I BELIEVE THEY MEAN WHAT THEY SAY.
HAND OVER CLARKIE AND THEIR STOCK RISES. CONTINUE TO HOLD OUT AND YOU'LL CUT THE GROUND FROM UNDER THEM. YOU'LL SET THE MUTANT CAUSE BACK TWENTY YEARS — AND THEN WE **WILL** SEE EXTERMINATIONS, BELIEVE ME.
THINK ABOUT IT.

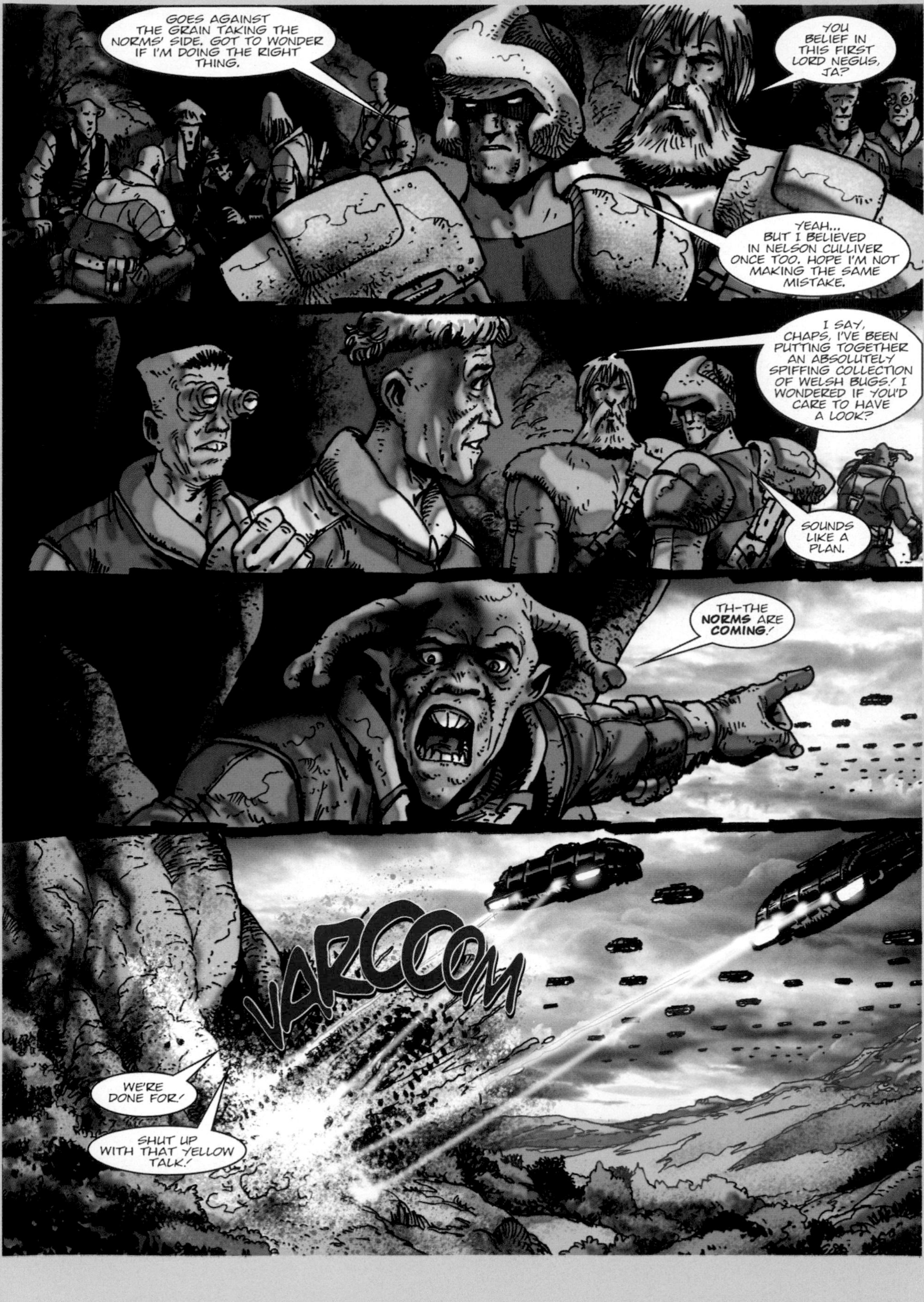
GOES AGAINST THE GRAIN TAKING THE NORMS' SIDE. GOT TO WONDER IF I'M DOING THE RIGHT THING.
YOU BELIEF IN THIS FIRST LORD NEGUS, JA?
YEAH... BUT I BELIEVED IN NELSON CULLIVER ONCE TOO. HOPE I'M NOT MAKING THE SAME MISTAKE.
I SAY, CHAPS, I'VE BEEN PUTTING TOGETHER AN ABSOLUTELY SPIFFING COLLECTION OF WELSH BUGS! I WONDERED IF YOU'D CARE TO HAVE A LOOK?
SOUNDS LIKE A PLAN.
TH-THE **NORMS** ARE **COMING**!
VARCCOM
WE'RE DONE FOR!
SHUT UP WITH THAT YELLOW TALK!

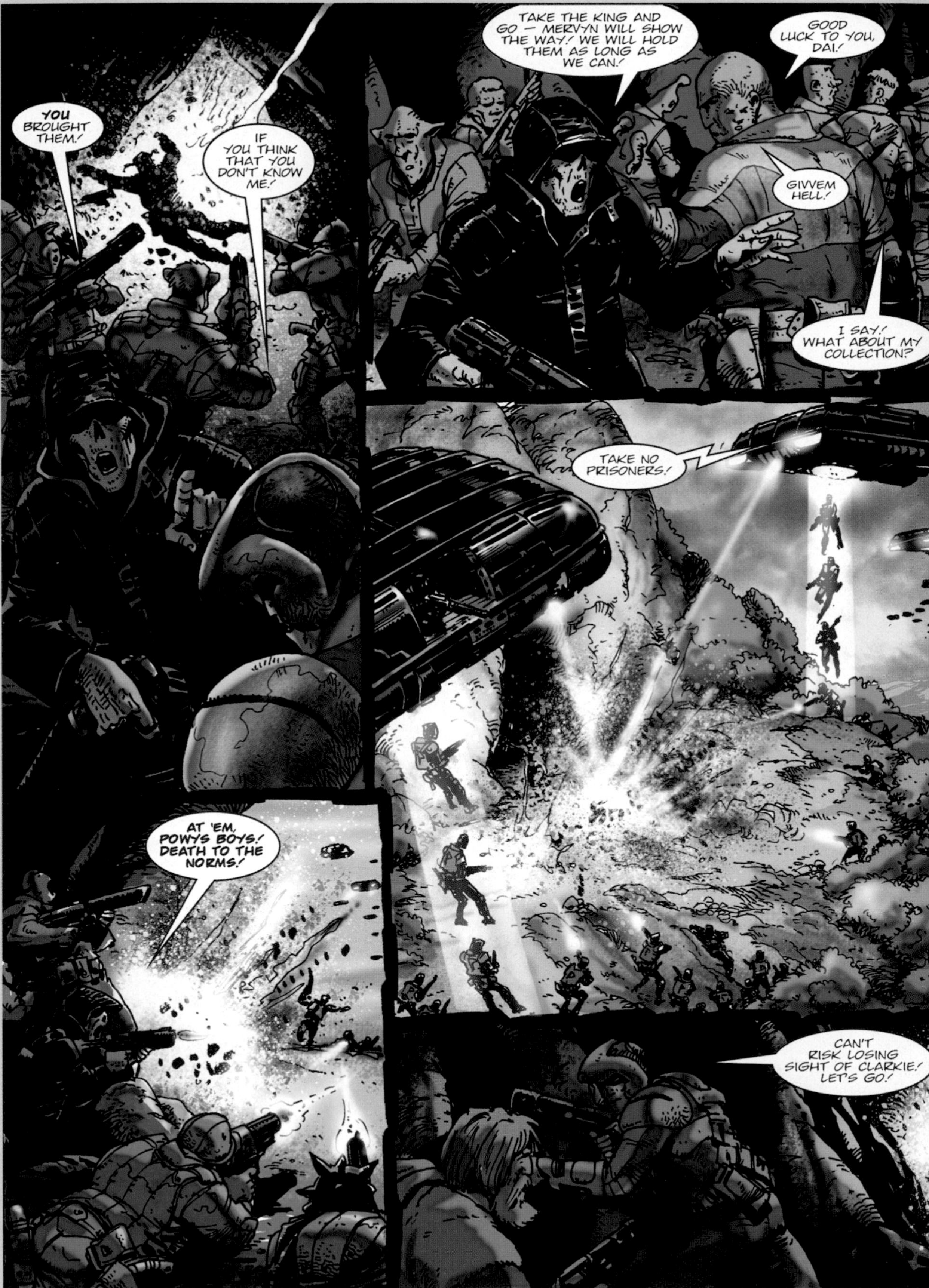
YOU BROUGHT THEM!
IF YOU THINK THAT YOU DON'T KNOW ME!
TAKE THE KING AND GO — MERVYN WILL SHOW THE WAY! WE WILL HOLD THEM AS LONG AS WE CAN!
GOOD LUCK TO YOU, DAI!
GIVVEM HELL!
I SAY! WHAT ABOUT MY COLLECTION?
TAKE NO PRISONERS!
AT 'EM, POWY'S BOYS! DEATH TO THE NORMS!
CAN'T RISK LOSING SIGHT OF CLARKIE! LET'S GO!

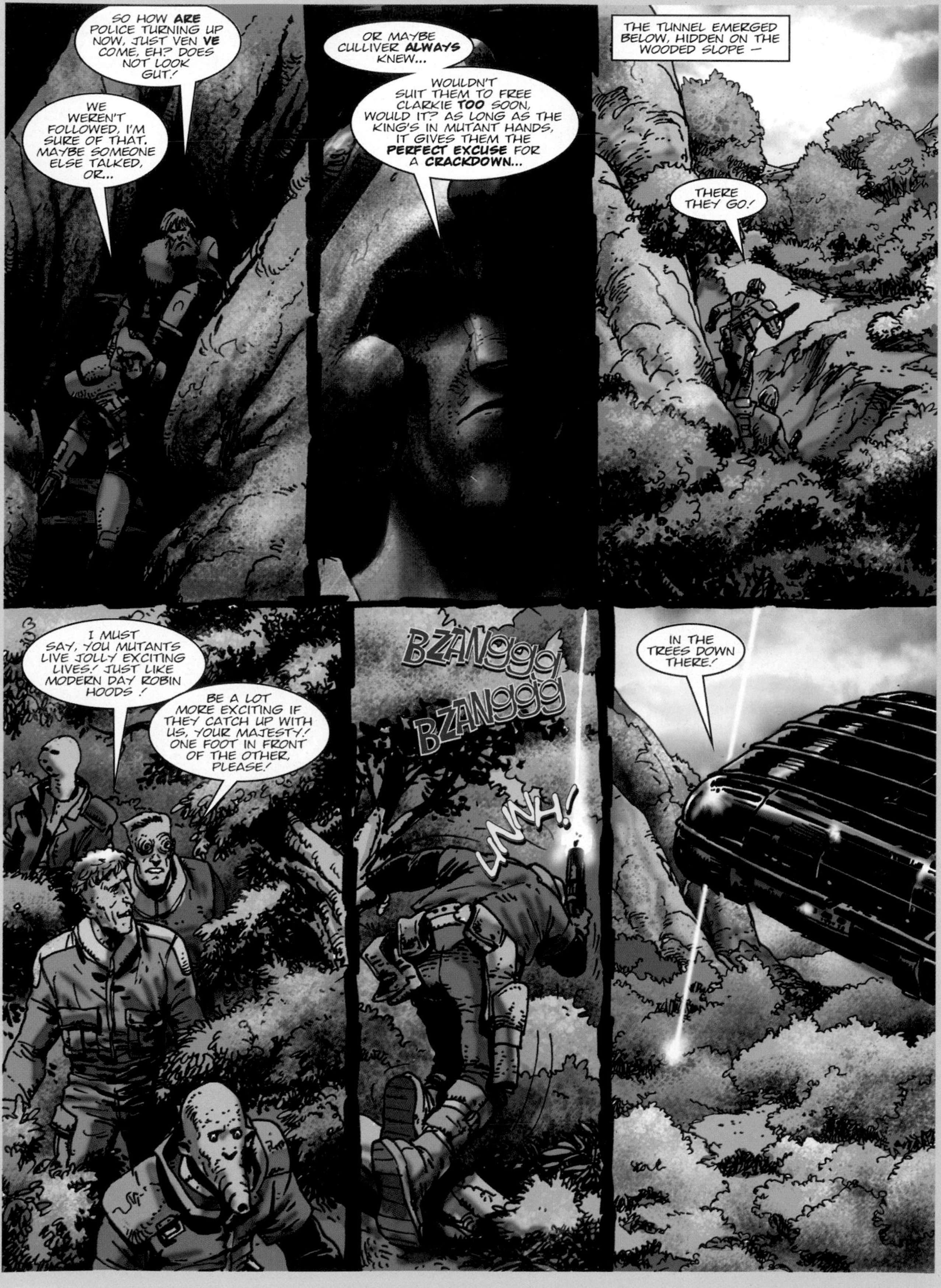
SO HOW **ARE** POLICE TURNING UP NOW, JUST VEN **VE** COME, EH? DOES NOT LOOK GUT!
WE WEREN'T FOLLOWED, I'M SURE OF THAT. MAYBE SOMEONE ELSE TALKED, OR...
OR MAYBE CULLIVER **ALWAYS** KNEW...
WOULDN'T SUIT THEM TO FREE CLARKIE **TOO** SOON, WOULD IT? AS LONG AS THE KING'S IN MUTANT HANDS, IT GIVES THEM THE **PERFECT EXCUSE** FOR A **CRACKDOWN**...
THE TUNNEL EMERGED BELOW, HIDDEN ON THE WOODED SLOPE —
THERE THEY GO!
I MUST SAY, YOU MUTANTS LIVE JOLLY EXCITING LIVES! JUST LIKE MODERN DAY ROBIN HOODS !
BE A LOT MORE EXCITING IF THEY CATCH UP WITH US, YOUR MAJESTY! ONE FOOT IN FRONT OF THE OTHER, PLEASE!
BZANggg
BZANggg
UNNH!
IN THE TREES DOWN THERE!

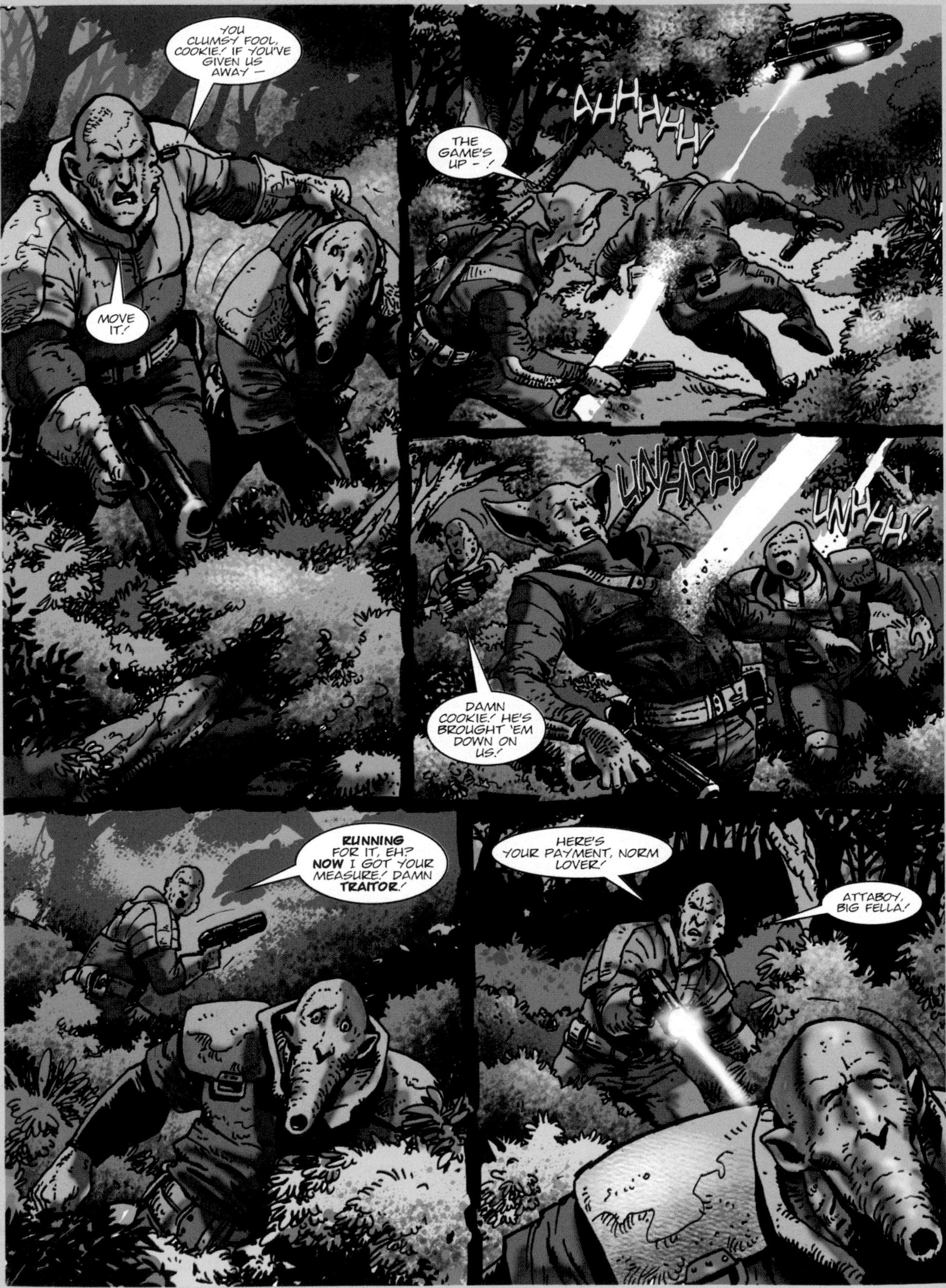
YOU CLUMSY FOOL, COOKIE! IF YOU'VE GIVEN US AWAY —
MOVE IT!
AHHHHHH!
THE GAME'S UP — !
UNHHH!
UNHHH!
DAMN COOKIE! HE'S BROUGHT 'EM DOWN ON US!
RUNNING FOR IT, EH? NOW I GOT YOUR MEASURE! DAMN TRAITOR!
HERE'S YOUR PAYMENT, NORM LOVER!
ATTABOY, BIG FELLA!

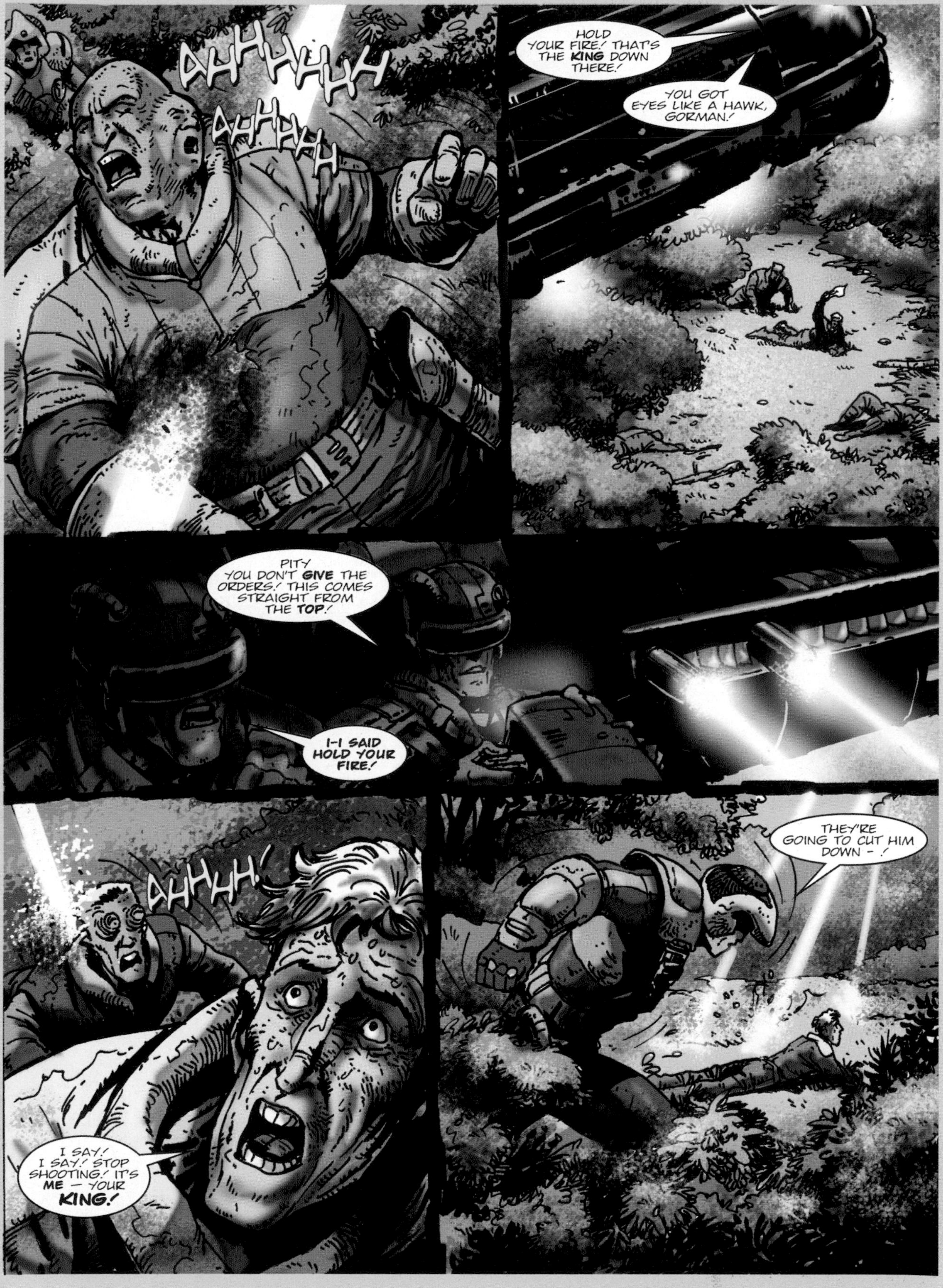
AHHHHHH
AHHHHH
HOLD YOUR FIRE! THAT'S THE KING DOWN THERE!
YOU GOT EYES LIKE A HAWK, GORMAN!
PITY YOU DON'T GIVE THE ORDERS! THIS COMES STRAIGHT FROM THE TOP!
I-I SAID HOLD YOUR FIRE!
AHHHH!
I SAY! I SAY! STOP SHOOTING! IT'S ME — YOUR KING!
THEY'RE GOING TO CUT HIM DOWN —!

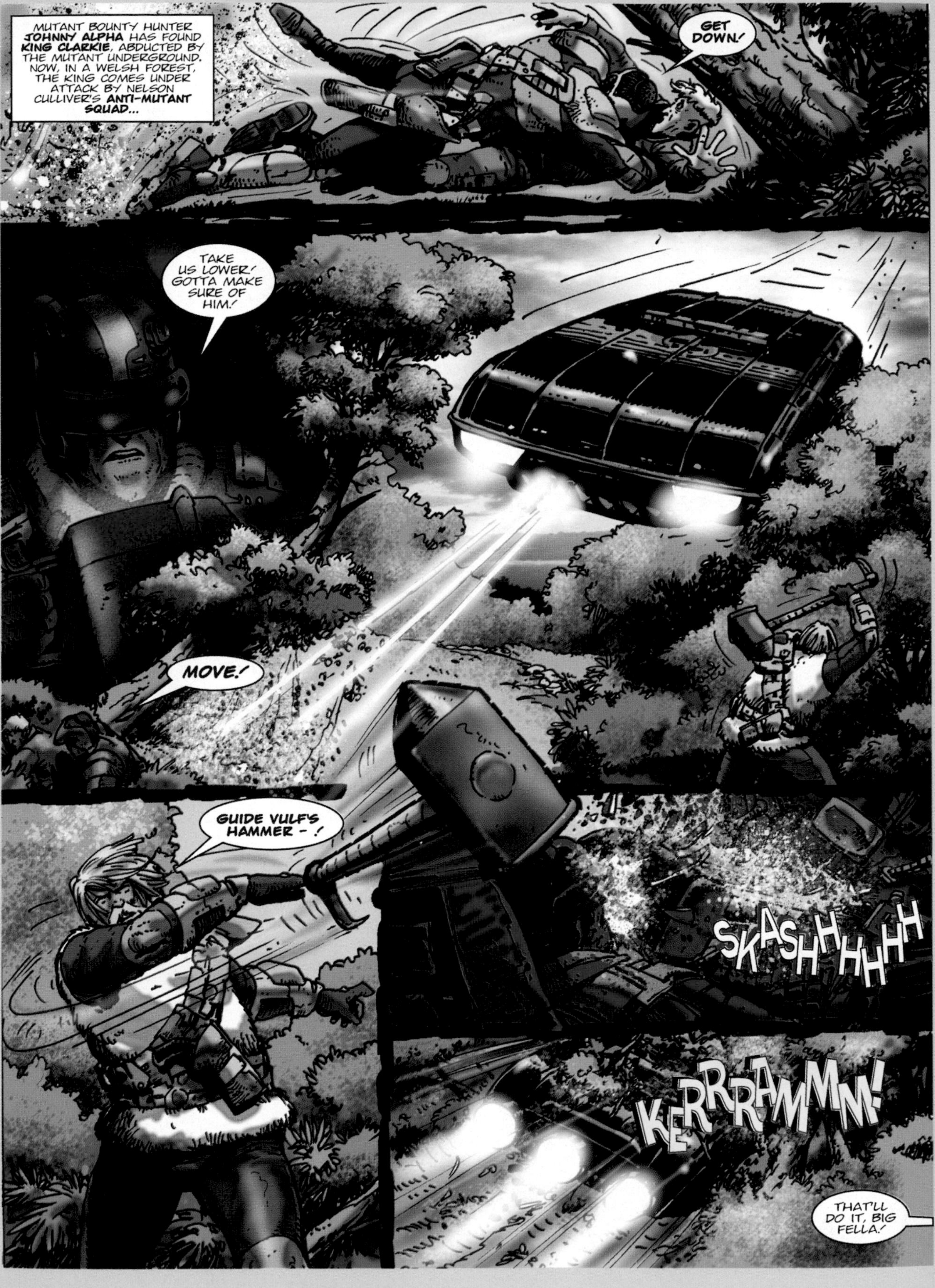
MUTANT BOUNTY HUNTER **JOHNNY ALPHA** HAS FOUND **KING CLARKIE**, ABDUCTED BY THE MUTANT UNDERGROUND. NOW, IN A WELSH FOREST, THE KING COMES UNDER ATTACK BY NELSON CULLIVER'S **ANTI-MUTANT SQUAD...**
GET DOWN!
TAKE US LOWER! GOTTA MAKE SURE OF HIM!
MOVE!
GUIDE VULF'S HAMMER -!
SKASHHHHHHH
KERRRAMMM!
THAT'LL DO IT, BIG FELLA!

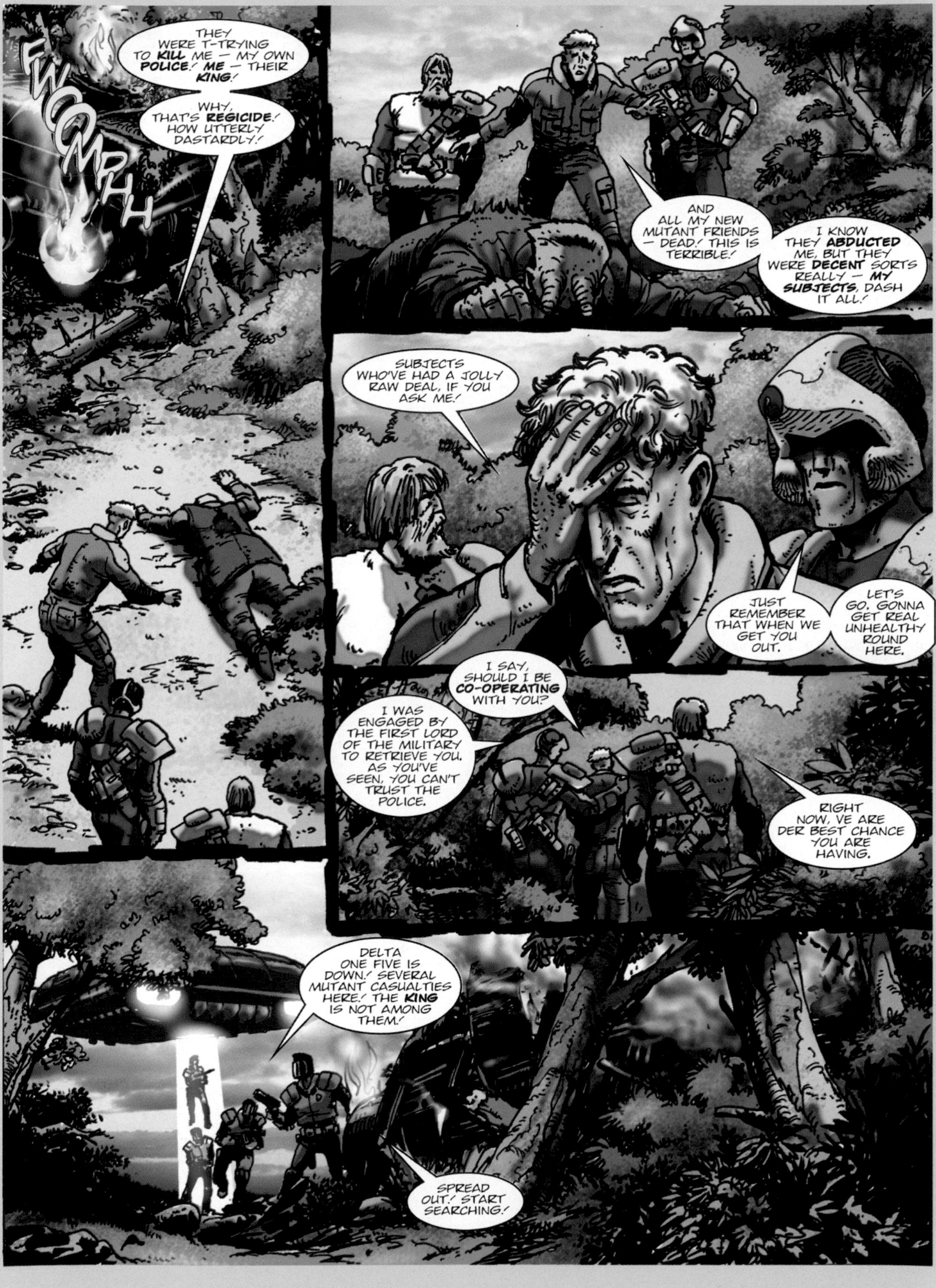
FWOOMPHH
THEY WERE T-TRYING TO KILL ME — MY OWN POLICE! ME — THEIR KING!
WHY, THAT'S REGICIDE! HOW UTTERLY DASTARDLY!
AND ALL MY NEW MUTANT FRIENDS — DEAD! THIS IS TERRIBLE!
I KNOW THEY ABDUCTED ME, BUT THEY WERE DECENT SORTS REALLY — MY SUBJECTS, DASH IT ALL!
SUBJECTS WHO'VE HAD A JOLLY RAW DEAL, IF YOU ASK ME!
JUST REMEMBER THAT WHEN WE GET YOU OUT.
LET'S GO. GONNA GET REAL UNHEALTHY ROUND HERE.
I SAY, SHOULD I BE CO-OPERATING WITH YOU?
I WAS ENGAGED BY THE FIRST LORD OF THE MILITARY TO RETRIEVE YOU. AS YOU'VE SEEN, YOU CAN'T TRUST THE POLICE.
RIGHT NOW, VE ARE DER BEST CHANCE YOU ARE HAVING.
DELTA ONE FIVE IS DOWN! SEVERAL MUTANT CASUALTIES HERE! THE KING IS NOT AMONG THEM!
SPREAD OUT! START SEARCHING!

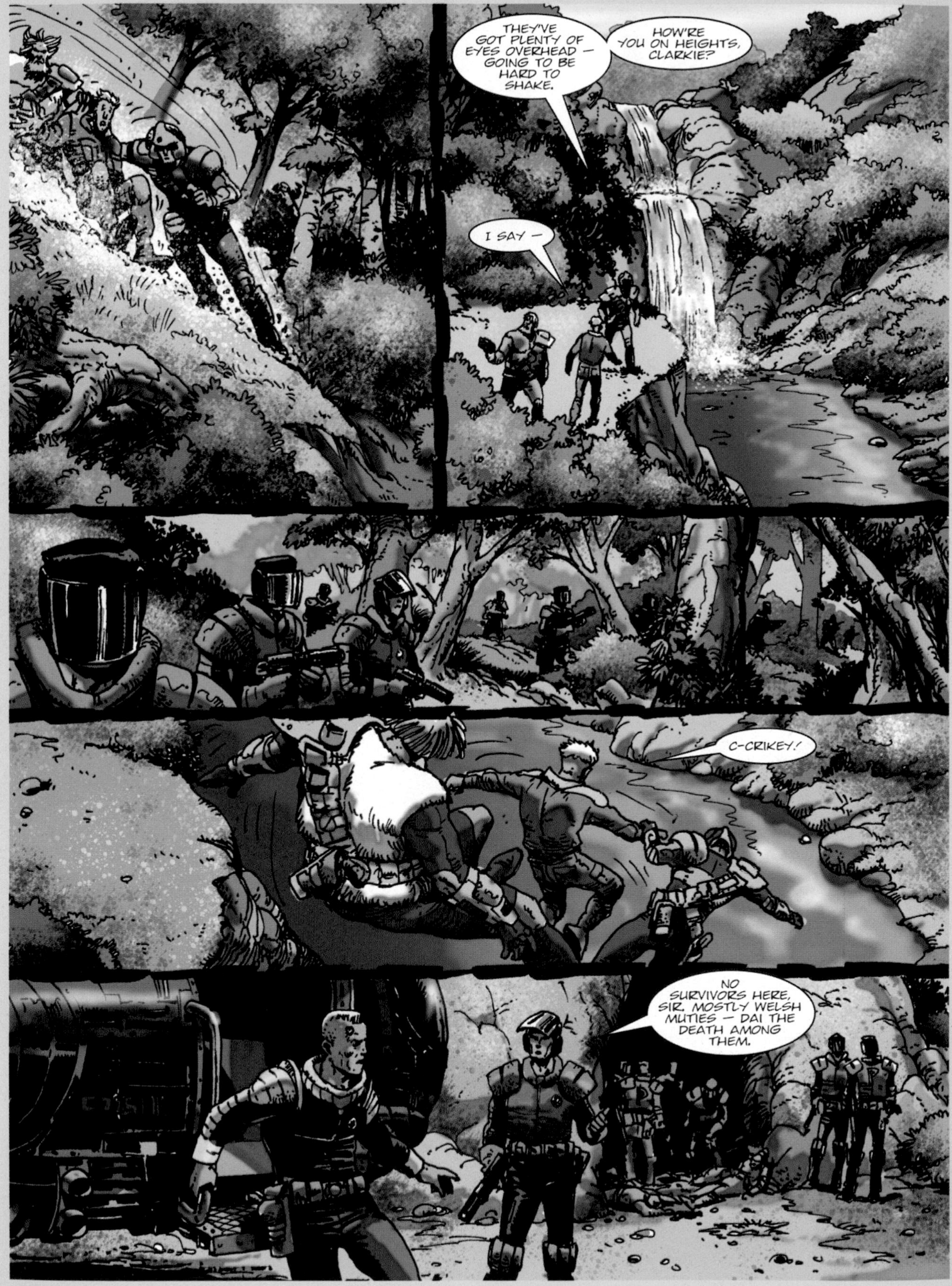
THEY'VE GOT PLENTY OF EYES OVERHEAD — GOING TO BE HARD TO SHAKE.
HOW'RE YOU ON HEIGHTS, CLARKIE?
I SAY —
C-CRIKEY!
NO SURVIVORS HERE, SIR. MOSTLY WELSH MUTIES — DAI THE DEATH AMONG THEM.

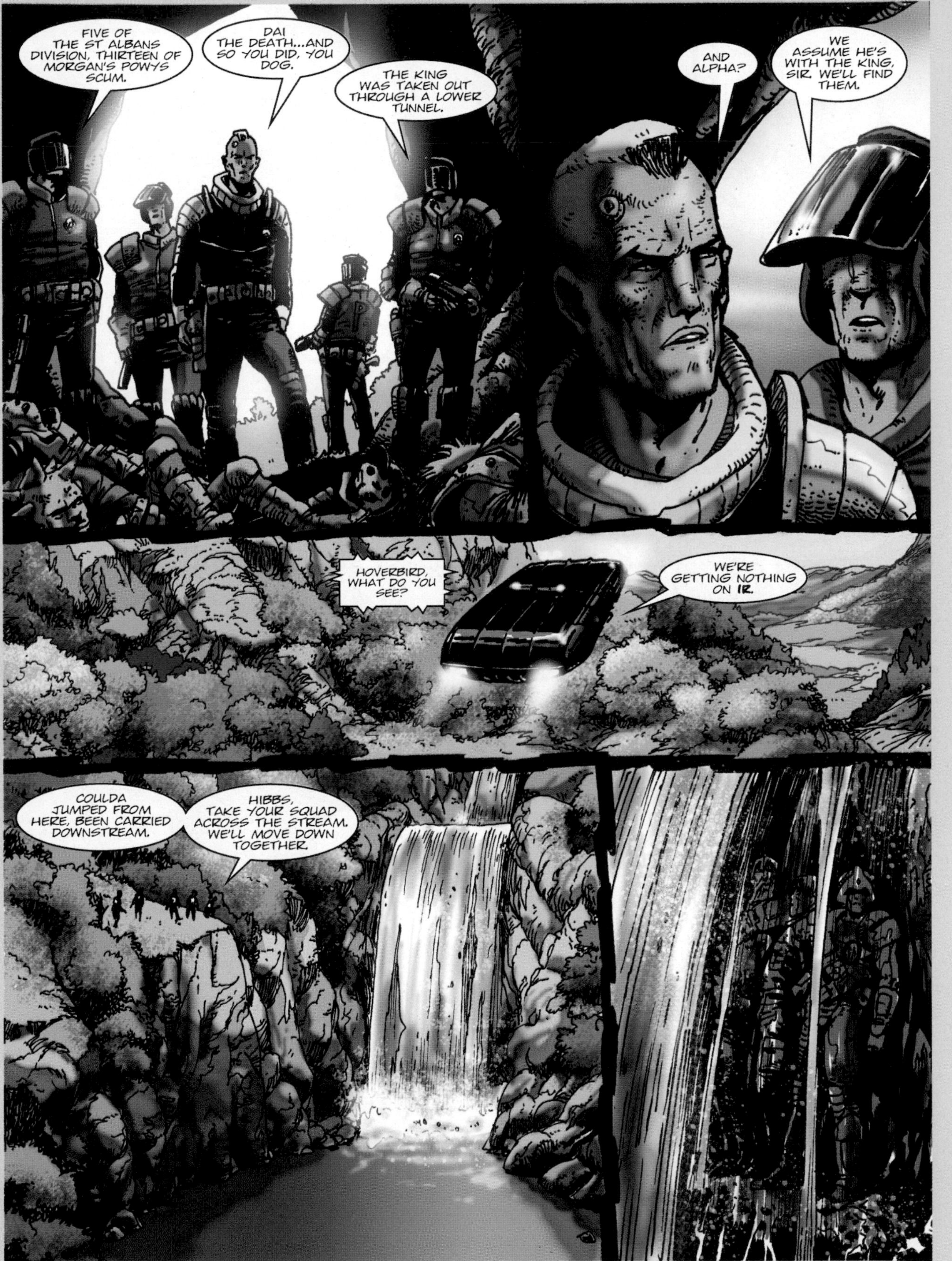
FIVE OF THE ST ALBANS DIVISION, THIRTEEN OF MORGAN'S POWYS SCUM.
DAI THE DEATH...AND SO YOU DID, YOU DOG.
THE KING WAS TAKEN OUT THROUGH A LOWER TUNNEL.
AND ALPHA?
WE ASSUME HE'S WITH THE KING, SIR. WE'LL FIND THEM.
HOVERBIRD, WHAT DO YOU SEE?
WE'RE GETTING NOTHING ON IR.
COULDA JUMPED FROM HERE, BEEN CARRIED DOWNSTREAM.
HIBBS, TAKE YOUR SQUAD ACROSS THE STREAM. WE'LL MOVE DOWN TOGETHER.

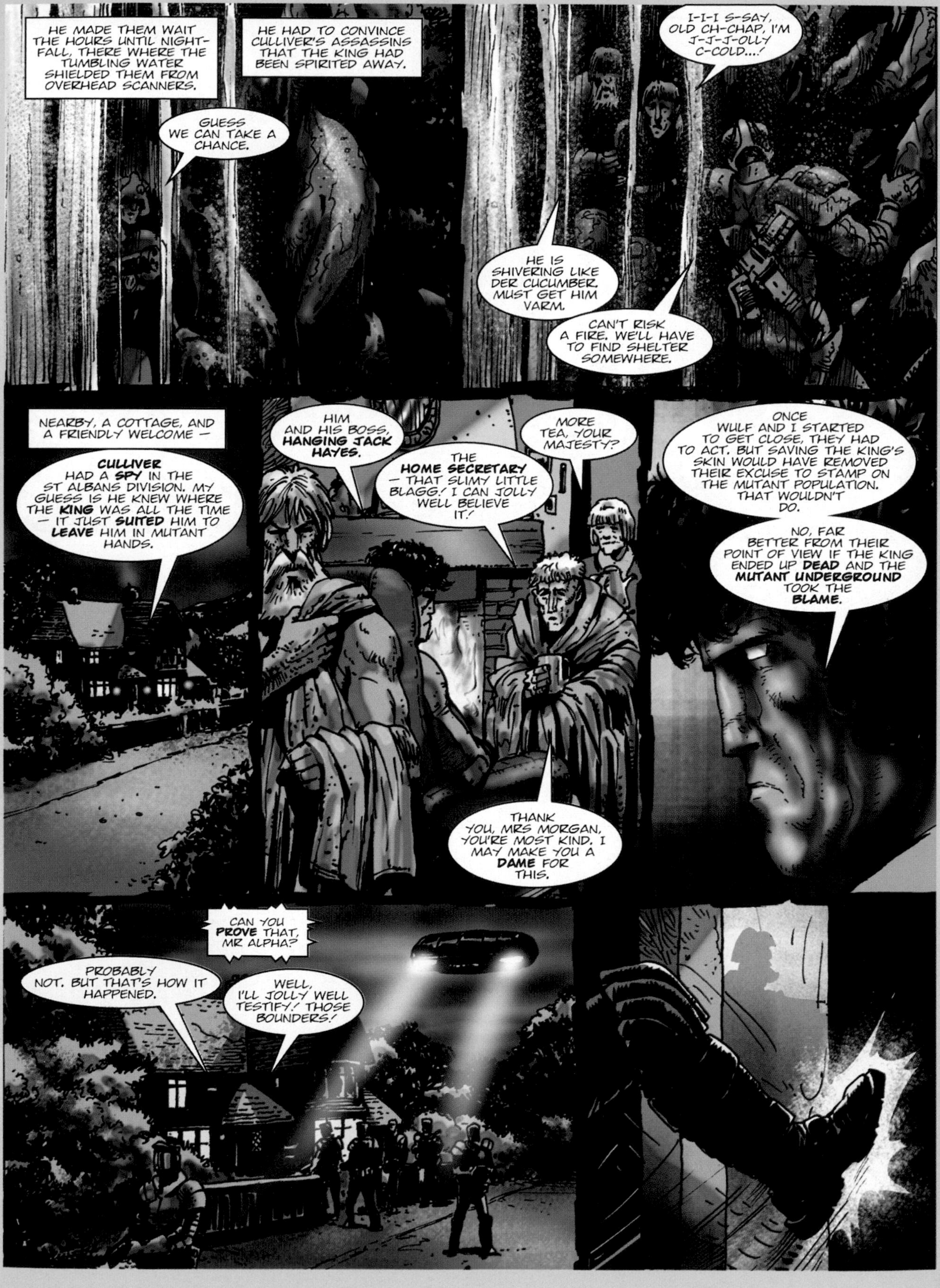

HE MADE THEM WAIT THE HOURS UNTIL NIGHT-FALL, THERE WHERE THE TUMBLING WATER SHIELDED THEM FROM OVERHEAD SCANNERS.
GUESS WE CAN TAKE A CHANCE.
HE HAD TO CONVINCE CULLIVER'S ASSASSINS THAT THE KING HAD BEEN SPIRITED AWAY.
I-I-I S-SAY, OLD CH-CHAP, I'M J-J-J-OLLY C-COLD...!
HE IS SHIVERING LIKE DER CUCUMBER. MUST GET HIM VARM.
CAN'T RISK A FIRE. WE'LL HAVE TO FIND SHELTER SOMEWHERE.
NEARBY, A COTTAGE, AND A FRIENDLY WELCOME —
CULLIVER HAD A SPY IN THE ST ALBANS DIVISION. MY GUESS IS HE KNEW WHERE THE KING WAS ALL THE TIME — IT JUST SUITED HIM TO LEAVE HIM IN MUTANT HANDS.
HIM AND HIS BOSS, HANGING JACK HAYES.
THE HOME SECRETARY — THAT SLIMY LITTLE BLAGG! I CAN JOLLY WELL BELIEVE IT!
MORE TEA, YOUR MAJESTY?
THANK YOU, MRS MORGAN, YOU'RE MOST KIND. I MAY MAKE YOU A DAME FOR THIS.
ONCE WULF AND I STARTED TO GET CLOSE, THEY HAD TO ACT. BUT SAVING THE KING'S SKIN WOULD HAVE REMOVED THEIR EXCUSE TO STAMP ON THE MUTANT POPULATION. THAT WOULDN'T DO.
NO, FAR BETTER FROM THEIR POINT OF VIEW IF THE KING ENDED UP DEAD AND THE MUTANT UNDERGROUND TOOK THE BLAME.
CAN YOU PROVE THAT, MR ALPHA?
PROBABLY NOT. BUT THAT'S HOW IT HAPPENED.
WELL, I'LL JOLLY WELL TESTIFY! THOSE BOUNDERS!

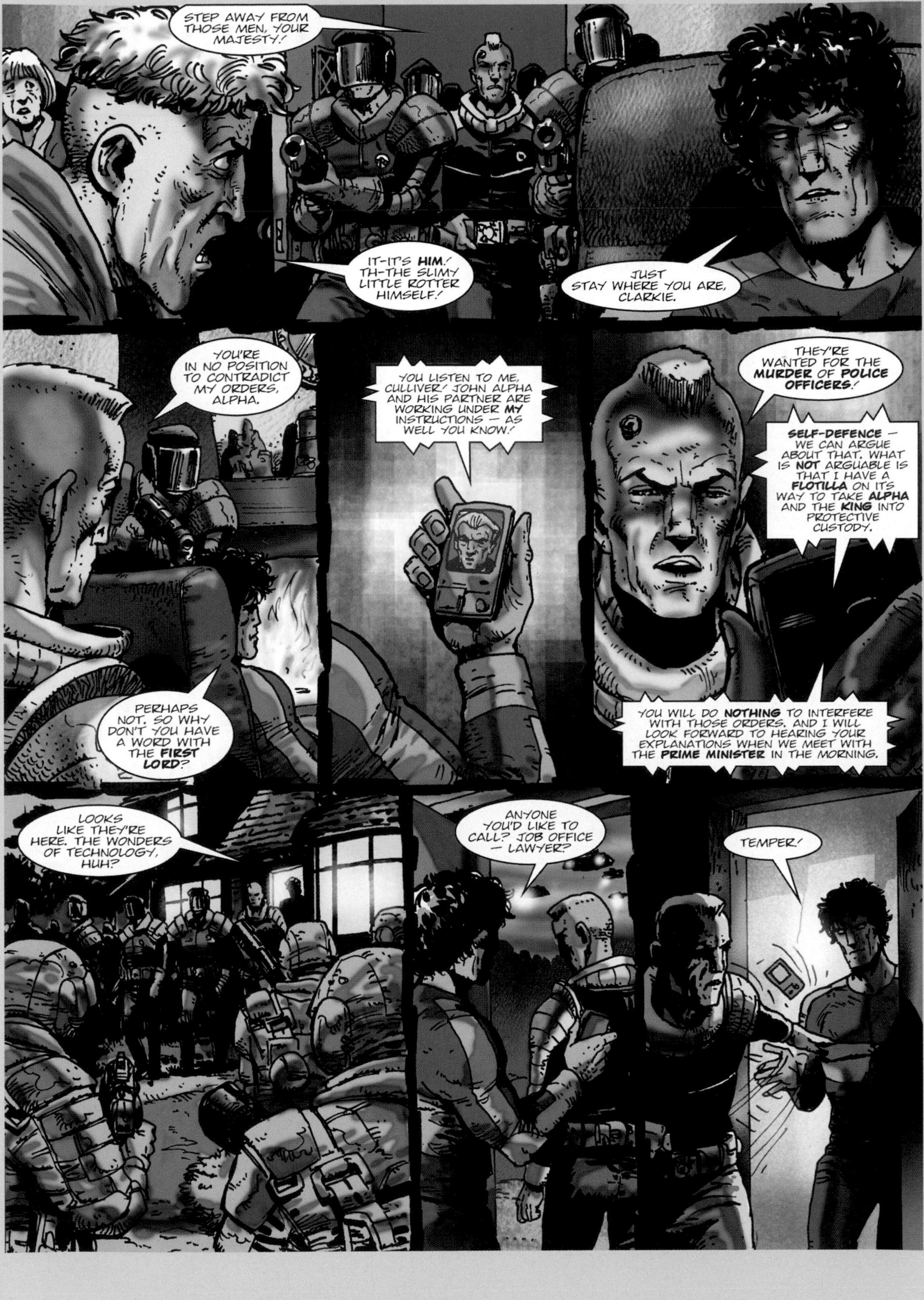

STEP AWAY FROM THOSE MEN, YOUR MAJESTY!
IT-IT'S **HIM**! TH-THE SLIMY LITTLE ROTTER HIMSELF!
JUST STAY WHERE YOU ARE, CLARKIE.
YOU'RE IN NO POSITION TO CONTRADICT MY ORDERS, ALPHA.
PERHAPS NOT. SO WHY DON'T YOU HAVE A WORD WITH THE **FIRST LORD**?
YOU LISTEN TO ME, CULLIVER! JOHN ALPHA AND HIS PARTNER ARE WORKING UNDER **MY** INSTRUCTIONS — AS WELL YOU KNOW!
THEY'RE WANTED FOR THE **MURDER** OF **POLICE OFFICERS**!
SELF-DEFENCE — WE CAN ARGUE ABOUT THAT. WHAT IS **NOT** ARGUABLE IS THAT I HAVE A **FLOTILLA** ON ITS WAY TO TAKE **ALPHA** AND THE **KING** INTO PROTECTIVE CUSTODY.
YOU WILL DO **NOTHING** TO INTERFERE WITH THOSE ORDERS. AND I WILL LOOK FORWARD TO HEARING YOUR EXPLANATIONS WHEN WE MEET WITH THE **PRIME MINISTER** IN THE MORNING.
LOOKS LIKE THEY'RE HERE. THE WONDERS OF TECHNOLOGY, HUH?
ANYONE YOU'D LIKE TO CALL? JOB OFFICE — LAWYER?
TEMPER!

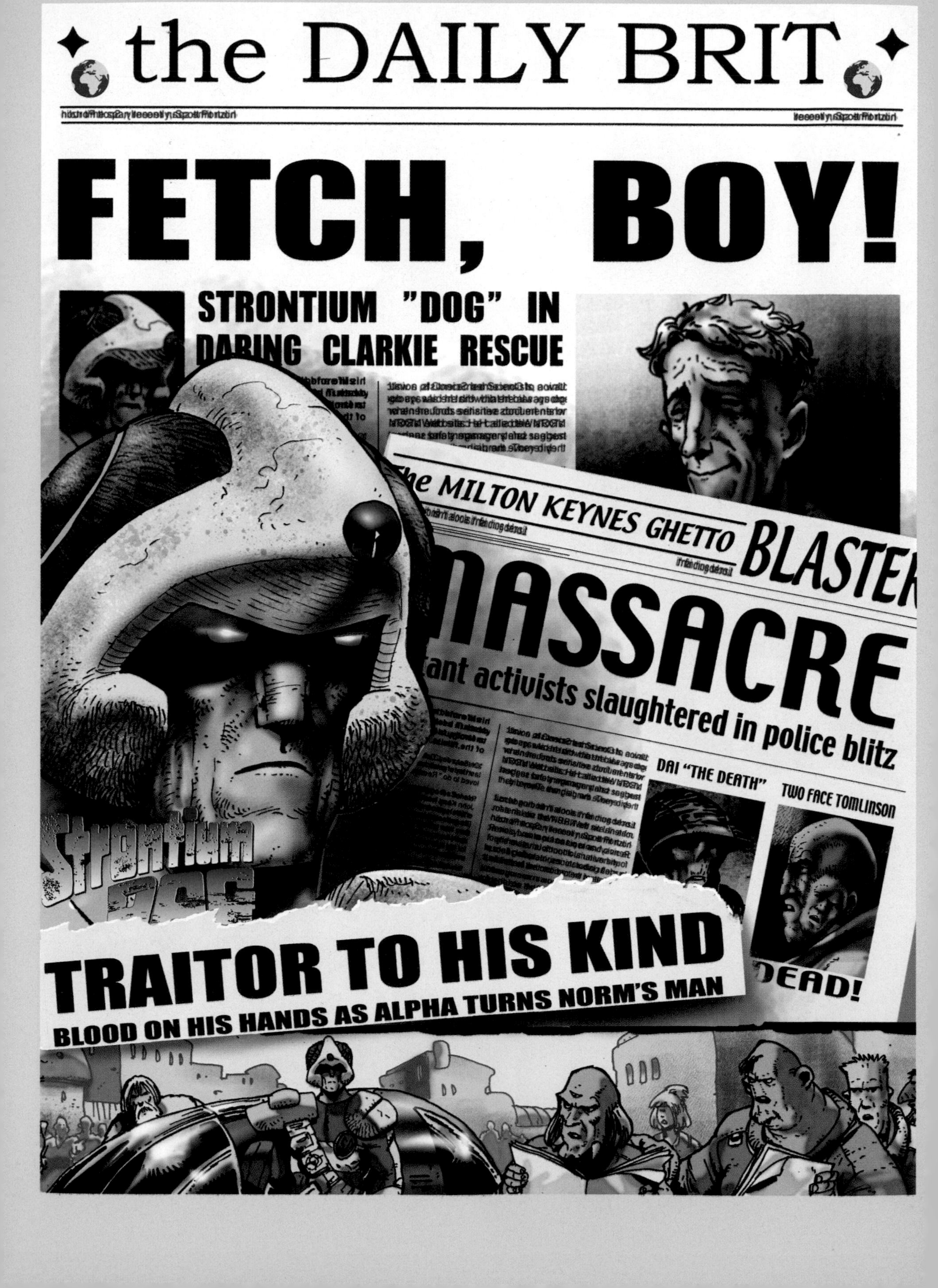

the DAILY BRIT
FETCH, BOY!
STRONTIUM "DOG" IN DARING CLARKIE RESCUE
The MILTON KEYNES GHETTO BLASTER
MASSACRE
ant activists slaughtered in police blitz
DAI "THE DEATH"
TWO FACE TOMLINSON
DEAD!
Strontium Dog
TRAITOR TO HIS KIND
BLOOD ON HIS HANDS AS ALPHA TURNS NORM'S MAN

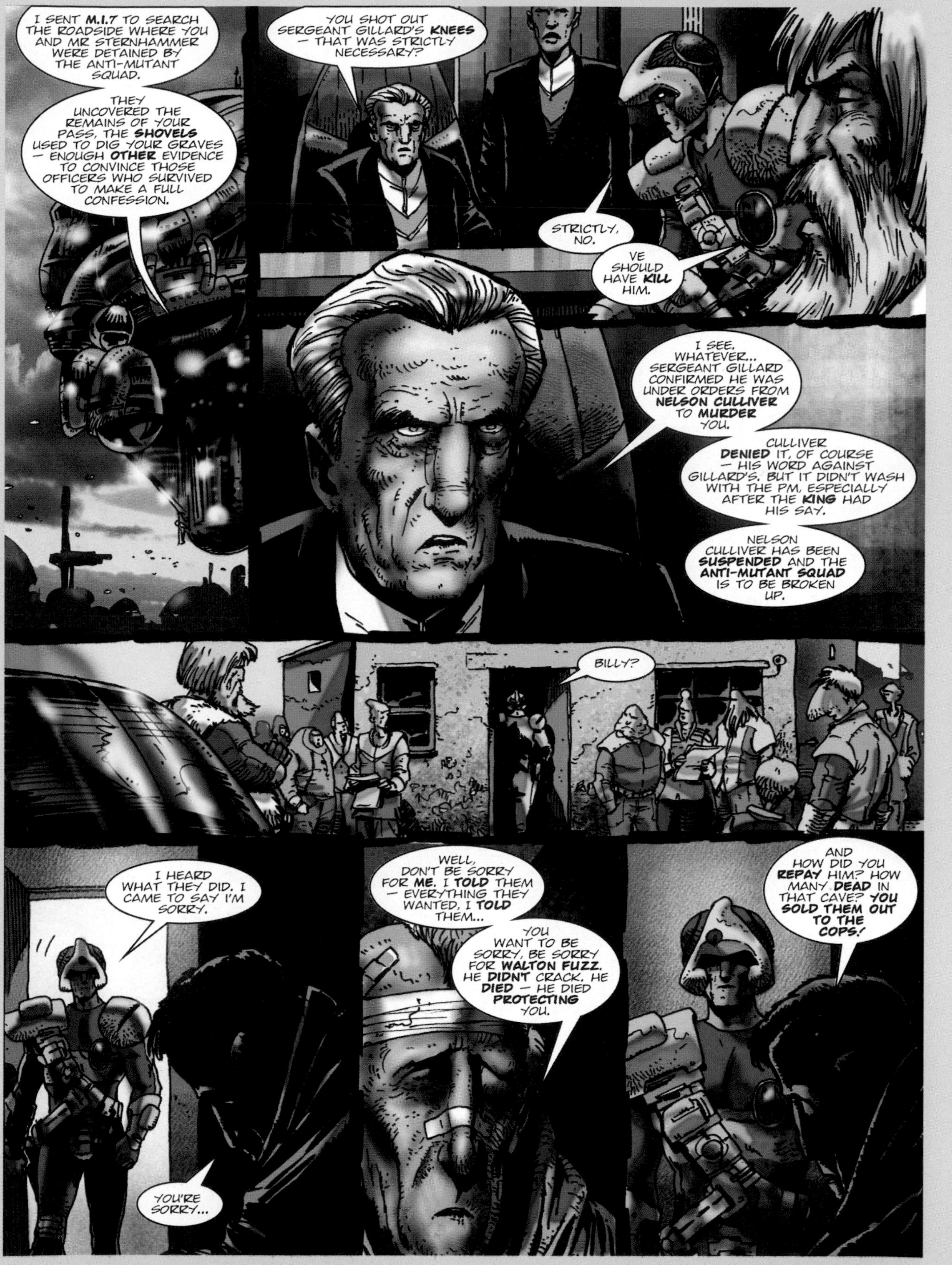
I SENT M.I.7 TO SEARCH THE ROADSIDE WHERE YOU AND MR STERNHAMMER WERE DETAINED BY THE ANTI-MUTANT SQUAD.
THEY UNCOVERED THE REMAINS OF YOUR PASS, THE SHOVELS USED TO DIG YOUR GRAVES — ENOUGH OTHER EVIDENCE TO CONVINCE THOSE OFFICERS WHO SURVIVED TO MAKE A FULL CONFESSION.
YOU SHOT OUT SERGEANT GILLARD'S KNEES — THAT WAS STRICTLY NECESSARY?
STRICTLY, NO.
VE SHOULD HAVE KILL HIM.
I SEE. WHATEVER... SERGEANT GILLARD CONFIRMED HE WAS UNDER ORDERS FROM NELSON CULLIVER TO MURDER YOU.
CULLIVER DENIED IT, OF COURSE — HIS WORD AGAINST GILLARD'S. BUT IT DIDN'T WASH WITH THE PM, ESPECIALLY AFTER THE KING HAD HIS SAY.
NELSON CULLIVER HAS BEEN SUSPENDED AND THE ANTI-MUTANT SQUAD IS TO BE BROKEN UP.
BILLY?
I HEARD WHAT THEY DID. I CAME TO SAY I'M SORRY.
YOU'RE SORRY...
WELL, DON'T BE SORRY FOR ME. I TOLD THEM — EVERYTHING THEY WANTED, I TOLD THEM...
YOU WANT TO BE SORRY, BE SORRY FOR WALTON FUZZ. HE DIDN'T CRACK. HE DIED — HE DIED PROTECTING YOU.
AND HOW DID YOU REPAY HIM? HOW MANY DEAD IN THAT CAVE? YOU SOLD THEM OUT TO THE COPS!

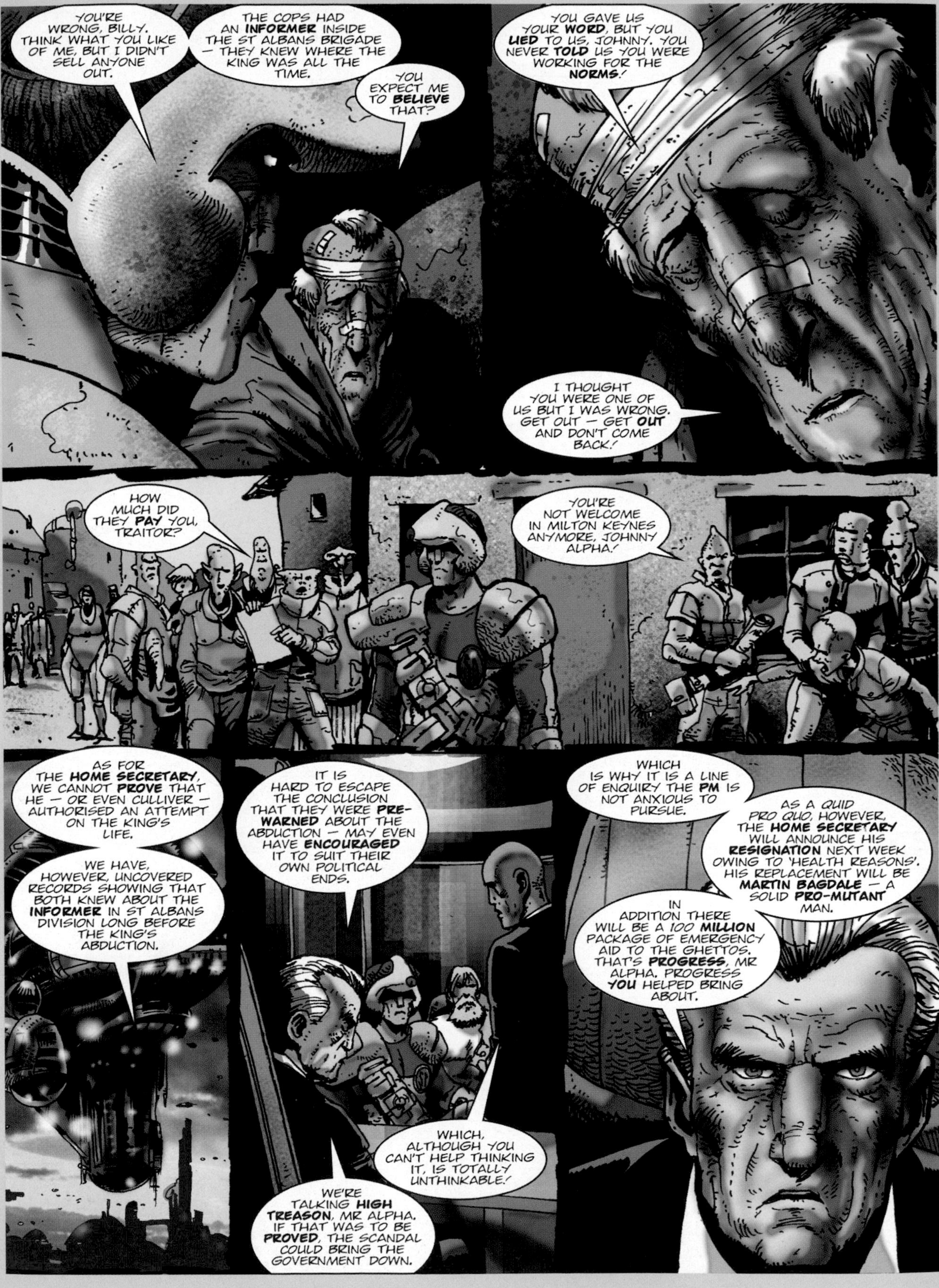

YOU'RE WRONG, BILLY. THINK WHAT YOU LIKE OF ME, BUT I DIDN'T SELL ANYONE OUT.
THE COPS HAD AN INFORMER INSIDE THE ST ALBANS BRIGADE — THEY KNEW WHERE THE KING WAS ALL THE TIME.
YOU EXPECT ME TO BELIEVE THAT?
YOU GAVE US YOUR WORD, BUT YOU LIED TO US, JOHNNY. YOU NEVER TOLD US YOU WERE WORKING FOR THE NORMS!
I THOUGHT YOU WERE ONE OF US BUT I WAS WRONG. GET OUT — GET OUT AND DON'T COME BACK!
HOW MUCH DID THEY PAY YOU, TRAITOR?
YOU'RE NOT WELCOME IN MILTON KEYNES ANYMORE, JOHNNY ALPHA!
AS FOR THE HOME SECRETARY, WE CANNOT PROVE THAT HE — OR EVEN CULLIVER — AUTHORISED AN ATTEMPT ON THE KING'S LIFE.
WE HAVE, HOWEVER, UNCOVERED RECORDS SHOWING THAT BOTH KNEW ABOUT THE INFORMER IN ST ALBANS DIVISION LONG BEFORE THE KING'S ABDUCTION.
IT IS HARD TO ESCAPE THE CONCLUSION THAT THEY WERE PRE-WARNED ABOUT THE ABDUCTION — MAY EVEN HAVE ENCOURAGED IT TO SUIT THEIR OWN POLITICAL ENDS.
WE'RE TALKING HIGH TREASON, MR ALPHA. IF THAT WAS TO BE PROVED, THE SCANDAL COULD BRING THE GOVERNMENT DOWN.
WHICH, ALTHOUGH YOU CAN'T HELP THINKING IT, IS TOTALLY UNTHINKABLE!
WHICH IS WHY IT IS A LINE OF ENQUIRY THE PM IS NOT ANXIOUS TO PURSUE.
AS A QUID PRO QUO, HOWEVER, THE HOME SECRETARY WILL ANNOUNCE HIS RESIGNATION NEXT WEEK OWING TO 'HEALTH REASONS'. HIS REPLACEMENT WILL BE MARTIN BAGDALE — A SOLID PRO-MUTANT MAN.
IN ADDITION THERE WILL BE A 100 MILLION PACKAGE OF EMERGENCY AID TO THE GHETTOS. THAT'S PROGRESS, MR ALPHA. PROGRESS YOU HELPED BRING ABOUT.

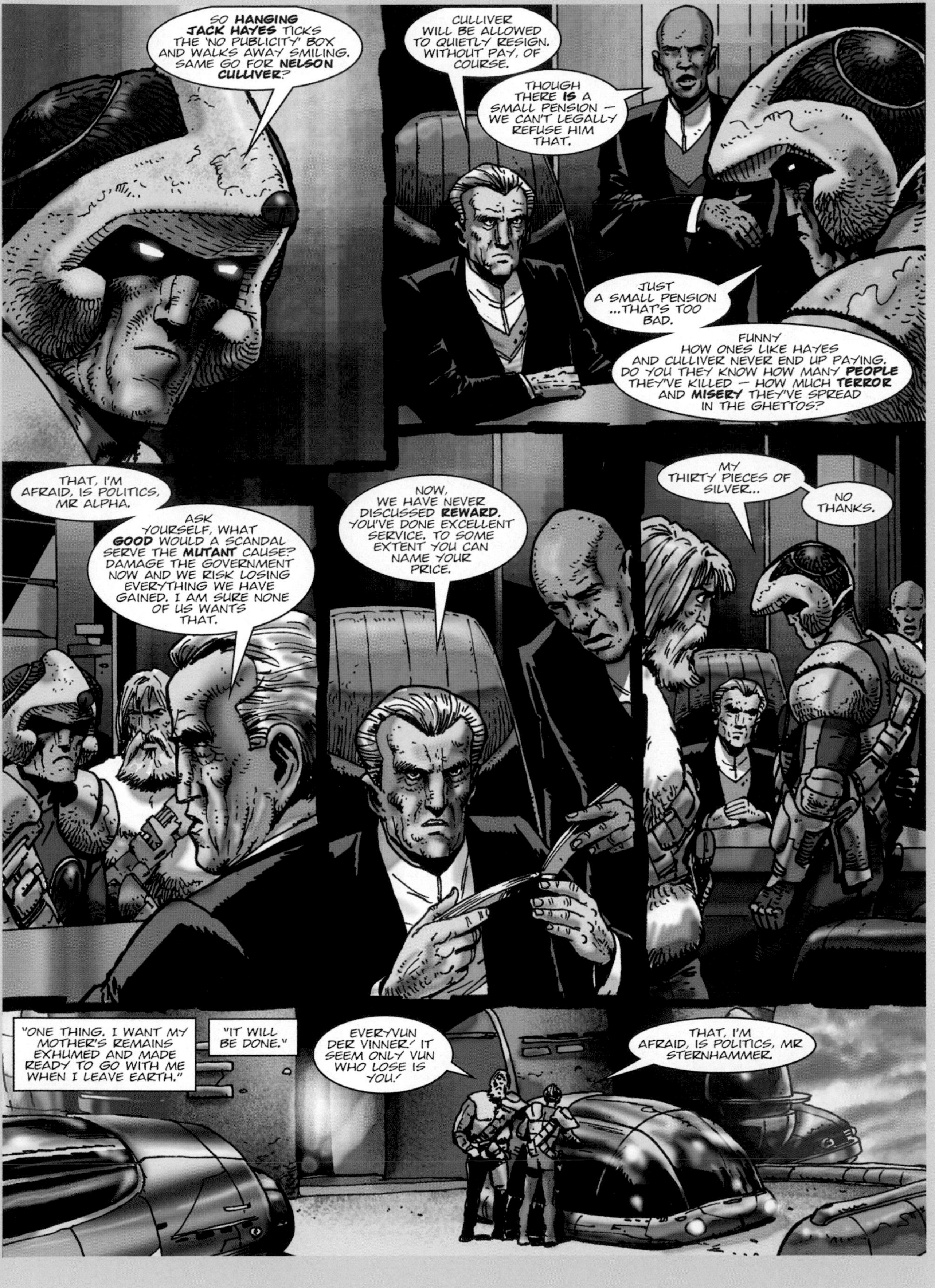
SO HANGING JACK HAYES TICKS THE 'NO PUBLICITY' BOX AND WALKS AWAY SMILING. SAME GO FOR NELSON CULLIVER?
CULLIVER WILL BE ALLOWED TO QUIETLY RESIGN. WITHOUT PAY, OF COURSE.
THOUGH THERE IS A SMALL PENSION — WE CAN'T LEGALLY REFUSE HIM THAT.
JUST A SMALL PENSION ...THAT'S TOO BAD.
FUNNY HOW ONES LIKE HAYES AND CULLIVER NEVER END UP PAYING. DO YOU THEY KNOW HOW MANY PEOPLE THEY'VE KILLED — HOW MUCH TERROR AND MISERY THEY'VE SPREAD IN THE GHETTOS?
THAT, I'M AFRAID, IS POLITICS, MR ALPHA.
ASK YOURSELF, WHAT GOOD WOULD A SCANDAL SERVE THE MUTANT CAUSE? DAMAGE THE GOVERNMENT NOW AND WE RISK LOSING EVERYTHING WE HAVE GAINED. I AM SURE NONE OF US WANTS THAT.
NOW, WE HAVE NEVER DISCUSSED REWARD. YOU'VE DONE EXCELLENT SERVICE. TO SOME EXTENT YOU CAN NAME YOUR PRICE.
MY THIRTY PIECES OF SILVER...
NO THANKS.
"ONE THING. I WANT MY MOTHER'S REMAINS EXHUMED AND MADE READY TO GO WITH ME WHEN I LEAVE EARTH."
"IT WILL BE DONE."
EVERYVUN DER VINNER! IT SEEM ONLY VUN WHO LOSE IS YOU!
THAT, I'M AFRAID, IS POLITICS, MR STERNHAMMER.

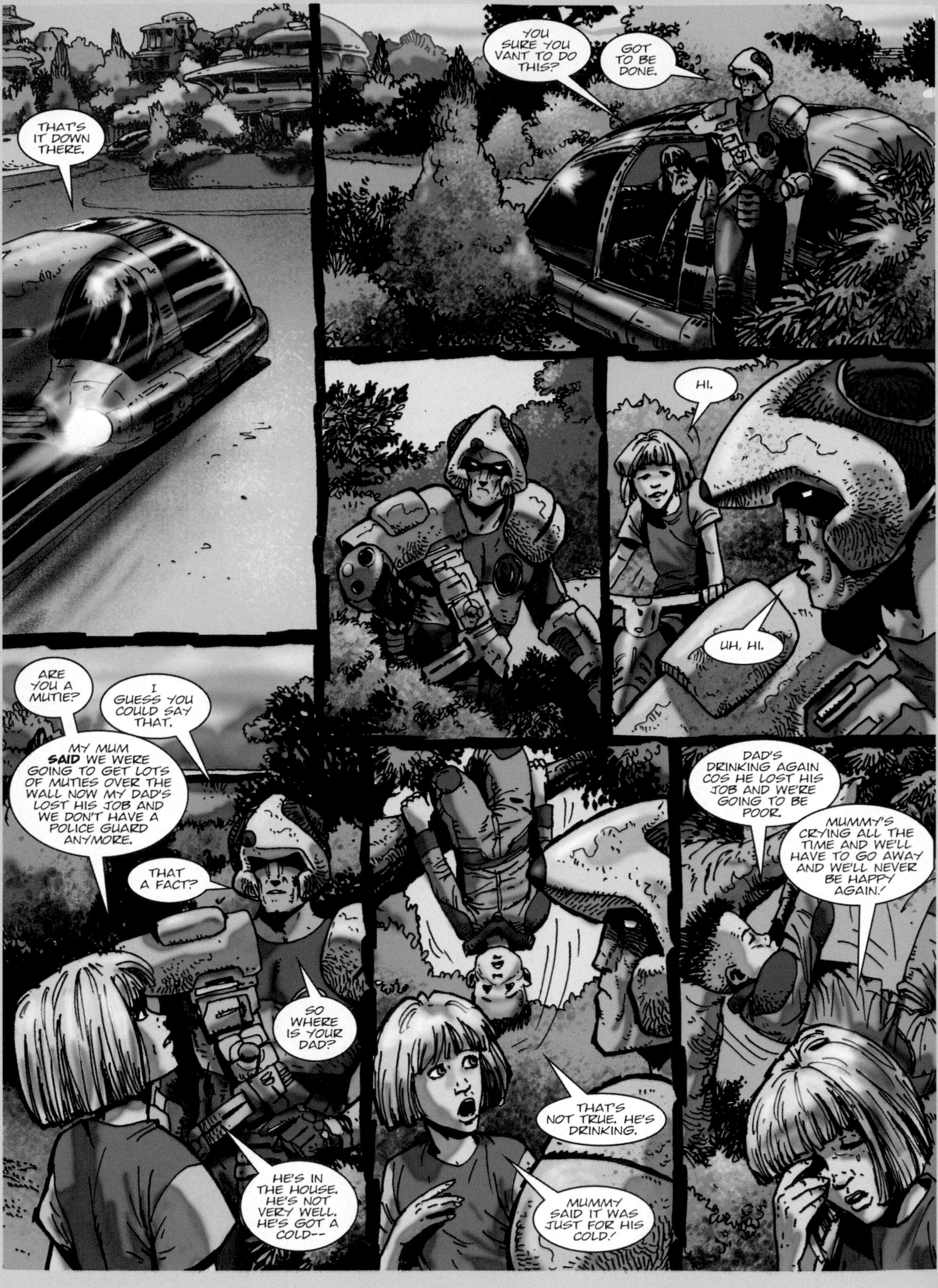
THAT'S IT DOWN THERE.
YOU SURE YOU VANT TO DO THIS?
GOT TO BE DONE.
HI.
UH, HI.
ARE YOU A MUTIE?
I GUESS YOU COULD SAY THAT.
MY MUM **SAID** WE WERE GOING TO GET LOTS OF MUTIES OVER THE WALL NOW MY DAD'S LOST HIS JOB AND WE DON'T HAVE A POLICE GUARD ANYMORE.
THAT A FACT?
SO WHERE IS YOUR DAD?
HE'S IN THE HOUSE. HE'S NOT VERY WELL. HE'S GOT A COLD--
THAT'S NOT TRUE. HE'S DRINKING.
MUMMY SAID IT WAS JUST FOR HIS COLD!
DAD'S DRINKING AGAIN COS HE LOST HIS JOB AND WE'RE GOING TO BE POOR.
MUMMY'S CRYING ALL THE TIME AND WE'LL HAVE TO GO AWAY AND WE'LL NEVER BE HAPPY AGAIN!

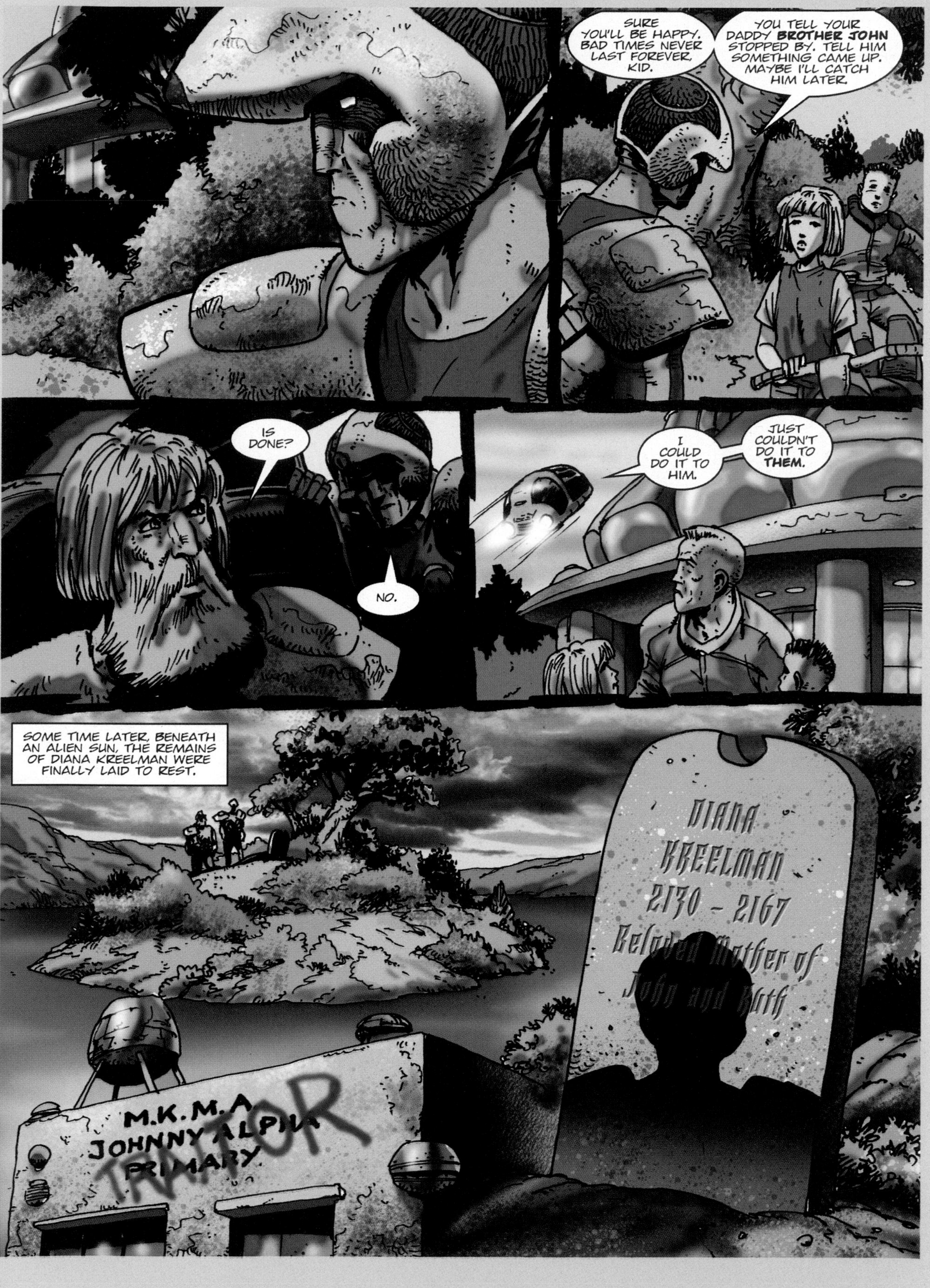
SURE YOU'LL BE HAPPY. BAD TIMES NEVER LAST FOREVER, KID.
YOU TELL YOUR DADDY **BROTHER JOHN** STOPPED BY. TELL HIM SOMETHING CAME UP. MAYBE I'LL CATCH HIM LATER.
IS DONE?
NO.
I COULD DO IT TO HIM.
JUST COULDN'T DO IT TO **THEM.**
SOME TIME LATER, BENEATH AN ALIEN SUN, THE REMAINS OF DIANA KREELMAN WERE FINALLY LAID TO REST.
DIANA
KREELMAN
2130 - 2167
M.K.M.A
JOHNNY ALPHA
PRIMARY
TRAITOR

SHAGGY DOG STORY

Script: John Wagner
Art: Carlos Ezquerra
Letters: Annie Parkhouse

Originally published in *2000 AD* Progs 2006, 1469-1472

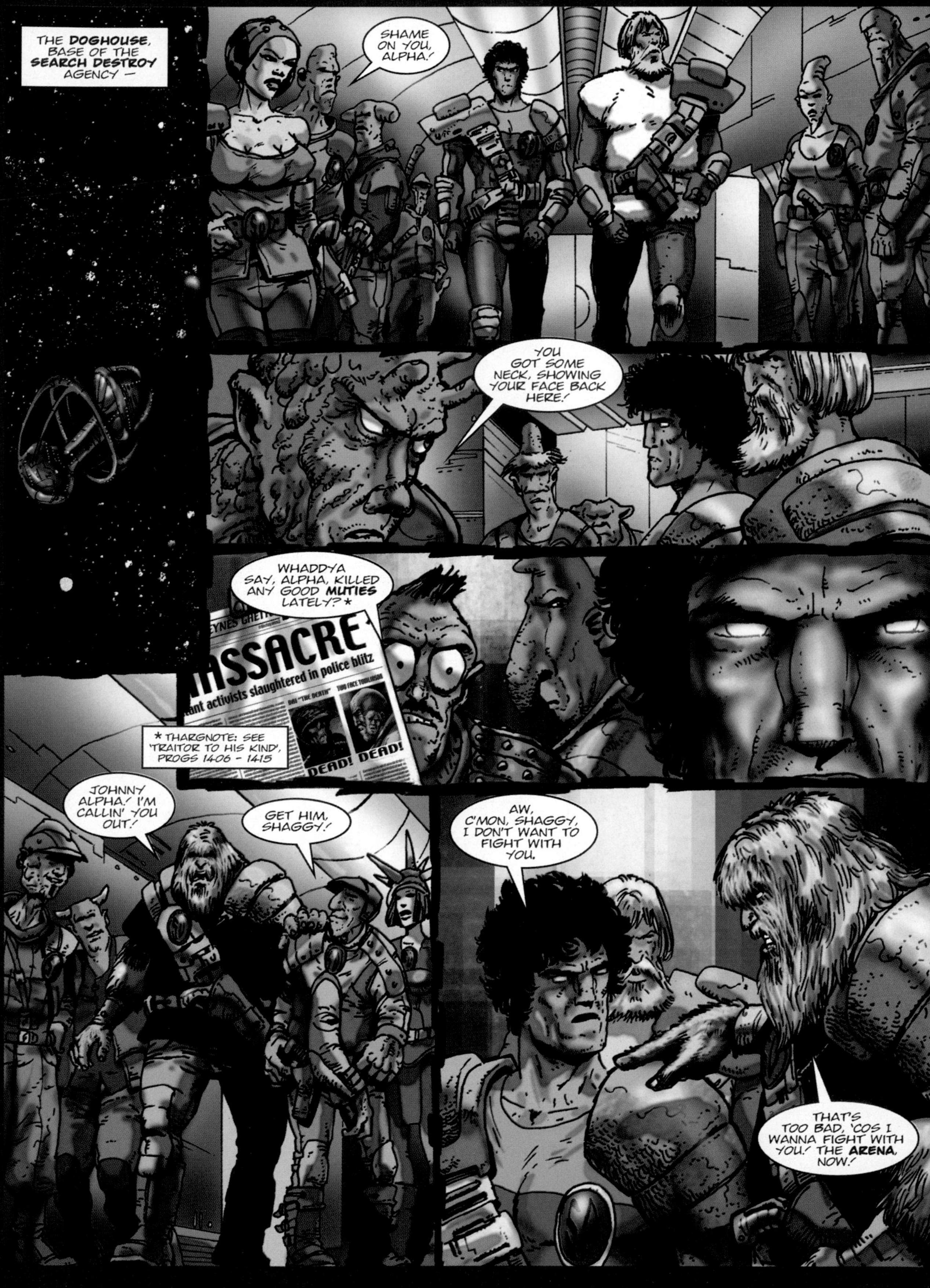
THE DOGHOUSE, BASE OF THE SEARCH DESTROY AGENCY —
SHAME ON YOU, ALPHA!
YOU GOT SOME NECK, SHOWING YOUR FACE BACK HERE!
WHADDYA SAY, ALPHA, KILLED ANY GOOD MUTIES LATELY? *
ASSACRE
ant activists slaughtered in police blitz
DEAD! DEAD!
* THARGNOTE: SEE 'TRAITOR TO HIS KIND', PROGS 1406 - 1415
JOHNNY ALPHA! I'M CALLIN' YOU OUT!
GET HIM, SHAGGY!
AW, C'MON, SHAGGY, I DON'T WANT TO FIGHT WITH YOU.
THAT'S TOO BAD, 'COS I WANNA FIGHT WITH YOU! THE ARENA, NOW!

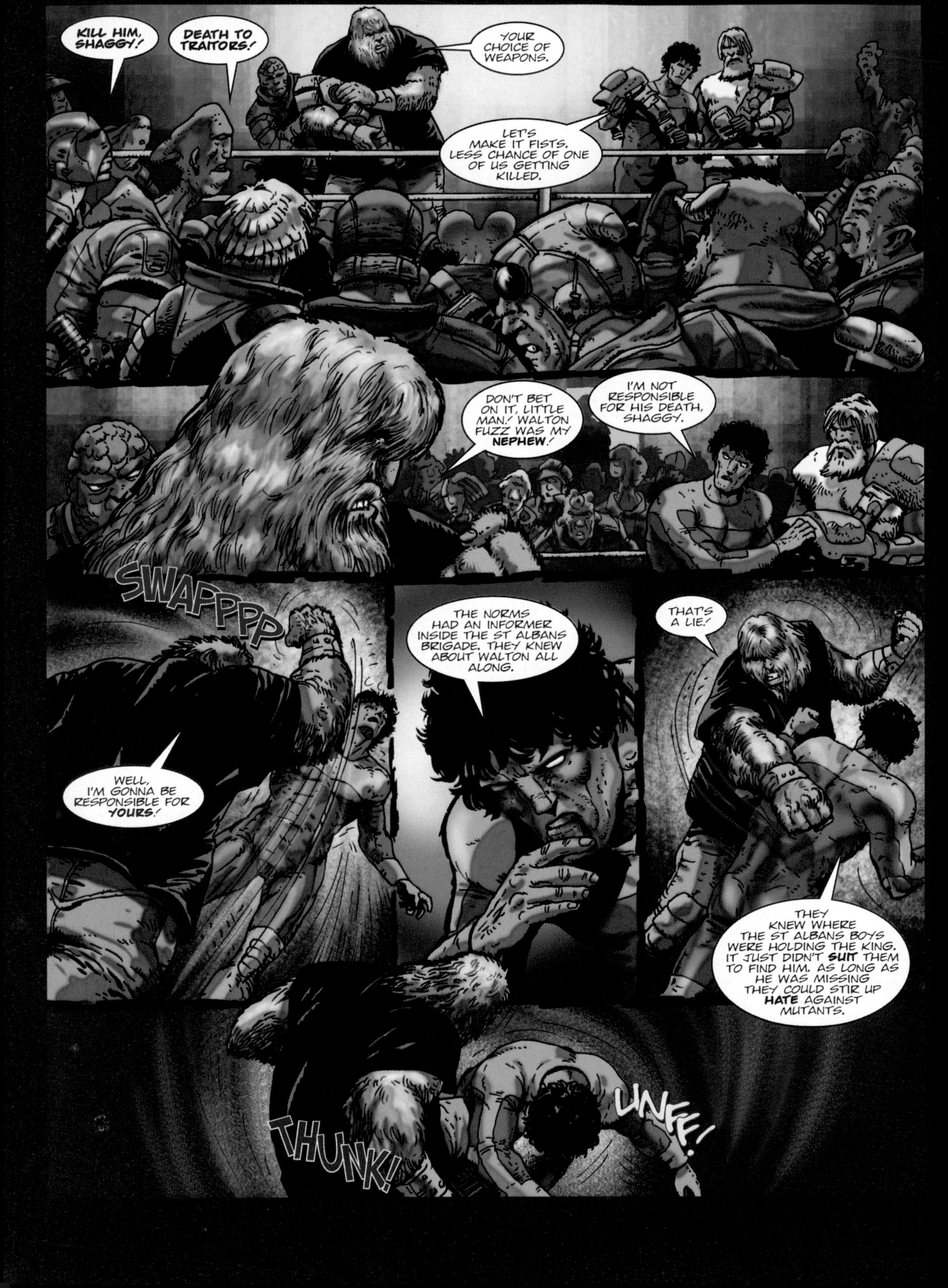
KILL HIM, SHAGGY!
DEATH TO TRAITORS!
YOUR CHOICE OF WEAPONS.
LET'S MAKE IT FISTS. LESS CHANCE OF ONE OF US GETTING KILLED.
DON'T BET ON IT, LITTLE MAN! WALTON FUZZ WAS MY NEPHEW!
I'M NOT RESPONSIBLE FOR HIS DEATH, SHAGGY.
SWAPPPP
WELL, I'M GONNA BE RESPONSIBLE FOR YOURS!
THE NORMS HAD AN INFORMER INSIDE THE ST ALBANS BRIGADE. THEY KNEW ABOUT WALTON ALL ALONG.
THAT'S A LIE!
THEY KNEW WHERE THE ST ALBANS BOYS WERE HOLDING THE KING. IT JUST DIDN'T SUIT THEM TO FIND HIM. AS LONG AS HE WAS MISSING THEY COULD STIR UP HATE AGAINST MUTANTS.
THUNK!
UNFF!

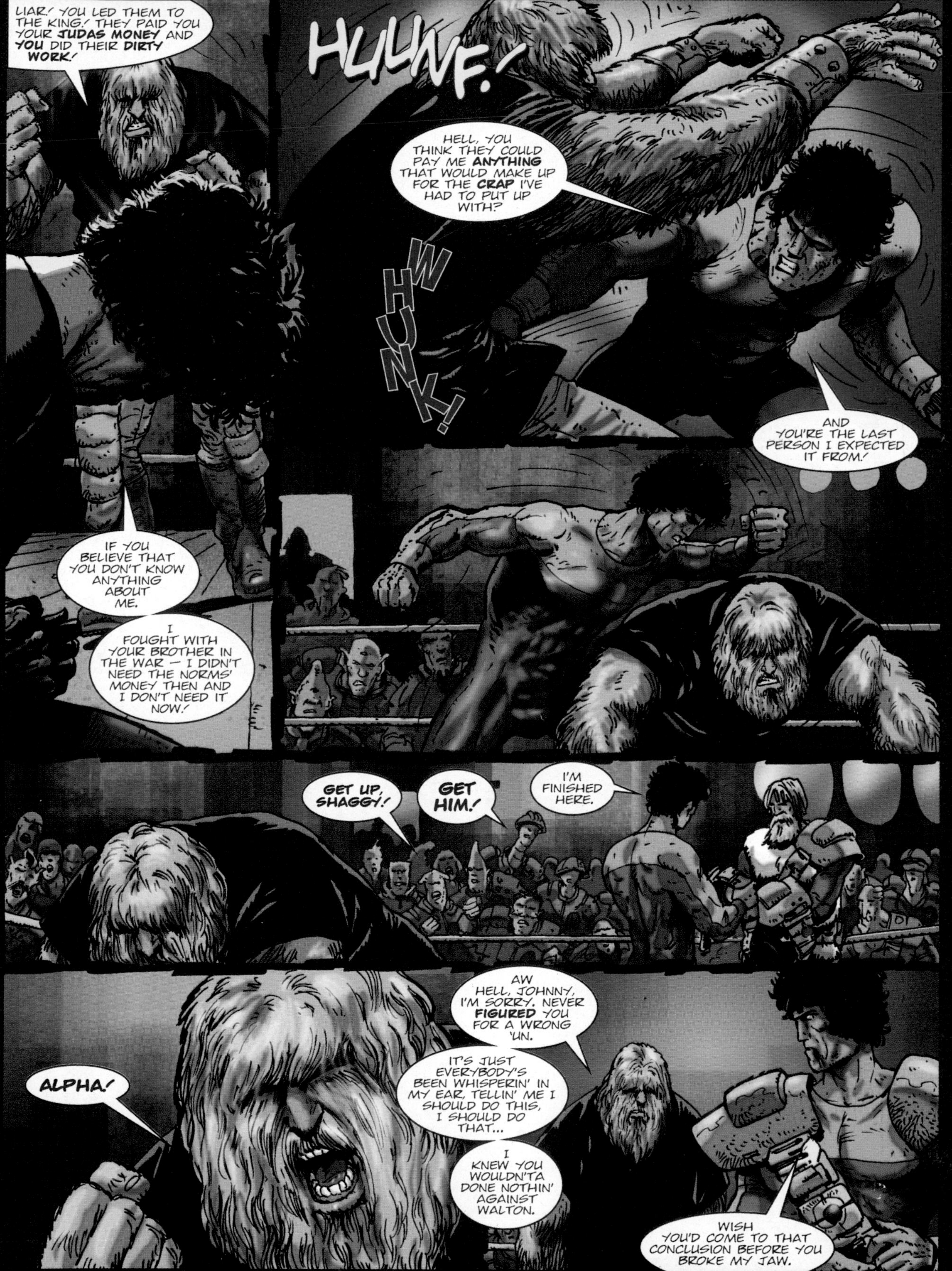
LIAR! YOU LED THEM TO THE KING! THEY PAID YOU YOUR JUDAS MONEY AND YOU DID THEIR DIRTY WORK!
HUUNF!
HELL, YOU THINK THEY COULD PAY ME ANYTHING THAT WOULD MAKE UP FOR THE CRAP I'VE HAD TO PUT UP WITH?
WHHUNK!
AND YOU'RE THE LAST PERSON I EXPECTED IT FROM!
IF YOU BELIEVE THAT YOU DON'T KNOW ANYTHING ABOUT ME.
I FOUGHT WITH YOUR BROTHER IN THE WAR — I DIDN'T NEED THE NORMS' MONEY THEN AND I DON'T NEED IT NOW!
GET UP, SHAGGY!
GET HIM!
I'M FINISHED HERE.
ALPHA!
AW HELL, JOHNNY, I'M SORRY. NEVER FIGURED YOU FOR A WRONG 'UN.
IT'S JUST EVERYBODY'S BEEN WHISPERIN' IN MY EAR, TELLIN' ME I SHOULD DO THIS, I SHOULD DO THAT...
I KNEW YOU WOULDN'TA DONE NOTHIN' AGAINST WALTON.
WISH YOU'D COME TO THAT CONCLUSION BEFORE YOU BROKE MY JAW.

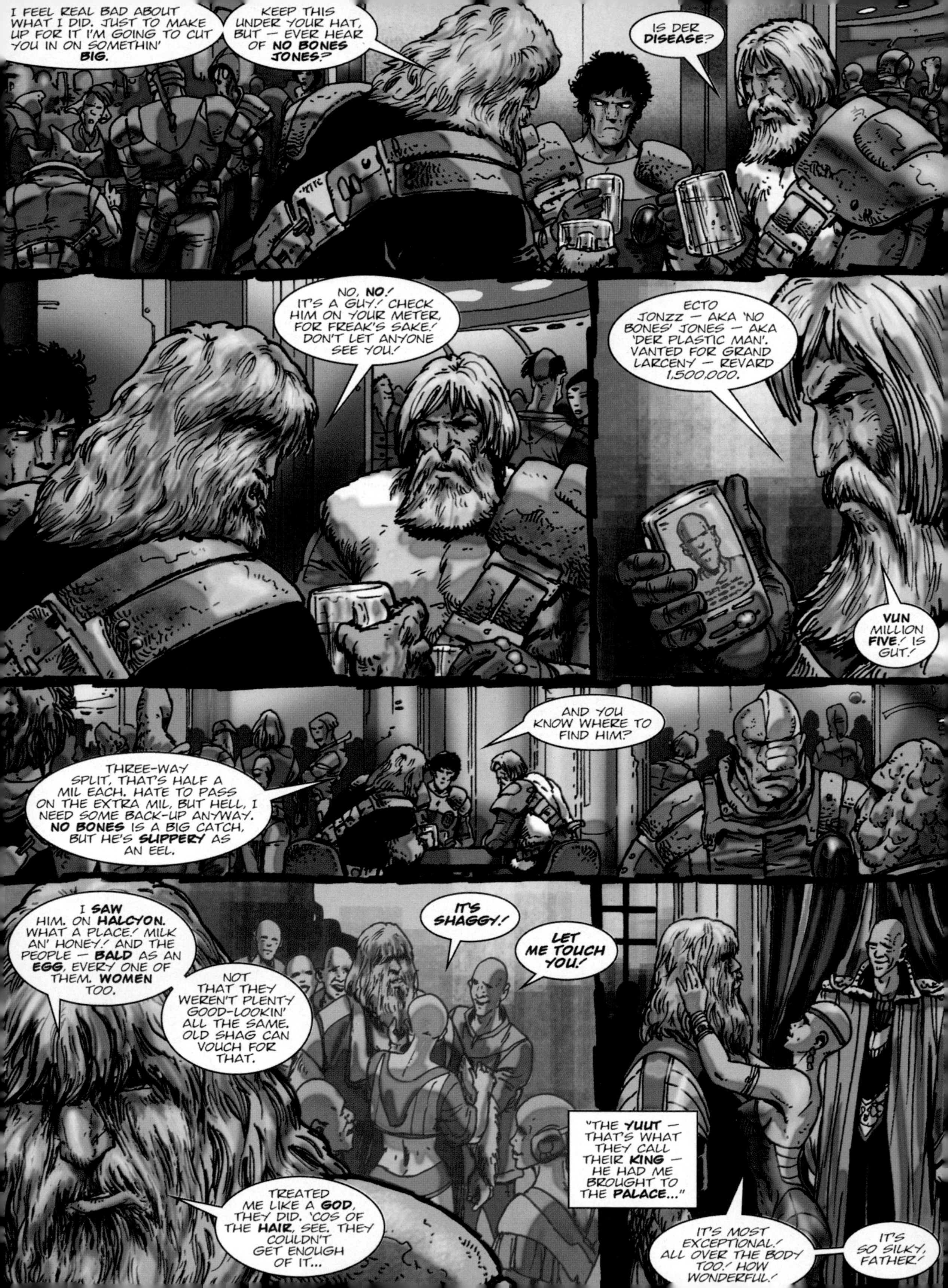

I FEEL REAL BAD ABOUT WHAT I DID. JUST TO MAKE UP FOR IT I'M GOING TO CUT YOU IN ON SOMETHIN' BIG.
KEEP THIS UNDER YOUR HAT, BUT — EVER HEAR OF NO BONES JONES?
IS DER DISEASE?
NO, NO! IT'S A GUY! CHECK HIM ON YOUR METER, FOR FREAK'S SAKE! DON'T LET ANYONE SEE YOU!
ECTO JONZZ — AKA 'NO BONES' JONES — AKA 'DER PLASTIC MAN'. VANTED FOR GRAND LARCENY — REVARD 1,500,000.
VUN MILLION FIVE! IS GUT!
THREE-WAY SPLIT, THAT'S HALF A MIL EACH. HATE TO PASS ON THE EXTRA MIL, BUT HELL, I NEED SOME BACK-UP ANYWAY. NO BONES IS A BIG CATCH, BUT HE'S SLIPPERY AS AN EEL.
AND YOU KNOW WHERE TO FIND HIM?
I SAW HIM. ON HALCYON. WHAT A PLACE! MILK AN' HONEY! AND THE PEOPLE — BALD AS AN EGG, EVERY ONE OF THEM. WOMEN TOO.
NOT THAT THEY WEREN'T PLENTY GOOD-LOOKIN' ALL THE SAME. OLD SHAG CAN VOUCH FOR THAT.
IT'S SHAGGY!
LET ME TOUCH YOU!
TREATED ME LIKE A GOD, THEY DID. 'COS OF THE HAIR, SEE. THEY COULDN'T GET ENOUGH OF IT...
"THE YUUT — THAT'S WHAT THEY CALL THEIR KING — HE HAD ME BROUGHT TO THE PALACE..."
IT'S MOST EXCEPTIONAL! ALL OVER THE BODY TOO! HOW WONDERFUL!
IT'S SO SILKY, FATHER!

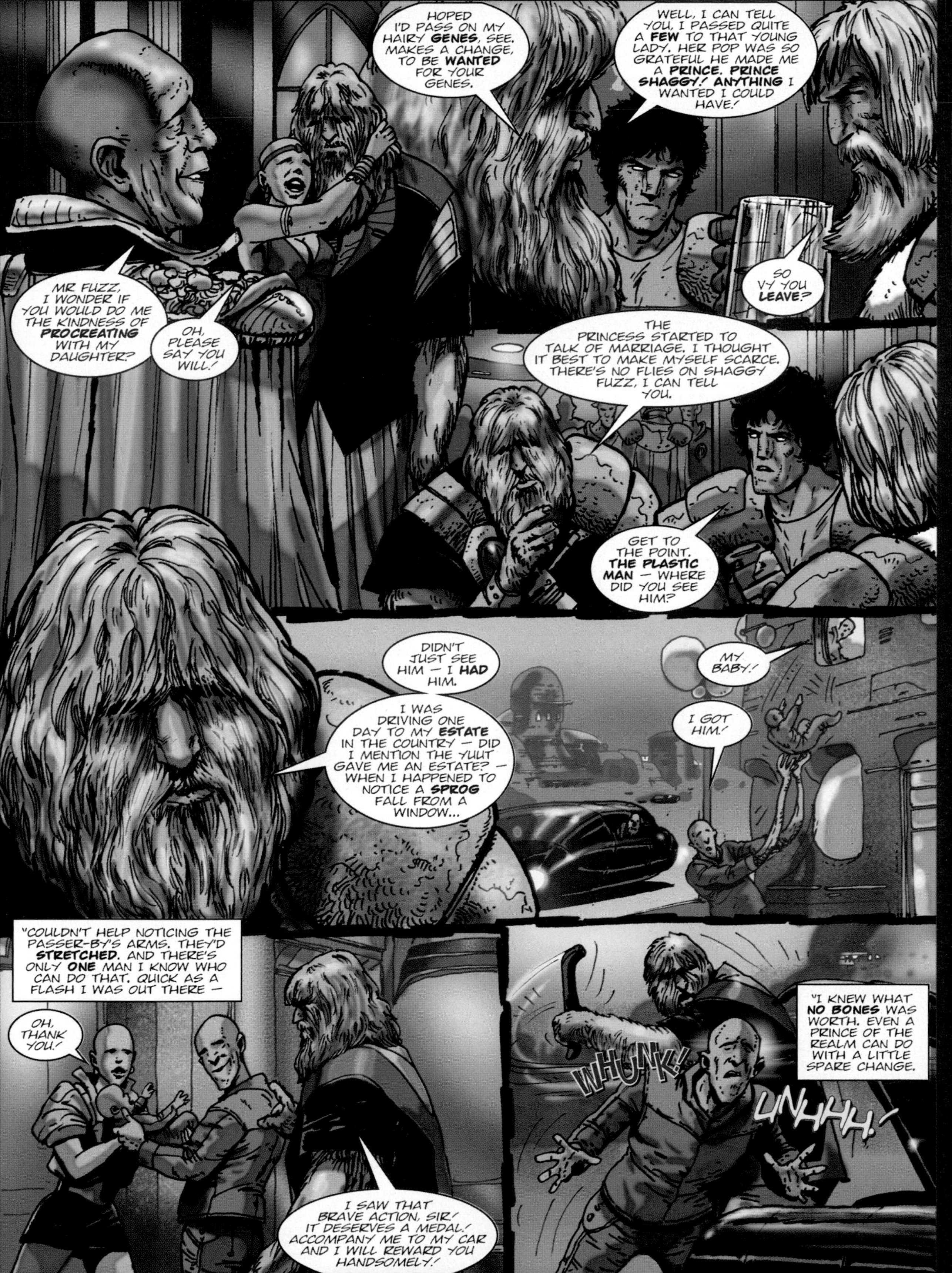
MR FUZZ, I WONDER IF YOU WOULD DO ME THE KINDNESS OF PROCREATING WITH MY DAUGHTER?
OH, PLEASE SAY YOU WILL!
HOPED I'D PASS ON MY HAIRY GENES, SEE. MAKES A CHANGE, TO BE WANTED FOR YOUR GENES.
WELL, I CAN TELL YOU, I PASSED QUITE A FEW TO THAT YOUNG LADY. HER POP WAS SO GRATEFUL HE MADE ME A PRINCE. PRINCE SHAGGY! ANYTHING I WANTED I COULD HAVE!
SO VY YOU LEAVE?
THE PRINCESS STARTED TO TALK OF MARRIAGE. I THOUGHT IT BEST TO MAKE MYSELF SCARCE. THERE'S NO FLIES ON SHAGGY FUZZ, I CAN TELL YOU.
GET TO THE POINT. THE PLASTIC MAN — WHERE DID YOU SEE HIM?
DIDN'T JUST SEE HIM — I HAD HIM.
I WAS DRIVING ONE DAY TO MY ESTATE IN THE COUNTRY — DID I MENTION THE YUUT GAVE ME AN ESTATE? — WHEN I HAPPENED TO NOTICE A SPROG FALL FROM A WINDOW...
MY BABY!
I GOT HIM!
"COULDN'T HELP NOTICING THE PASSER-BY'S ARMS. THEY'D STRETCHED. AND THERE'S ONLY ONE MAN I KNOW WHO CAN DO THAT. QUICK AS A FLASH I WAS OUT THERE —
OH, THANK YOU!
I SAW THAT BRAVE ACTION, SIR! IT DESERVES A MEDAL! ACCOMPANY ME TO MY CAR AND I WILL REWARD YOU HANDSOMELY!
"I KNEW WHAT NO BONES WAS WORTH. EVEN A PRINCE OF THE REALM CAN DO WITH A LITTLE SPARE CHANGE.
WHUNK!
UNHHH!

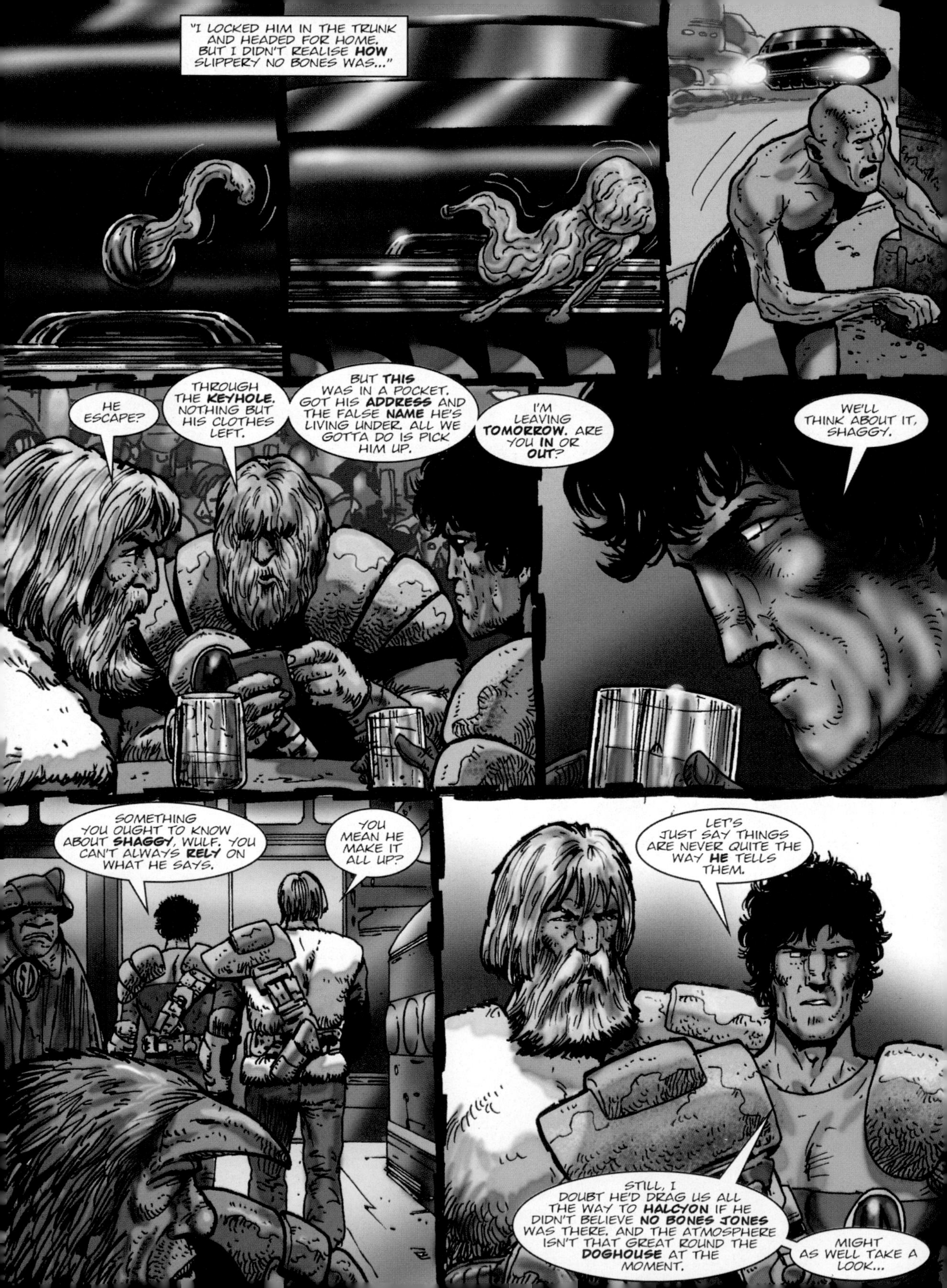
"I LOCKED HIM IN THE TRUNK AND HEADED FOR HOME. BUT I DIDN'T REALISE HOW SLIPPERY NO BONES WAS..."
HE ESCAPE?
THROUGH THE KEYHOLE. NOTHING BUT HIS CLOTHES LEFT.
BUT THIS WAS IN A POCKET. GOT HIS ADDRESS AND THE FALSE NAME HE'S LIVING UNDER. ALL WE GOTTA DO IS PICK HIM UP.
I'M LEAVING TOMORROW. ARE YOU IN OR OUT?
WE'LL THINK ABOUT IT, SHAGGY.
SOMETHING YOU OUGHT TO KNOW ABOUT SHAGGY, WULF. YOU CAN'T ALWAYS RELY ON WHAT HE SAYS.
YOU MEAN HE MAKE IT ALL UP?
LET'S JUST SAY THINGS ARE NEVER QUITE THE WAY HE TELLS THEM.
STILL, I DOUBT HE'D DRAG US ALL THE WAY TO HALCYON IF HE DIDN'T BELIEVE NO BONES JONES WAS THERE. AND THE ATMOSPHERE ISN'T THAT GREAT ROUND THE DOGHOUSE AT THE MOMENT.
MIGHT AS WELL TAKE A LOOK...

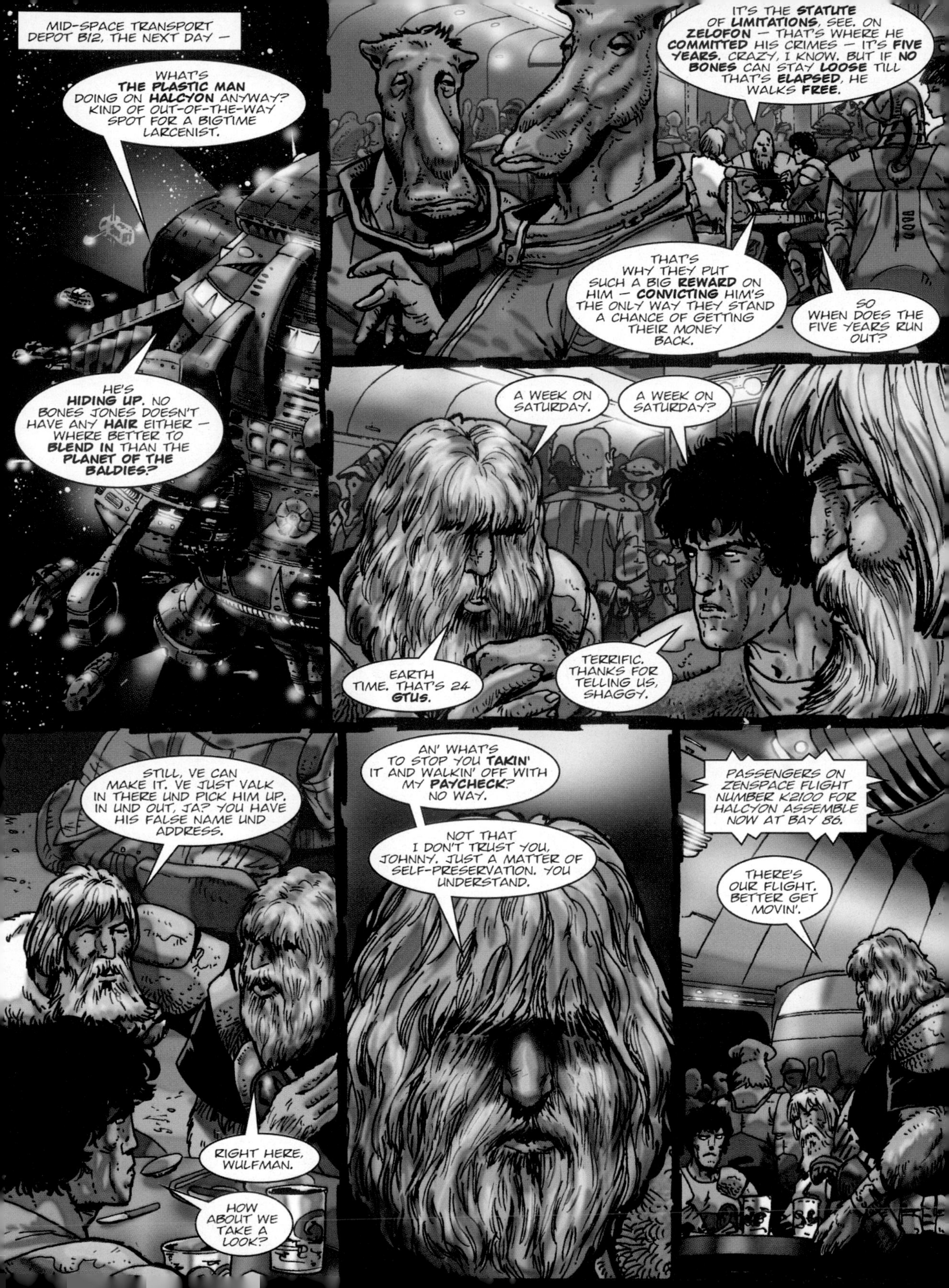
MID-SPACE TRANSPORT DEPOT B12, THE NEXT DAY —
WHAT'S THE PLASTIC MAN DOING ON HALCYON ANYWAY? KIND OF OUT-OF-THE-WAY SPOT FOR A BIGTIME LARCENIST.
HE'S HIDING UP. NO BONES JONES DOESN'T HAVE ANY HAIR EITHER — WHERE BETTER TO BLEND IN THAN THE PLANET OF THE BALDIES?
IT'S THE STATUTE OF LIMITATIONS, SEE. ON ZELOFON — THAT'S WHERE HE COMMITTED HIS CRIMES — IT'S FIVE YEARS. CRAZY, I KNOW. BUT IF NO BONES CAN STAY LOOSE TILL THAT'S ELAPSED, HE WALKS FREE.
THAT'S WHY THEY PUT SUCH A BIG REWARD ON HIM — CONVICTING HIM'S THE ONLY WAY THEY STAND A CHANCE OF GETTING THEIR MONEY BACK.
SO WHEN DOES THE FIVE YEARS RUN OUT?
A WEEK ON SATURDAY.
A WEEK ON SATURDAY?
EARTH TIME. THAT'S 24 GTUS.
TERRIFIC. THANKS FOR TELLING US, SHAGGY.
STILL, VE CAN MAKE IT. VE JUST VALK IN THERE UND PICK HIM UP. IN UND OUT, JA? YOU HAVE HIS FALSE NAME UND ADDRESS.
RIGHT HERE, WULFMAN.
HOW ABOUT WE TAKE A LOOK?
AN' WHAT'S TO STOP YOU TAKIN' IT AND WALKIN' OFF WITH MY PAYCHECK? NO WAY.
NOT THAT I DON'T TRUST YOU, JOHNNY. JUST A MATTER OF SELF-PRESERVATION. YOU UNDERSTAND.
PASSENGERS ON ZENSPACE FLIGHT NUMBER K2100 FOR HALCYON ASSEMBLE NOW AT BAY 86.
THERE'S OUR FLIGHT. BETTER GET MOVIN'.

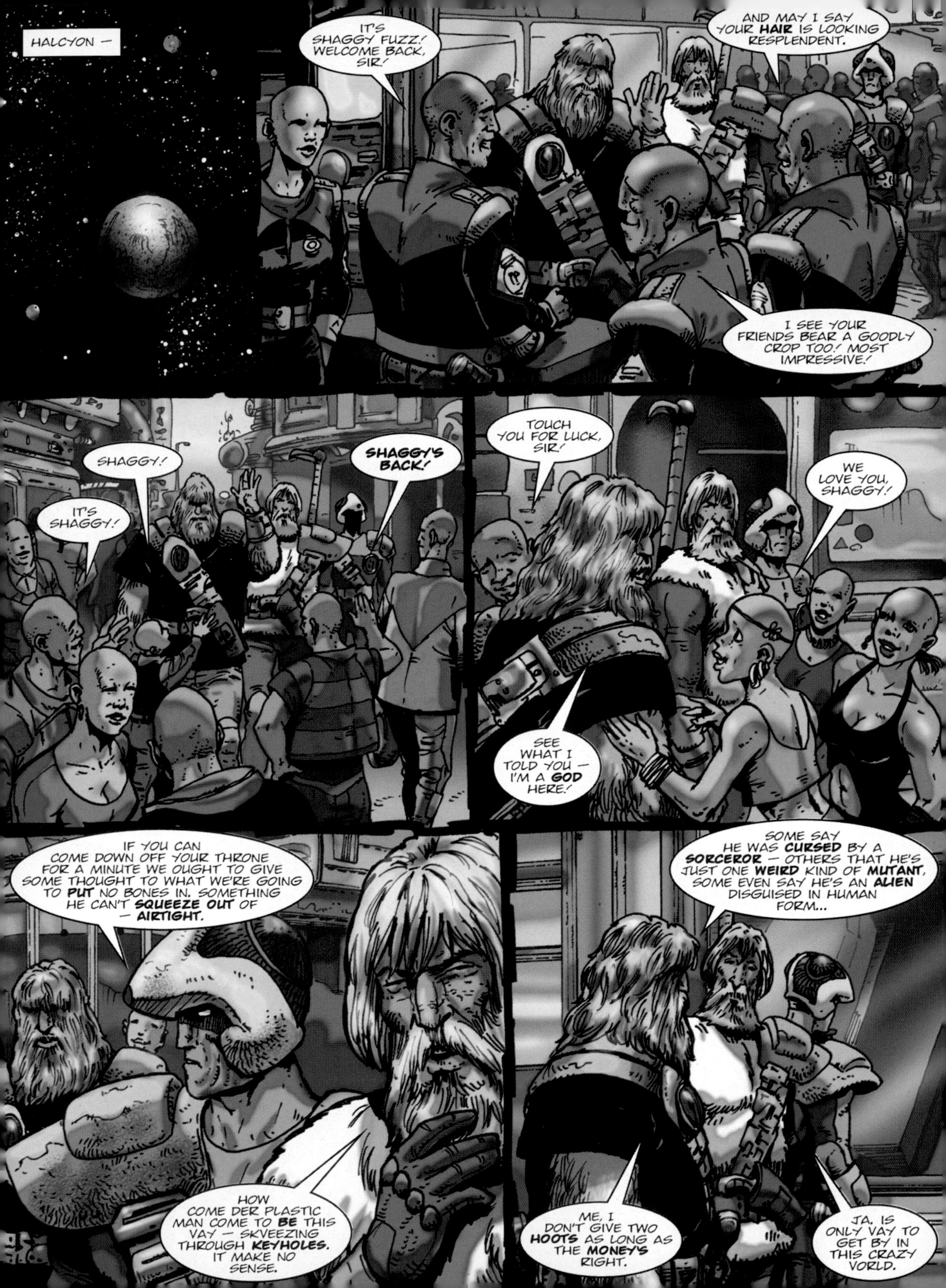
HALCYON —
IT'S SHAGGY FUZZ! WELCOME BACK, SIR!
AND MAY I SAY YOUR HAIR IS LOOKING RESPLENDENT.
I SEE YOUR FRIENDS BEAR A GOODLY CROP TOO! MOST IMPRESSIVE!
SHAGGY!
IT'S SHAGGY!
SHAGGY'S BACK!
TOUCH YOU FOR LUCK, SIR!
WE LOVE YOU, SHAGGY!
SEE WHAT I TOLD YOU — I'M A GOD HERE!
IF YOU CAN COME DOWN OFF YOUR THRONE FOR A MINUTE WE OUGHT TO GIVE SOME THOUGHT TO WHAT WE'RE GOING TO PUT NO BONES IN. SOMETHING HE CAN'T SQUEEZE OUT OF — AIRTIGHT.
HOW COME DER PLASTIC MAN COME TO BE THIS VAY — SKVEEZING THROUGH KEYHOLES. IT MAKE NO SENSE.
SOME SAY HE WAS CURSED BY A SORCEROR — OTHERS THAT HE'S JUST ONE WEIRD KIND OF MUTANT, SOME EVEN SAY HE'S AN ALIEN DISGUISED IN HUMAN FORM...
ME, I DON'T GIVE TWO HOOTS AS LONG AS THE MONEY'S RIGHT.
JA, IS ONLY VAY TO GET BY IN THIS CRAZY VORLD.

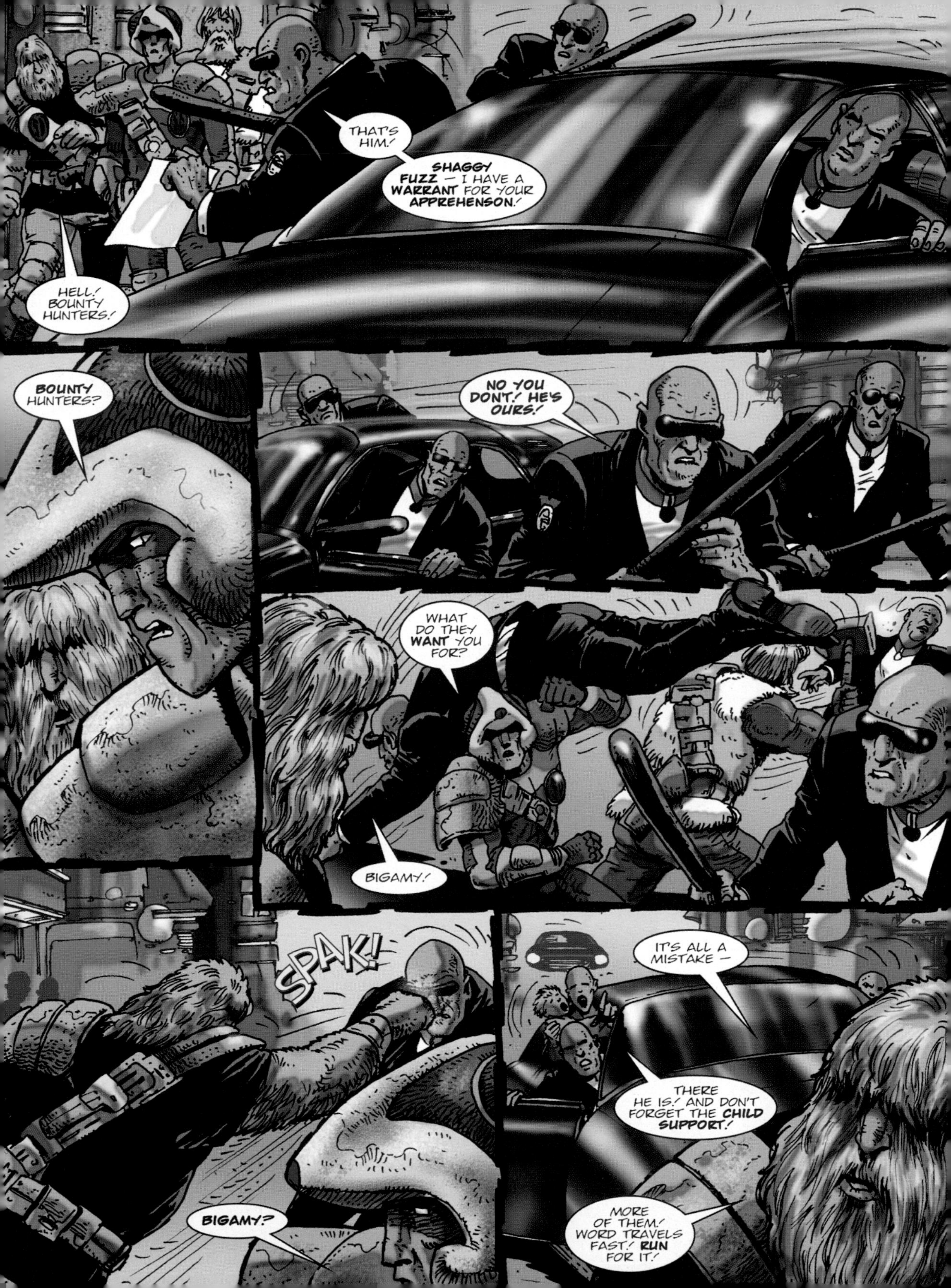
THAT'S HIM!
SHAGGY FUZZ — I HAVE A WARRANT FOR YOUR APPREHENSON!
HELL! BOUNTY HUNTERS!
BOUNTY HUNTERS?
NO YOU DON'T! HE'S OURS!
WHAT DO THEY WANT YOU FOR?
BIGAMY!
SPAK!
BIGAMY?
IT'S ALL A MISTAKE —
THERE HE IS! AND DON'T FORGET THE CHILD SUPPORT!
MORE OF THEM! WORD TRAVELS FAST! RUN FOR IT!

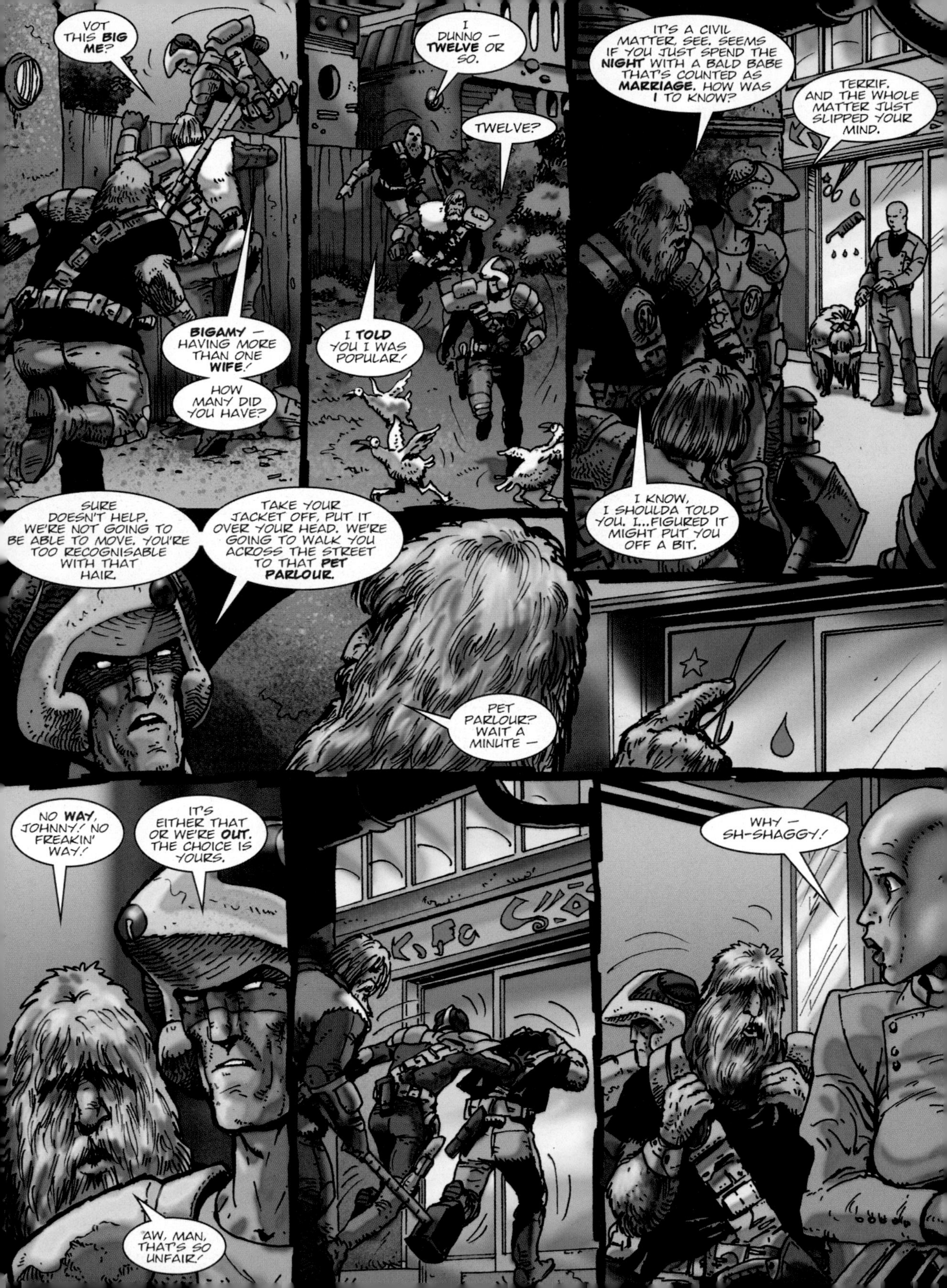
VOT THIS BIG ME?
BIGAMY — HAVING MORE THAN ONE WIFE!
HOW MANY DID YOU HAVE?
I DUNNO — TWELVE OR SO.
TWELVE?
I TOLD YOU I WAS POPULAR!
IT'S A CIVIL MATTER, SEE. SEEMS IF YOU JUST SPEND THE NIGHT WITH A BALD BABE THAT'S COUNTED AS MARRIAGE. HOW WAS I TO KNOW?
TERRIF. AND THE WHOLE MATTER JUST SLIPPED YOUR MIND.
I KNOW, I SHOULDA TOLD YOU. I...FIGURED IT MIGHT PUT YOU OFF A BIT.
SURE DOESN'T HELP. WE'RE NOT GOING TO BE ABLE TO MOVE. YOU'RE TOO RECOGNISABLE WITH THAT HAIR.
TAKE YOUR JACKET OFF, PUT IT OVER YOUR HEAD. WE'RE GOING TO WALK YOU ACROSS THE STREET TO THAT PET PARLOUR.
PET PARLOUR? WAIT A MINUTE —
NO WAY, JOHNNY! NO FREAKIN' WAY!
IT'S EITHER THAT OR WE'RE OUT. THE CHOICE IS YOURS.
AW, MAN, THAT'S SO UNFAIR!
WHY — SH-SHAGGY!

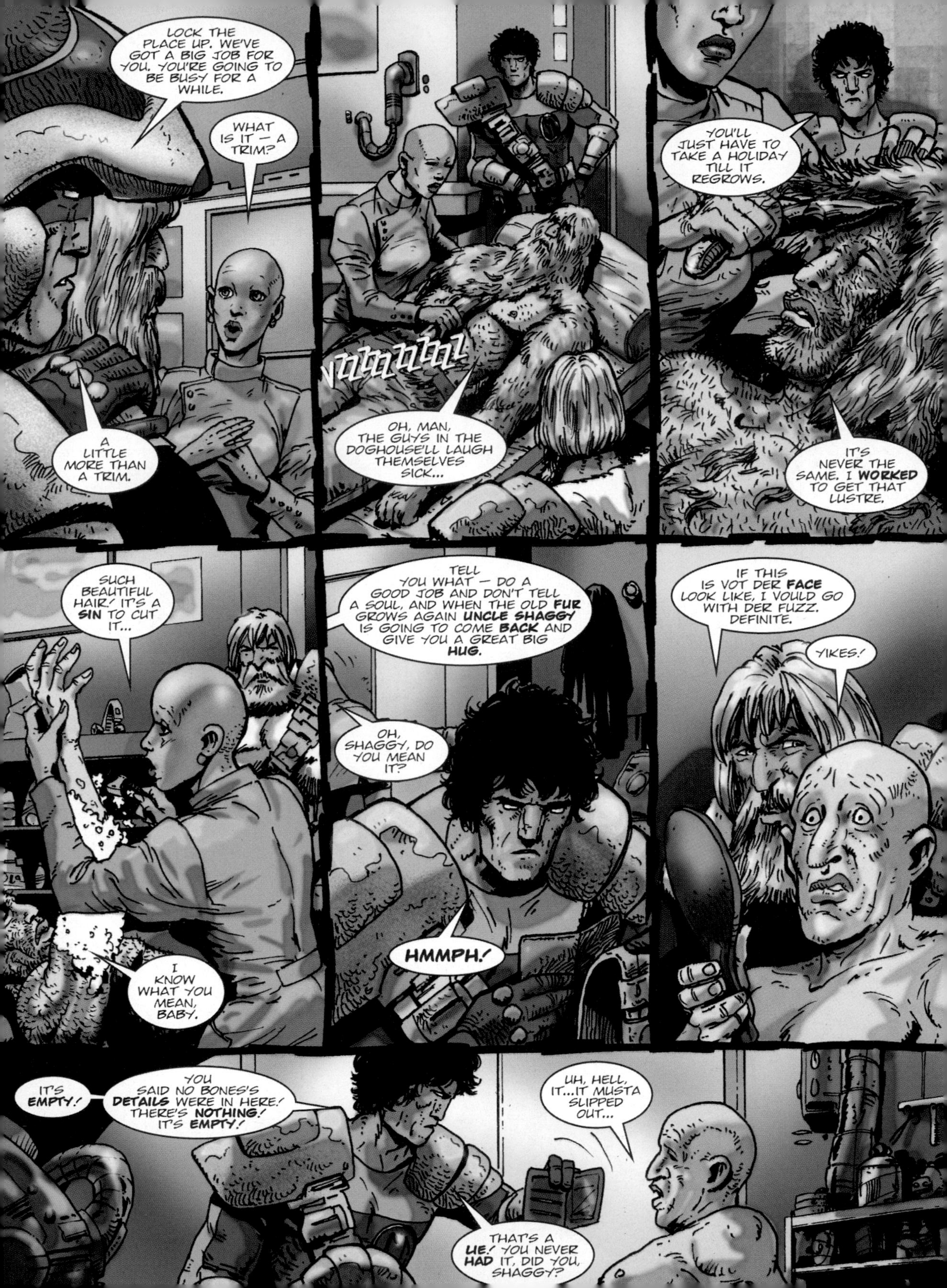
LOCK THE PLACE UP. WE'VE GOT A BIG JOB FOR YOU. YOU'RE GOING TO BE BUSY FOR A WHILE.
WHAT IS IT — A TRIM?
A LITTLE MORE THAN A TRIM.
VZZZZZZZ
OH, MAN, THE GUYS IN THE DOGHOUSE'LL LAUGH THEMSELVES SICK...
YOU'LL JUST HAVE TO TAKE A HOLIDAY TILL IT REGROWS.
IT'S NEVER THE SAME. I **WORKED** TO GET THAT LUSTRE.
SUCH BEAUTIFUL HAIR! IT'S A **SIN** TO CUT IT...
I KNOW WHAT YOU MEAN, BABY.
TELL YOU WHAT — DO A GOOD JOB AND DON'T TELL A SOUL, AND WHEN THE OLD **FUR** GROWS AGAIN **UNCLE SHAGGY** IS GOING TO COME **BACK** AND GIVE YOU A GREAT BIG **HUG**.
OH, SHAGGY, DO YOU MEAN IT?
HMMPH!
IF THIS IS VOT DER **FACE** LOOK LIKE, I VOULD GO WITH DER FUZZ. DEFINITE.
YIKES!
IT'S **EMPTY!**
YOU SAID NO BONES'S **DETAILS** WERE IN HERE! THERE'S **NOTHING!** IT'S **EMPTY!**
UH, HELL, IT...IT MUSTA SLIPPED OUT...
THAT'S A **LIE!** YOU NEVER **HAD** IT, DID YOU, SHAGGY?

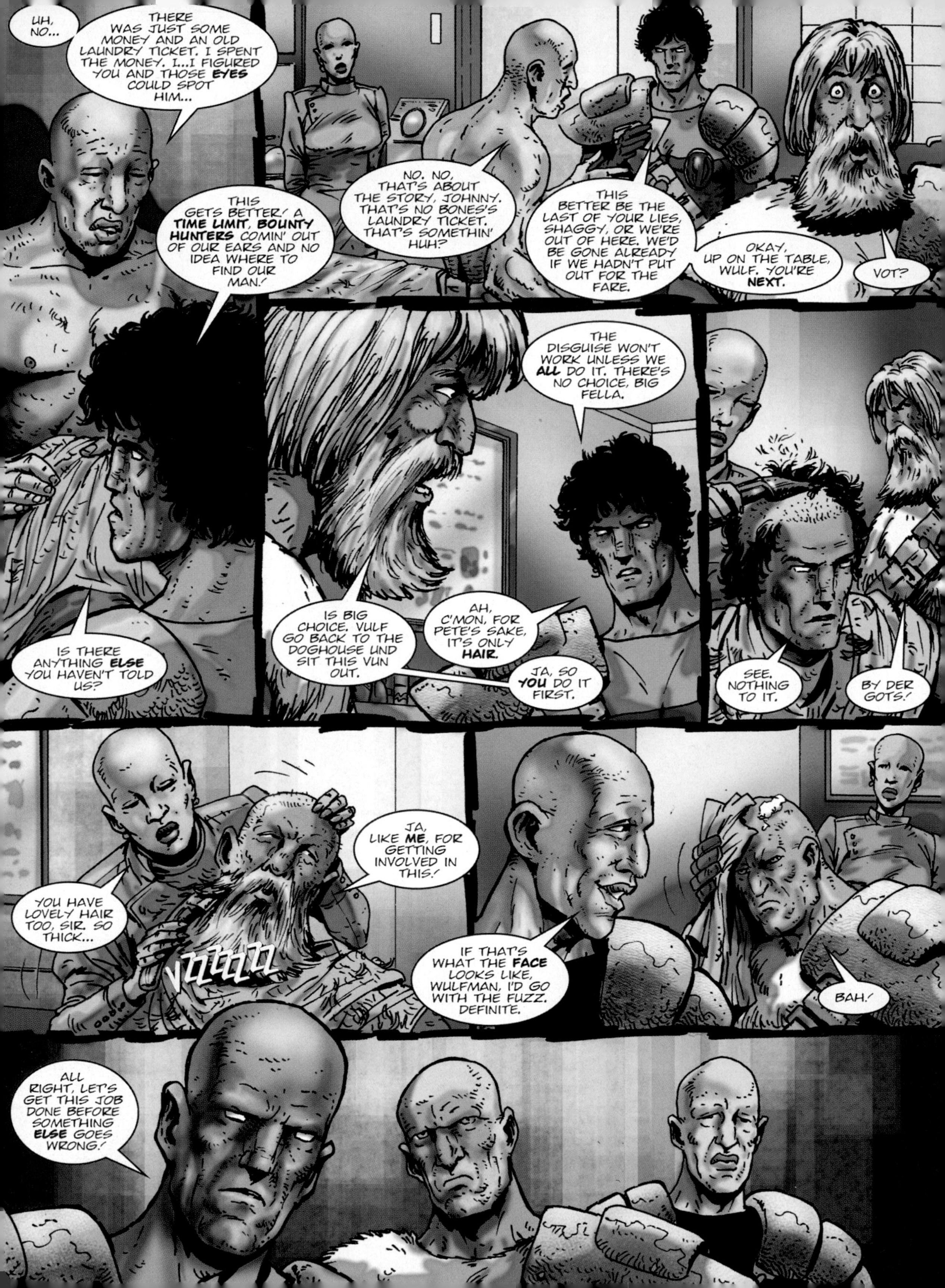
UH, NO...
THERE WAS JUST SOME MONEY AND AN OLD LAUNDRY TICKET. I SPENT THE MONEY. I...I FIGURED YOU AND THOSE EYES COULD SPOT HIM...
THIS GETS BETTER! A TIME LIMIT, BOUNTY HUNTERS COMIN' OUT OF OUR EARS AND NO IDEA WHERE TO FIND OUR MAN!
NO. NO, THAT'S ABOUT THE STORY, JOHNNY. THAT'S NO BONES'S LAUNDRY TICKET. THAT'S SOMETHIN' HUH?
THIS BETTER BE THE LAST OF YOUR LIES, SHAGGY, OR WE'RE OUT OF HERE. WE'D BE GONE ALREADY IF WE HADN'T PUT OUT FOR THE FARE.
OKAY, UP ON THE TABLE, WULF. YOU'RE NEXT.
VOT?
IS THERE ANYTHING ELSE YOU HAVEN'T TOLD US?
IS BIG CHOICE. VULF GO BACK TO THE DOGHOUSE UND SIT THIS VUN OUT.
THE DISGUISE WON'T WORK UNLESS WE ALL DO IT. THERE'S NO CHOICE, BIG FELLA.
AH, C'MON, FOR PETE'S SAKE, IT'S ONLY HAIR.
JA, SO YOU DO IT FIRST.
SEE. NOTHING TO IT.
BY DER GOTS!
YOU HAVE LOVELY HAIR TOO, SIR. SO THICK...
VZZZZZZ
JA, LIKE ME, FOR GETTING INVOLVED IN THIS!
IF THAT'S WHAT THE FACE LOOKS LIKE, WULFMAN, I'D GO WITH THE FUZZ. DEFINITE.
BAH!
ALL RIGHT, LET'S GET THIS JOB DONE BEFORE SOMETHING ELSE GOES WRONG!

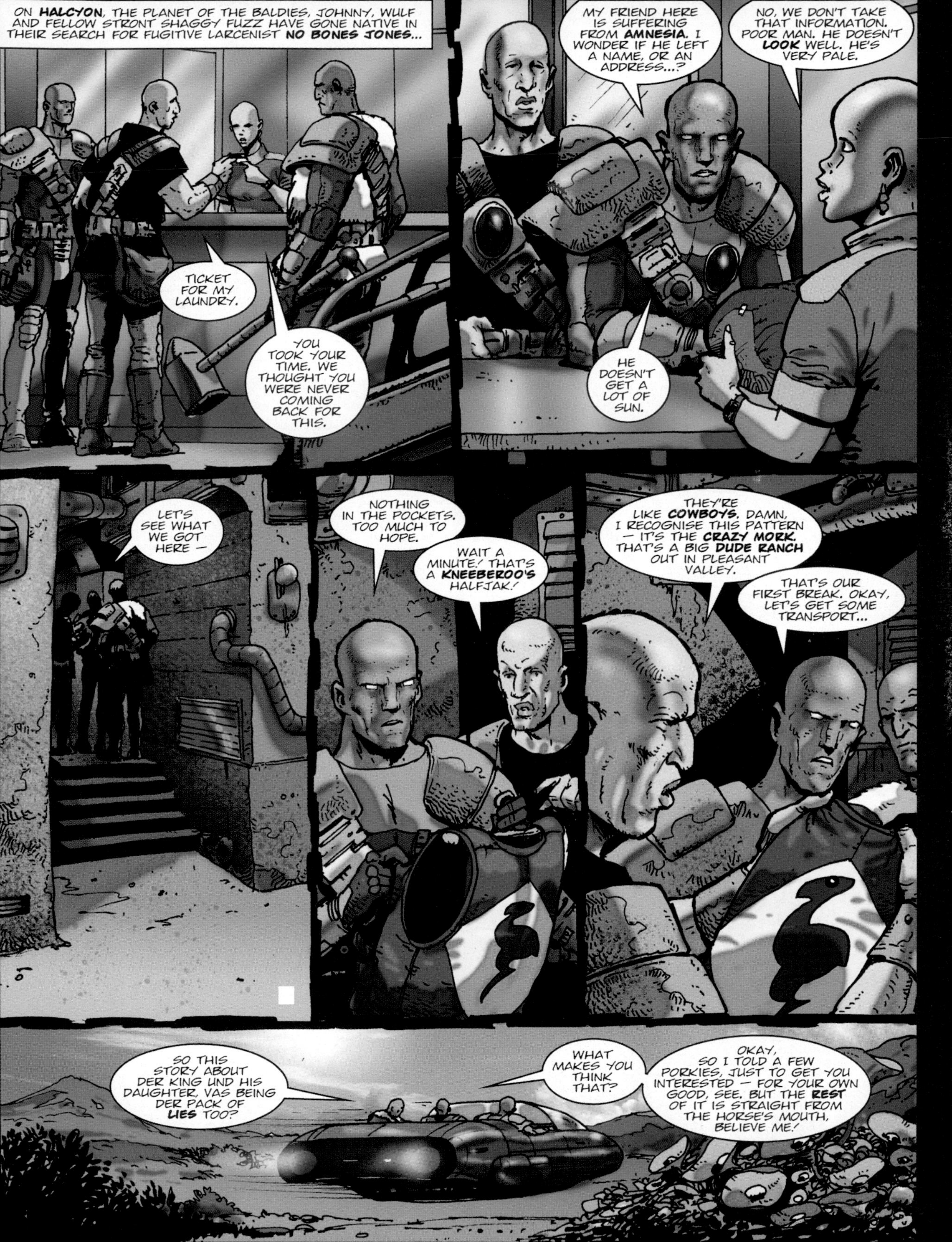
ON HALCYON, THE PLANET OF THE BALDIES, JOHNNY, WULF AND FELLOW STRONT SHAGGY FUZZ HAVE GONE NATIVE IN THEIR SEARCH FOR FUGITIVE LARCENIST NO BONES JONES...
TICKET FOR MY LAUNDRY.
YOU TOOK YOUR TIME. WE THOUGHT YOU WERE NEVER COMING BACK FOR THIS.
MY FRIEND HERE IS SUFFERING FROM AMNESIA. I WONDER IF HE LEFT A NAME, OR AN ADDRESS...?
NO, WE DON'T TAKE THAT INFORMATION. POOR MAN. HE DOESN'T LOOK WELL. HE'S VERY PALE.
HE DOESN'T GET A LOT OF SUN.
LET'S SEE WHAT WE GOT HERE —
NOTHING IN THE POCKETS. TOO MUCH TO HOPE.
WAIT A MINUTE! THAT'S A KNEEBEROO'S HALFJAK!
THEY'RE LIKE COWBOYS. DAMN, I RECOGNISE THIS PATTERN — IT'S THE CRAZY MORK. THAT'S A BIG DUDE RANCH OUT IN PLEASANT VALLEY.
THAT'S OUR FIRST BREAK. OKAY, LET'S GET SOME TRANSPORT...
SO THIS STORY ABOUT DER KING AND HIS DAUGHTER, VAS BEING DER PACK OF LIES TOO?
WHAT MAKES YOU THINK THAT?
OKAY, SO I TOLD A FEW PORKIES, JUST TO GET YOU INTERESTED — FOR YOUR OWN GOOD, SEE. BUT THE REST OF IT IS STRAIGHT FROM THE HORSE'S MOUTH, BELIEVE ME!

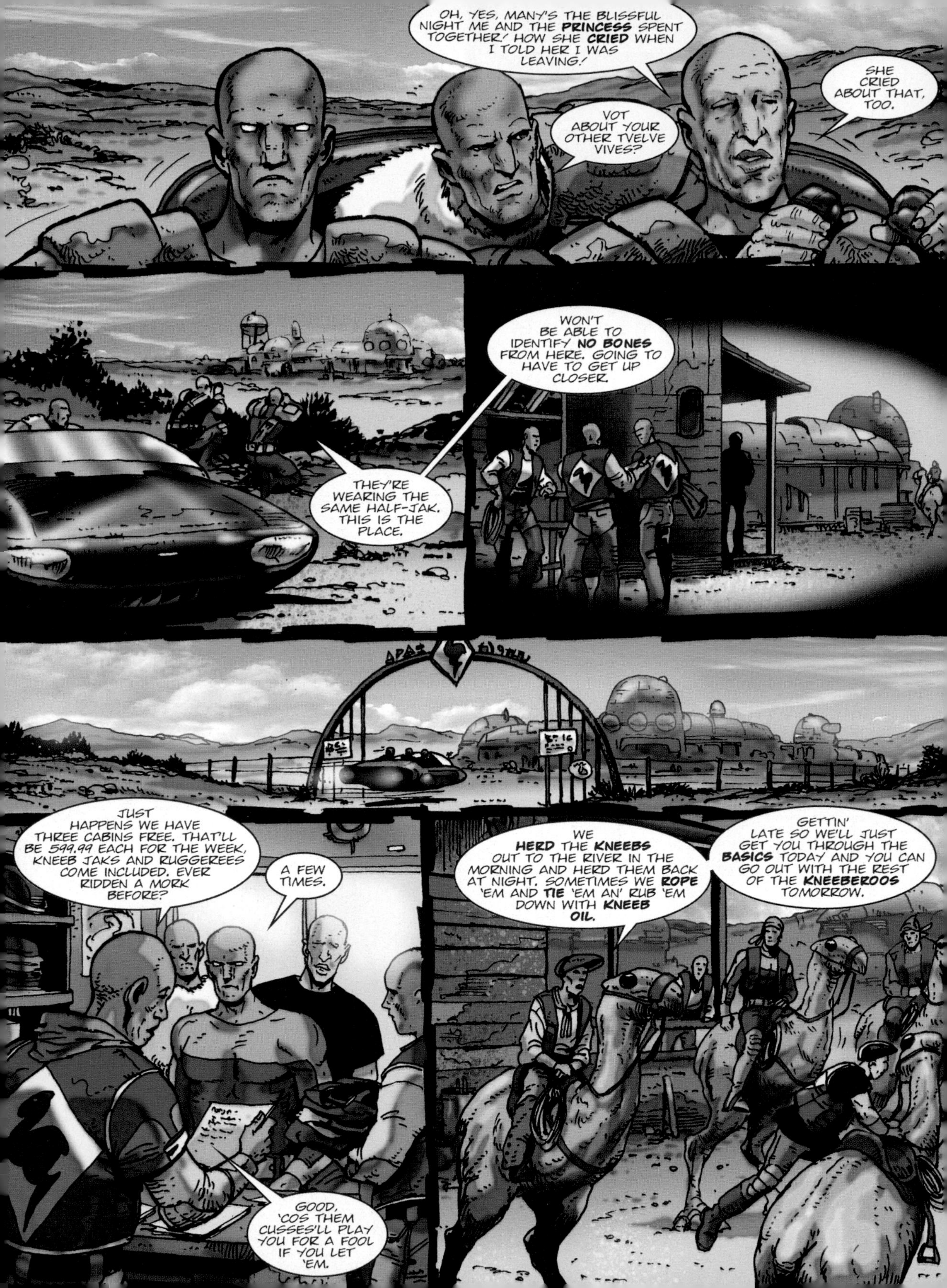
OH, YES, MANY'S THE BLISSFUL NIGHT ME AND THE PRINCESS SPENT TOGETHER! HOW SHE CRIED WHEN I TOLD HER I WAS LEAVING!
VOT ABOUT YOUR OTHER TVELVE VIVES?
SHE CRIED ABOUT THAT, TOO.
THEY'RE WEARING THE SAME HALF-JAK. THIS IS THE PLACE.
WON'T BE ABLE TO IDENTIFY NO BONES FROM HERE. GOING TO HAVE TO GET UP CLOSER.
JUST HAPPENS WE HAVE THREE CABINS FREE. THAT'LL BE 599.99 EACH FOR THE WEEK, KNEEB JAKS AND RUGGEREES COME INCLUDED. EVER RIDDEN A MORK BEFORE?
A FEW TIMES.
GOOD, 'COS THEM CUSSES'LL PLAY YOU FOR A FOOL IF YOU LET 'EM.
WE HERD THE KNEEBS OUT TO THE RIVER IN THE MORNING AND HERD THEM BACK AT NIGHT. SOMETIMES WE ROPE 'EM AND TIE 'EM AN' RUB 'EM DOWN WITH KNEEB OIL.
GETTIN' LATE SO WE'LL JUST GET YOU THROUGH THE BASICS TODAY AND YOU CAN GO OUT WITH THE REST OF THE KNEEBEROOS TOMORROW.

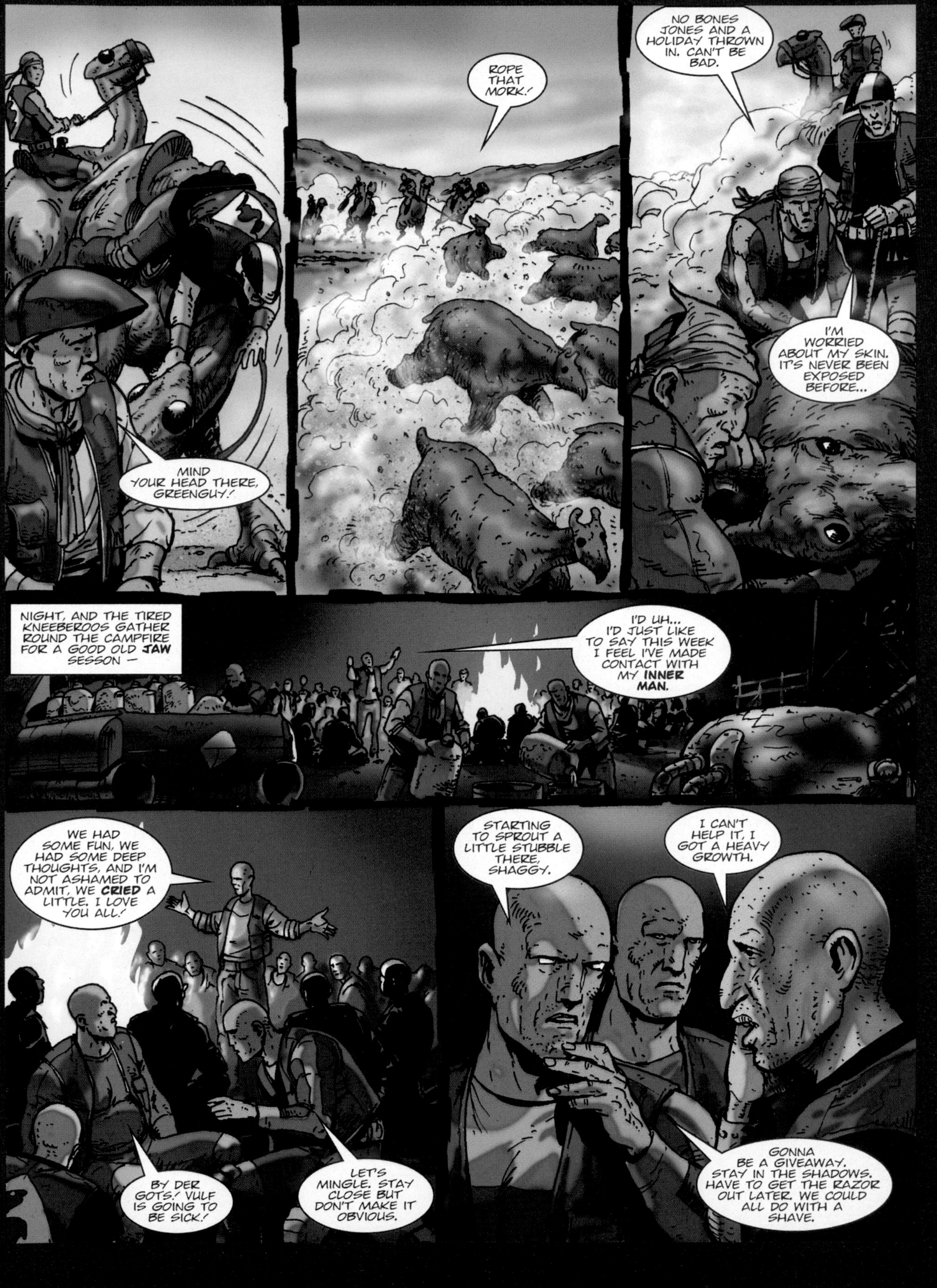
MIND YOUR HEAD THERE, GREENGUY!
ROPE THAT MORK!
NO BONES JONES AND A HOLIDAY THROWN IN. CAN'T BE BAD.
I'M WORRIED ABOUT MY SKIN. IT'S NEVER BEEN EXPOSED BEFORE...
NIGHT, AND THE TIRED KNEEBEROOS GATHER ROUND THE CAMPFIRE FOR A GOOD OLD JAW SESSON —
I'D UH... I'D JUST LIKE TO SAY THIS WEEK I FEEL I'VE MADE CONTACT WITH MY INNER MAN.
WE HAD SOME FUN, WE HAD SOME DEEP THOUGHTS, AND I'M NOT ASHAMED TO ADMIT, WE CRIED A LITTLE. I LOVE YOU ALL!
BY DER GOTS! VULF IS GOING TO BE SICK!
LET'S MINGLE. STAY CLOSE BUT DON'T MAKE IT OBVIOUS.
STARTING TO SPROUT A LITTLE STUBBLE THERE, SHAGGY.
I CAN'T HELP IT, I GOT A HEAVY GROWTH.
GONNA BE A GIVEAWAY. STAY IN THE SHADOWS. HAVE TO GET THE RAZOR OUT LATER. WE COULD ALL DO WITH A SHAVE.

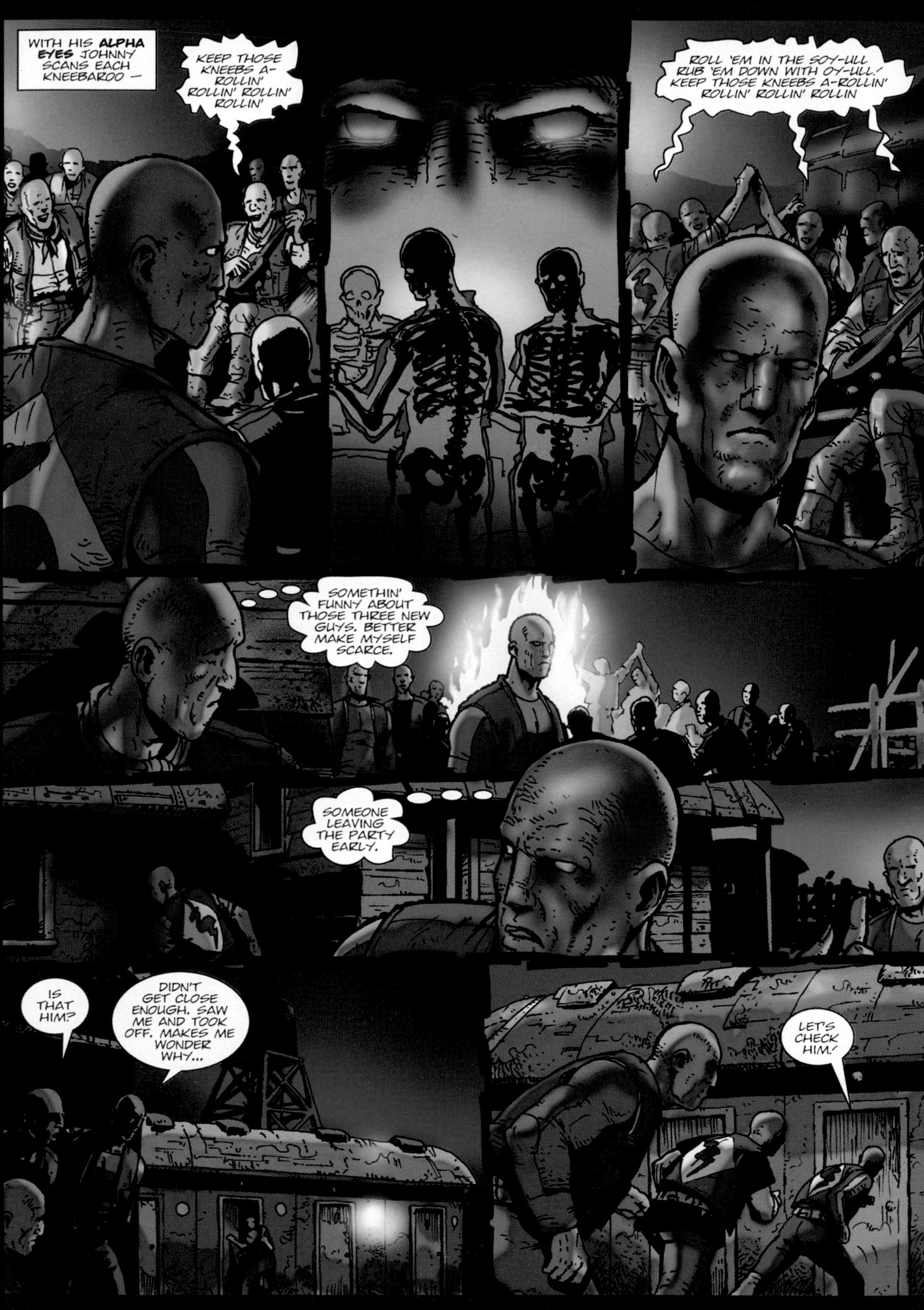
WITH HIS ALPHA EYES JOHNNY SCANS EACH KNEEBAROO —
KEEP THOSE KNEEBS A-ROLLIN' ROLLIN' ROLLIN' ROLLIN'
ROLL 'EM IN THE SOY-ULL RUB 'EM DOWN WITH OY-ULL! KEEP THOSE KNEEBS A-ROLLIN' ROLLIN' ROLLIN' ROLLIN
SOMETHIN' FUNNY ABOUT THOSE THREE NEW GUYS. BETTER MAKE MYSELF SCARCE.
SOMEONE LEAVING THE PARTY EARLY.
IS THAT HIM?
DIDN'T GET CLOSE ENOUGH. SAW ME AND TOOK OFF. MAKES ME WONDER WHY...
LET'S CHECK HIM!

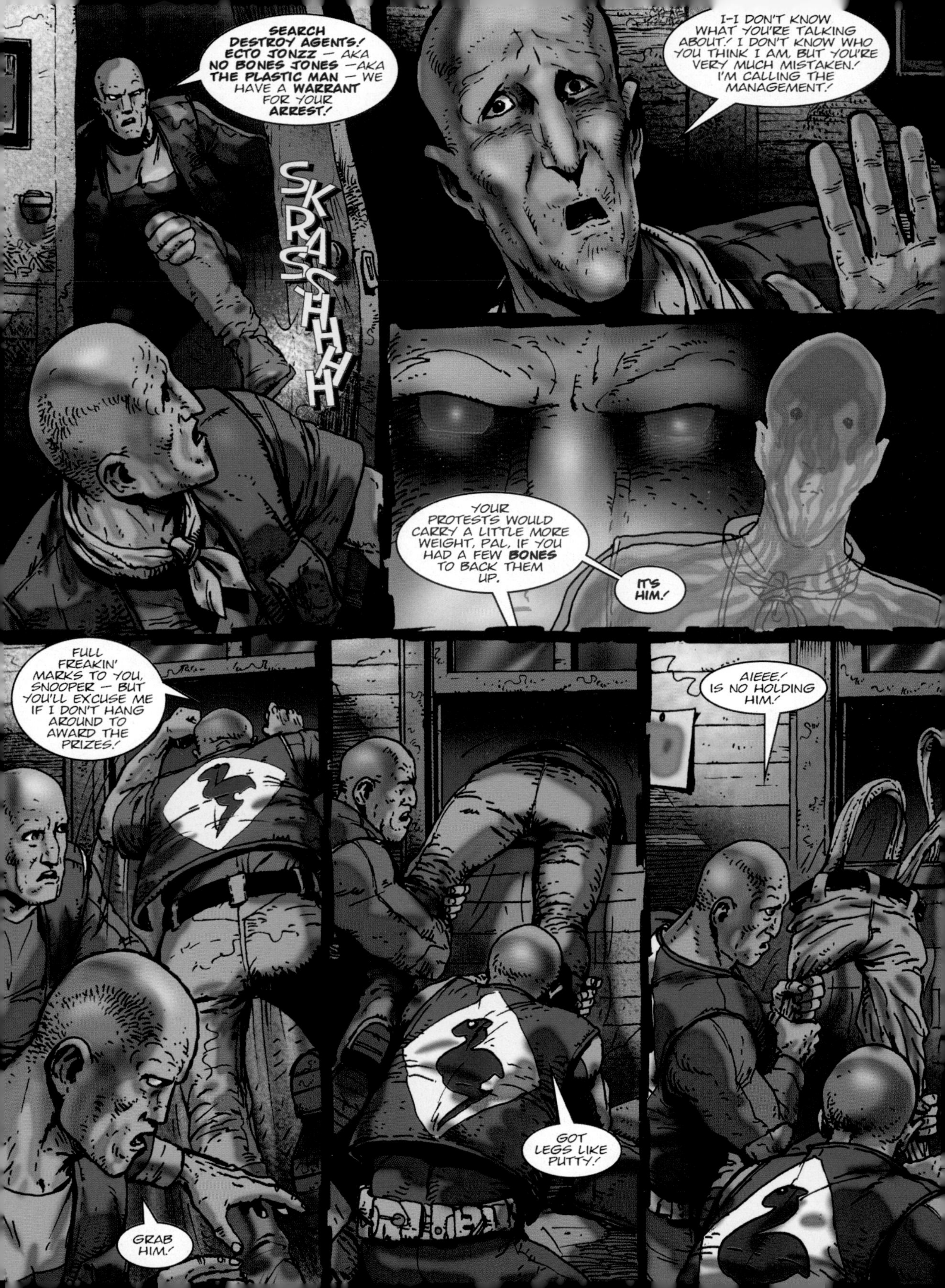
SEARCH DESTROY AGENTS! ECTO JONZZ — AKA NO BONES JONES — AKA THE PLASTIC MAN — WE HAVE A WARRANT FOR YOUR ARREST!
SKRASSHHH
I-I DON'T KNOW WHAT YOU'RE TALKING ABOUT! I DON'T KNOW WHO YOU THINK I AM, BUT YOU'RE VERY MUCH MISTAKEN! I'M CALLING THE MANAGEMENT!
YOUR PROTESTS WOULD CARRY A LITTLE MORE WEIGHT, PAL, IF YOU HAD A FEW BONES TO BACK THEM UP.
IT'S HIM!
FULL FREAKIN' MARKS TO YOU, SNOOPER — BUT YOU'LL EXCUSE ME IF I DON'T HANG AROUND TO AWARD THE PRIZES!
GRAB HIM!
GOT LEGS LIKE PUTTY!
AIEEE! IS NO HOLDING HIM!

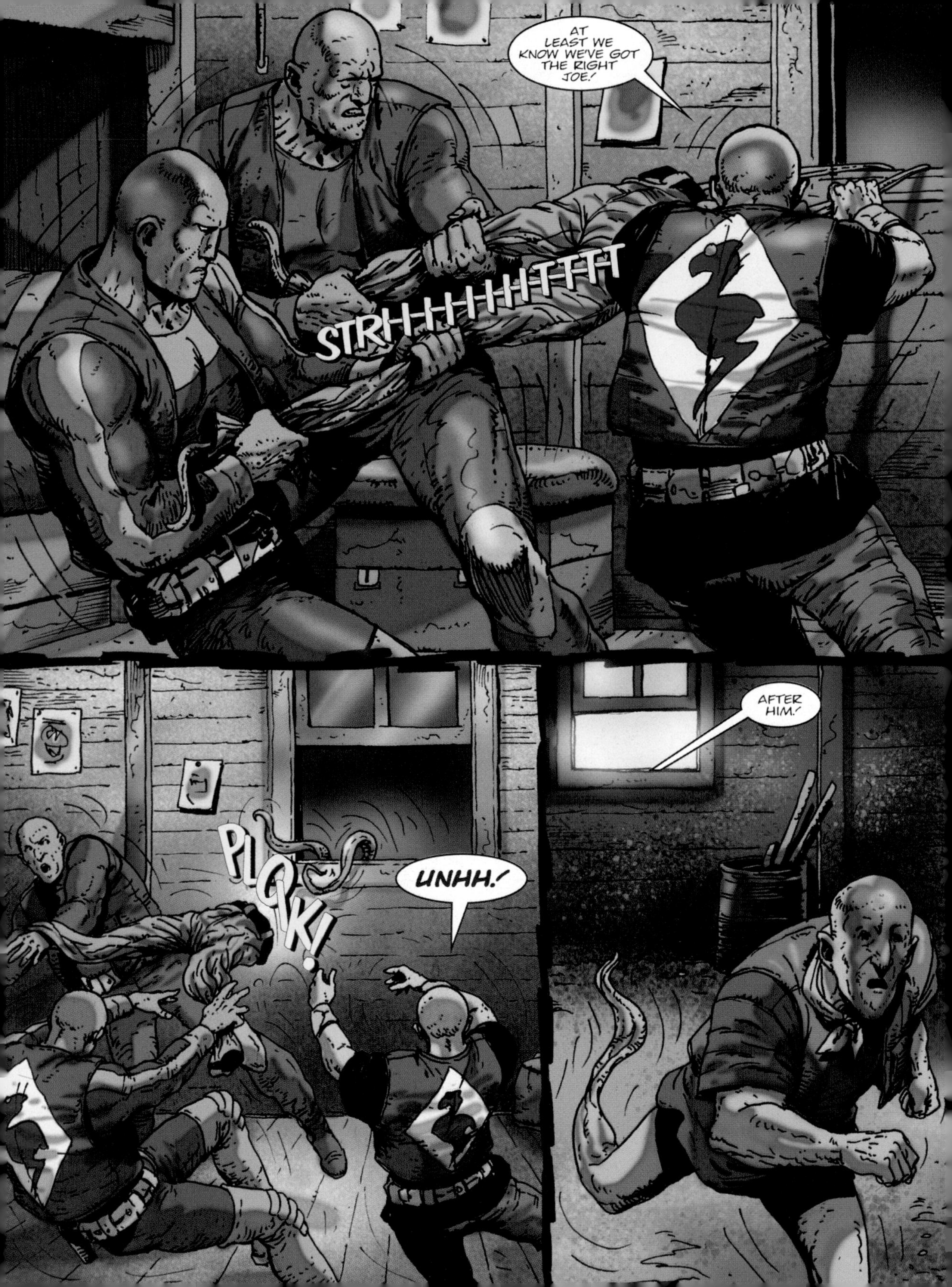
AT LEAST WE KNOW WE'VE GOT THE RIGHT JOE!
STRI-I-I-I-I-I-I-ITTTTT
PLOK!
UNHH!
AFTER HIM!

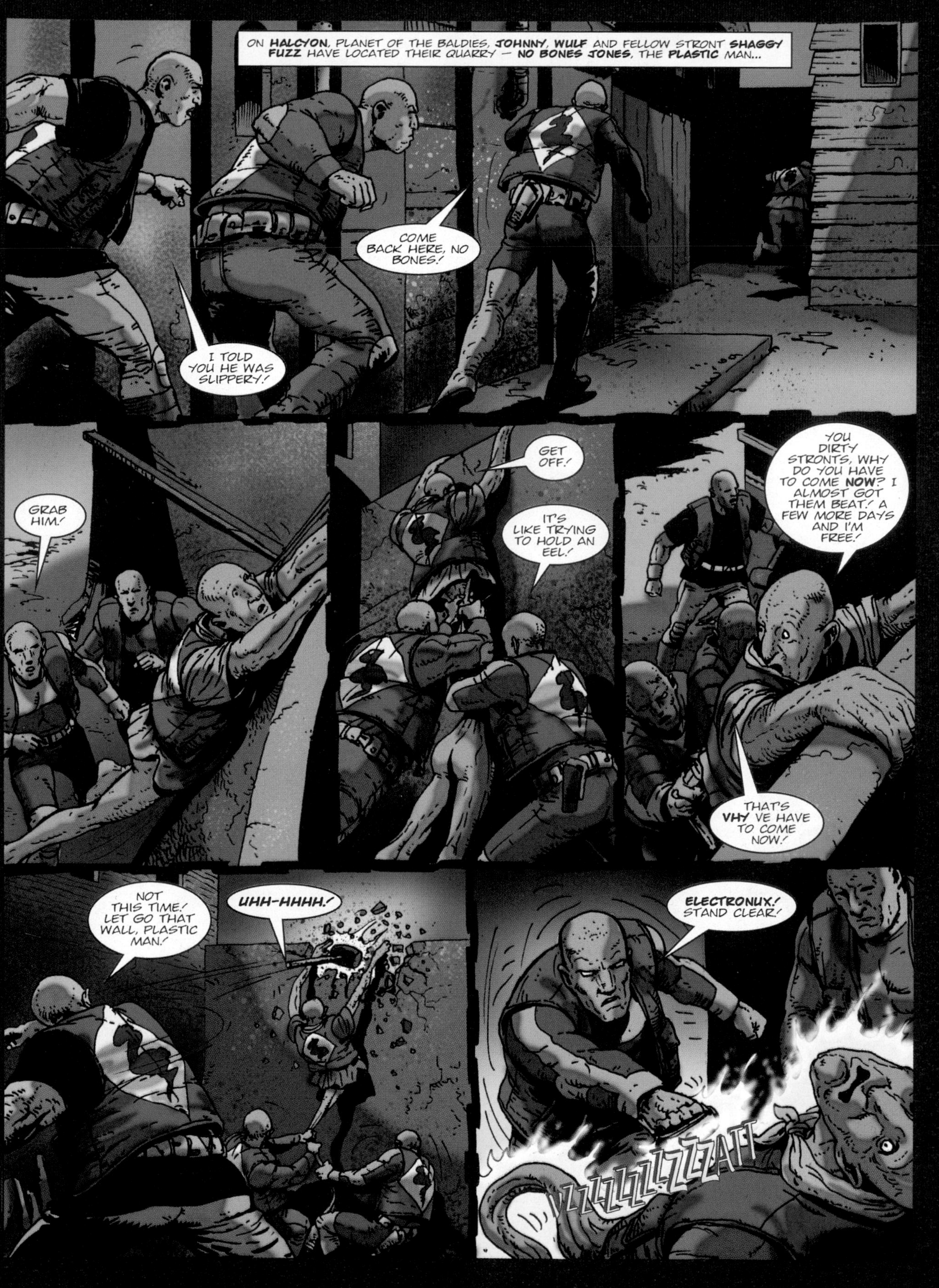
ON HALCYON, PLANET OF THE BALDIES, JOHNNY, WULF AND FELLOW STRONT SHAGGY FUZZ HAVE LOCATED THEIR QUARRY — NO BONES JONES, THE PLASTIC MAN...
COME BACK HERE, NO BONES!
I TOLD YOU HE WAS SLIPPERY!
GRAB HIM!
GET OFF!
IT'S LIKE TRYING TO HOLD AN EEL!
YOU DIRTY STRONTS, WHY DO YOU HAVE TO COME NOW? I ALMOST GOT THEM BEAT! A FEW MORE DAYS AND I'M FREE!
THAT'S VHY VE HAVE TO COME NOW!
NOT THIS TIME! LET GO THAT WALL, PLASTIC MAN!
UHH-HHHH!
ELECTRONUX! STAND CLEAR!
VZZZZZZZZZZZZATT

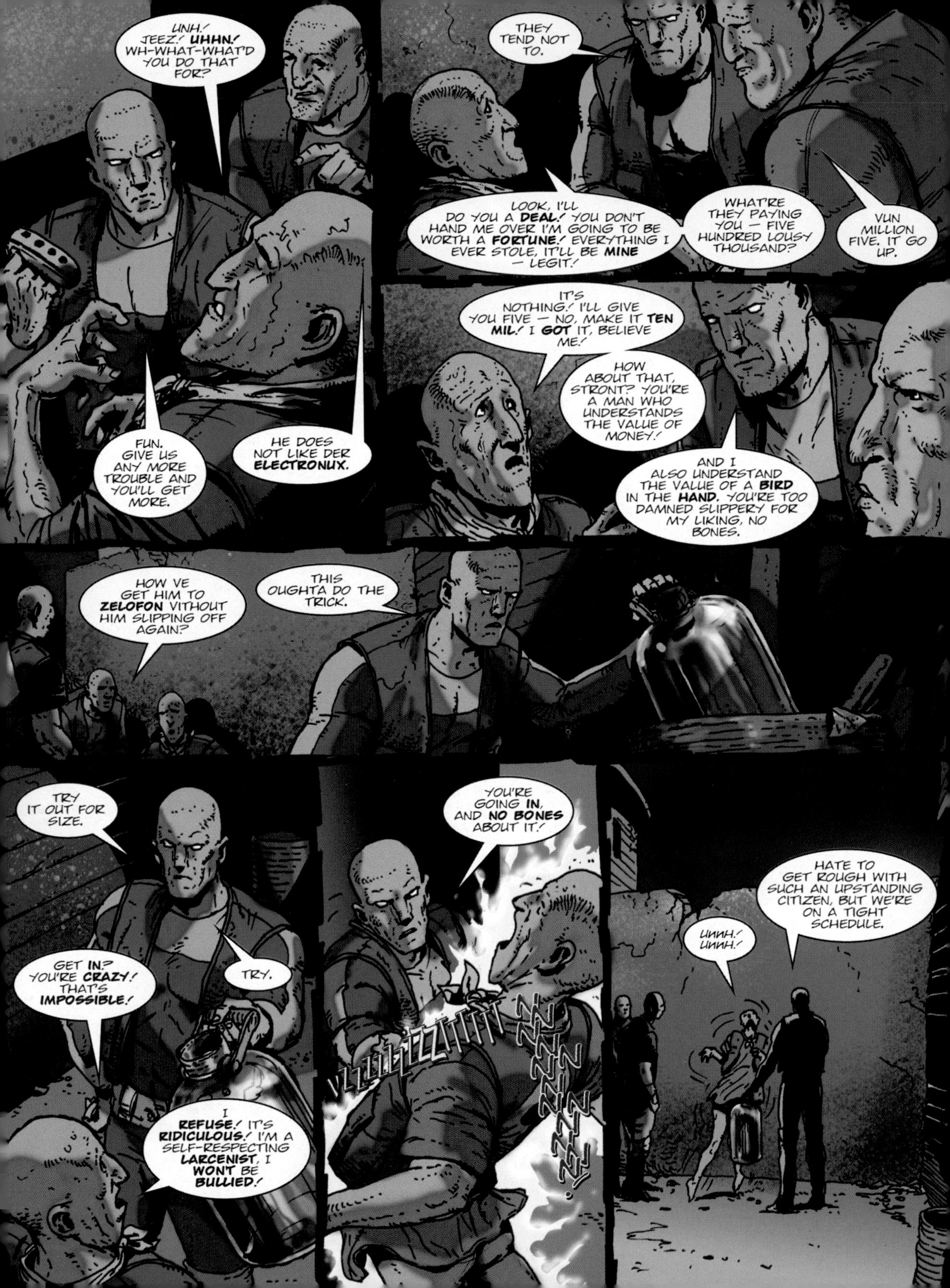
UNH! JEEZ! UHHN! WH-WHAT-WHAT'D YOU DO THAT FOR?
FUN. GIVE US ANY MORE TROUBLE AND YOU'LL GET MORE.
HE DOES NOT LIKE DER ELECTRONUX.
THEY TEND NOT TO.
LOOK, I'LL DO YOU A DEAL! YOU DON'T HAND ME OVER I'M GOING TO BE WORTH A FORTUNE! EVERYTHING I EVER STOLE, IT'LL BE MINE — LEGIT!
WHAT'RE THEY PAYING YOU — FIVE HUNDRED LOUSY THOUSAND?
VUN MILLION FIVE. IT GO UP.
IT'S NOTHING! I'LL GIVE YOU FIVE — NO, MAKE IT TEN MIL! I GOT IT, BELIEVE ME!
HOW ABOUT THAT, STRONT? YOU'RE A MAN WHO UNDERSTANDS THE VALUE OF MONEY!
AND I ALSO UNDERSTAND THE VALUE OF A BIRD IN THE HAND. YOU'RE TOO DAMNED SLIPPERY FOR MY LIKING, NO BONES.
HOW VE GET HIM TO ZELOFON VITHOUT HIM SLIPPING OFF AGAIN?
THIS OUGHTA DO THE TRICK.
TRY IT OUT FOR SIZE.
GET IN? YOU'RE CRAZY! THAT'S IMPOSSIBLE!
TRY.
I REFUSE! IT'S RIDICULOUS! I'M A SELF-RESPECTING LARCENIST, I WON'T BE BULLIED!
YOU'RE GOING IN, AND NO BONES ABOUT IT!
VZZZZZZZZZZZZZT
ZZZZZZZZZZZZZZ!
UNNH! UNNH!
HATE TO GET ROUGH WITH SUCH AN UPSTANDING CITIZEN, BUT WE'RE ON A TIGHT SCHEDULE.

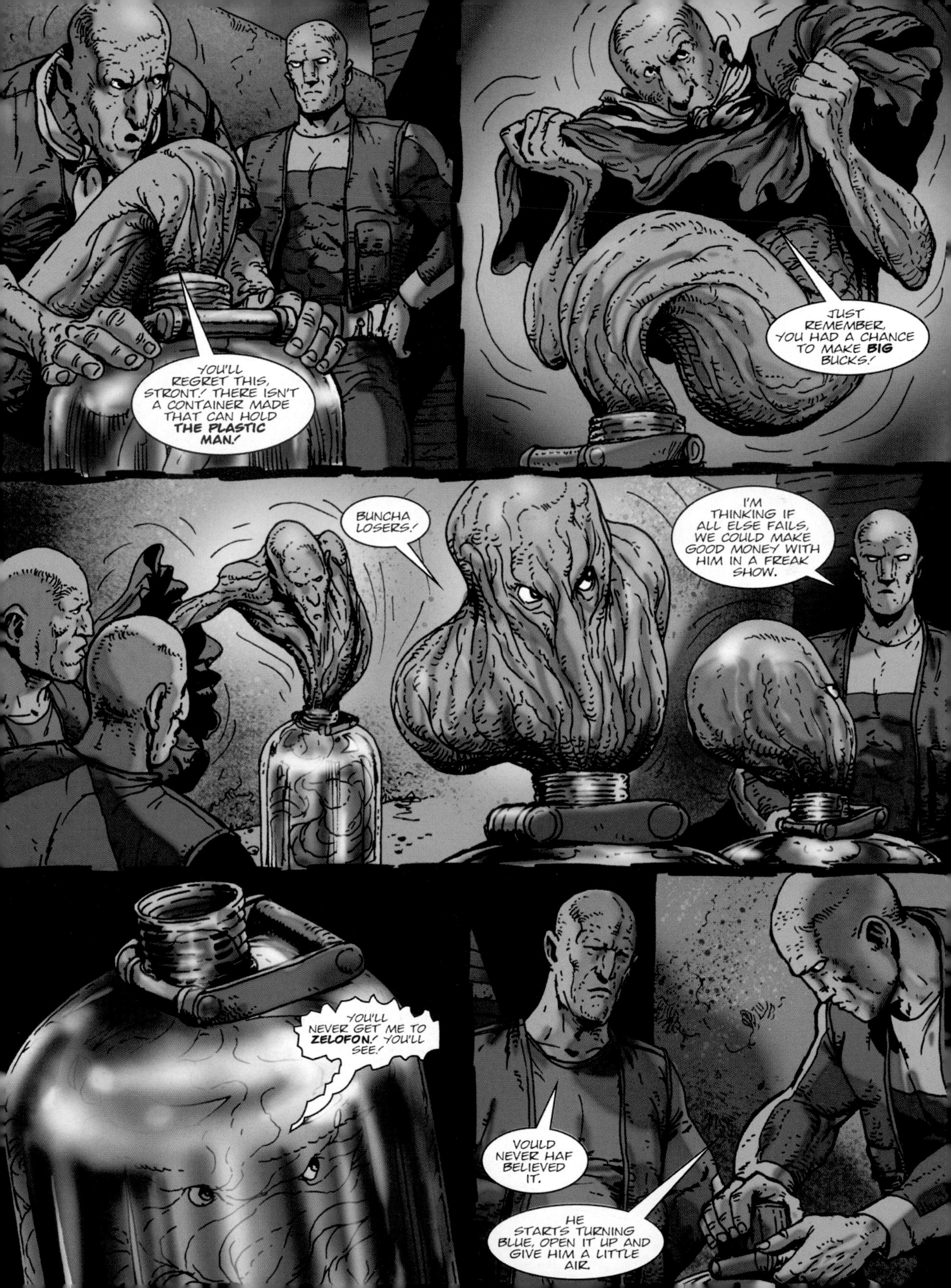
YOU'LL REGRET THIS, STRONT! THERE ISN'T A CONTAINER MADE THAT CAN HOLD THE PLASTIC MAN!
JUST REMEMBER, YOU HAD A CHANCE TO MAKE BIG BUCKS!
BUNCHA LOSERS!
I'M THINKING IF ALL ELSE FAILS, WE COULD MAKE GOOD MONEY WITH HIM IN A FREAK SHOW.
YOU'LL NEVER GET ME TO ZELOFON! YOU'LL SEE!
VOULD NEVER HAF BELIEVED IT.
HE STARTS TURNING BLUE, OPEN IT UP AND GIVE HIM A LITTLE AIR.

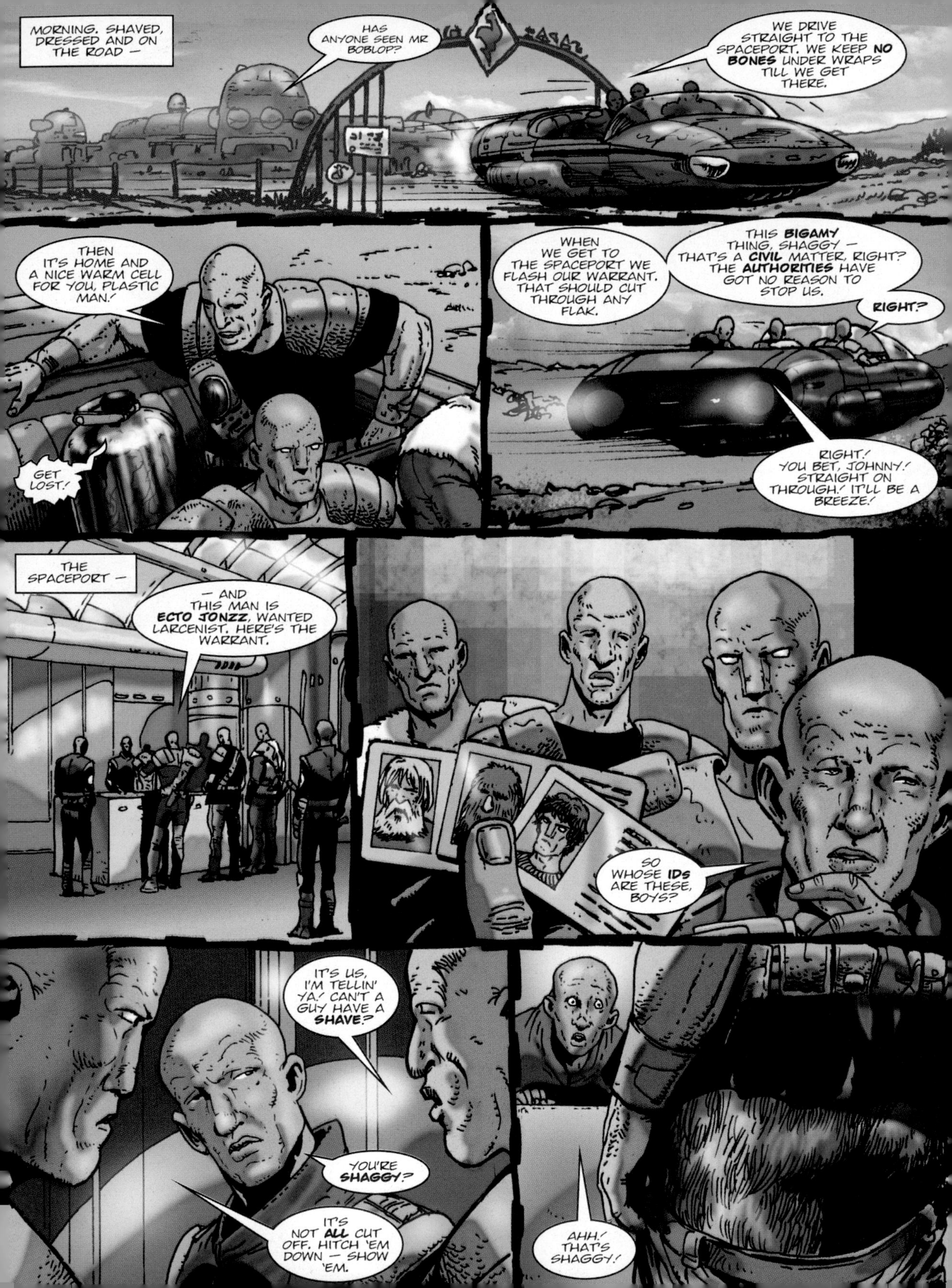
MORNING. SHAVED, DRESSED AND ON THE ROAD —
HAS ANYONE SEEN MR BOBLOP?
WE DRIVE STRAIGHT TO THE SPACEPORT. WE KEEP NO BONES UNDER WRAPS TILL WE GET THERE.
THEN IT'S HOME AND A NICE WARM CELL FOR YOU, PLASTIC MAN.
GET LOST.
WHEN WE GET TO THE SPACEPORT WE FLASH OUR WARRANT. THAT SHOULD CUT THROUGH ANY FLAK.
THIS BIGAMY THING, SHAGGY — THAT'S A CIVIL MATTER, RIGHT? THE AUTHORITIES HAVE GOT NO REASON TO STOP US.
RIGHT?
RIGHT. YOU BET, JOHNNY. STRAIGHT ON THROUGH. IT'LL BE A BREEZE.
THE SPACEPORT —
— AND THIS MAN IS ECTO JONZZ, WANTED LARCENIST. HERE'S THE WARRANT.
SO WHOSE IDS ARE THESE, BOYS?
IT'S US, I'M TELLIN' YA. CAN'T A GUY HAVE A SHAVE?
YOU'RE SHAGGY?
IT'S NOT ALL CUT OFF. HITCH 'EM DOWN — SHOW 'EM.
AHH. THAT'S SHAGGY.

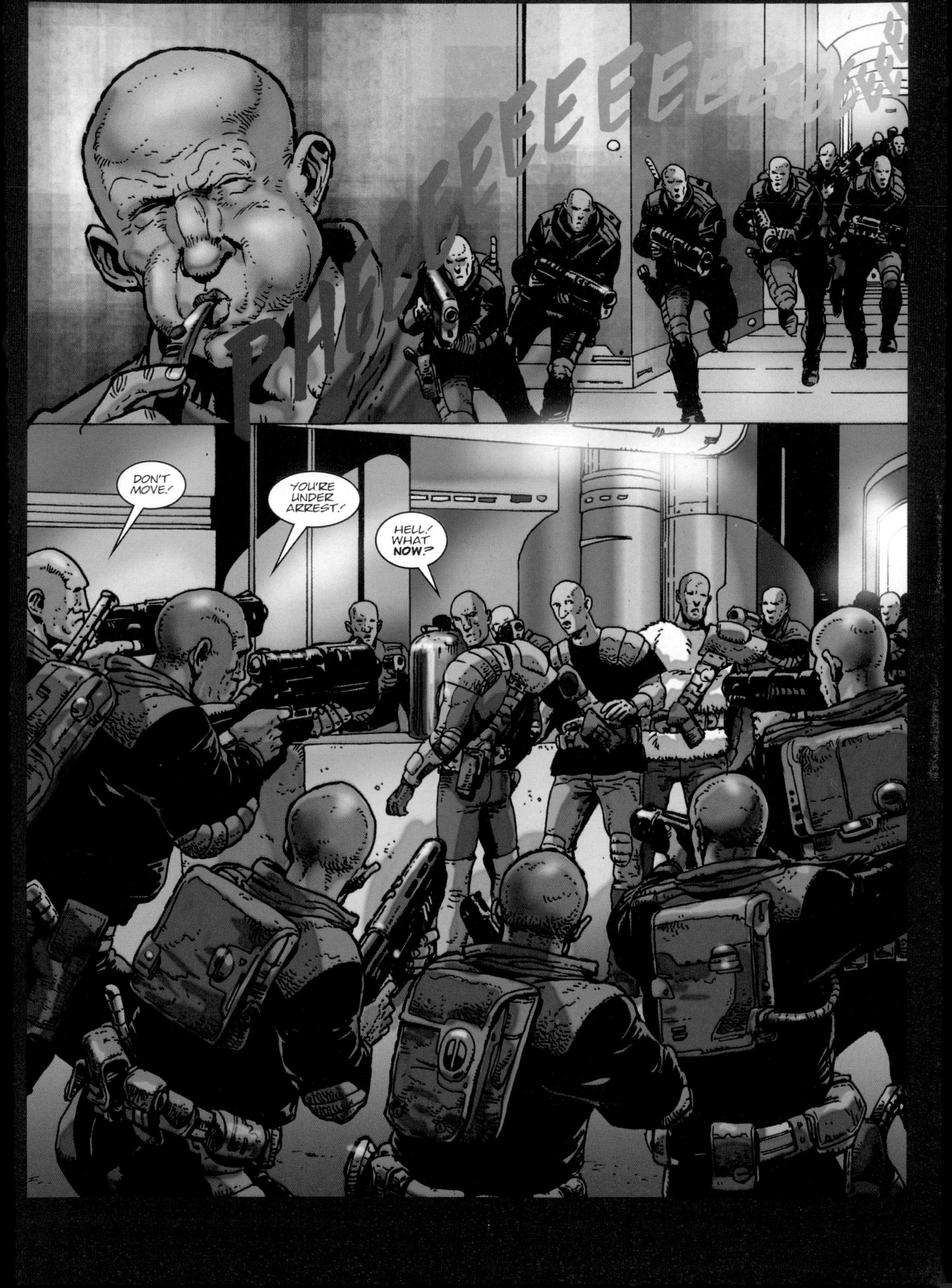
PHEEEEEEEEEEEEEEEW
DON'T MOVE!
YOU'RE UNDER ARREST!
HELL! WHAT **NOW**?

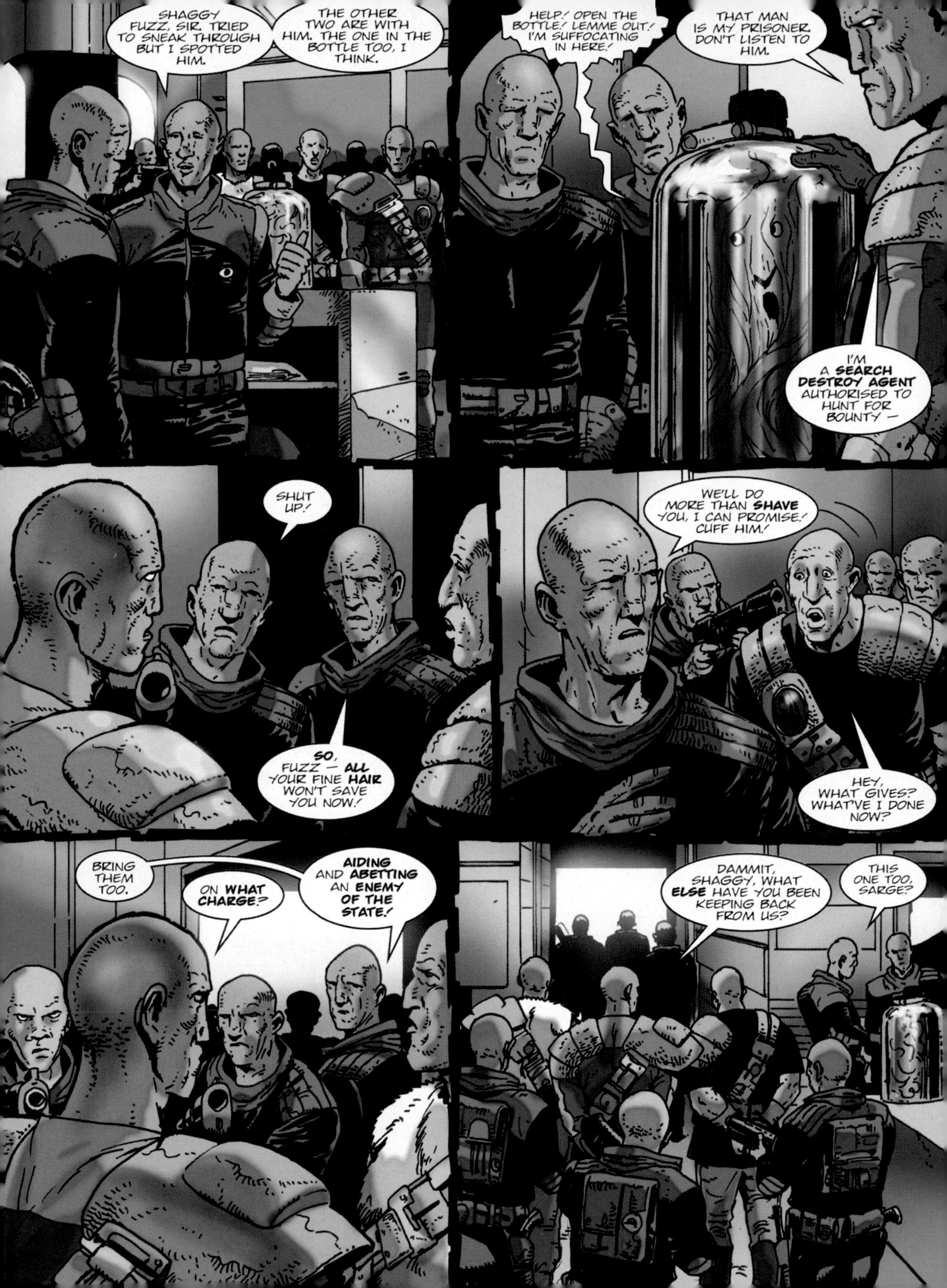
SHAGGY FUZZ, SIR, TRIED TO SNEAK THROUGH BUT I SPOTTED HIM.
THE OTHER TWO ARE WITH HIM. THE ONE IN THE BOTTLE TOO, I THINK.
HELP! OPEN THE BOTTLE! LEMME OUT! I'M SUFFOCATING IN HERE!
THAT MAN IS MY PRISONER. DON'T LISTEN TO HIM.
I'M A SEARCH DESTROY AGENT AUTHORISED TO HUNT FOR BOUNTY —
SHUT UP!
SO, FUZZ — ALL YOUR FINE HAIR WON'T SAVE YOU NOW!
WE'LL DO MORE THAN SHAVE YOU, I CAN PROMISE! CUFF HIM!
HEY, WHAT GIVES? WHAT'VE I DONE NOW?
BRING THEM TOO.
ON WHAT CHARGE?
AIDING AND ABETTING AN ENEMY OF THE STATE!
DAMMIT, SHAGGY, WHAT ELSE HAVE YOU BEEN KEEPING BACK FROM US?
THIS ONE TOO, SARGE?

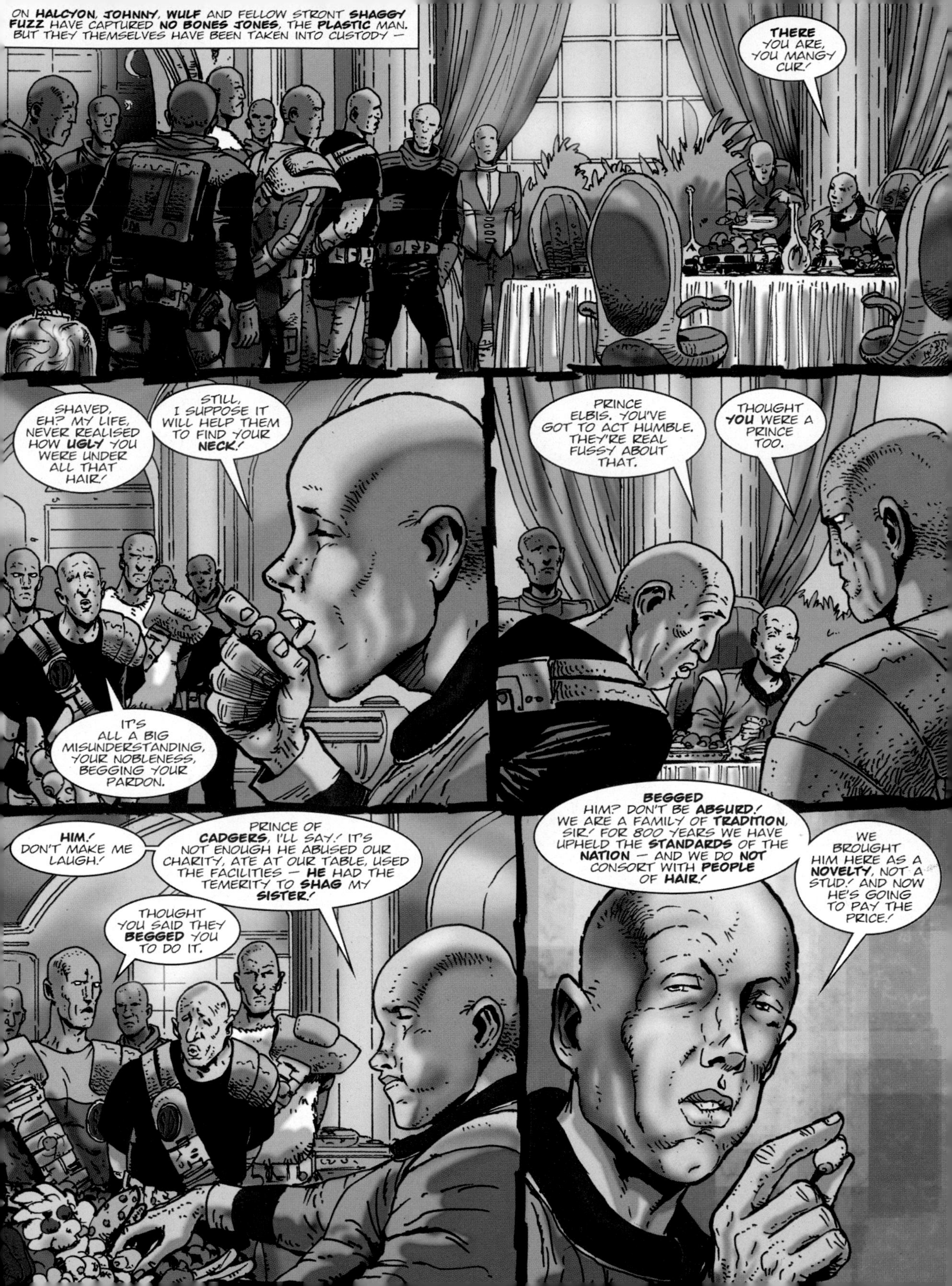

ON HALCYON, JOHNNY, WULF AND FELLOW STRONT SHAGGY FUZZ HAVE CAPTURED NO BONES JONES, THE PLASTIC MAN. BUT THEY THEMSELVES HAVE BEEN TAKEN INTO CUSTODY —
THERE YOU ARE, YOU MANGY CUR!
SHAVED, EH? MY LIFE, NEVER REALISED HOW UGLY YOU WERE UNDER ALL THAT HAIR!
STILL, I SUPPOSE IT WILL HELP THEM TO FIND YOUR NECK!
IT'S ALL A BIG MISUNDERSTANDING, YOUR NOBLENESS, BEGGING YOUR PARDON.
PRINCE ELBIS. YOU'VE GOT TO ACT HUMBLE. THEY'RE REAL FUSSY ABOUT THAT.
THOUGHT YOU WERE A PRINCE TOO.
HIM! DON'T MAKE ME LAUGH!
PRINCE OF CADGERS, I'LL SAY! IT'S NOT ENOUGH HE ABUSED OUR CHARITY, ATE AT OUR TABLE, USED THE FACILITIES — HE HAD THE TEMERITY TO SHAG MY SISTER!
THOUGHT YOU SAID THEY BEGGED YOU TO DO IT.
BEGGED HIM? DON'T BE ABSURD! WE ARE A FAMILY OF TRADITION, SIR! FOR 800 YEARS WE HAVE UPHELD THE STANDARDS OF THE NATION — AND WE DO NOT CONSORT WITH PEOPLE OF HAIR!
WE BROUGHT HIM HERE AS A NOVELTY, NOT A STUD! AND NOW HE'S GOING TO PAY THE PRICE!

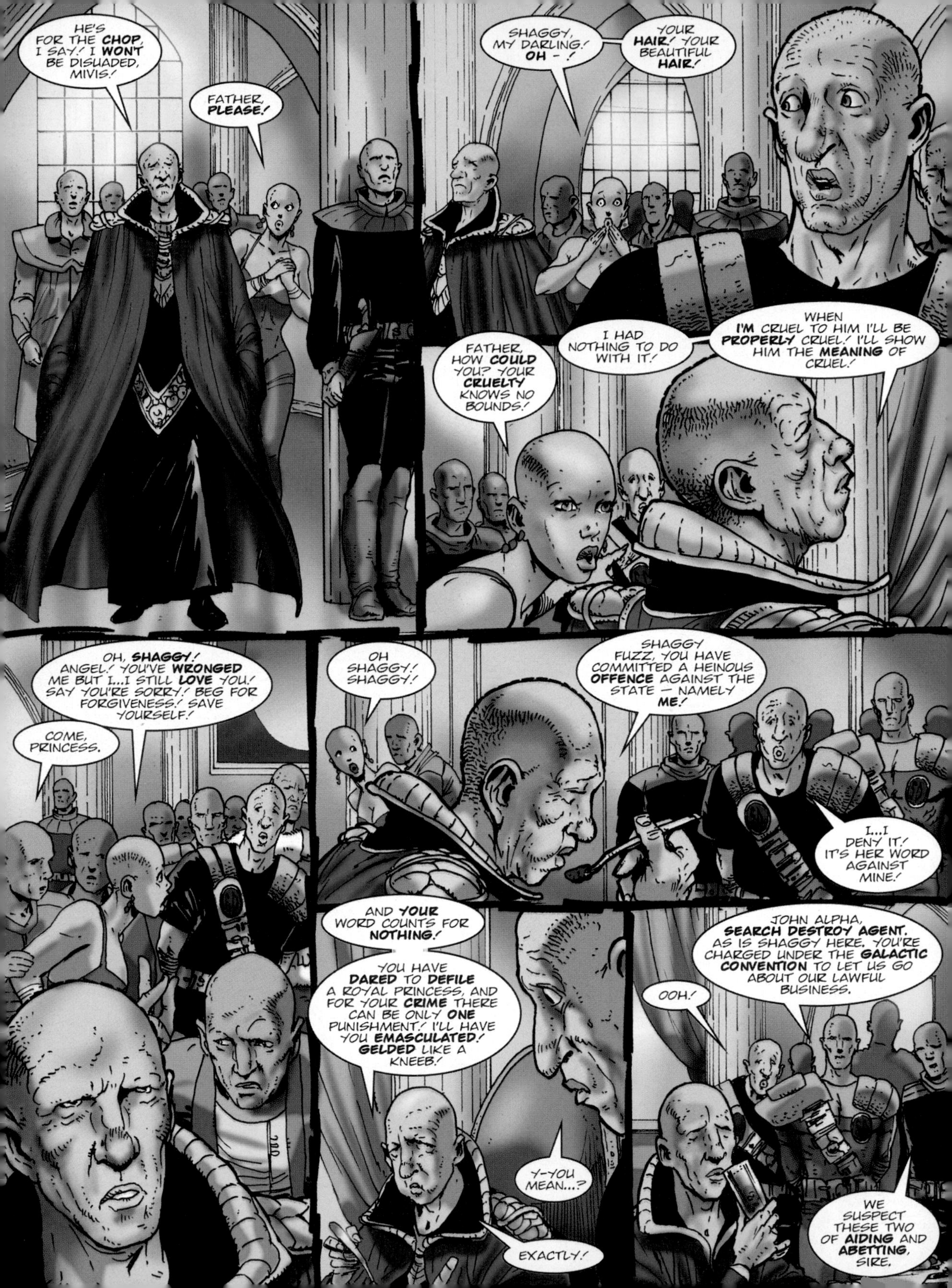
HE'S FOR THE CHOP, I SAY! I WON'T BE DISUADED, MIVIS!
FATHER, PLEASE!
SHAGGY, MY DARLING! OH - !
YOUR HAIR! YOUR BEAUTIFUL HAIR!
FATHER, HOW COULD YOU? YOUR CRUELTY KNOWS NO BOUNDS!
I HAD NOTHING TO DO WITH IT!
WHEN I'M CRUEL TO HIM I'LL BE PROPERLY CRUEL! I'LL SHOW HIM THE MEANING OF CRUEL!
OH, SHAGGY! ANGEL! YOU'VE WRONGED ME BUT I...I STILL LOVE YOU! SAY YOU'RE SORRY! BEG FOR FORGIVENESS! SAVE YOURSELF!
COME, PRINCESS.
OH SHAGGY! SHAGGY!
SHAGGY FUZZ, YOU HAVE COMMITTED A HEINOUS OFFENCE AGAINST THE STATE — NAMELY ME!
I...I DENY IT! IT'S HER WORD AGAINST MINE!
AND YOUR WORD COUNTS FOR NOTHING!
YOU HAVE DARED TO DEFILE A ROYAL PRINCESS, AND FOR YOUR CRIME THERE CAN BE ONLY ONE PUNISHMENT! I'LL HAVE YOU EMASCULATED! GELDED LIKE A KNEEB!
Y-YOU MEAN...?
EXACTLY!
JOHN ALPHA, SEARCH DESTROY AGENT. AS IS SHAGGY HERE. YOU'RE CHARGED UNDER THE GALACTIC CONVENTION TO LET US GO ABOUT OUR LAWFUL BUSINESS.
OOH!
WE SUSPECT THESE TWO OF AIDING AND ABETTING, SIRE.

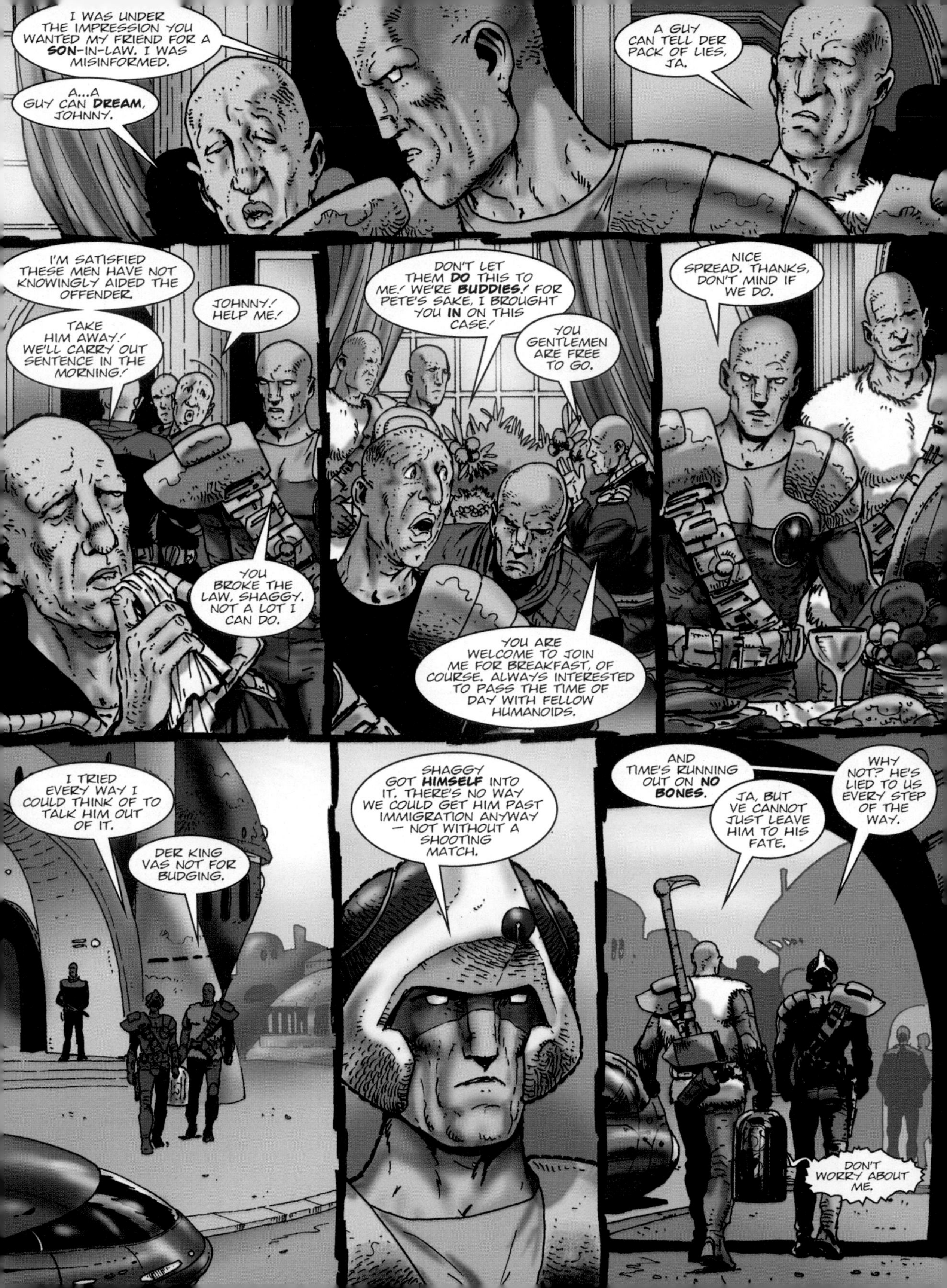

I WAS UNDER THE IMPRESSION YOU WANTED MY FRIEND FOR A **SON**-IN-LAW. I WAS MISINFORMED.
A...A GUY CAN **DREAM**, JOHNNY.
A GUY CAN TELL DER PACK OF LIES, JA.
I'M SATISFIED THESE MEN HAVE NOT KNOWINGLY AIDED THE OFFENDER.
TAKE HIM AWAY! WE'LL CARRY OUT SENTENCE IN THE MORNING!
JOHNNY! HELP ME!
YOU BROKE THE LAW, SHAGGY. NOT A LOT I CAN DO.
DON'T LET THEM **DO** THIS TO ME! WE'RE **BUDDIES**! FOR PETE'S SAKE, I BROUGHT YOU **IN** ON THIS CASE!
YOU GENTLEMEN ARE FREE TO GO.
YOU ARE WELCOME TO JOIN ME FOR BREAKFAST, OF COURSE. ALWAYS INTERESTED TO PASS THE TIME OF DAY WITH FELLOW HUMANOIDS.
NICE SPREAD. THANKS, DON'T MIND IF WE DO.
I TRIED EVERY WAY I COULD THINK OF TO TALK HIM OUT OF IT.
DER KING VAS NOT FOR BUDGING.
SHAGGY GOT **HIMSELF** INTO IT. THERE'S NO WAY WE COULD GET HIM PAST IMMIGRATION ANYWAY — NOT WITHOUT A SHOOTING MATCH.
AND TIME'S RUNNING OUT ON **NO BONES**.
JA, BUT VE CANNOT JUST LEAVE HIM TO HIS FATE.
WHY NOT? HE'S LIED TO US EVERY STEP OF THE WAY.
DON'T WORRY ABOUT ME.

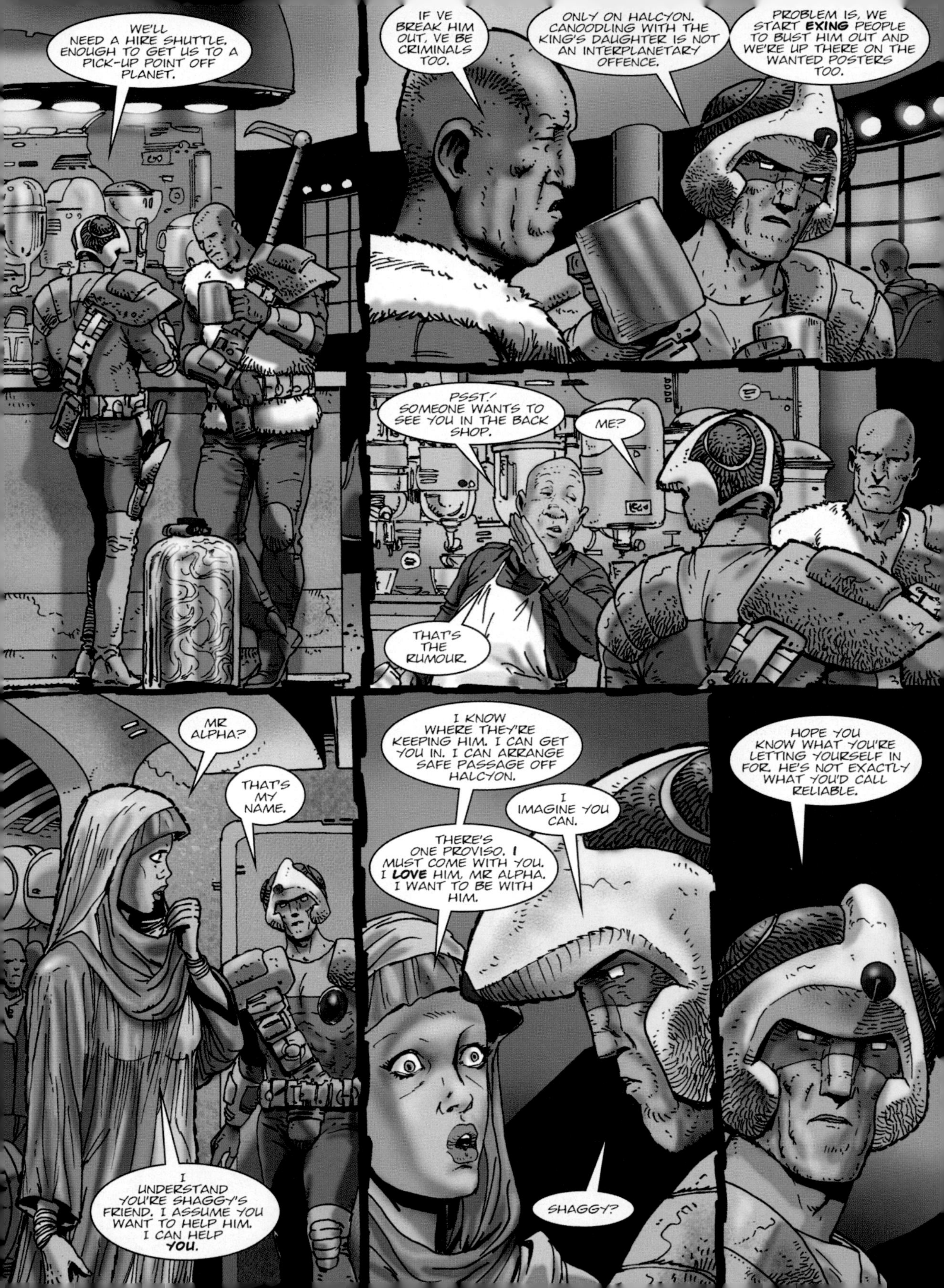
WE'LL NEED A HIRE SHUTTLE. ENOUGH TO GET US TO A PICK-UP POINT OFF PLANET.
IF VE BREAK HIM OUT, VE BE CRIMINALS TOO.
ONLY ON HALCYON. CANOODLING WITH THE KING'S DAUGHTER IS NOT AN INTERPLANETARY OFFENCE.
PROBLEM IS, WE START **EXING** PEOPLE TO BUST HIM OUT AND WE'RE UP THERE ON THE WANTED POSTERS TOO.
PSST! SOMEONE WANTS TO SEE YOU IN THE BACK SHOP.
ME?
THAT'S THE RUMOUR.
MR ALPHA?
THAT'S MY NAME.
I UNDERSTAND YOU'RE SHAGGY'S FRIEND. I ASSUME YOU WANT TO HELP HIM. I CAN HELP **YOU**.
I KNOW WHERE THEY'RE KEEPING HIM. I CAN GET YOU IN. I CAN ARRANGE SAFE PASSAGE OFF HALCYON.
I IMAGINE YOU CAN.
THERE'S ONE PROVISO. I MUST COME WITH YOU. I **LOVE** HIM, MR ALPHA. I WANT TO BE WITH HIM.
SHAGGY?
HOPE YOU KNOW WHAT YOU'RE LETTING YOURSELF IN FOR. HE'S NOT EXACTLY WHAT YOU'D CALL RELIABLE.

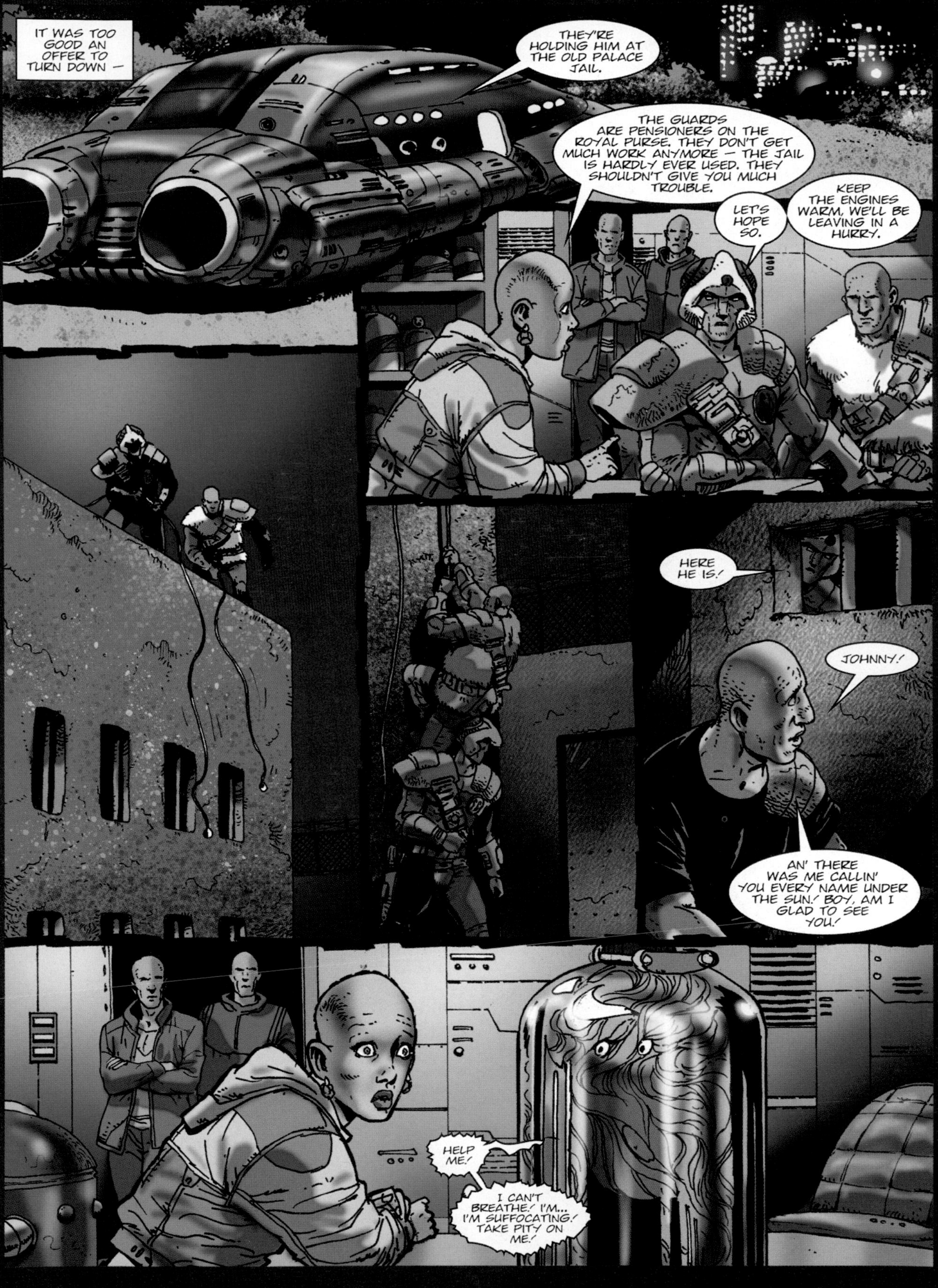
IT WAS TOO GOOD AN OFFER TO TURN DOWN —
THEY'RE HOLDING HIM AT THE OLD PALACE JAIL.
THE GUARDS ARE PENSIONERS ON THE ROYAL PURSE. THEY DON'T GET MUCH WORK ANYMORE — THE JAIL IS HARDLY EVER USED. THEY SHOULDN'T GIVE YOU MUCH TROUBLE.
LET'S HOPE SO.
KEEP THE ENGINES WARM, WE'LL BE LEAVING IN A HURRY.
HERE HE IS!
JOHNNY!
AN' THERE WAS ME CALLIN' YOU EVERY NAME UNDER THE SUN! BOY, AM I GLAD TO SEE YOU!
HELP ME!
I CAN'T BREATHE! I'M... I'M SUFFOCATING! TAKE PITY ON ME!

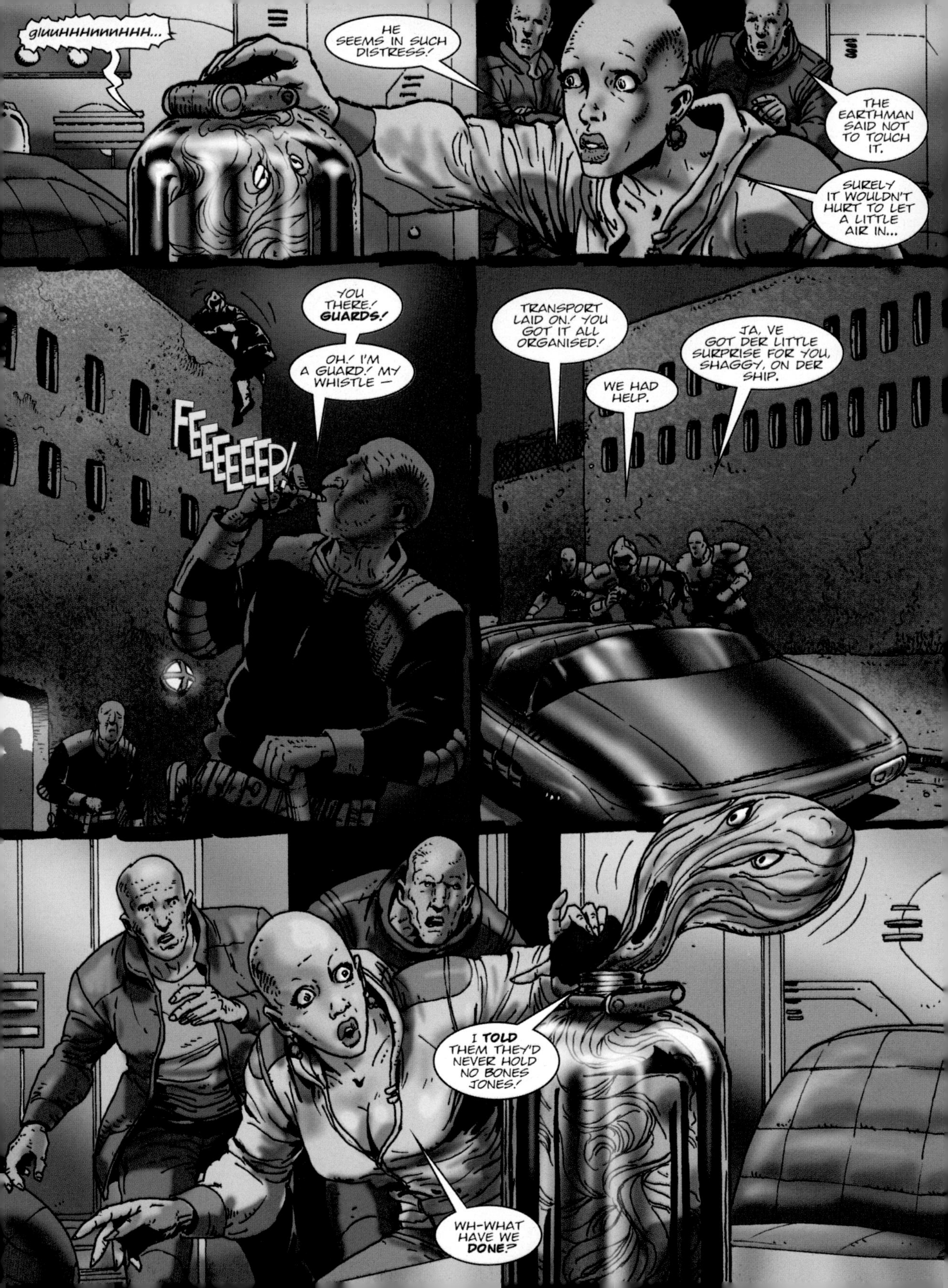
gluuHHHHHHHHH...
HE SEEMS IN SUCH DISTRESS!
THE EARTHMAN SAID NOT TO TOUCH IT.
SURELY IT WOULDN'T HURT TO LET A LITTLE AIR IN...
YOU THERE! GUARDS!
OH! I'M A GUARD! MY WHISTLE —
FEEEEEEP!
TRANSPORT LAID ON! YOU GOT IT ALL ORGANISED!
WE HAD HELP.
JA, VE GOT DER LITTLE SURPRISE FOR YOU, SHAGGY, ON DER SHIP.
I TOLD THEM THEY'D NEVER HOLD NO BONES JONES!
WH-WHAT HAVE WE DONE?

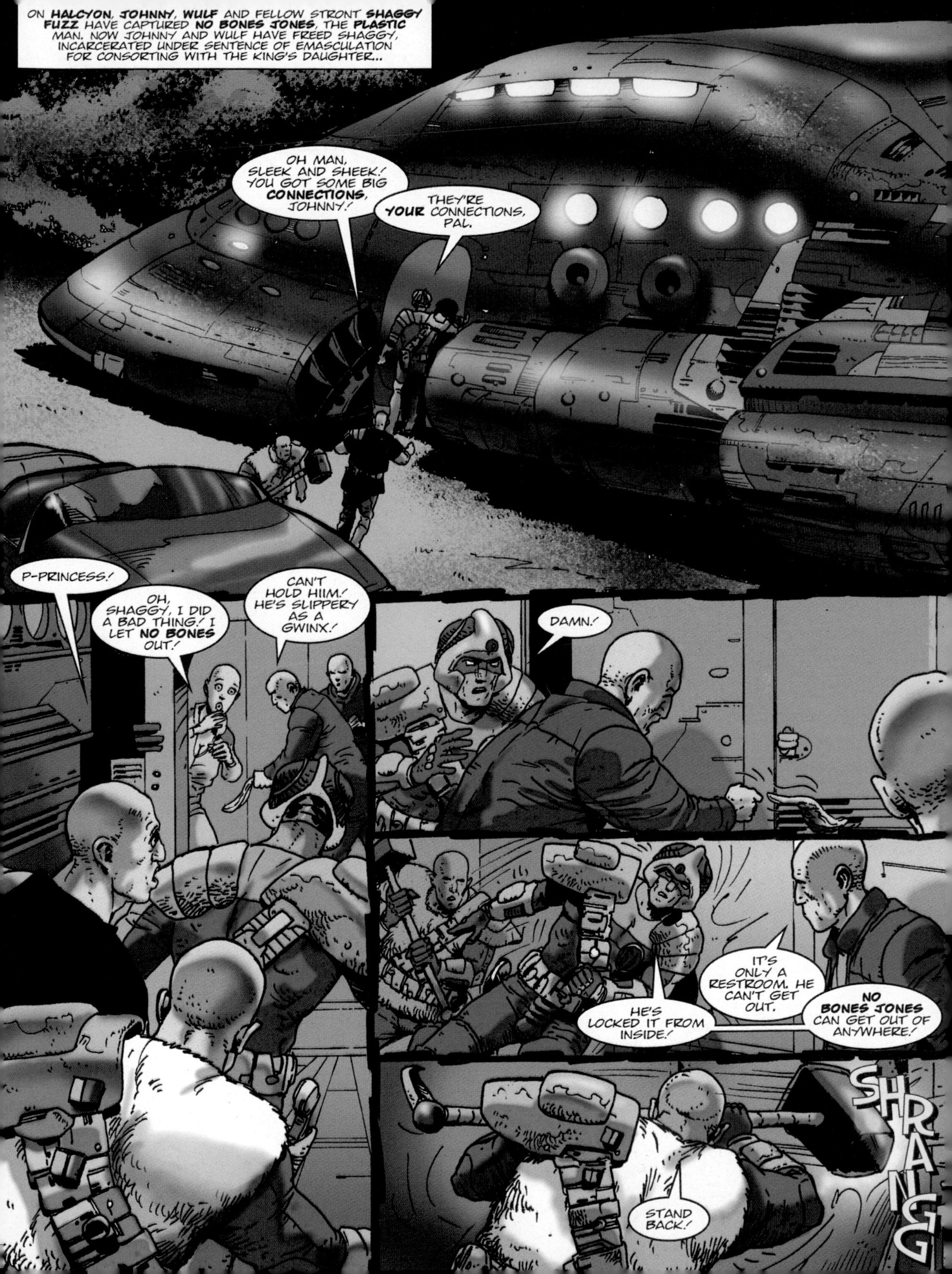
ON HALCYON, JOHNNY, WULF AND FELLOW STRONT SHAGGY FUZZ HAVE CAPTURED NO BONES JONES, THE PLASTIC MAN. NOW JOHNNY AND WULF HAVE FREED SHAGGY, INCARCERATED UNDER SENTENCE OF EMASCULATION FOR CONSORTING WITH THE KING'S DAUGHTER...
OH MAN, SLEEK AND SHEEK! YOU GOT SOME BIG CONNECTIONS, JOHNNY!
THEY'RE YOUR CONNECTIONS, PAL.
P-PRINCESS!
OH, SHAGGY, I DID A BAD THING! I LET NO BONES OUT!
CAN'T HOLD HIIM! HE'S SLIPPERY AS A GWINX!
DAMN!
IT'S ONLY A RESTROOM. HE CAN'T GET OUT.
HE'S LOCKED IT FROM INSIDE!
NO BONES JONES CAN GET OUT OF ANYWHERE!
SHRAIGG
STAND BACK!

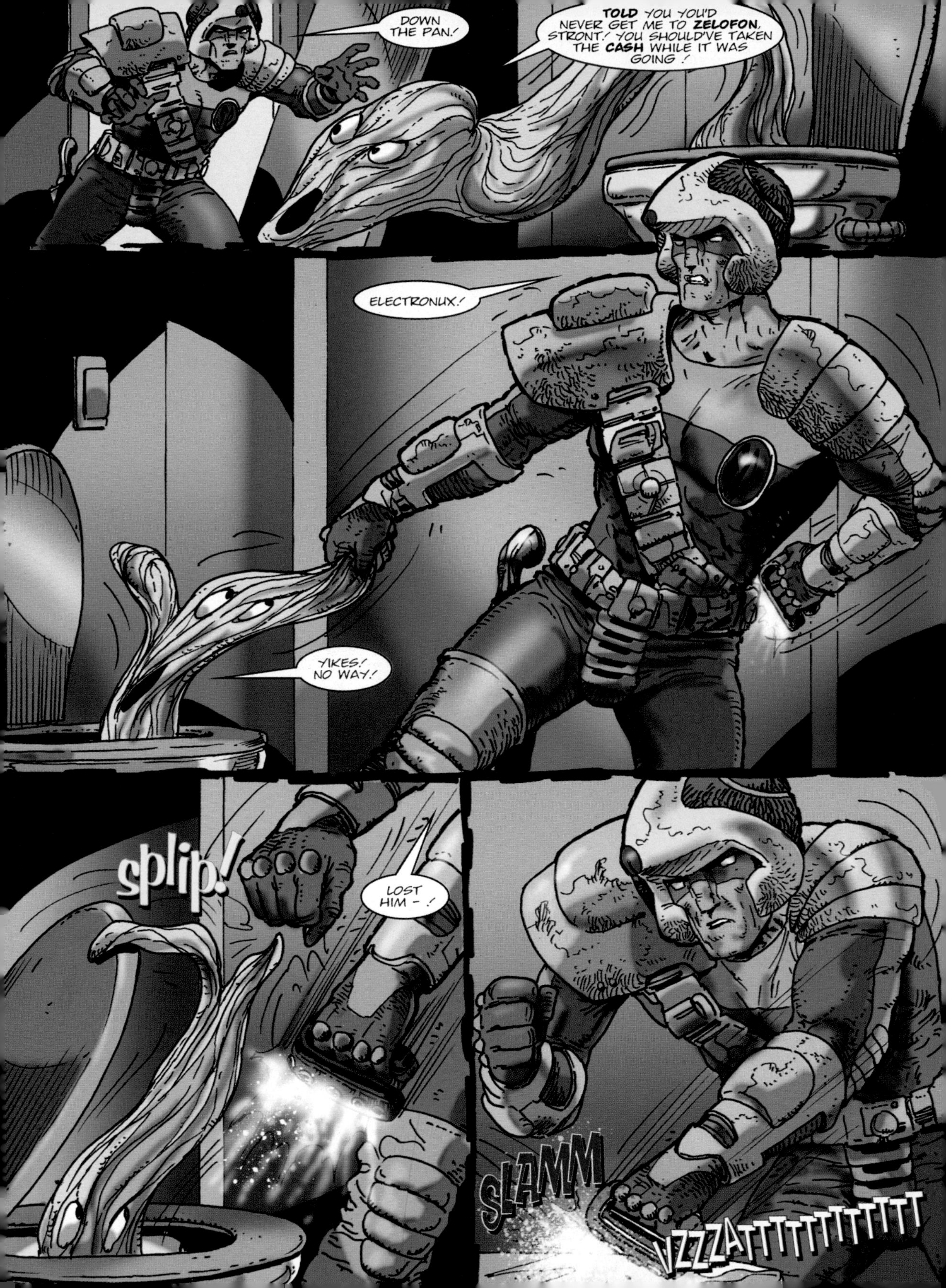
DOWN THE PAN!
TOLD YOU YOU'D NEVER GET ME TO ZELOFON, STRONT! YOU SHOULD'VE TAKEN THE CASH WHILE IT WAS GOING!
ELECTRONUX!
YIKES! NO WAY!
splip!
LOST HIM - !
SLAMM
VZZZATTTTTTTTTTTT

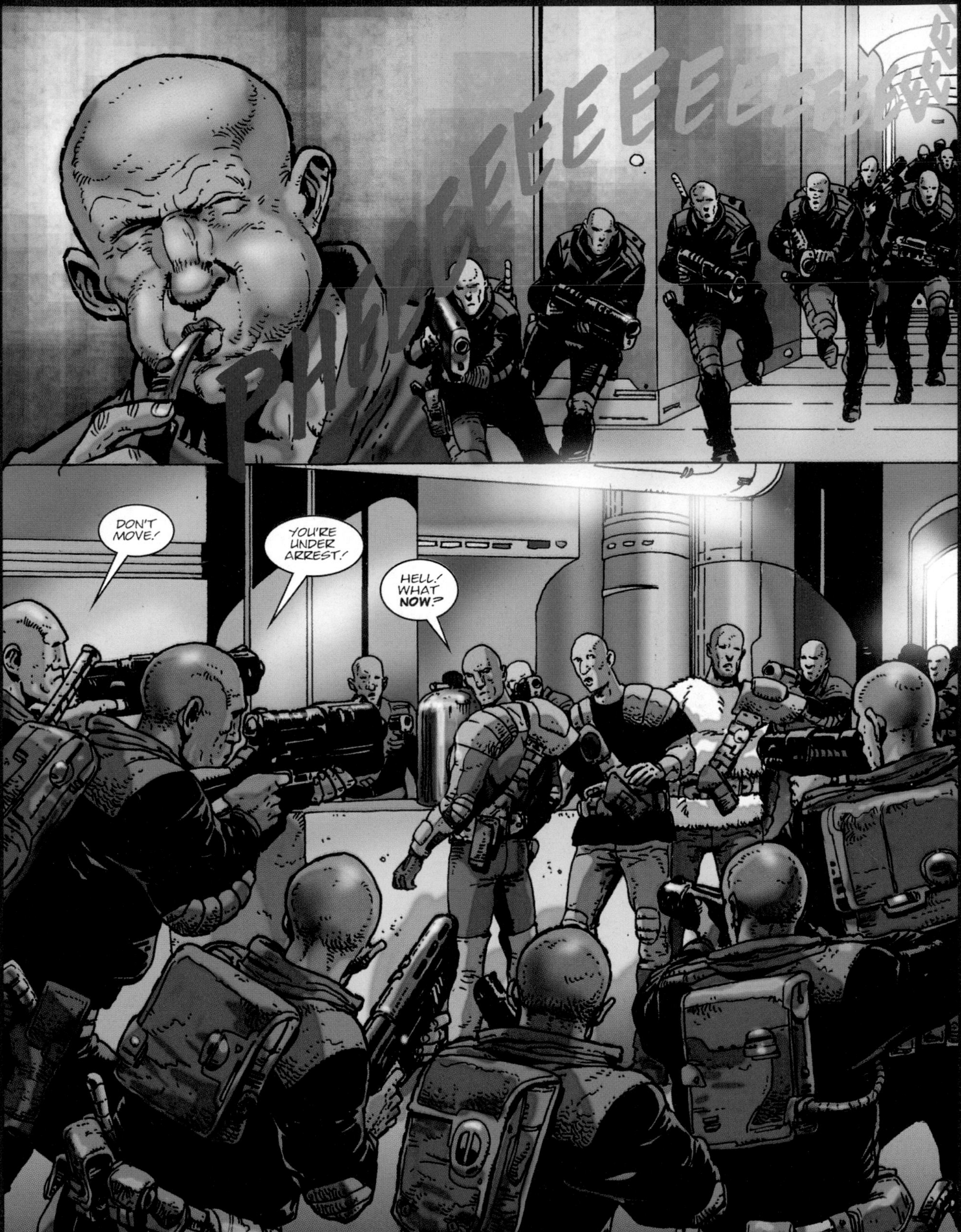
PHEEEEEEEEEEEEW
DON'T MOVE!
YOU'RE UNDER ARREST!
HELL! WHAT **NOW**?

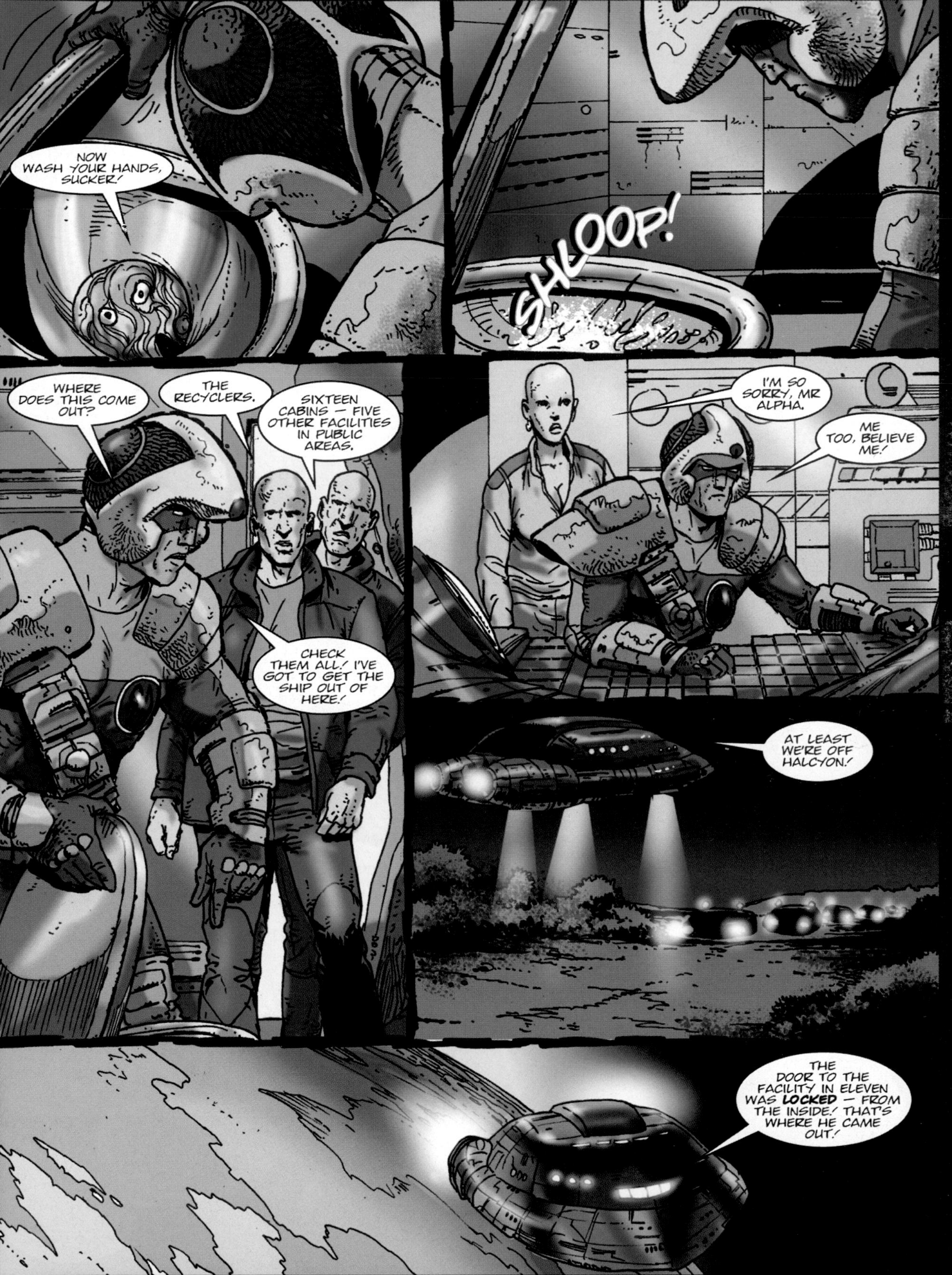
NOW WASH YOUR HANDS, SUCKER!
SHLOOP!
WHERE DOES THIS COME OUT?
THE RECYCLERS.
SIXTEEN CABINS — FIVE OTHER FACILITIES IN PUBLIC AREAS.
CHECK THEM ALL! I'VE GOT TO GET THE SHIP OUT OF HERE!
I'M SO SORRY, MR ALPHA.
ME TOO, BELIEVE ME!
AT LEAST WE'RE OFF HALCYON!
THE DOOR TO THE FACILITY IN ELEVEN WAS **LOCKED** — FROM THE INSIDE! THAT'S WHERE HE CAME OUT!

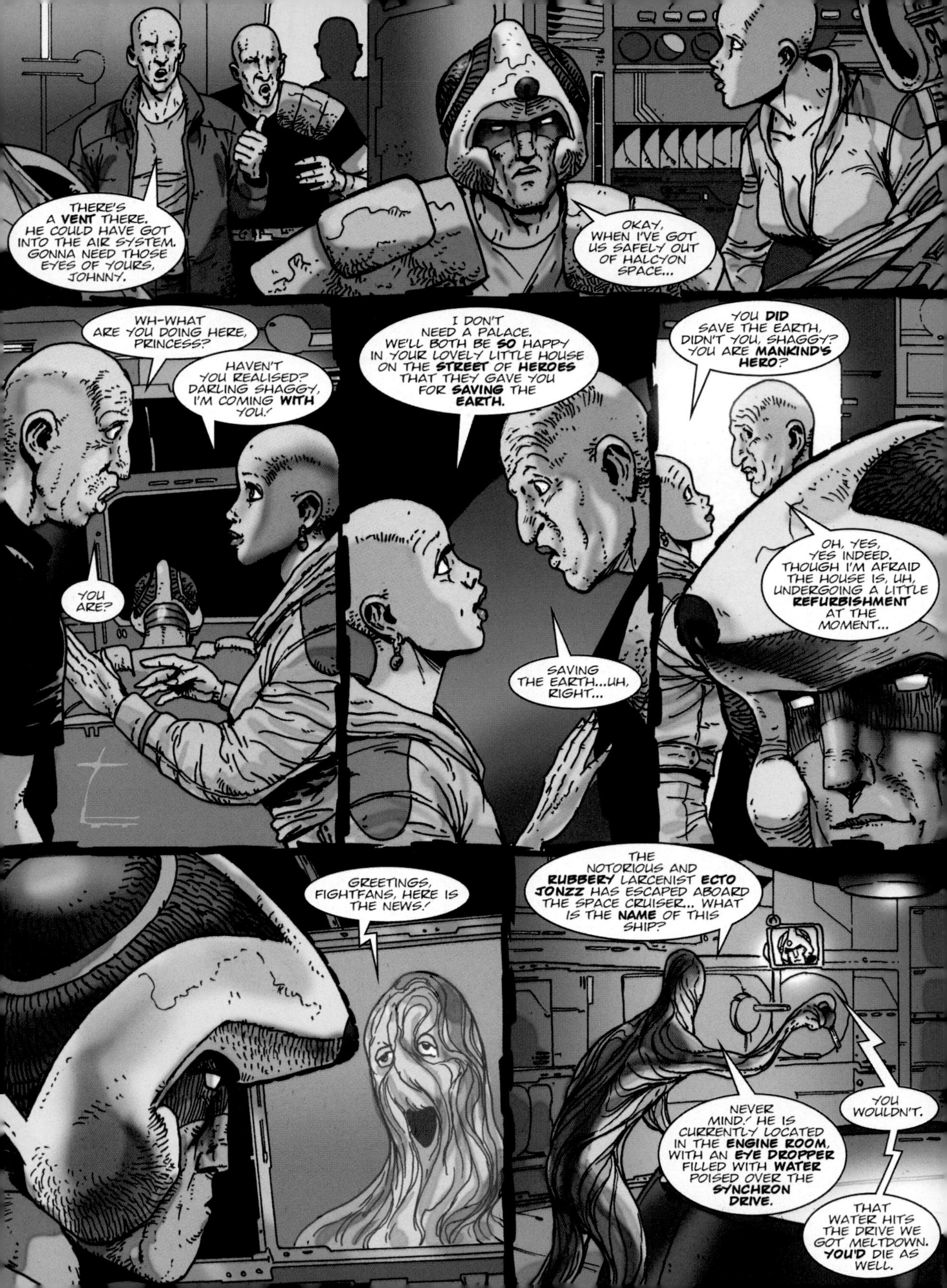
THERE'S A VENT THERE. HE COULD HAVE GOT INTO THE AIR SYSTEM. GONNA NEED THOSE EYES OF YOURS, JOHNNY.
OKAY, WHEN I'VE GOT US SAFELY OUT OF HALCYON SPACE...
WH-WHAT ARE YOU DOING HERE, PRINCESS?
HAVEN'T YOU REALISED? DARLING SHAGGY, I'M COMING WITH YOU!
YOU ARE?
I DON'T NEED A PALACE. WE'LL BOTH BE SO HAPPY IN YOUR LOVELY LITTLE HOUSE ON THE STREET OF HEROES THAT THEY GAVE YOU FOR SAVING THE EARTH.
SAVING THE EARTH...UH, RIGHT...
YOU DID SAVE THE EARTH, DIDN'T YOU, SHAGGY? YOU ARE MANKIND'S HERO?
OH, YES, YES INDEED. THOUGH I'M AFRAID THE HOUSE IS, UH, UNDERGOING A LITTLE REFURBISHMENT AT THE MOMENT...
GREETINGS, FIGHTFANS, HERE IS THE NEWS!
THE NOTORIOUS AND RUBBERY LARCENIST ECTO JONZZ HAS ESCAPED ABOARD THE SPACE CRUISER... WHAT IS THE NAME OF THIS SHIP?
NEVER MIND! HE IS CURRENTLY LOCATED IN THE ENGINE ROOM, WITH AN EYE DROPPER FILLED WITH WATER POISED OVER THE SYNCHRON DRIVE.
YOU WOULDN'T.
THAT WATER HITS THE DRIVE WE GOT MELTDOWN. YOU'D DIE AS WELL.

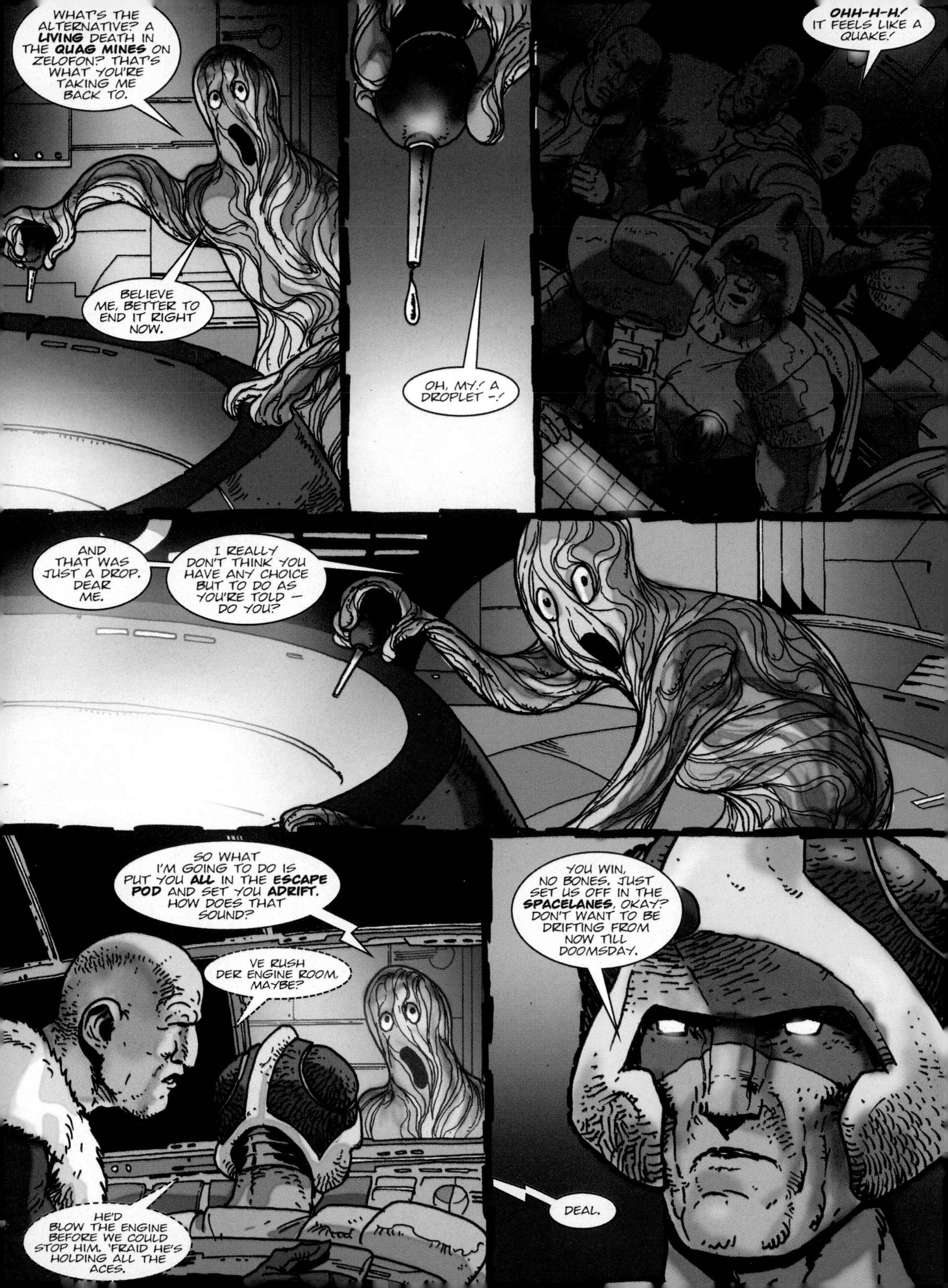
WHAT'S THE ALTERNATIVE? A LIVING DEATH IN THE QUAG MINES ON ZELOFON? THAT'S WHAT YOU'RE TAKING ME BACK TO.
BELIEVE ME, BETTER TO END IT RIGHT NOW.
OH, MY! A DROPLET -!
OHH-H-H! IT FEELS LIKE A QUAKE!
AND THAT WAS JUST A DROP. DEAR ME.
I REALLY DON'T THINK YOU HAVE ANY CHOICE BUT TO DO AS YOU'RE TOLD — DO YOU?
SO WHAT I'M GOING TO DO IS PUT YOU ALL IN THE ESCAPE POD AND SET YOU ADRIFT. HOW DOES THAT SOUND?
VE RUSH DER ENGINE ROOM, MAYBE?
HE'D BLOW THE ENGINE BEFORE WE COULD STOP HIM. 'FRAID HE'S HOLDING ALL THE ACES.
YOU WIN, NO BONES. JUST SET US OFF IN THE SPACELANES, OKAY? DON'T WANT TO BE DRIFTING FROM NOW TILL DOOMSDAY.
DEAL.

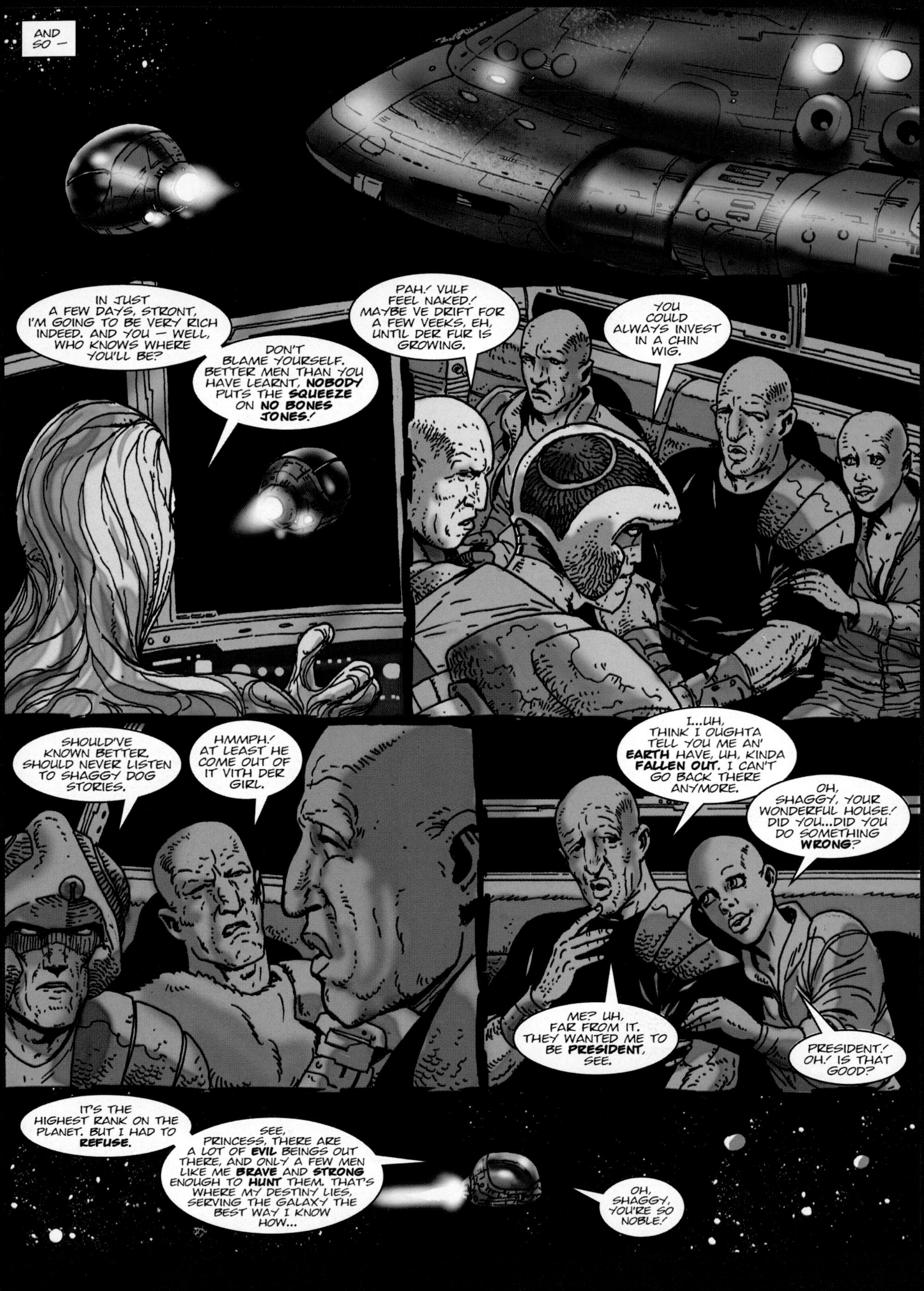
AND SO —
IN JUST A FEW DAYS, STRONT, I'M GOING TO BE VERY RICH INDEED. AND YOU — WELL, WHO KNOWS WHERE YOU'LL BE?
DON'T BLAME YOURSELF. BETTER MEN THAN YOU HAVE LEARNT, NOBODY PUTS THE SQUEEZE ON NO BONES JONES!
PAH! VULF FEEL NAKED! MAYBE VE DRIFT FOR A FEW VEEKS, EH, UNTIL DER FUR IS GROWING.
YOU COULD ALWAYS INVEST IN A CHIN WIG.
SHOULD'VE KNOWN BETTER. SHOULD NEVER LISTEN TO SHAGGY DOG STORIES.
HMMPH! AT LEAST HE COME OUT OF IT VITH DER GIRL.
I...UH, THINK I OUGHTA TELL YOU ME AN' EARTH HAVE, UH, KINDA FALLEN OUT. I CAN'T GO BACK THERE ANYMORE.
OH, SHAGGY, YOUR WONDERFUL HOUSE! DID YOU...DID YOU DO SOMETHING WRONG?
ME? UH, FAR FROM IT. THEY WANTED ME TO BE PRESIDENT, SEE.
PRESIDENT! OH! IS THAT GOOD?
IT'S THE HIGHEST RANK ON THE PLANET. BUT I HAD TO REFUSE.
SEE, PRINCESS, THERE ARE A LOT OF EVIL BEINGS OUT THERE, AND ONLY A FEW MEN LIKE ME BRAVE AND STRONG ENOUGH TO HUNT THEM. THAT'S WHERE MY DESTINY LIES, SERVING THE GALAXY THE BEST WAY I KNOW HOW...
OH, SHAGGY, YOU'RE SO NOBLE!

THE GLUM AFFAIR

Script: John Wagner
Art: Carlos Ezquerra
Letters: Ellie De Ville

Originally published in *2000 AD* Progs 2008, 1567-1576

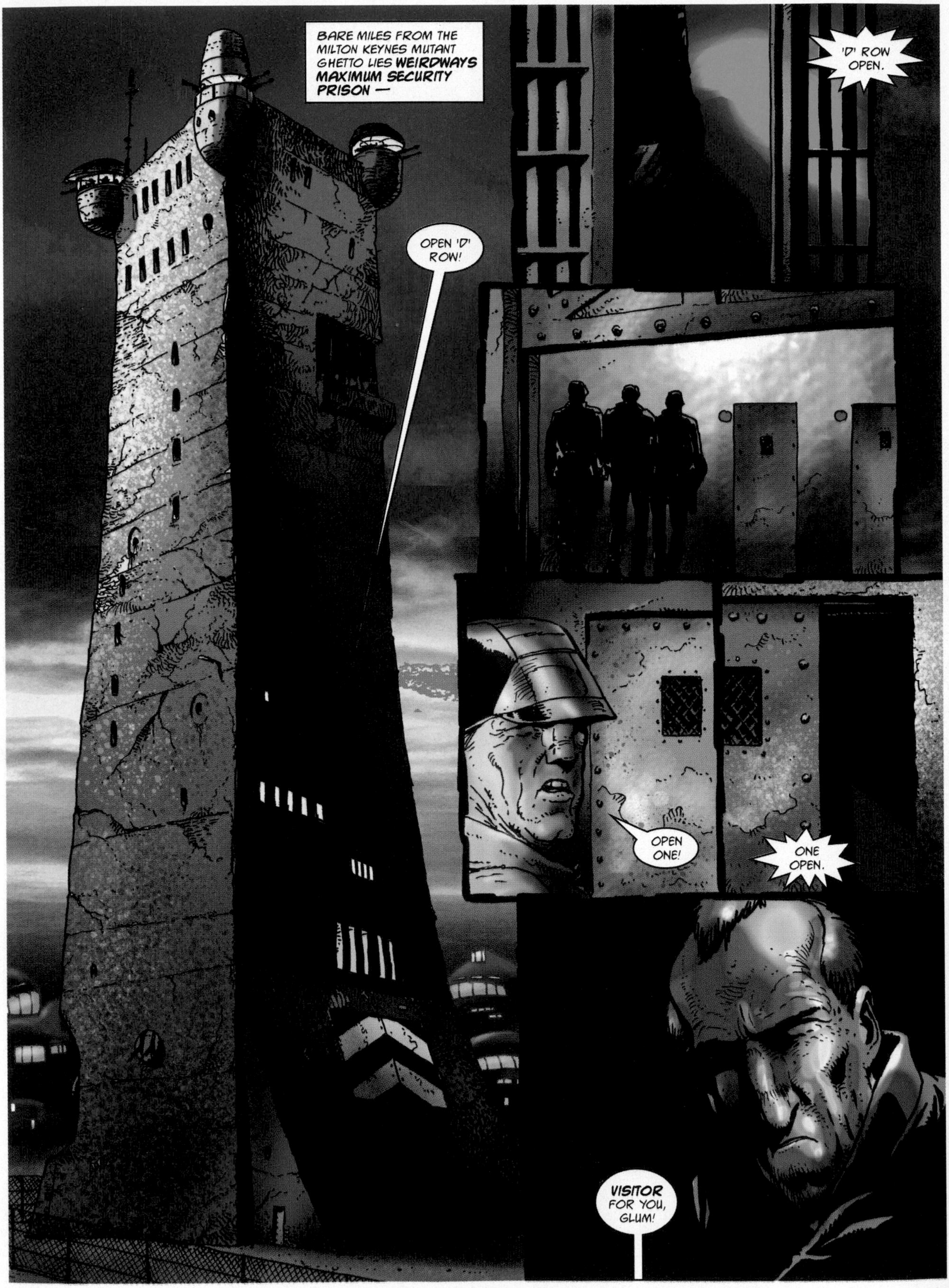
BARE MILES FROM THE MILTON KEYNES MUTANT GHETTO LIES WEIRDWAYS MAXIMUM SECURITY PRISON —
OPEN 'D' ROW!
'D' ROW OPEN.
OPEN ONE!
ONE OPEN.
VISITOR FOR YOU, GLUM!

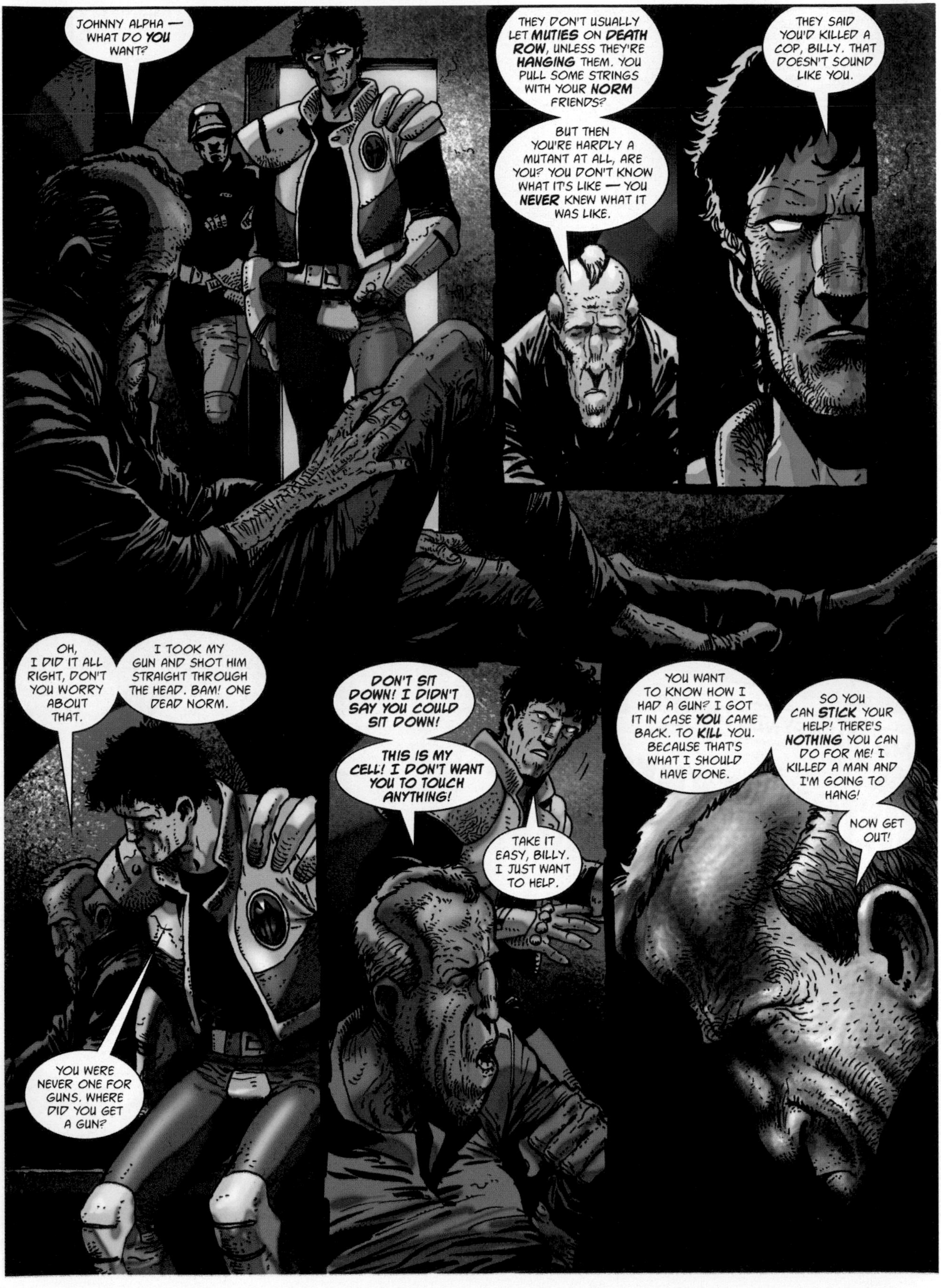
JOHNNY ALPHA — WHAT DO YOU WANT?
THEY DON'T USUALLY LET MUTIES ON DEATH ROW, UNLESS THEY'RE HANGING THEM. YOU PULL SOME STRINGS WITH YOUR NORM FRIENDS?
BUT THEN YOU'RE HARDLY A MUTANT AT ALL, ARE YOU? YOU DON'T KNOW WHAT IT'S LIKE — YOU NEVER KNEW WHAT IT WAS LIKE.
THEY SAID YOU'D KILLED A COP, BILLY. THAT DOESN'T SOUND LIKE YOU.
OH, I DID IT ALL RIGHT, DON'T YOU WORRY ABOUT THAT.
I TOOK MY GUN AND SHOT HIM STRAIGHT THROUGH THE HEAD. BAM! ONE DEAD NORM.
YOU WERE NEVER ONE FOR GUNS. WHERE DID YOU GET A GUN?
DON'T SIT DOWN! I DIDN'T SAY YOU COULD SIT DOWN!
THIS IS MY CELL! I DON'T WANT YOU TO TOUCH ANYTHING!
TAKE IT EASY, BILLY. I JUST WANT TO HELP.
YOU WANT TO KNOW HOW I HAD A GUN? I GOT IT IN CASE YOU CAME BACK. TO KILL YOU. BECAUSE THAT'S WHAT I SHOULD HAVE DONE.
SO YOU CAN STICK YOUR HELP! THERE'S NOTHING YOU CAN DO FOR ME! I KILLED A MAN AND I'M GOING TO HANG!
NOW GET OUT!

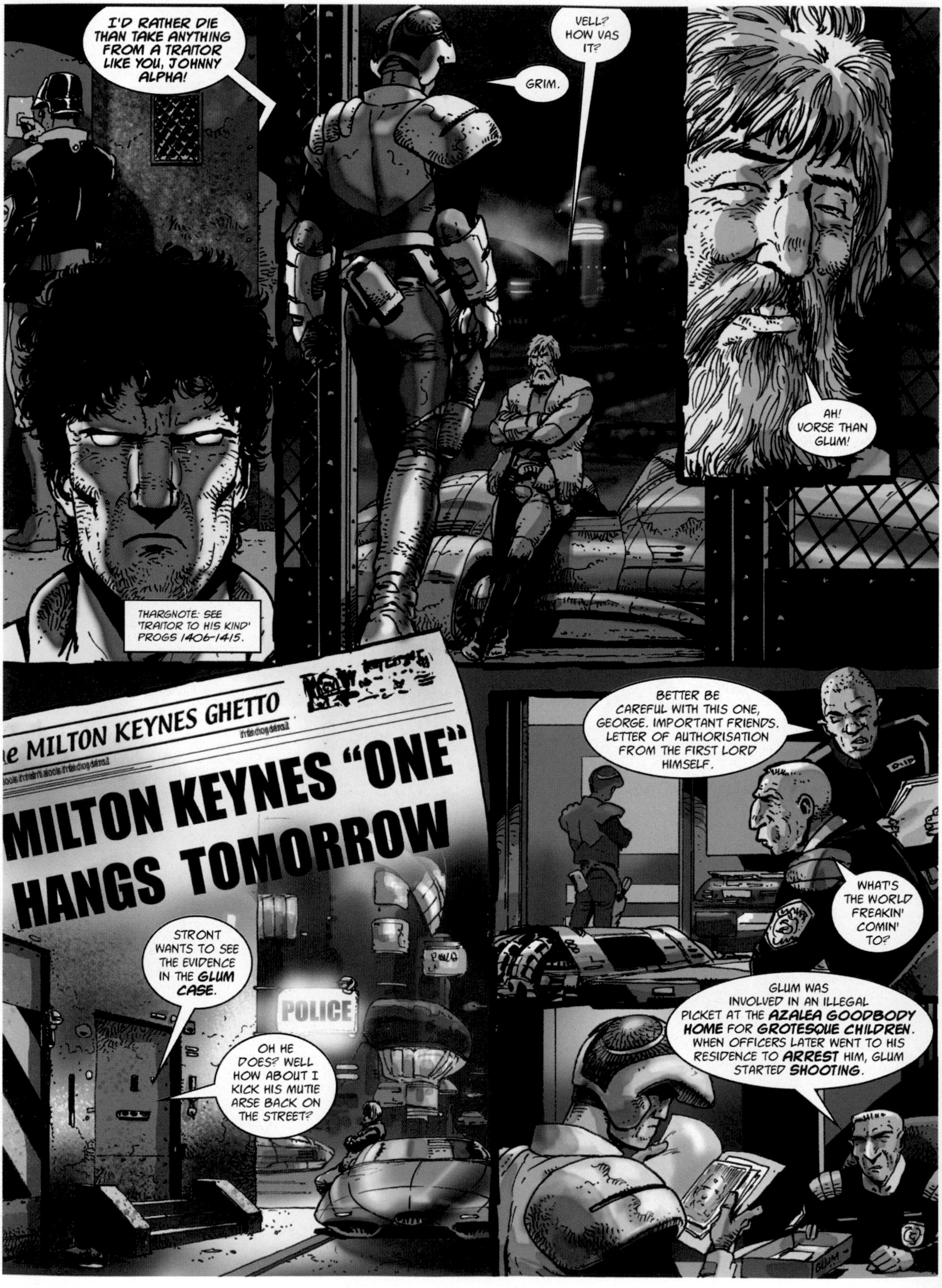
I'D RATHER DIE THAN TAKE ANYTHING FROM A TRAITOR LIKE YOU, JOHNNY ALPHA!
THARGNOTE: SEE 'TRAITOR TO HIS KIND' PROGS 1406-1415.
VELL? HOW VAS IT?
GRIM.
AH! VORSE THAN GLUM!
The MILTON KEYNES GHETTO
MILTON KEYNES "ONE" HANGS TOMORROW
STRONT WANTS TO SEE THE EVIDENCE IN THE GLUM CASE.
POLICE
OH HE DOES? WELL HOW ABOUT I KICK HIS MUTIE ARSE BACK ON THE STREET?
BETTER BE CAREFUL WITH THIS ONE, GEORGE. IMPORTANT FRIENDS. LETTER OF AUTHORISATION FROM THE FIRST LORD HIMSELF.
WHAT'S THE WORLD FREAKIN' COMIN' TO?
GLUM WAS INVOLVED IN AN ILLEGAL PICKET AT THE AZALEA GOODBODY HOME FOR GROTESQUE CHILDREN. WHEN OFFICERS LATER WENT TO HIS RESIDENCE TO ARREST HIM, GLUM STARTED SHOOTING.

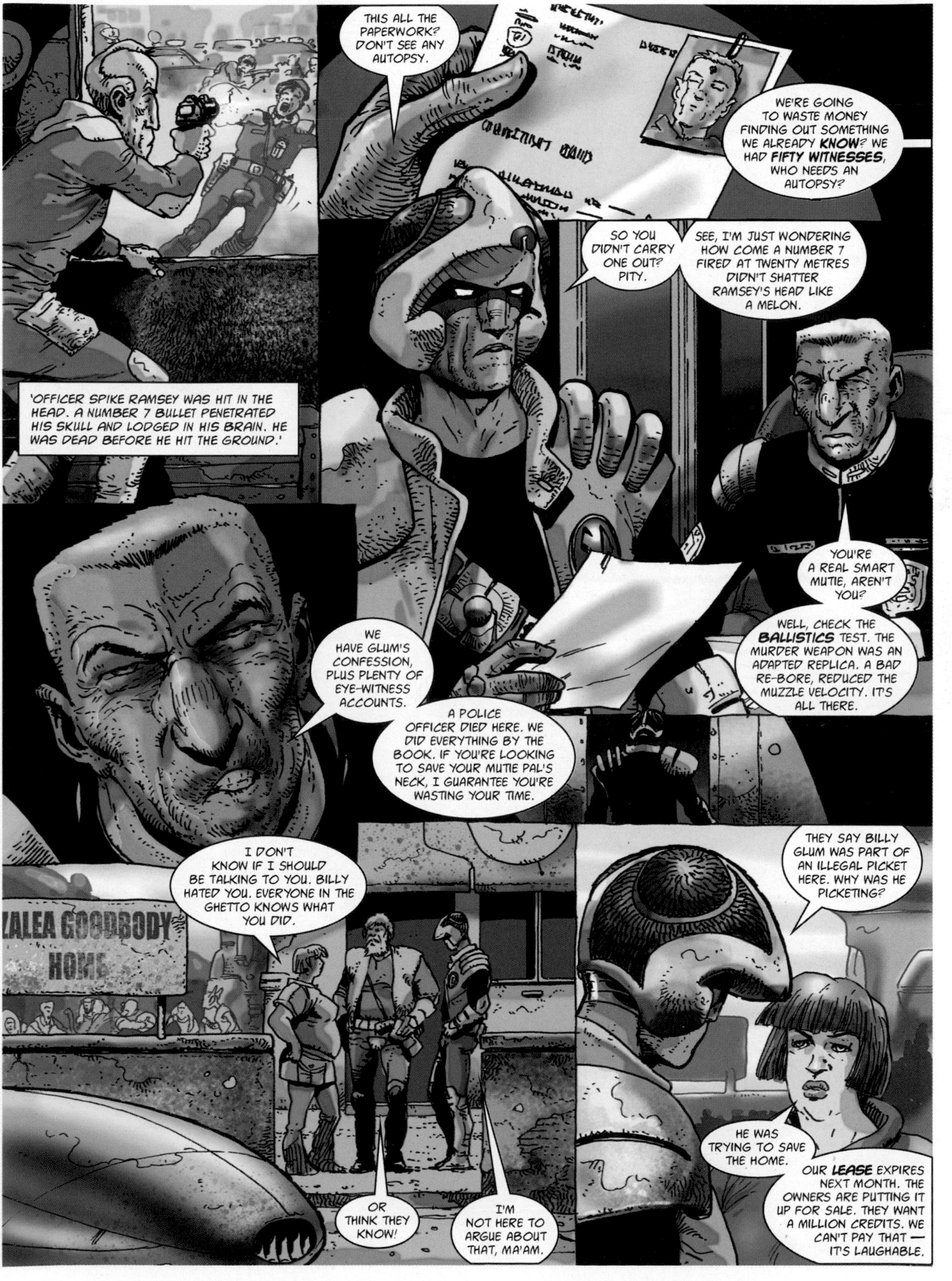
THIS ALL THE PAPERWORK? DON'T SEE ANY AUTOPSY.
WE'RE GOING TO WASTE MONEY FINDING OUT SOMETHING WE ALREADY KNOW? WE HAD FIFTY WITNESSES, WHO NEEDS AN AUTOPSY?
'OFFICER SPIKE RAMSEY WAS HIT IN THE HEAD. A NUMBER 7 BULLET PENETRATED HIS SKULL AND LODGED IN HIS BRAIN. HE WAS DEAD BEFORE HE HIT THE GROUND.'
SO YOU DIDN'T CARRY ONE OUT? PITY.
SEE, I'M JUST WONDERING HOW COME A NUMBER 7 FIRED AT TWENTY METRES DIDN'T SHATTER RAMSEY'S HEAD LIKE A MELON.
YOU'RE A REAL SMART MUTIE, AREN'T YOU?
WELL, CHECK THE BALLISTICS TEST. THE MURDER WEAPON WAS AN ADAPTED REPLICA. A BAD RE-BORE, REDUCED THE MUZZLE VELOCITY. IT'S ALL THERE.
WE HAVE GLUM'S CONFESSION, PLUS PLENTY OF EYE-WITNESS ACCOUNTS.
A POLICE OFFICER DIED HERE. WE DID EVERYTHING BY THE BOOK. IF YOU'RE LOOKING TO SAVE YOUR MUTIE PAL'S NECK, I GUARANTEE YOU'RE WASTING YOUR TIME.
I DON'T KNOW IF I SHOULD BE TALKING TO YOU. BILLY HATED YOU. EVERYONE IN THE GHETTO KNOWS WHAT YOU DID.
ZALEA GOODBODY HOME
OR THINK THEY KNOW!
I'M NOT HERE TO ARGUE ABOUT THAT, MA'AM.
THEY SAY BILLY GLUM WAS PART OF AN ILLEGAL PICKET HERE. WHY WAS HE PICKETING?
HE WAS TRYING TO SAVE THE HOME.
OUR LEASE EXPIRES NEXT MONTH. THE OWNERS ARE PUTTING IT UP FOR SALE. THEY WANT A MILLION CREDITS. WE CAN'T PAY THAT — IT'S LAUGHABLE.

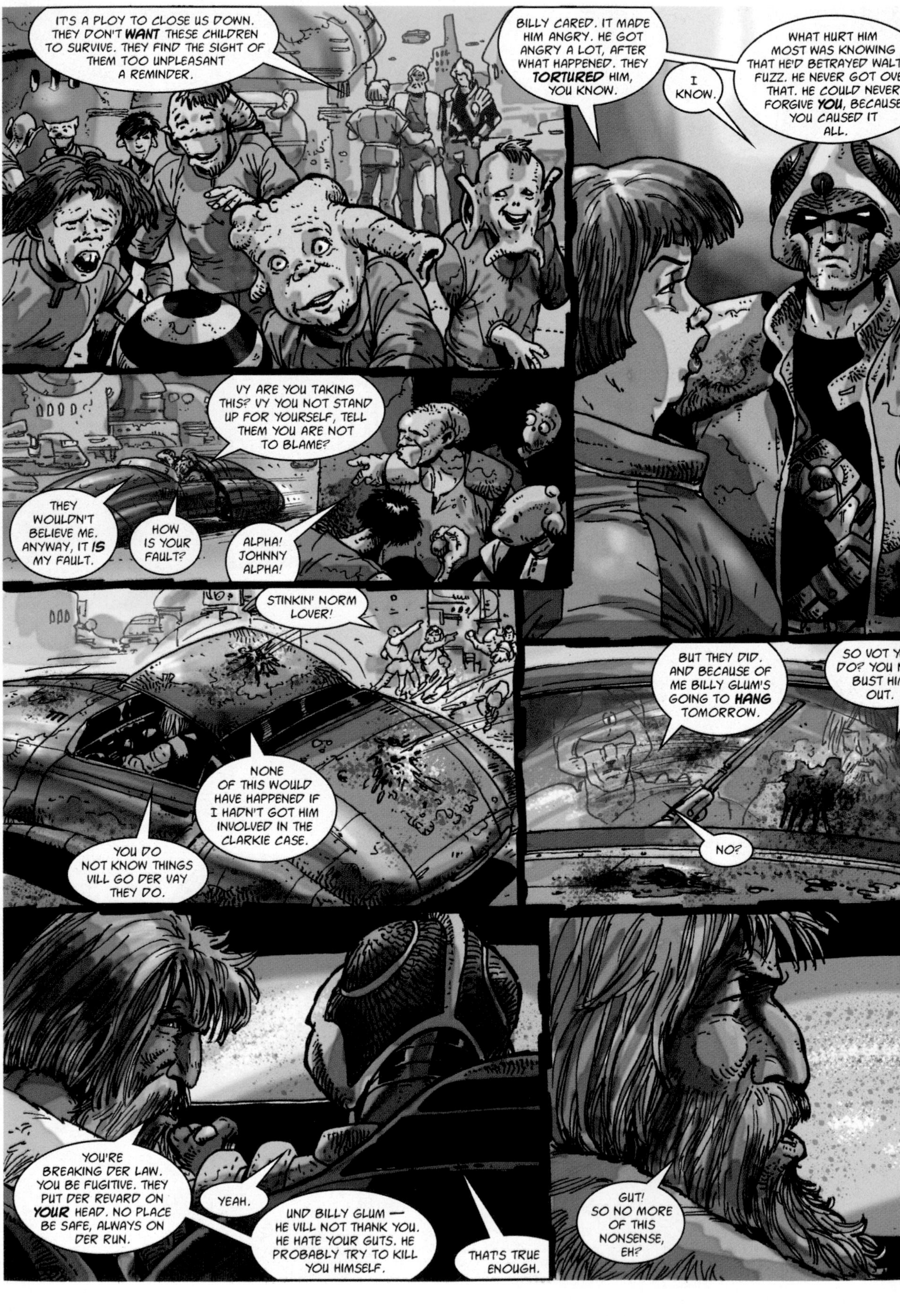
IT'S A PLOY TO CLOSE US DOWN. THEY DON'T **WANT** THESE CHILDREN TO SURVIVE. THEY FIND THE SIGHT OF THEM TOO UNPLEASANT A REMINDER.
BILLY CARED. IT MADE HIM ANGRY. HE GOT ANGRY A LOT, AFTER WHAT HAPPENED. THEY **TORTURED** HIM, YOU KNOW.
I KNOW.
WHAT HURT HIM MOST WAS KNOWING THAT HE'D BETRAYED WALTON FUZZ. HE NEVER GOT OVER THAT. HE COULD NEVER FORGIVE **YOU**, BECAUSE YOU CAUSED IT ALL.
VY ARE YOU TAKING THIS? VY YOU NOT STAND UP FOR YOURSELF, TELL THEM YOU ARE NOT TO BLAME?
THEY WOULDN'T BELIEVE ME. ANYWAY, IT **IS** MY FAULT.
HOW IS YOUR FAULT?
ALPHA! JOHNNY ALPHA!
STINKIN' NORM LOVER!
NONE OF THIS WOULD HAVE HAPPENED IF I HADN'T GOT HIM INVOLVED IN THE CLARKIE CASE.
YOU DO NOT KNOW THINGS VILL GO DER VAY THEY DO.
BUT THEY DID. AND BECAUSE OF ME BILLY GLUM'S GOING TO **HANG** TOMORROW.
SO VOT YOU DO? YOU NOT BUST HIM OUT.
NO?
YOU'RE BREAKING DER LAW. YOU BE FUGITIVE. THEY PUT DER REVARD ON **YOUR** HEAD. NO PLACE BE SAFE, ALWAYS ON DER RUN.
YEAH.
UND BILLY GLUM — HE VILL NOT THANK YOU. HE HATE YOUR GUTS. HE PROBABLY TRY TO KILL YOU HIMSELF.
THAT'S TRUE ENOUGH.
GUT! SO NO MORE OF THIS NONSENSE, EH?

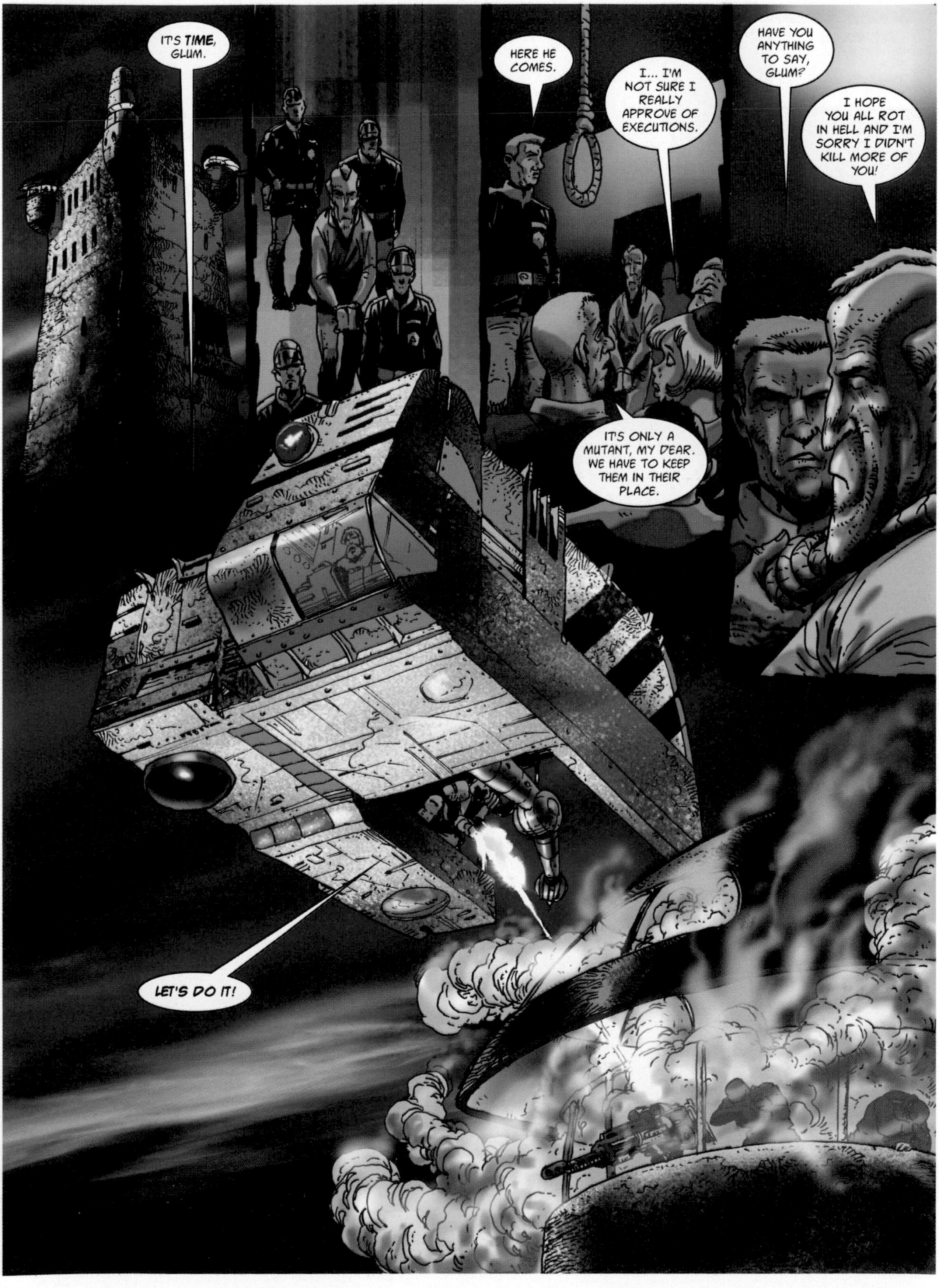
IT'S TIME, GLUM.
HERE HE COMES.
I... I'M NOT SURE I REALLY APPROVE OF EXECUTIONS.
HAVE YOU ANYTHING TO SAY, GLUM?
I HOPE YOU ALL ROT IN HELL AND I'M SORRY I DIDN'T KILL MORE OF YOU!
IT'S ONLY A MUTANT, MY DEAR. WE HAVE TO KEEP THEM IN THEIR PLACE.
LET'S DO IT!

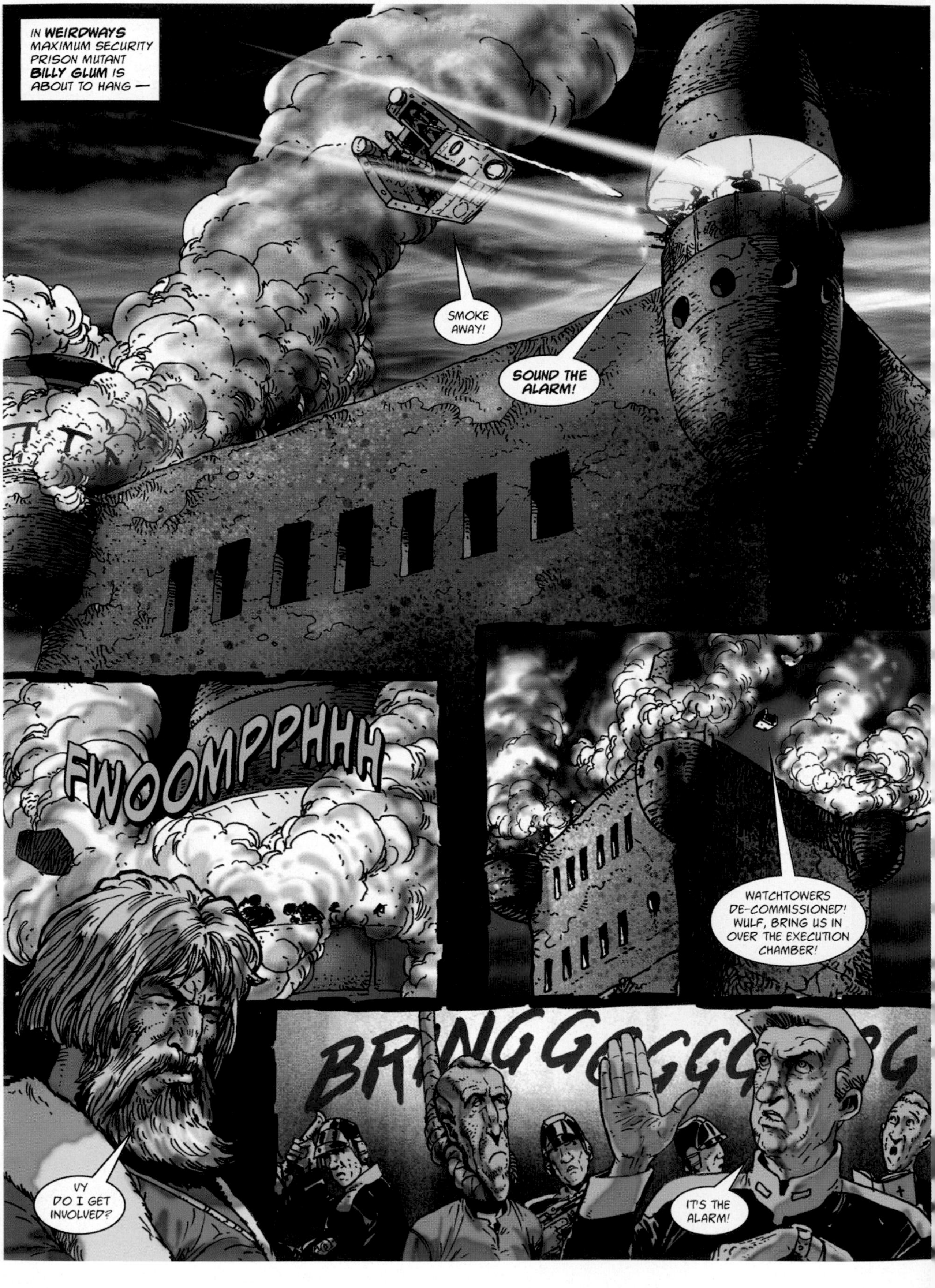

IN WEIRDWAYS MAXIMUM SECURITY PRISON MUTANT BILLY GLUM IS ABOUT TO HANG —
SMOKE AWAY!
SOUND THE ALARM!
FWOOMPPHHH
WATCHTOWERS DE-COMMISSIONED! WULF, BRING US IN OVER THE EXECUTION CHAMBER!
VY DO I GET INVOLVED?
IT'S THE ALARM!

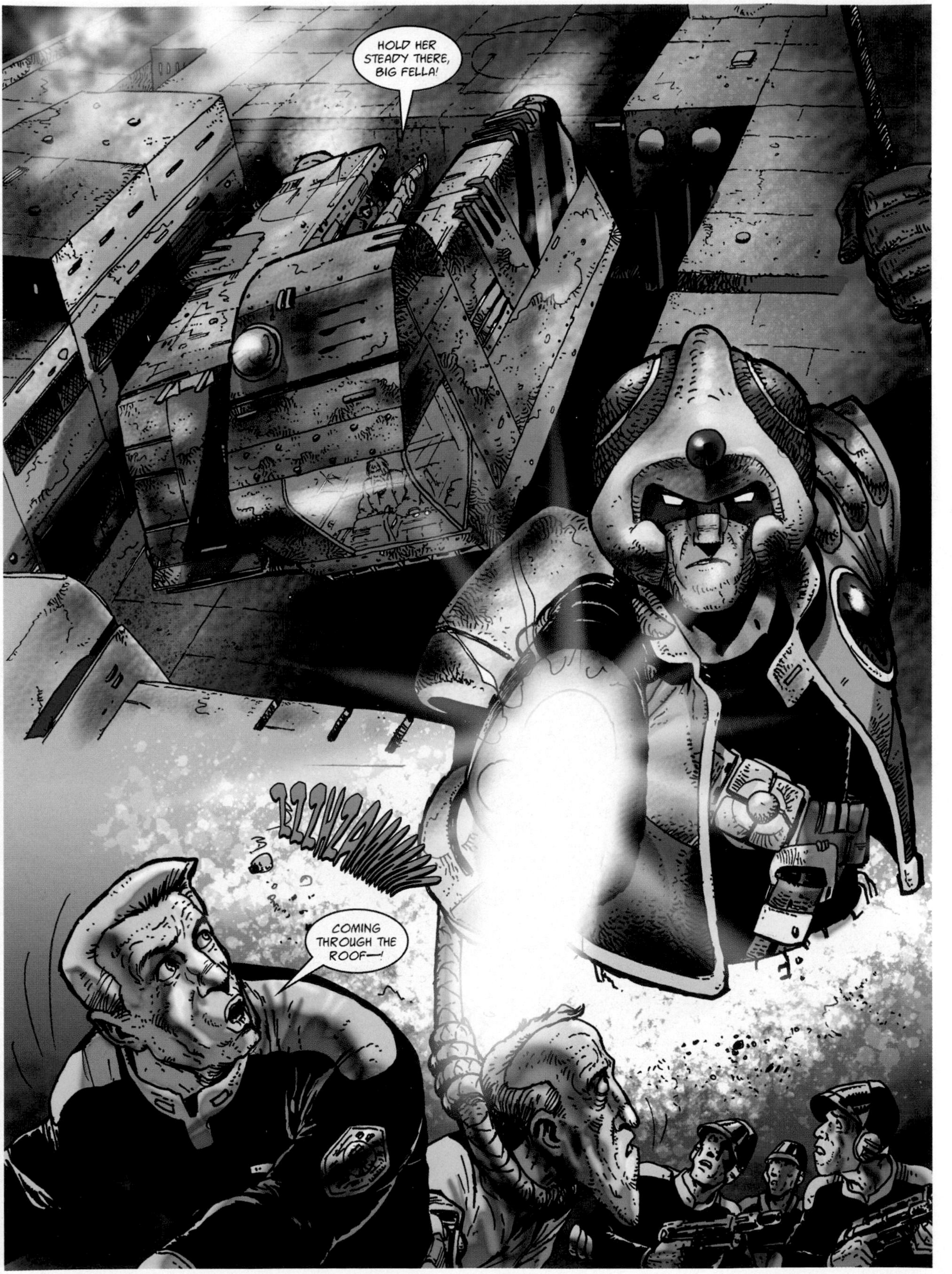
HOLD HER STEADY THERE, BIG FELLA!
ZZZHZAWWWW
COMING THROUGH THE ROOF—!

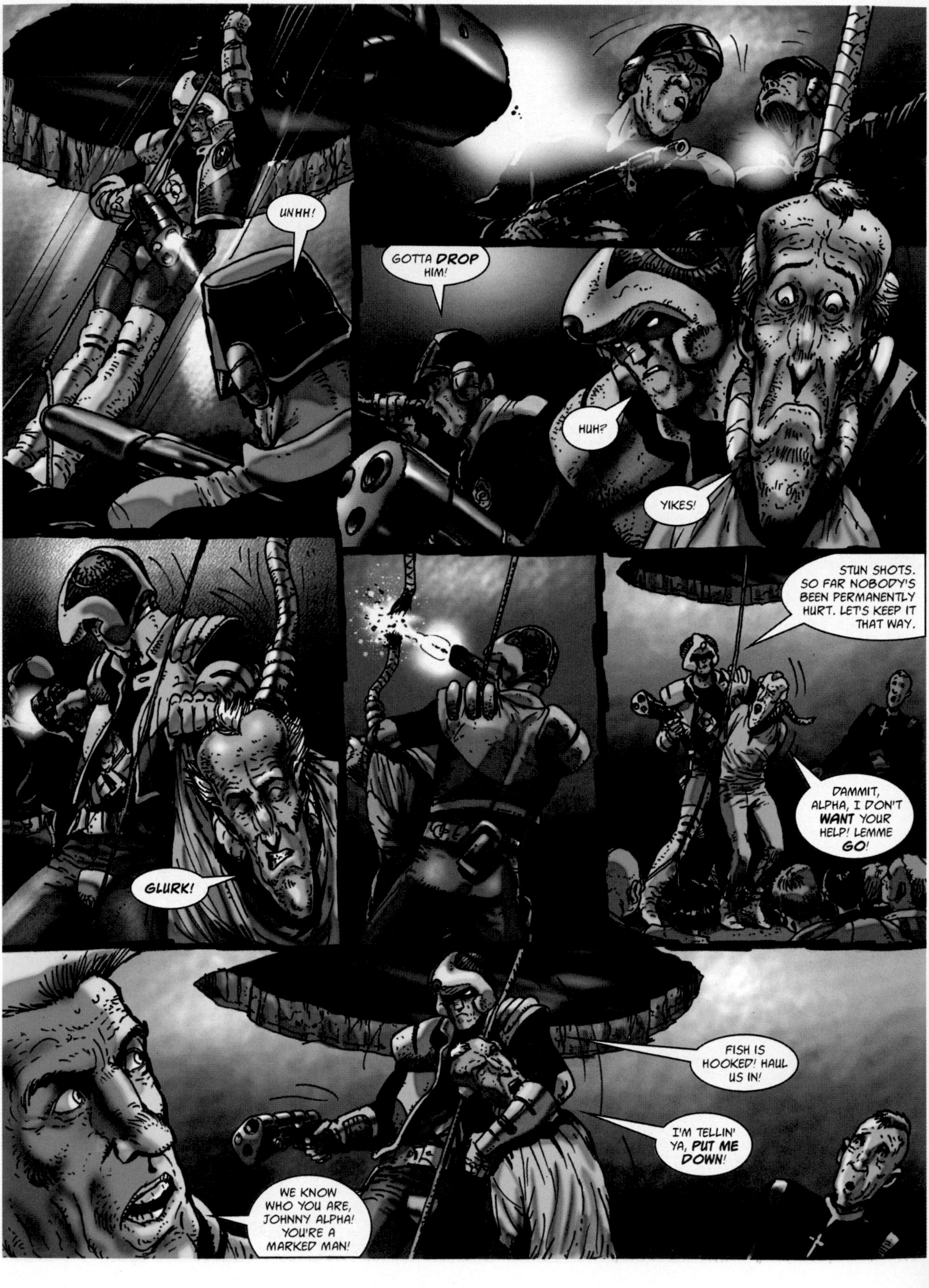
UNHH!
GOTTA DROP HIM!
HUH?
YIKES!
GLURK!
STUN SHOTS. SO FAR NOBODY'S BEEN PERMANENTLY HURT. LET'S KEEP IT THAT WAY.
DAMMIT, ALPHA, I DON'T WANT YOUR HELP! LEMME GO!
FISH IS HOOKED! HAUL US IN!
I'M TELLIN' YA, PUT ME DOWN!
WE KNOW WHO YOU ARE, JOHNNY ALPHA! YOU'RE A MARKED MAN!

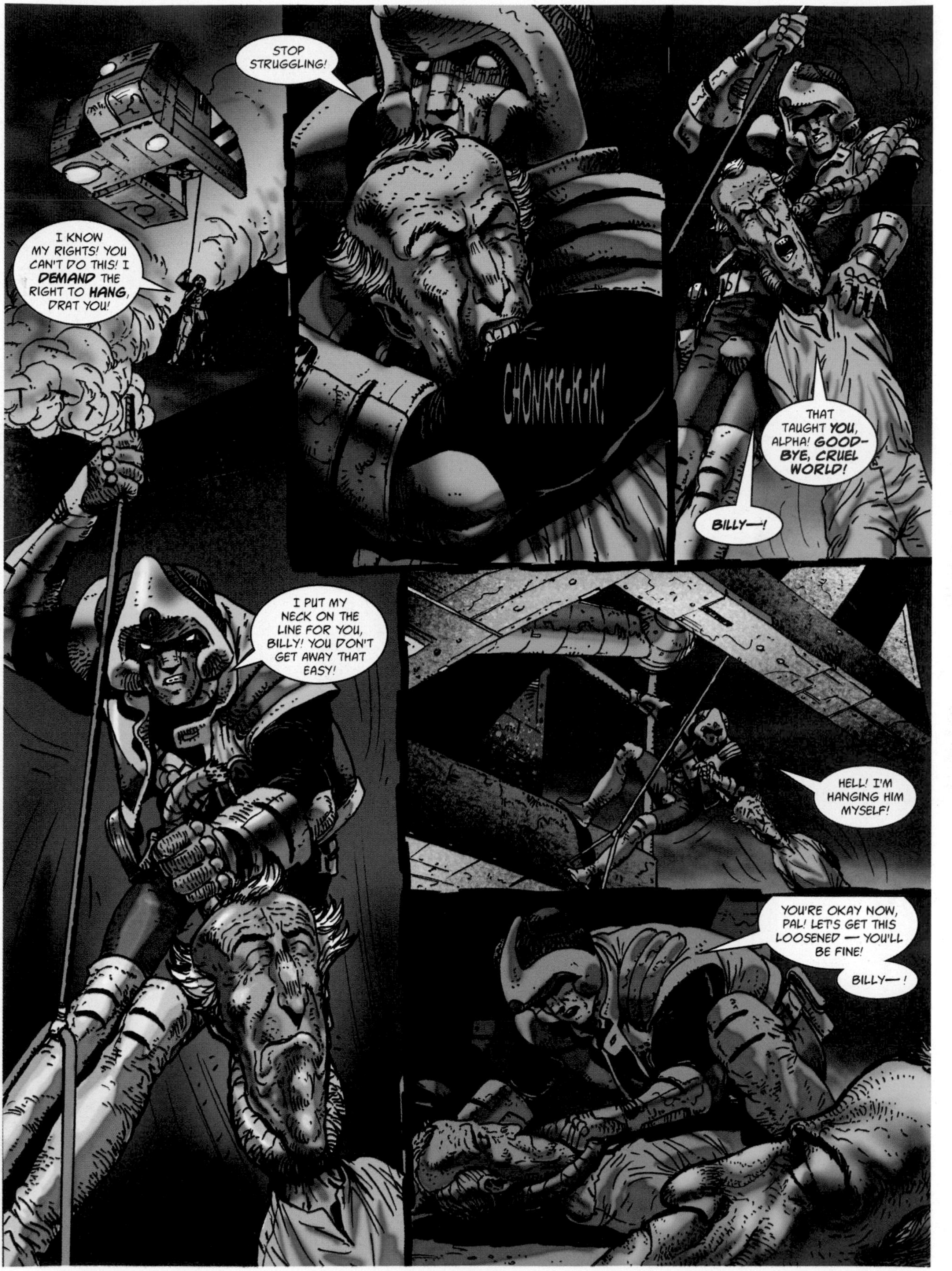
I KNOW MY RIGHTS! YOU CAN'T DO THIS! I **DEMAND** THE RIGHT TO **HANG**, DRAT YOU!
STOP STRUGGLING!
CHONKKK-K-K!
THAT TAUGHT **YOU**, ALPHA! **GOOD-BYE, CRUEL WORLD!**
BILLY—!
I PUT MY NECK ON THE LINE FOR YOU, BILLY! YOU DON'T GET AWAY THAT EASY!
HELL! I'M HANGING HIM MYSELF!
YOU'RE OKAY NOW, PAL! LET'S GET THIS LOOSENED — YOU'LL BE FINE!
BILLY—!

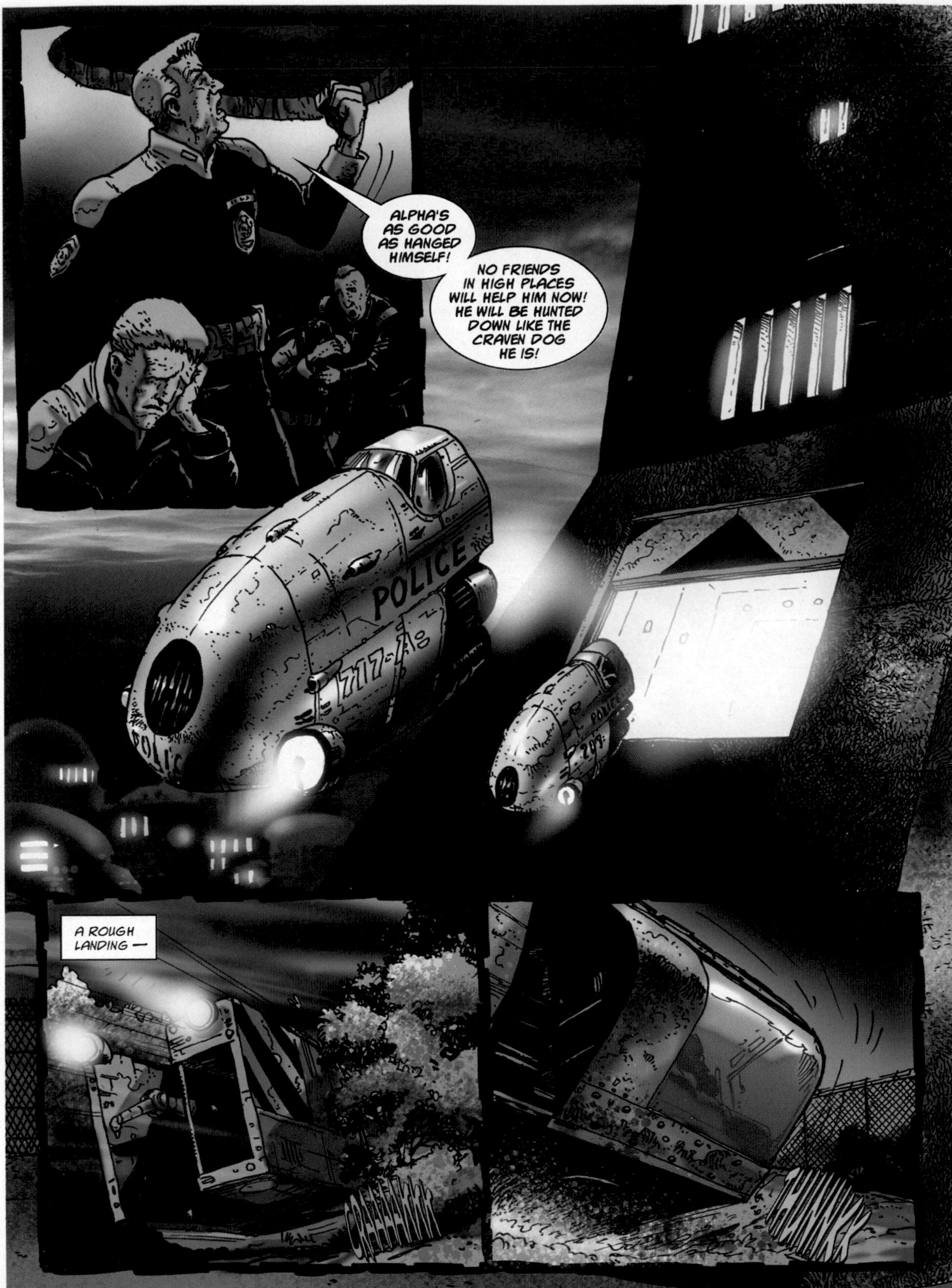
ALPHA'S AS GOOD AS HANGED HIMSELF!
NO FRIENDS IN HIGH PLACES WILL HELP HIM NOW! HE WILL BE HUNTED DOWN LIKE THE CRAVEN DOG HE IS!
POLICE
7717-Z
A ROUGH LANDING —
CRAAAAKKK
THUNKKK

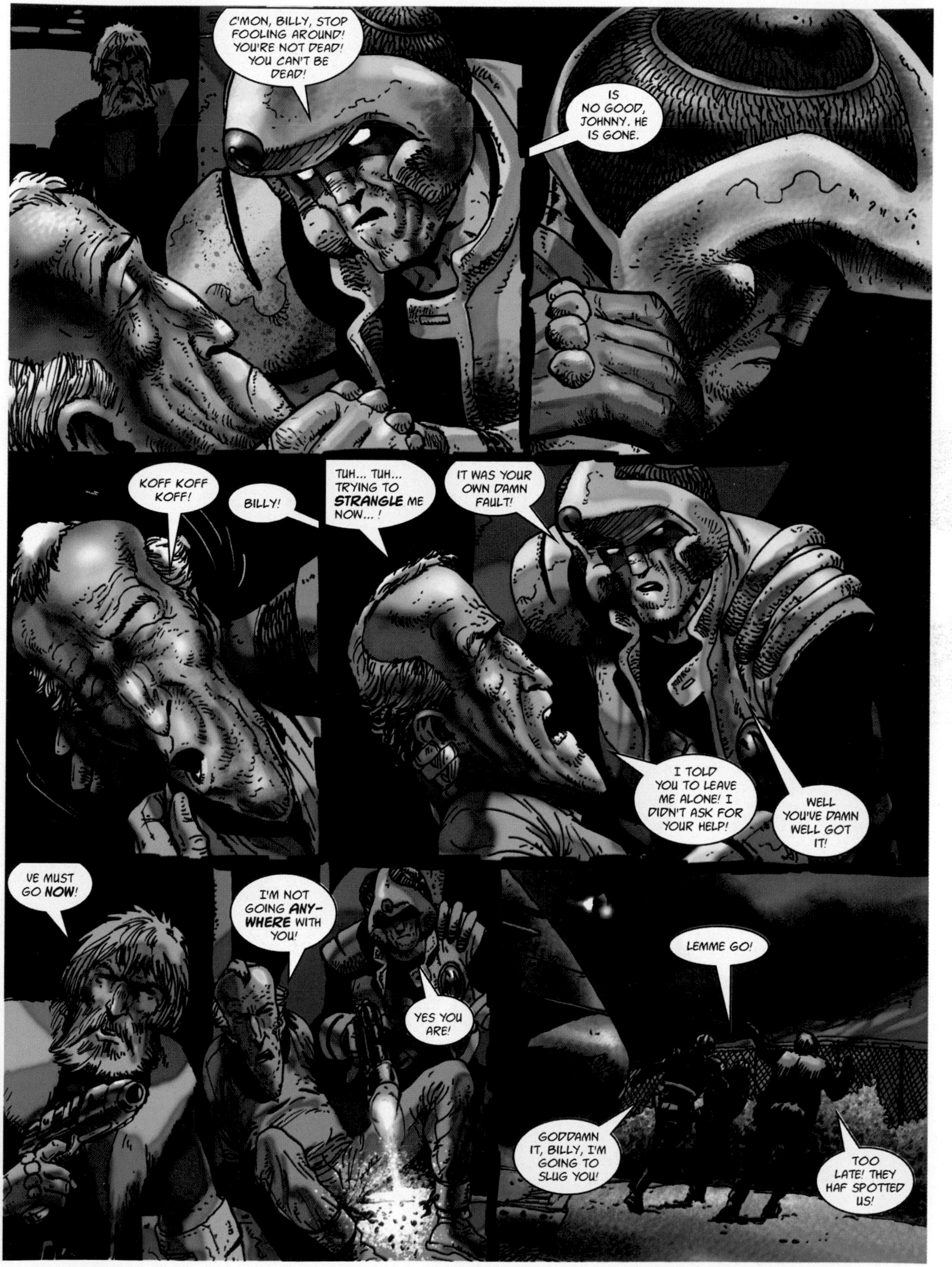

C'MON, BILLY, STOP FOOLING AROUND! YOU'RE NOT DEAD! YOU CAN'T BE DEAD!
IS NO GOOD, JOHNNY. HE IS GONE.
KOFF KOFF KOFF!
BILLY!
TUH... TUH... TRYING TO **STRANGLE** ME NOW... !
IT WAS YOUR OWN DAMN FAULT!
I TOLD YOU TO LEAVE ME ALONE! I DIDN'T ASK FOR YOUR HELP!
WELL YOU'VE DAMN WELL GOT IT!
VE MUST GO **NOW**!
I'M NOT GOING **ANY-WHERE** WITH YOU!
YES YOU ARE!
LEMME GO!
GODDAMN IT, BILLY, I'M GOING TO SLUG YOU!
TOO LATE! THEY HAF SPOTTED US!

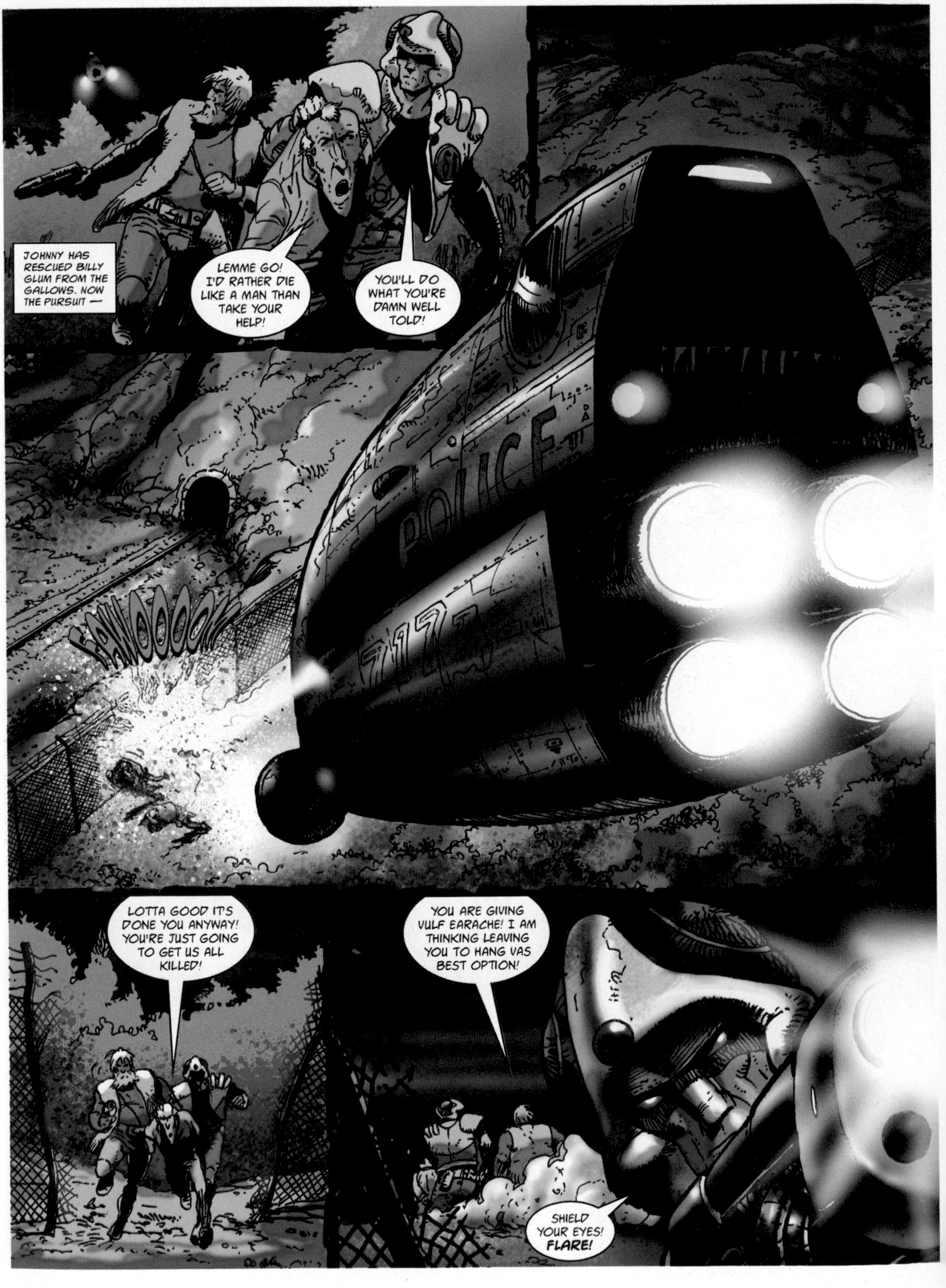
JOHNNY HAS RESCUED BILLY GLUM FROM THE GALLOWS. NOW THE PURSUIT —
LEMME GO! I'D RATHER DIE LIKE A MAN THAN TAKE YOUR HELP!
YOU'LL DO WHAT YOU'RE DAMN WELL TOLD!
POLICE
LOTTA GOOD IT'S DONE YOU ANYWAY! YOU'RE JUST GOING TO GET US ALL KILLED!
YOU ARE GIVING VULF EARACHE! I AM THINKING LEAVING YOU TO HANG VAS BEST OPTION!
SHIELD YOUR EYES! FLARE!

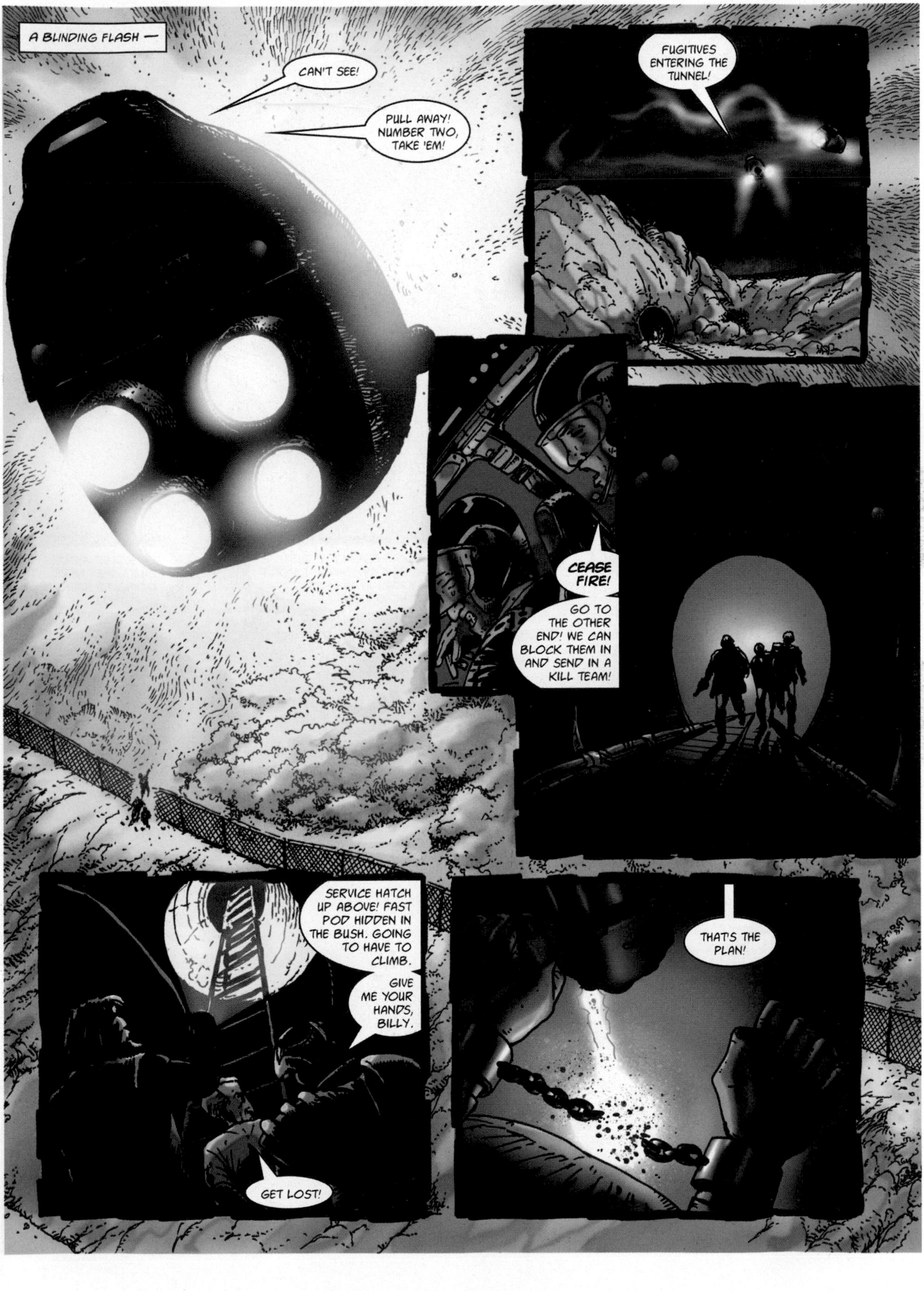
A BLINDING FLASH —
CAN'T SEE!
PULL AWAY! NUMBER TWO, TAKE 'EM!
FUGITIVES ENTERING THE TUNNEL!
CEASE FIRE!
GO TO THE OTHER END! WE CAN BLOCK THEM IN AND SEND IN A KILL TEAM!
SERVICE HATCH UP ABOVE! FAST POD HIDDEN IN THE BUSH. GOING TO HAVE TO CLIMB.
GIVE ME YOUR HANDS, BILLY.
GET LOST!
THAT'S THE PLAN!

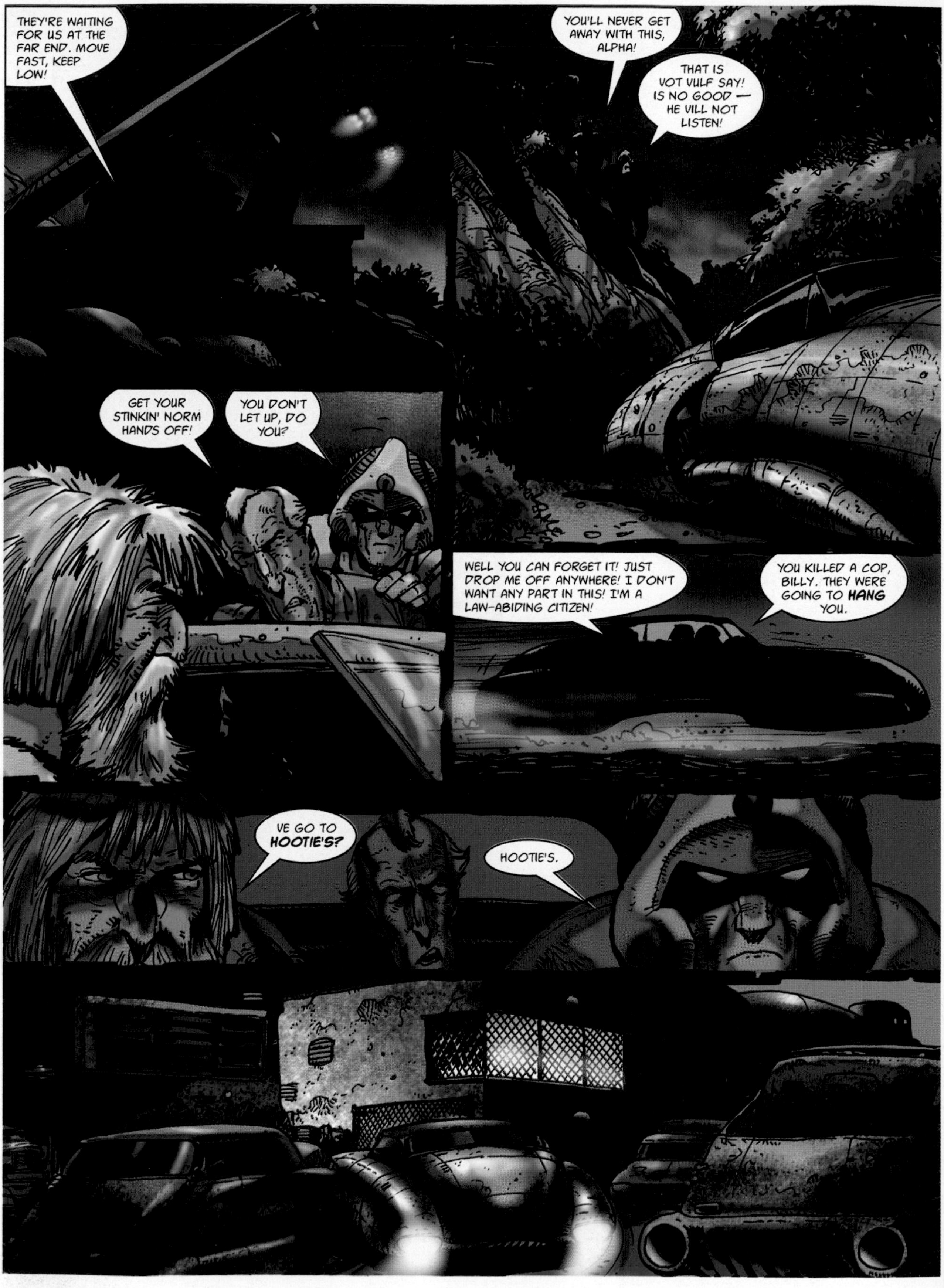
THEY'RE WAITING FOR US AT THE FAR END. MOVE FAST, KEEP LOW!
YOU'LL NEVER GET AWAY WITH THIS, ALPHA!
THAT IS VOT VULF SAY! IS NO GOOD — HE VILL NOT LISTEN!
GET YOUR STINKIN' NORM HANDS OFF!
YOU DON'T LET UP, DO YOU?
WELL YOU CAN FORGET IT! JUST DROP ME OFF ANYWHERE! I DON'T WANT ANY PART IN THIS! I'M A LAW-ABIDING CITIZEN!
YOU KILLED A COP, BILLY. THEY WERE GOING TO HANG YOU.
VE GO TO HOOTIE'S?
HOOTIE'S.

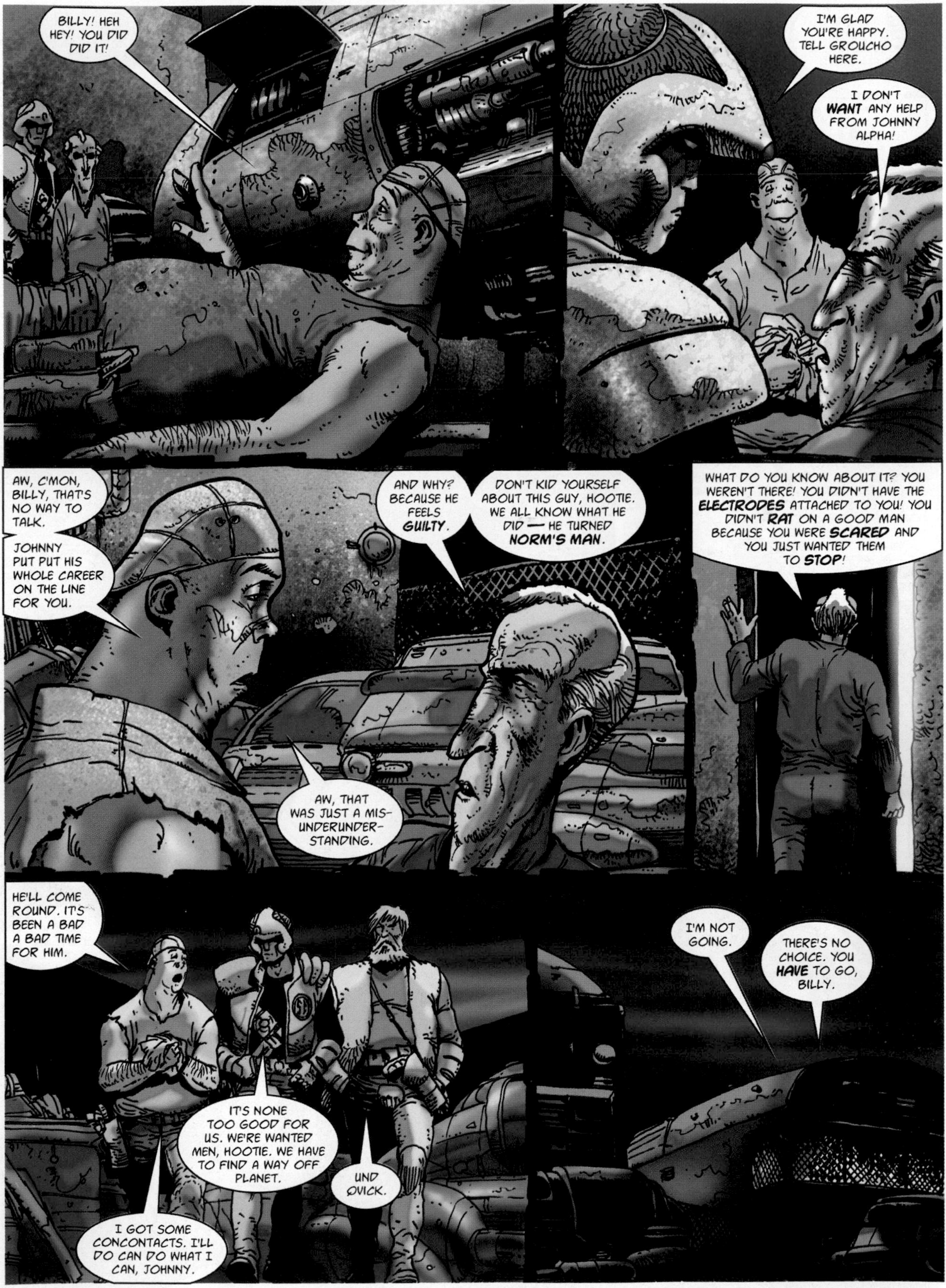
BILLY! HEH HEY! YOU DID DID IT!
I'M GLAD YOU'RE HAPPY. TELL GROUCHO HERE.
I DON'T **WANT** ANY HELP FROM JOHNNY ALPHA!
AW, C'MON, BILLY, THAT'S NO WAY TO TALK.
JOHNNY PUT PUT HIS WHOLE CAREER ON THE LINE FOR YOU.
AND WHY? BECAUSE HE FEELS **GUILTY**.
DON'T KID YOURSELF ABOUT THIS GUY, HOOTIE. WE ALL KNOW WHAT HE DID — HE TURNED **NORM'S MAN**.
AW, THAT WAS JUST A MIS-UNDERUNDER-STANDING.
WHAT DO YOU KNOW ABOUT IT? YOU WEREN'T THERE! YOU DIDN'T HAVE THE **ELECTRODES** ATTACHED TO YOU! YOU DIDN'T **RAT** ON A GOOD MAN BECAUSE YOU WERE **SCARED** AND YOU JUST WANTED THEM TO **STOP**!
HE'LL COME ROUND. IT'S BEEN A BAD A BAD TIME FOR HIM.
IT'S NONE TOO GOOD FOR US. WE'RE WANTED MEN, HOOTIE. WE HAVE TO FIND A WAY OFF PLANET.
UND QVICK.
I GOT SOME CONCONTACTS. I'LL DO CAN DO WHAT I CAN, JOHNNY.
I'M NOT GOING.
THERE'S NO CHOICE. YOU **HAVE** TO GO, BILLY.

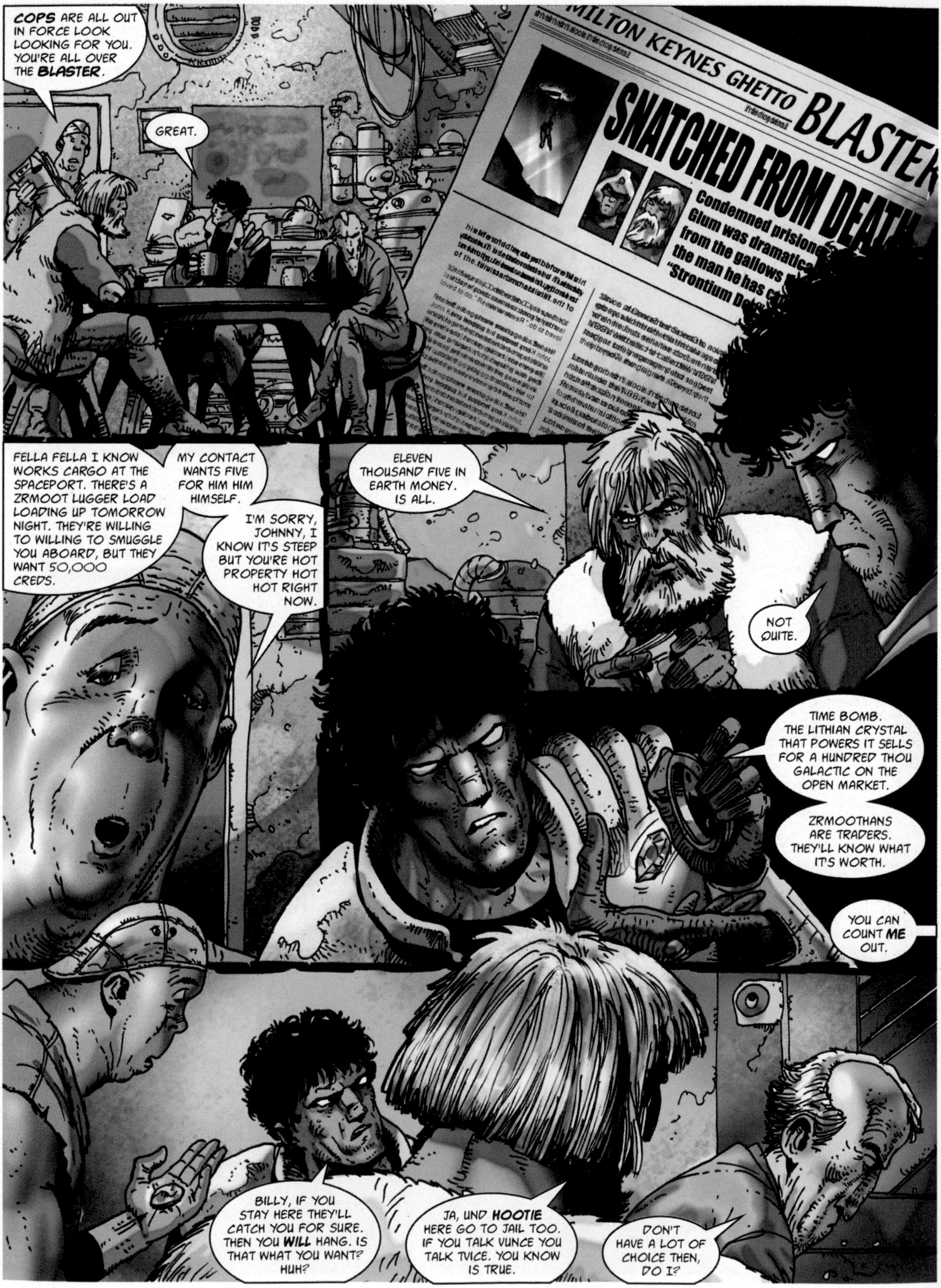
COPS ARE ALL OUT IN FORCE LOOK LOOKING FOR YOU. YOU'RE ALL OVER THE BLASTER.
GREAT.
MILTON KEYNES GHETTO BLASTER
SNATCHED FROM DEAT
FELLA FELLA I KNOW WORKS CARGO AT THE SPACEPORT. THERE'S A ZRMOOT LUGGER LOAD LOADING UP TOMORROW NIGHT. THEY'RE WILLING TO WILLING TO SMUGGLE YOU ABOARD, BUT THEY WANT 50,000 CREDS.
MY CONTACT WANTS FIVE FOR HIM HIM HIMSELF.
I'M SORRY, JOHNNY, I KNOW IT'S STEEP BUT YOU'RE HOT PROPERTY HOT HOT RIGHT NOW.
ELEVEN THOUSAND FIVE IN EARTH MONEY. IS ALL.
NOT QUITE.
TIME BOMB. THE LITHIAN CRYSTAL THAT POWERS IT SELLS FOR A HUNDRED THOU GALACTIC ON THE OPEN MARKET.
ZRMOOTHANS ARE TRADERS. THEY'LL KNOW WHAT IT'S WORTH.
YOU CAN COUNT ME OUT.
BILLY, IF YOU STAY HERE THEY'LL CATCH YOU FOR SURE. THEN YOU WILL HANG. IS THAT WHAT YOU WANT? HUH?
JA, UND HOOTIE HERE GO TO JAIL TOO. IF YOU TALK VUNCE YOU TALK TVICE. YOU KNOW IS TRUE.
DON'T HAVE A LOT OF CHOICE THEN, DO I?

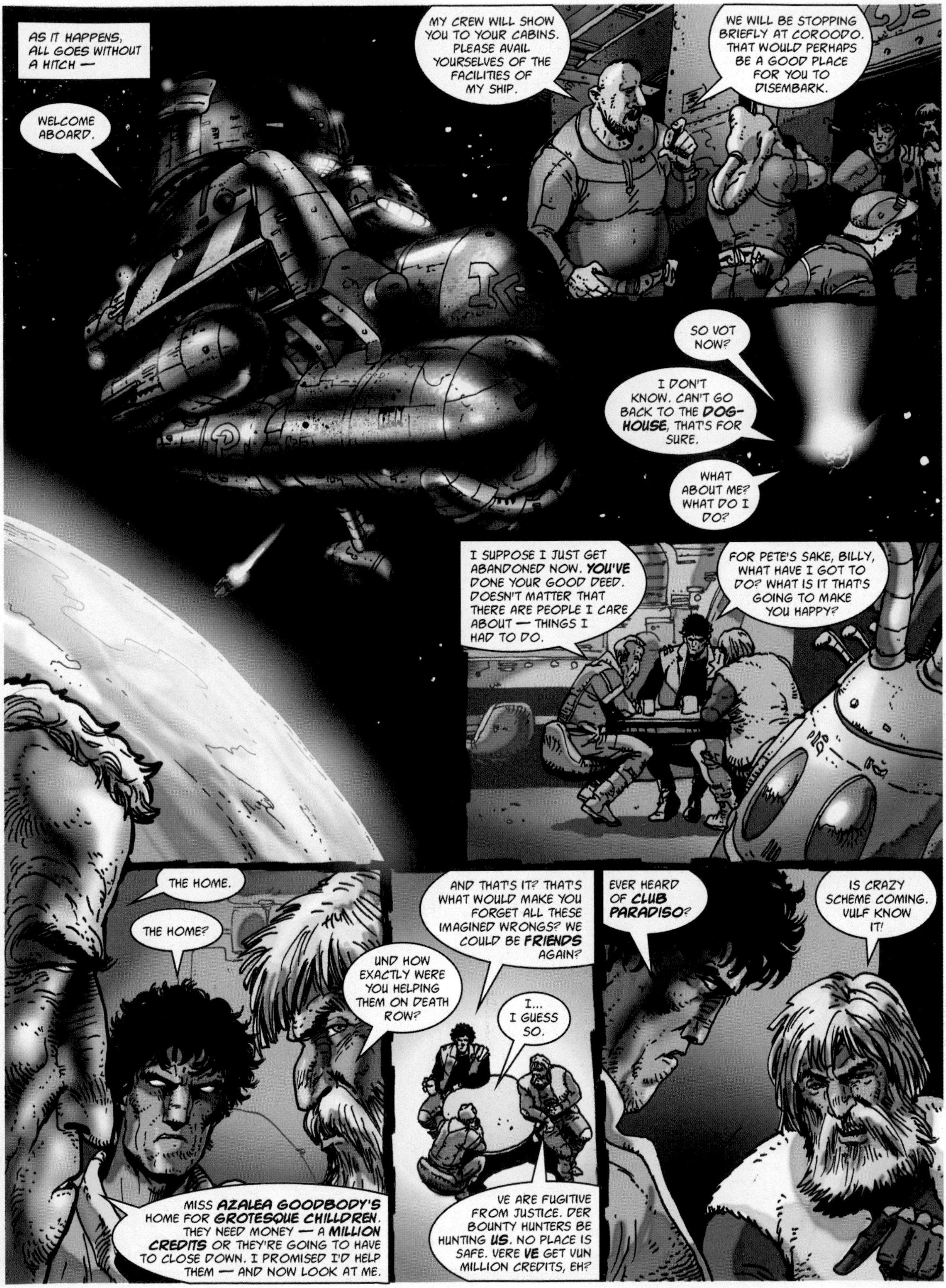
AS IT HAPPENS, ALL GOES WITHOUT A HITCH —
WELCOME ABOARD.
MY CREW WILL SHOW YOU TO YOUR CABINS. PLEASE AVAIL YOURSELVES OF THE FACILITIES OF MY SHIP.
WE WILL BE STOPPING BRIEFLY AT COROODO. THAT WOULD PERHAPS BE A GOOD PLACE FOR YOU TO DISEMBARK.
SO VOT NOW?
I DON'T KNOW. CAN'T GO BACK TO THE DOG-HOUSE, THAT'S FOR SURE.
WHAT ABOUT ME? WHAT DO I DO?
I SUPPOSE I JUST GET ABANDONED NOW. YOU'VE DONE YOUR GOOD DEED. DOESN'T MATTER THAT THERE ARE PEOPLE I CARE ABOUT — THINGS I HAD TO DO.
FOR PETE'S SAKE, BILLY, WHAT HAVE I GOT TO DO? WHAT IS IT THAT'S GOING TO MAKE YOU HAPPY?
THE HOME.
THE HOME?
UND HOW EXACTLY WERE YOU HELPING THEM ON DEATH ROW?
MISS AZALEA GOODBODY'S HOME FOR GROTESQUE CHILLDREN. THEY NEED MONEY — A MILLION CREDITS OR THEY'RE GOING TO HAVE TO CLOSE DOWN. I PROMISED I'D HELP THEM — AND NOW LOOK AT ME.
AND THAT'S IT? THAT'S WHAT WOULD MAKE YOU FORGET ALL THESE IMAGINED WRONGS? WE COULD BE FRIENDS AGAIN?
I... I GUESS SO.
VE ARE FUGITIVE FROM JUSTICE. DER BOUNTY HUNTERS BE HUNTING US. NO PLACE IS SAFE. VERE VE GET VUN MILLION CREDITS, EH?
EVER HEARD OF CLUB PARADISO?
IS CRAZY SCHEME COMING. VULF KNOW IT!

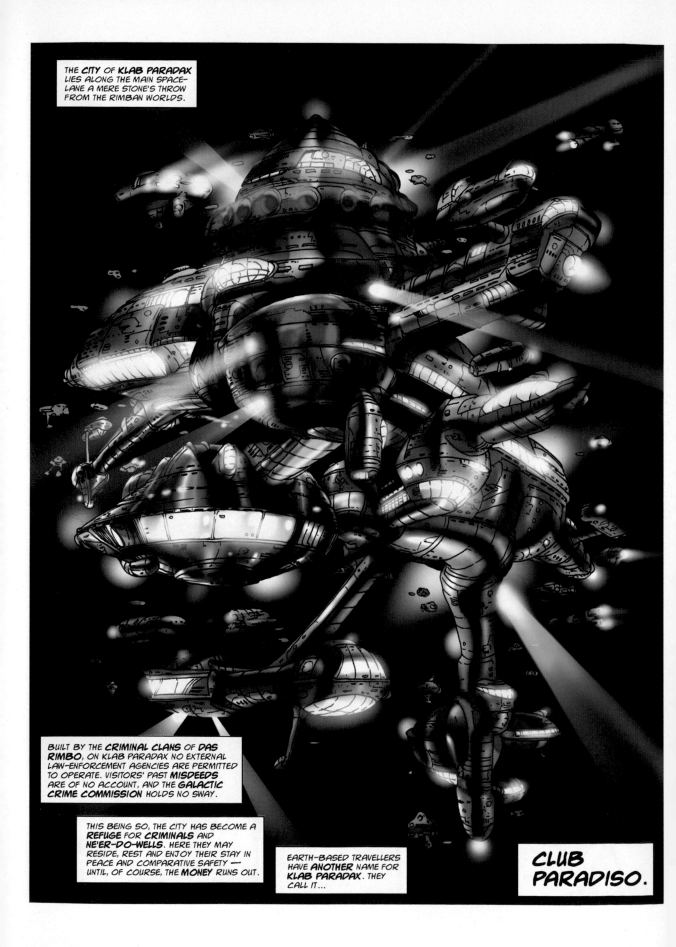

THE **CITY** OF **KLAB PARADAX**
LIES ALONG THE MAIN SPACE-
LANE A MERE STONE'S THROW
FROM THE RIMBAN WORLDS.

BUILT BY THE **CRIMINAL CLANS** OF **DAS
RIMBO**, ON KLAB PARADAX NO EXTERNAL
LAW-ENFORCEMENT AGENCIES ARE PERMITTED
TO OPERATE. VISITORS' PAST **MISDEEDS**
ARE OF NO ACCOUNT, AND THE **GALACTIC
CRIME COMMISSION** HOLDS NO SWAY.

THIS BEING SO, THE CITY HAS BECOME A
REFUGE FOR **CRIMINALS** AND
NE'ER-DO-WELLS. HERE THEY MAY
RESIDE, REST AND ENJOY THEIR STAY IN
PEACE AND COMPARATIVE SAFETY —
UNTIL, OF COURSE, THE **MONEY** RUNS OUT.

EARTH-BASED TRAVELLERS
HAVE **ANOTHER** NAME FOR
KLAB PARADAX. THEY
CALL IT...

CLUB
PARADISO.

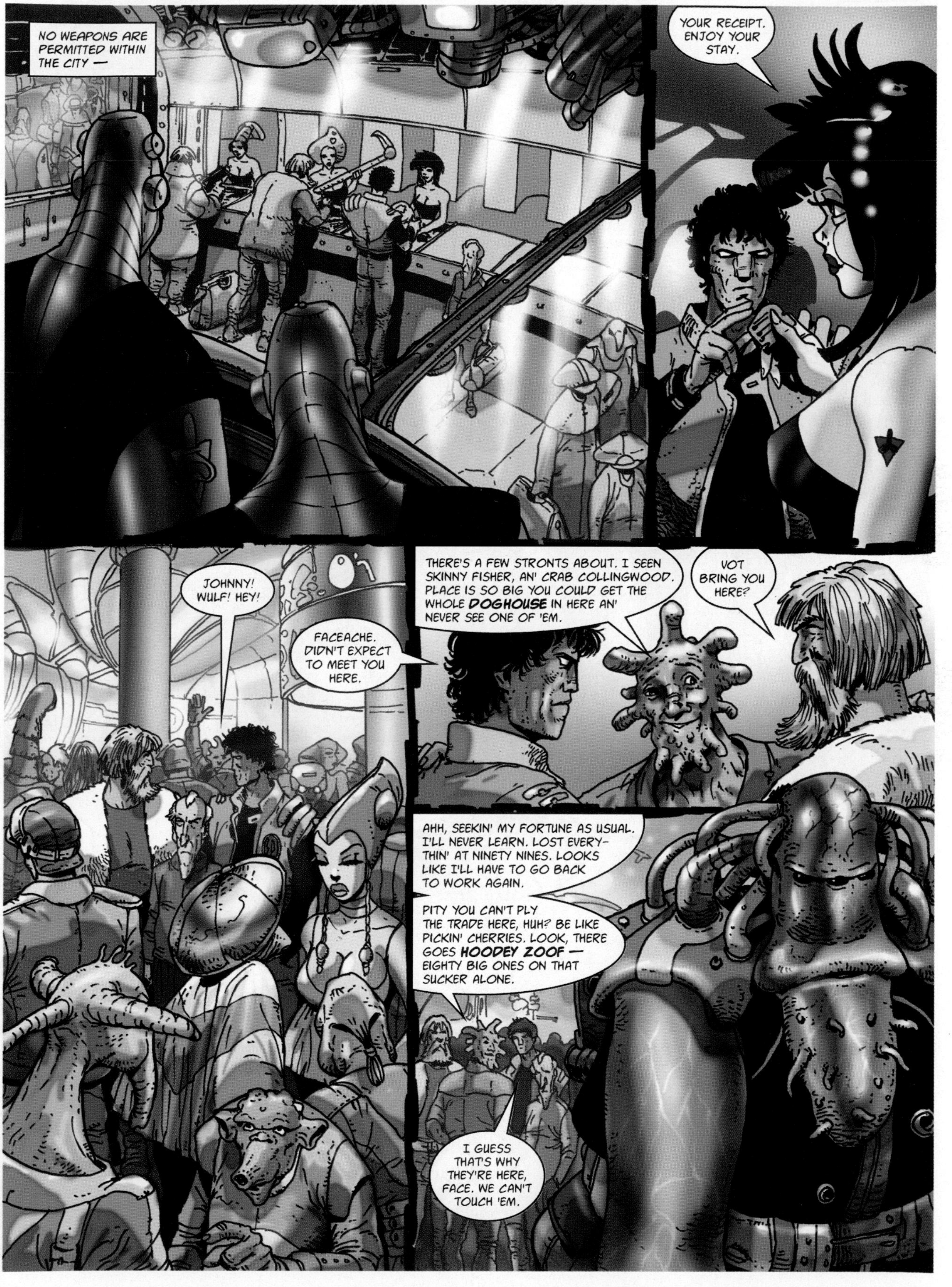

NO WEAPONS ARE PERMITTED WITHIN THE CITY —
YOUR RECEIPT. ENJOY YOUR STAY.
JOHNNY! WULF! HEY!
FACEACHE. DIDN'T EXPECT TO MEET YOU HERE.
THERE'S A FEW STRONTS ABOUT. I SEEN SKINNY FISHER, AN' CRAB COLLINGWOOD. PLACE IS SO BIG YOU COULD GET THE WHOLE DOGHOUSE IN HERE AN' NEVER SEE ONE OF 'EM.
VOT BRING YOU HERE?
AHH, SEEKIN' MY FORTUNE AS USUAL. I'LL NEVER LEARN. LOST EVERY-THIN' AT NINETY NINES. LOOKS LIKE I'LL HAVE TO GO BACK TO WORK AGAIN.
PITY YOU CAN'T PLY THE TRADE HERE, HUH? BE LIKE PICKIN' CHERRIES. LOOK, THERE GOES HOODEY ZOOF — EIGHTY BIG ONES ON THAT SUCKER ALONE.
I GUESS THAT'S WHY THEY'RE HERE, FACE. WE CAN'T TOUCH 'EM.

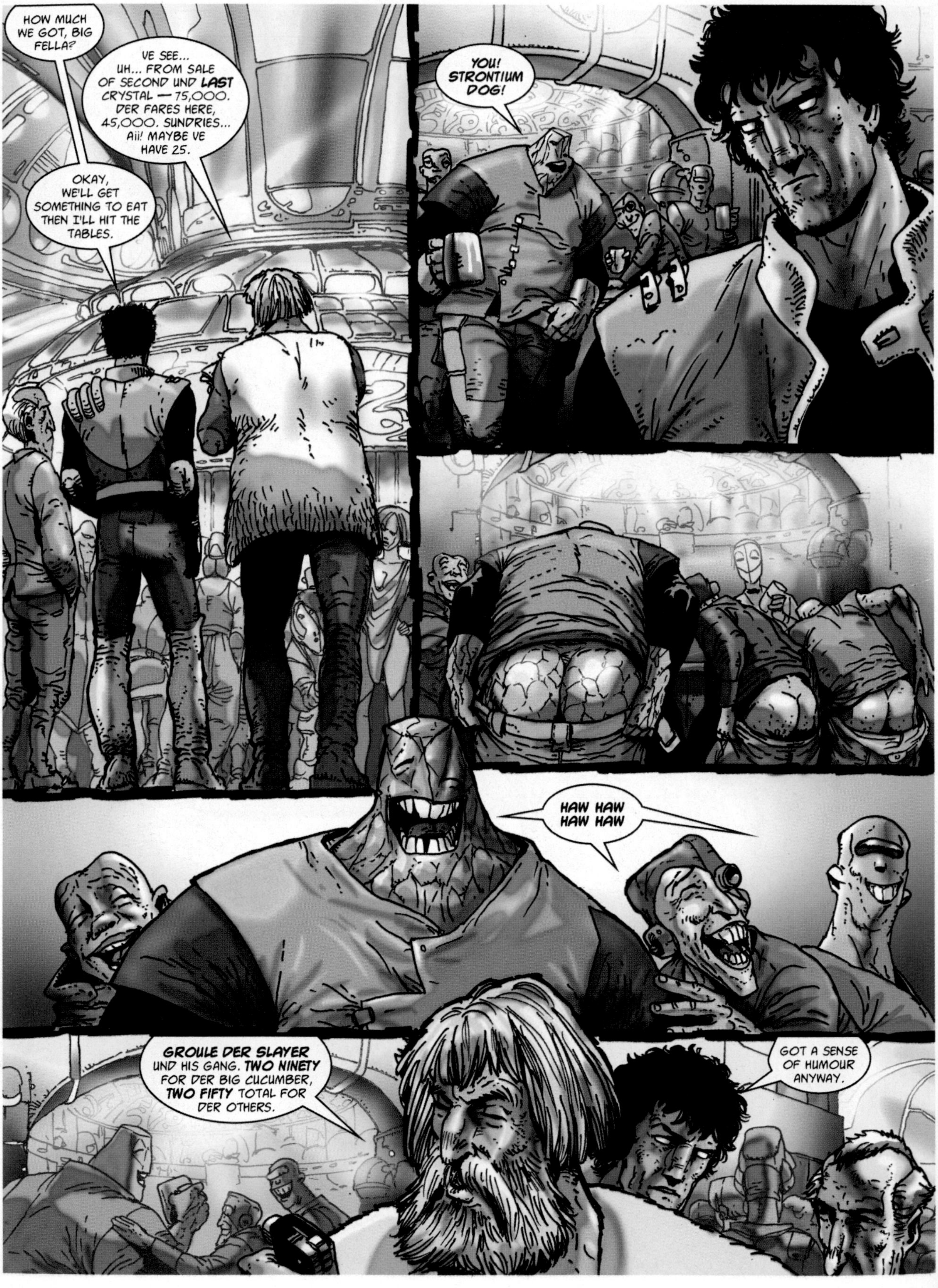
HOW MUCH WE GOT, BIG FELLA?
VE SEE... UH... FROM SALE OF SECOND UND LAST CRYSTAL — 75,000. DER FARES HERE, 45,000. SUNDRIES... Aii! MAYBE VE HAVE 25.
OKAY, WE'LL GET SOMETHING TO EAT THEN I'LL HIT THE TABLES.
YOU! STRONTIUM DOG!
HAW HAW HAW HAW
GROULE DER SLAYER UND HIS GANG. TWO NINETY FOR DER BIG CUCUMBER, TWO FIFTY TOTAL FOR DER OTHERS.
GOT A SENSE OF HUMOUR ANYWAY.

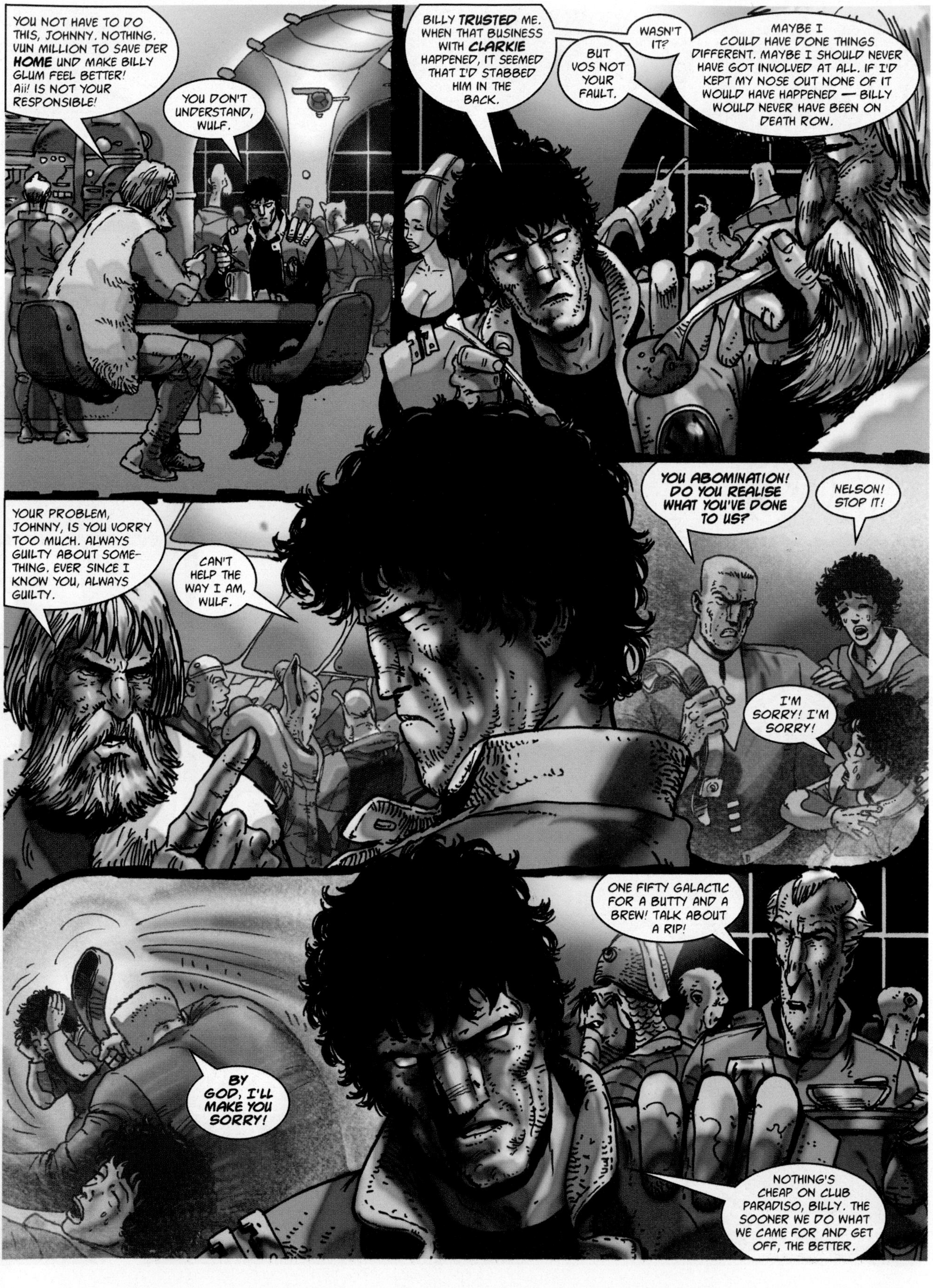
YOU NOT HAVE TO DO THIS, JOHNNY. NOTHING. VUN MILLION TO SAVE DER HOME UND MAKE BILLY GLUM FEEL BETTER! Aii! IS NOT YOUR RESPONSIBLE!
YOU DON'T UNDERSTAND, WULF.
BILLY TRUSTED ME. WHEN THAT BUSINESS WITH CLARKIE HAPPENED, IT SEEMED THAT I'D STABBED HIM IN THE BACK.
BUT VOS NOT YOUR FAULT.
WASN'T IT?
MAYBE I COULD HAVE DONE THINGS DIFFERENT. MAYBE I SHOULD NEVER HAVE GOT INVOLVED AT ALL. IF I'D KEPT MY NOSE OUT NONE OF IT WOULD HAVE HAPPENED — BILLY WOULD NEVER HAVE BEEN ON DEATH ROW.
YOUR PROBLEM, JOHNNY, IS YOU VORRY TOO MUCH. ALWAYS GUILTY ABOUT SOME-THING. EVER SINCE I KNOW YOU, ALWAYS GUILTY.
CAN'T HELP THE WAY I AM, WULF.
YOU ABOMINATION! DO YOU REALISE WHAT YOU'VE DONE TO US?
NELSON! STOP IT!
I'M SORRY! I'M SORRY!
BY GOD, I'LL MAKE YOU SORRY!
ONE FIFTY GALACTIC FOR A BUTTY AND A BREW! TALK ABOUT A RIP!
NOTHING'S CHEAP ON CLUB PARADISO, BILLY. THE SOONER WE DO WHAT WE CAME FOR AND GET OFF, THE BETTER.

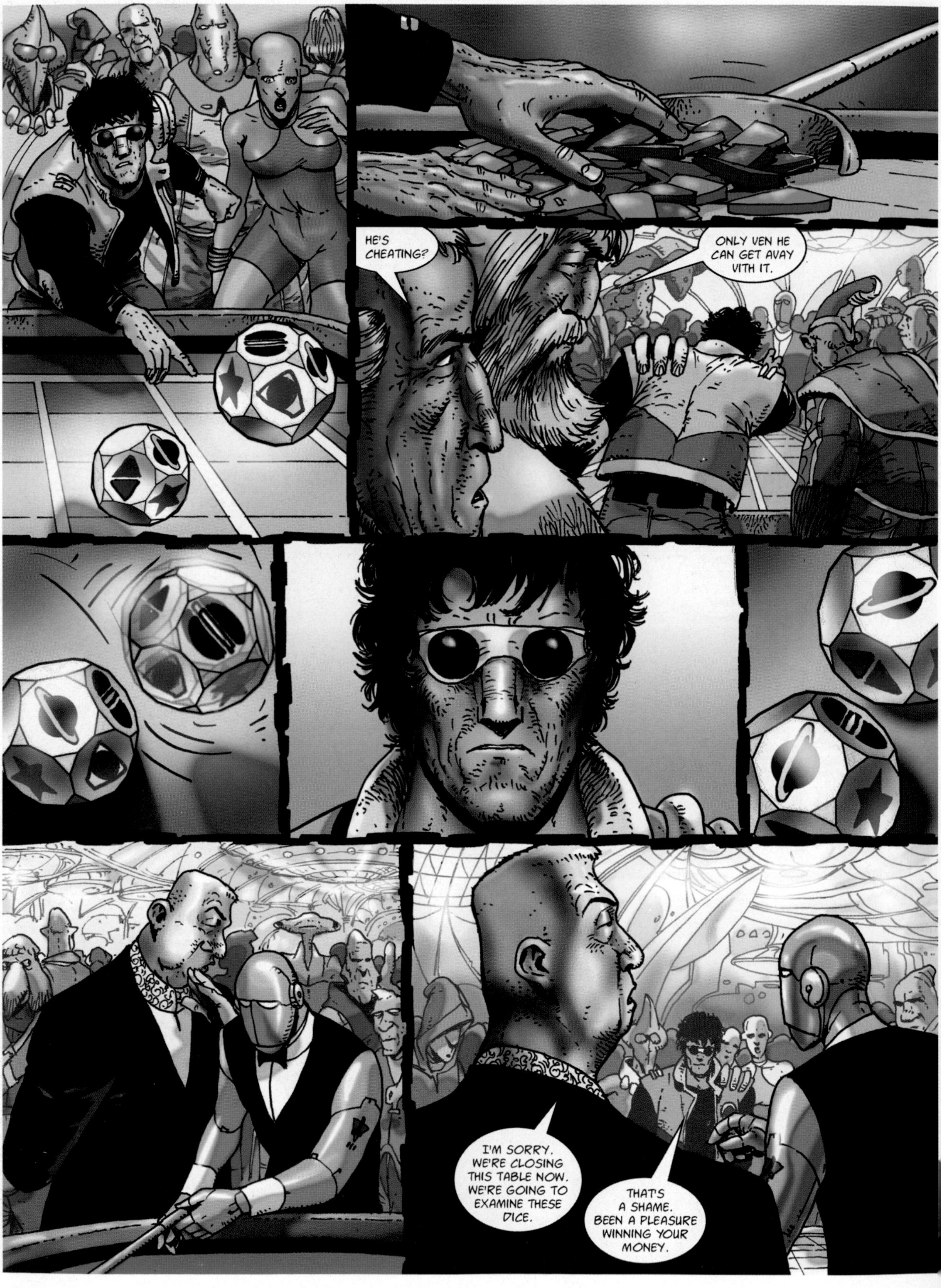
HE'S CHEATING?
ONLY VEN HE CAN GET AVAY VITH IT.
I'M SORRY. WE'RE CLOSING THIS TABLE NOW. WE'RE GOING TO EXAMINE THESE DICE.
THAT'S A SHAME. BEEN A PLEASURE WINNING YOUR MONEY.

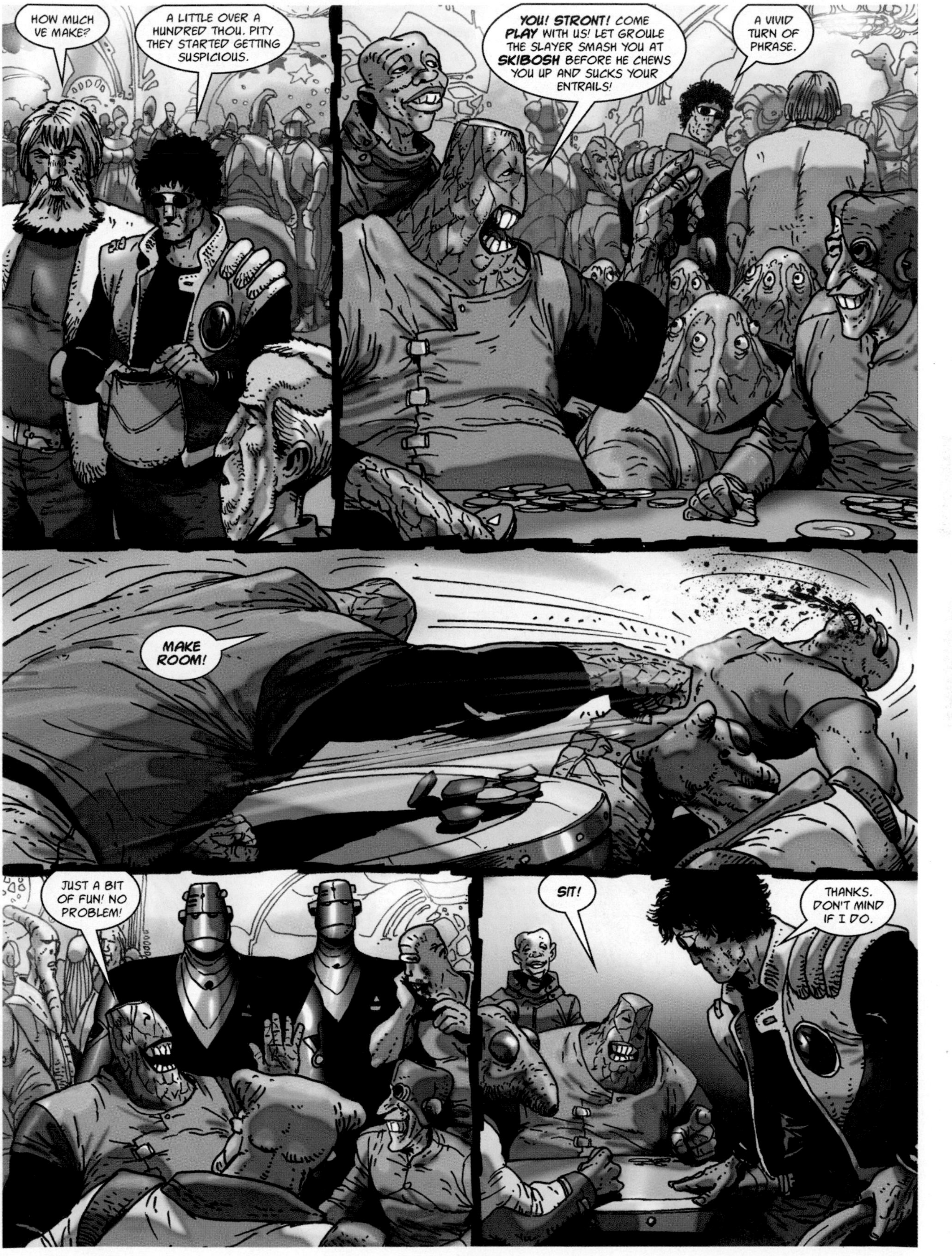
HOW MUCH VE MAKE?
A LITTLE OVER A HUNDRED THOU. PITY THEY STARTED GETTING SUSPICIOUS.
YOU! STRONT! COME PLAY WITH US! LET GROULE THE SLAYER SMASH YOU AT SKIBOSH BEFORE HE CHEWS YOU UP AND SUCKS YOUR ENTRAILS!
A VIVID TURN OF PHRASE.
MAKE ROOM!
JUST A BIT OF FUN! NO PROBLEM!
SIT!
THANKS. DON'T MIND IF I DO.

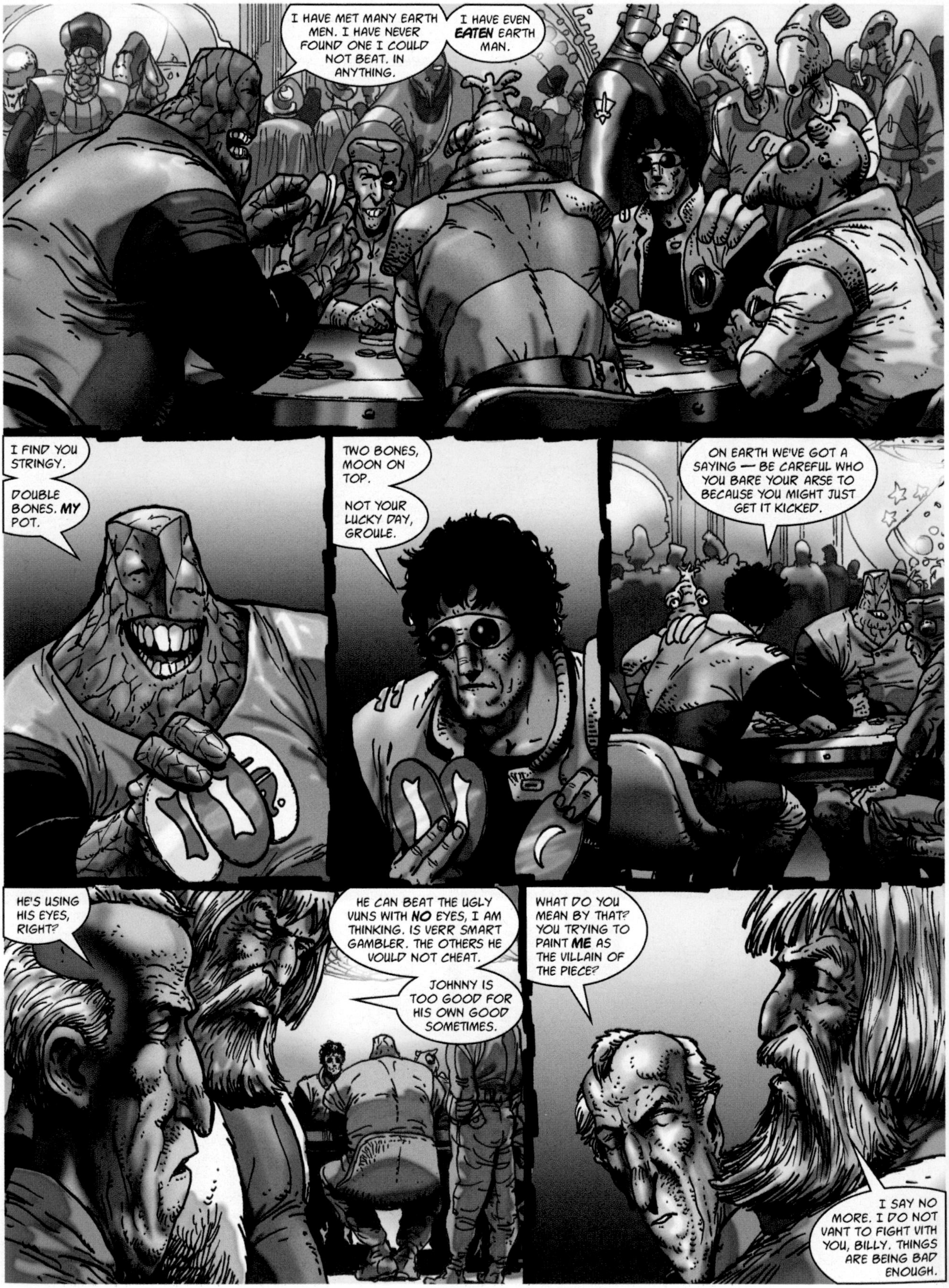
I HAVE MET MANY EARTH MEN. I HAVE NEVER FOUND ONE I COULD NOT BEAT. IN ANYTHING.
I HAVE EVEN EATEN EARTH MAN.
I FIND YOU STRINGY.
DOUBLE BONES. MY POT.
TWO BONES, MOON ON TOP.
NOT YOUR LUCKY DAY, GROULE.
ON EARTH WE'VE GOT A SAYING — BE CAREFUL WHO YOU BARE YOUR ARSE TO BECAUSE YOU MIGHT JUST GET IT KICKED.
HE'S USING HIS EYES, RIGHT?
HE CAN BEAT THE UGLY VUNS WITH NO EYES, I AM THINKING. IS VERR SMART GAMBLER. THE OTHERS HE VOULD NOT CHEAT.
JOHNNY IS TOO GOOD FOR HIS OWN GOOD SOMETIMES.
WHAT DO YOU MEAN BY THAT? YOU TRYING TO PAINT ME AS THE VILLAIN OF THE PIECE?
I SAY NO MORE. I DO NOT VANT TO FIGHT VITH YOU, BILLY. THINGS ARE BEING BAD ENOUGH.

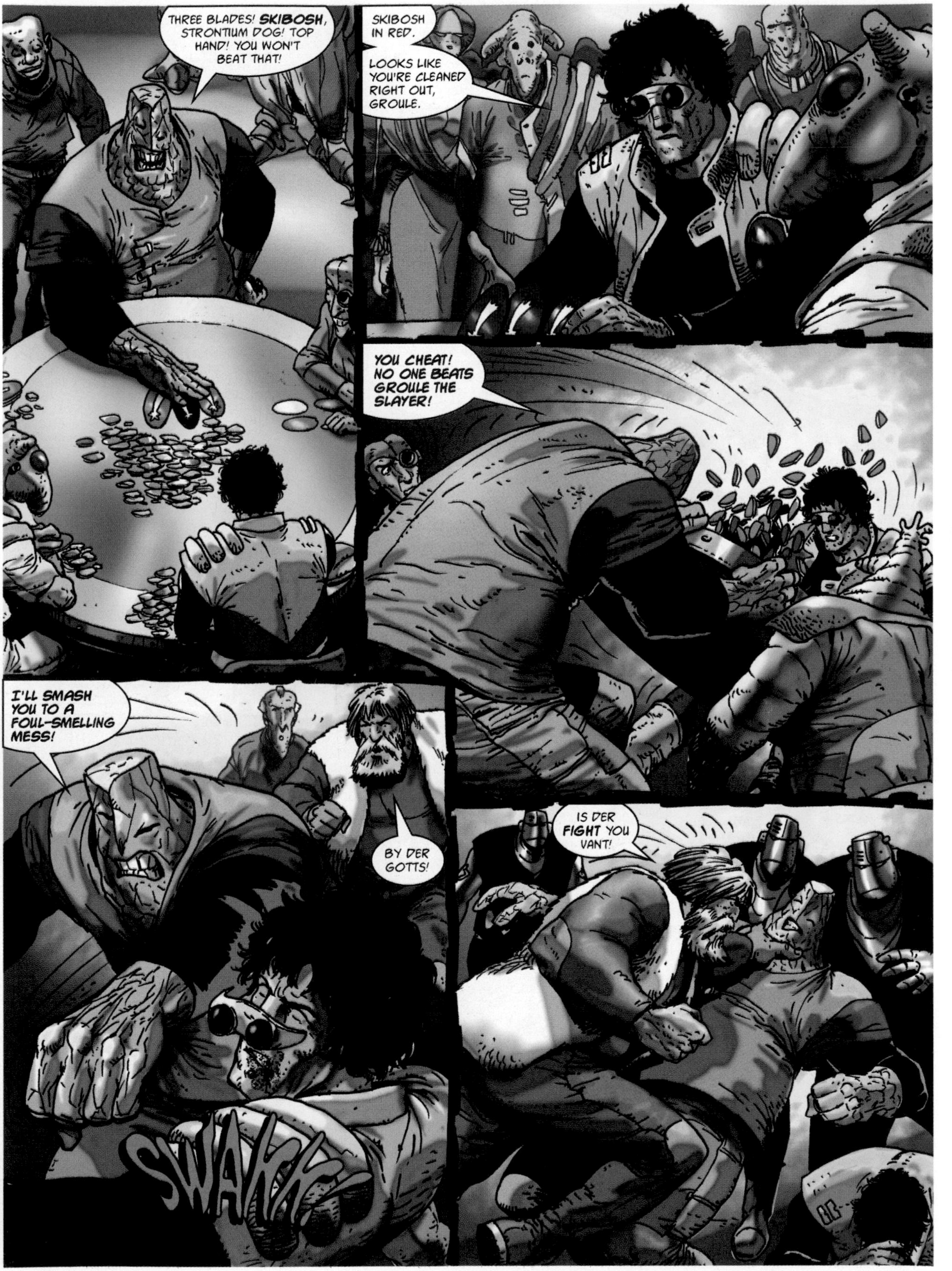

THREE BLADES! SKIBOSH, STRONTIUM DOG! TOP HAND! YOU WON'T BEAT THAT!
SKIBOSH IN RED.
LOOKS LIKE YOU'RE CLEANED RIGHT OUT, GROULE.
YOU CHEAT! NO ONE BEATS GROULE THE SLAYER!
I'LL SMASH YOU TO A FOUL-SMELLING MESS!
BY DER GOTTS!
SWAKK!
IS DER FIGHT YOU VANT!

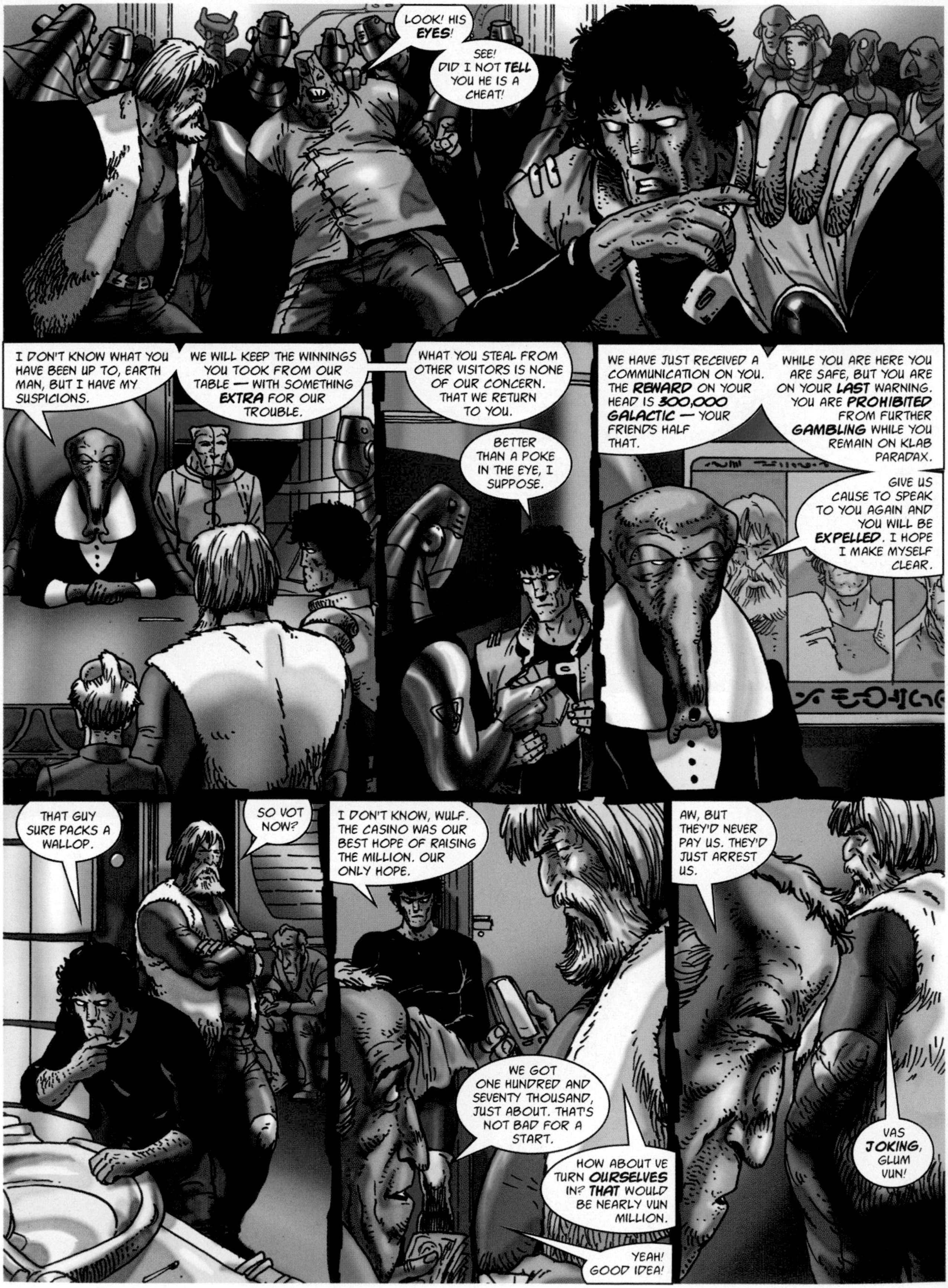

LOOK! HIS **EYES**!
SEE! DID I NOT **TELL** YOU HE IS A CHEAT!
I DON'T KNOW WHAT YOU HAVE BEEN UP TO, EARTH MAN, BUT I HAVE MY SUSPICIONS.
WE WILL KEEP THE WINNINGS YOU TOOK FROM OUR TABLE — WITH SOMETHING **EXTRA** FOR OUR TROUBLE.
WHAT YOU STEAL FROM OTHER VISITORS IS NONE OF OUR CONCERN. THAT WE RETURN TO YOU.
BETTER THAN A POKE IN THE EYE, I SUPPOSE.
WE HAVE JUST RECEIVED A COMMUNICATION ON YOU. THE **REWARD** ON YOUR HEAD IS **300,000 GALACTIC** — YOUR FRIENDS HALF THAT.
WHILE YOU ARE HERE YOU ARE SAFE, BUT YOU ARE ON YOUR **LAST** WARNING. YOU ARE **PROHIBITED** FROM FURTHER **GAMBLING** WHILE YOU REMAIN ON KLAB PARADAX.
GIVE US CAUSE TO SPEAK TO YOU AGAIN AND YOU WILL BE **EXPELLED**. I HOPE I MAKE MYSELF CLEAR.
THAT GUY SURE PACKS A WALLOP.
SO VOT NOW?
I DON'T KNOW, WULF. THE CASINO WAS OUR BEST HOPE OF RAISING THE MILLION. OUR ONLY HOPE.
WE GOT ONE HUNDRED AND SEVENTY THOUSAND, JUST ABOUT. THAT'S NOT BAD FOR A START.
HOW ABOUT VE TURN **OURSELVES** IN? **THAT** WOULD BE NEARLY VUN MILLION.
YEAH! GOOD IDEA!
AW, BUT THEY'D NEVER PAY US. THEY'D JUST ARREST US.
VAS **JOKING**, GLUM VUN!

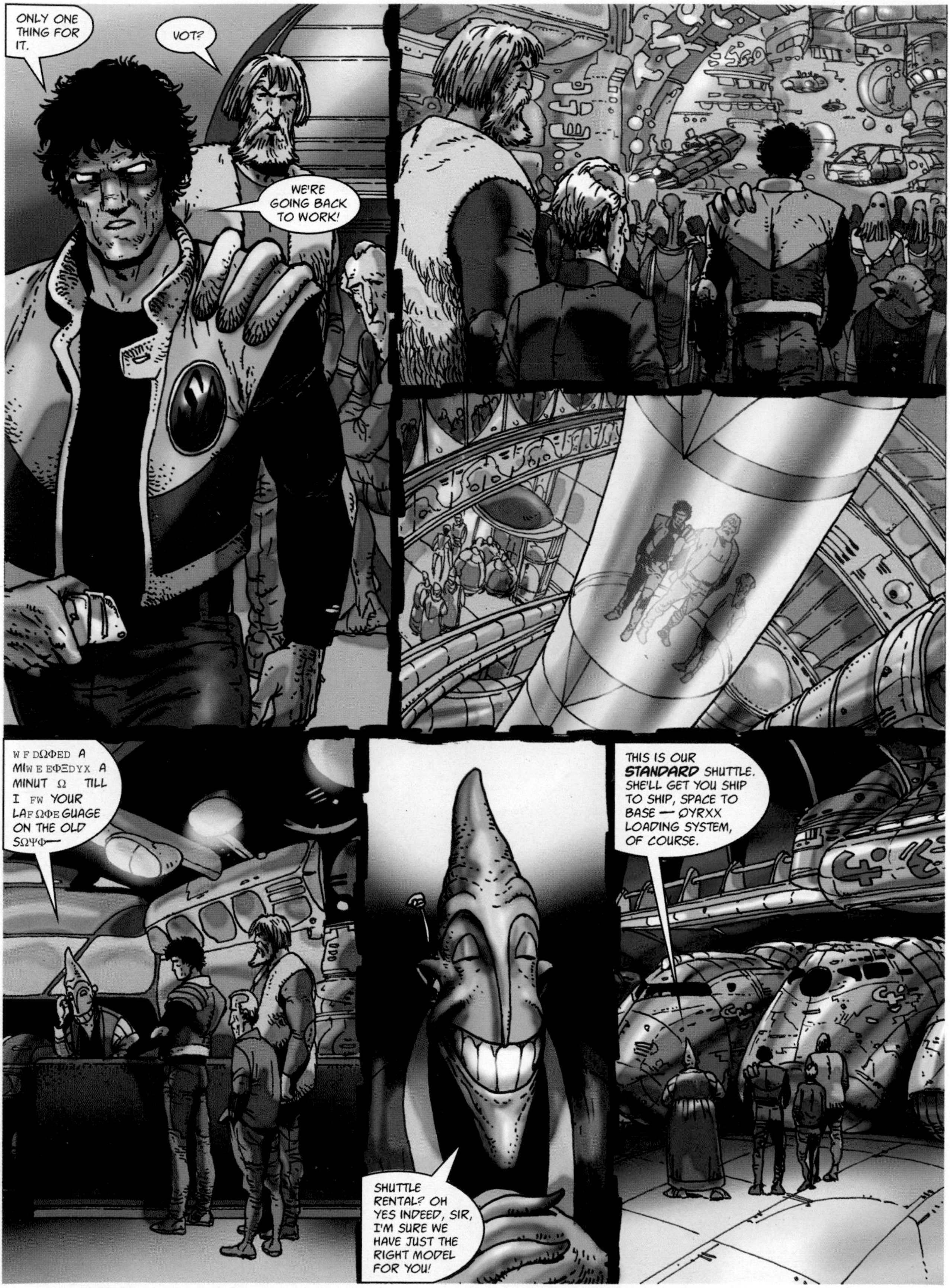
ONLY ONE THING FOR IT.
VOT?
WE'RE GOING BACK TO WORK!
W F DΩΦED A MIW E EΦΞDYX A MINUT Ω TILL I FW YOUR LAF ΩΦE GUAGE ON THE OLD SΩΨΦ—
SHUTTLE RENTAL? OH YES INDEED, SIR, I'M SURE WE HAVE JUST THE RIGHT MODEL FOR YOU!
THIS IS OUR **STANDARD** SHUTTLE. SHE'LL GET YOU SHIP TO SHIP, SPACE TO BASE — ØYRXX LOADING SYSTEM, OF COURSE.

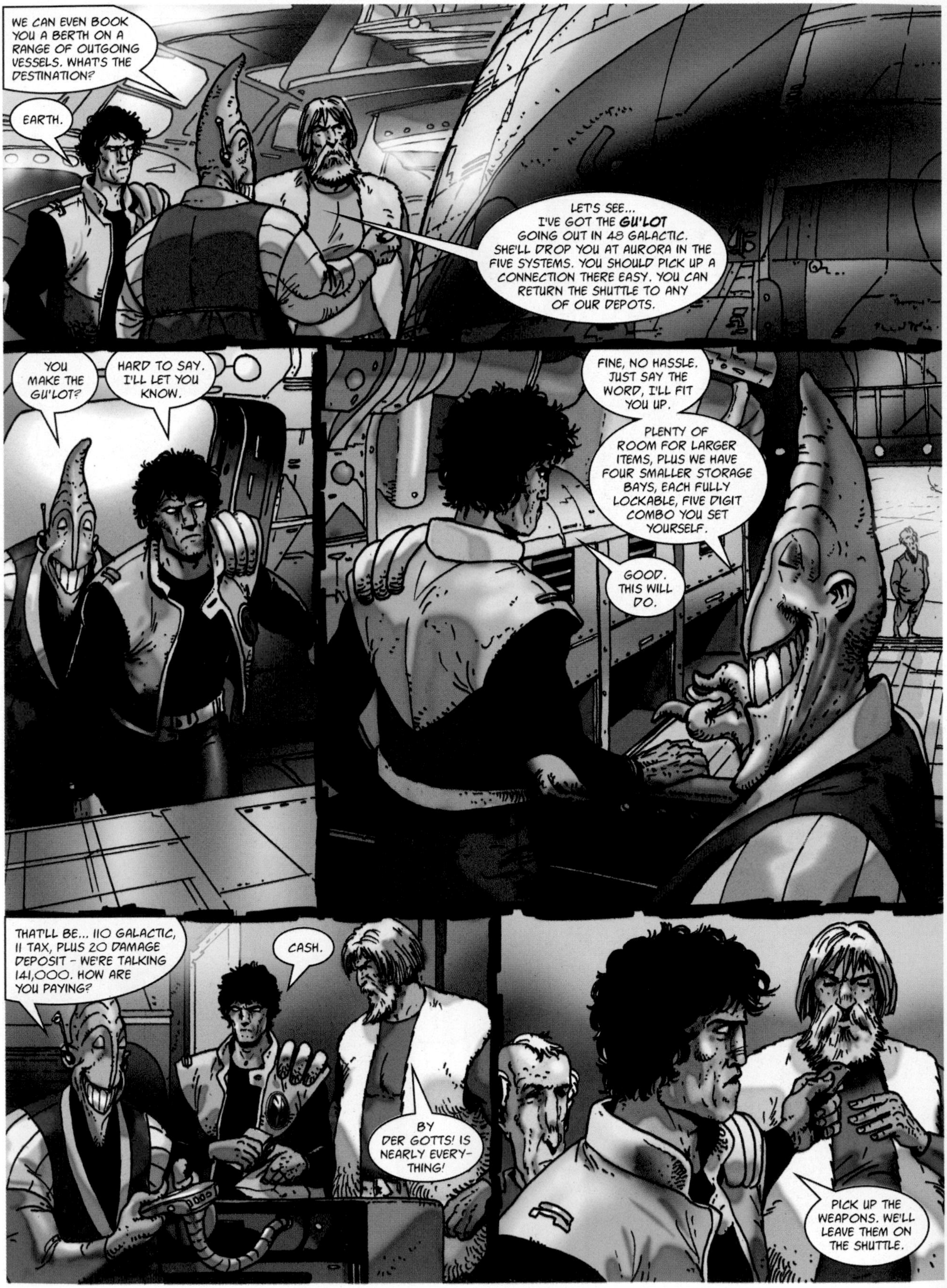
WE CAN EVEN BOOK YOU A BERTH ON A RANGE OF OUTGOING VESSELS. WHAT'S THE DESTINATION?
EARTH.
LET'S SEE... I'VE GOT THE GU'LOT GOING OUT IN 48 GALACTIC. SHE'LL DROP YOU AT AURORA IN THE FIVE SYSTEMS. YOU SHOULD PICK UP A CONNECTION THERE EASY. YOU CAN RETURN THE SHUTTLE TO ANY OF OUR DEPOTS.
YOU MAKE THE GU'LOT?
HARD TO SAY. I'LL LET YOU KNOW.
FINE, NO HASSLE. JUST SAY THE WORD, I'LL FIT YOU UP.
PLENTY OF ROOM FOR LARGER ITEMS, PLUS WE HAVE FOUR SMALLER STORAGE BAYS, EACH FULLY LOCKABLE, FIVE DIGIT COMBO YOU SET YOURSELF.
GOOD. THIS WILL DO.
THAT'LL BE... 110 GALACTIC, 11 TAX, PLUS 20 DAMAGE DEPOSIT - WE'RE TALKING 141,000. HOW ARE YOU PAYING?
CASH.
BY DER GOTTS! IS NEARLY EVERY-THING!
PICK UP THE WEAPONS. WE'LL LEAVE THEM ON THE SHUTTLE.

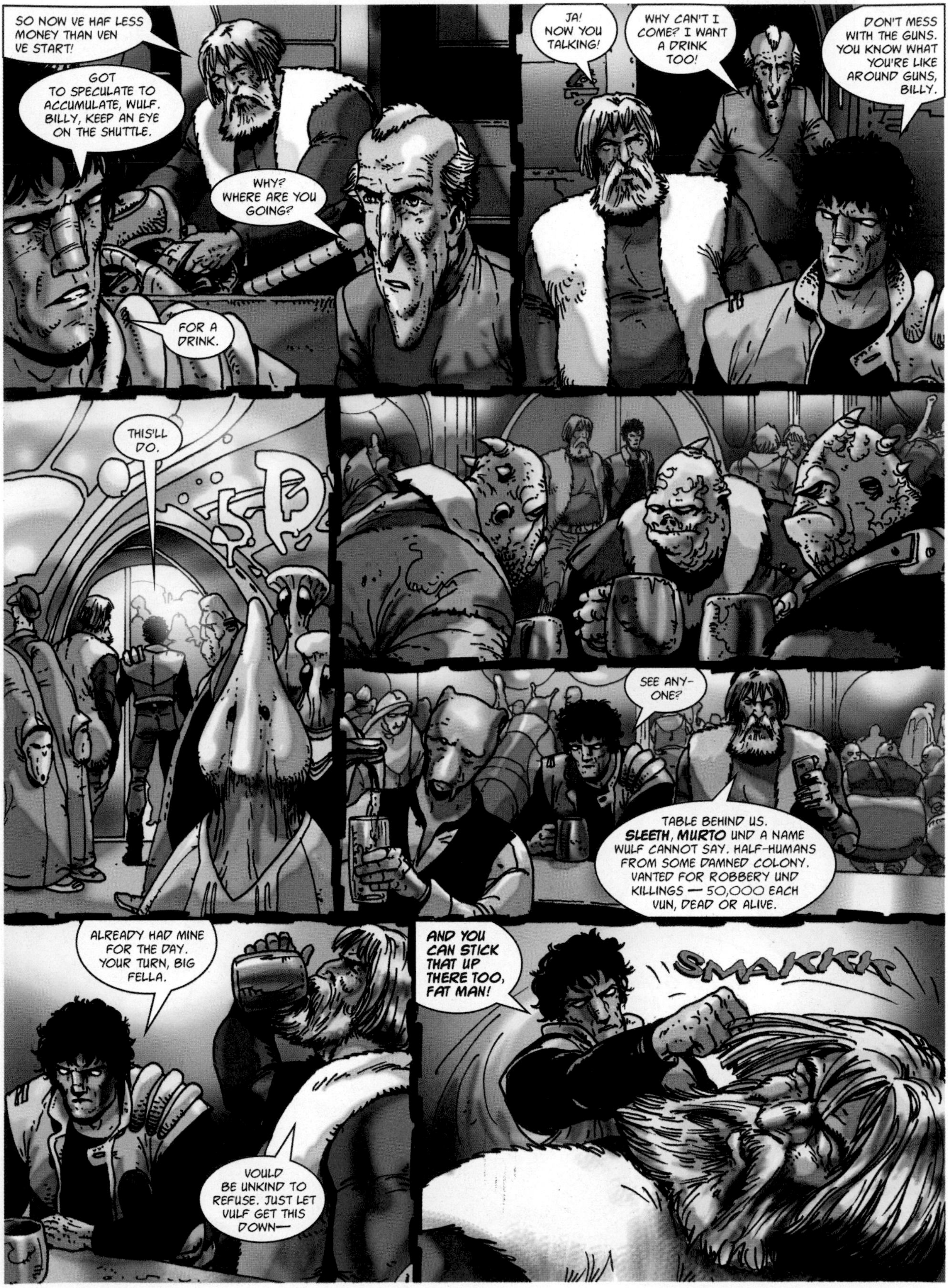

SO NOW VE HAF LESS MONEY THAN VEN VE START!
GOT TO SPECULATE TO ACCUMULATE, WULF. BILLY, KEEP AN EYE ON THE SHUTTLE.
WHY? WHERE ARE YOU GOING?
FOR A DRINK.
JA! NOW YOU TALKING!
WHY CAN'T I COME? I WANT A DRINK TOO!
DON'T MESS WITH THE GUNS. YOU KNOW WHAT YOU'RE LIKE AROUND GUNS, BILLY.
THIS'LL DO.
SEE ANY-ONE?
TABLE BEHIND US. **SLEETH, MURTO** UND A NAME WULF CANNOT SAY. HALF-HUMANS FROM SOME DAMNED COLONY. VANTED FOR ROBBERY UND KILLINGS — 50,000 EACH VUN, DEAD OR ALIVE.
ALREADY HAD MINE FOR THE DAY. YOUR TURN, BIG FELLA.
VOULD BE UNKIND TO REFUSE. JUST LET VULF GET THIS DOWN—
AND YOU CAN STICK THAT UP THERE TOO, FAT MAN!
SMAKKK

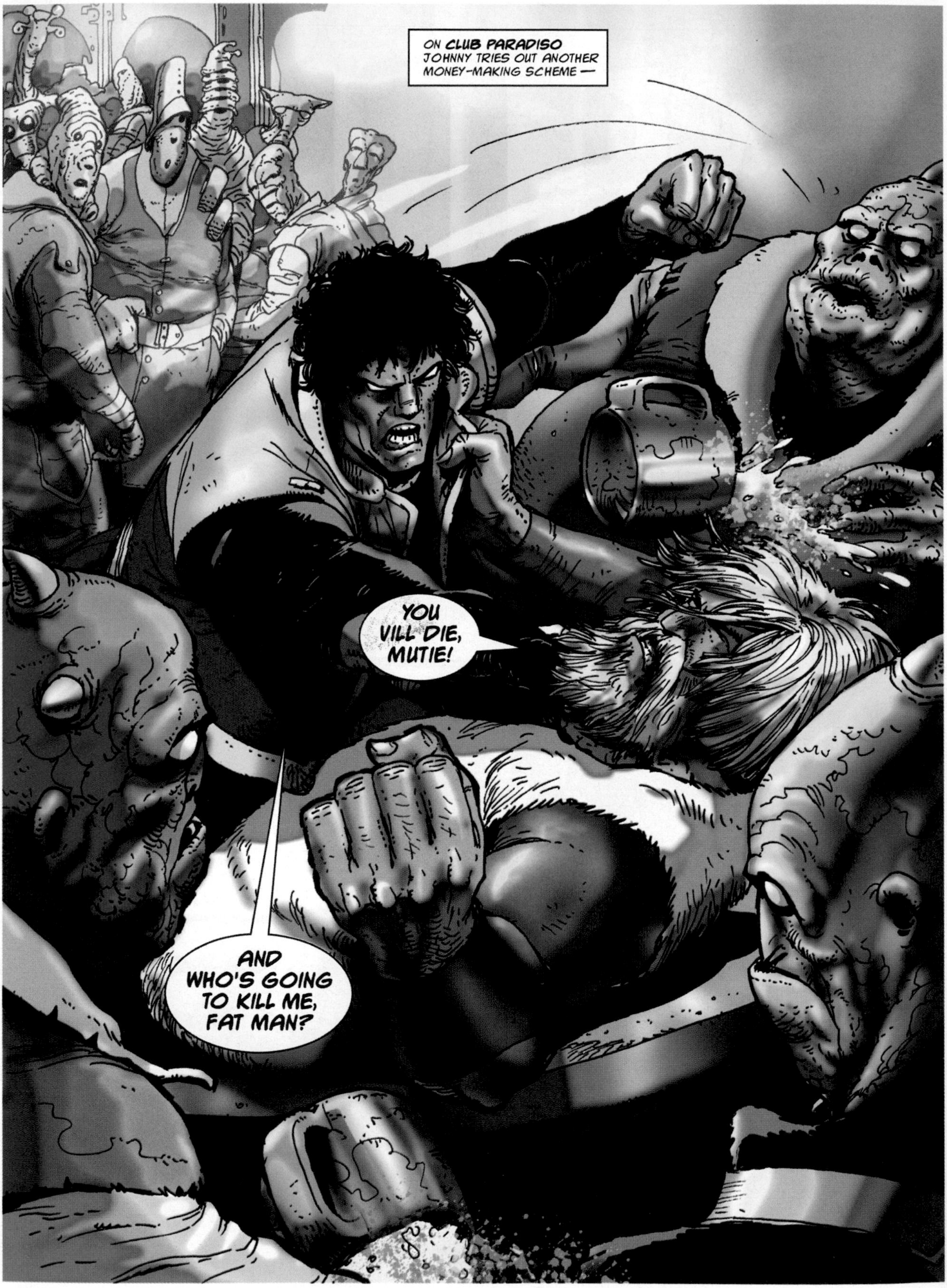
ON CLUB PARADISO JOHNNY TRIES OUT ANOTHER MONEY-MAKING SCHEME —
YOU VILL DIE, MUTIE!
AND WHO'S GOING TO KILL ME, FAT MAN?

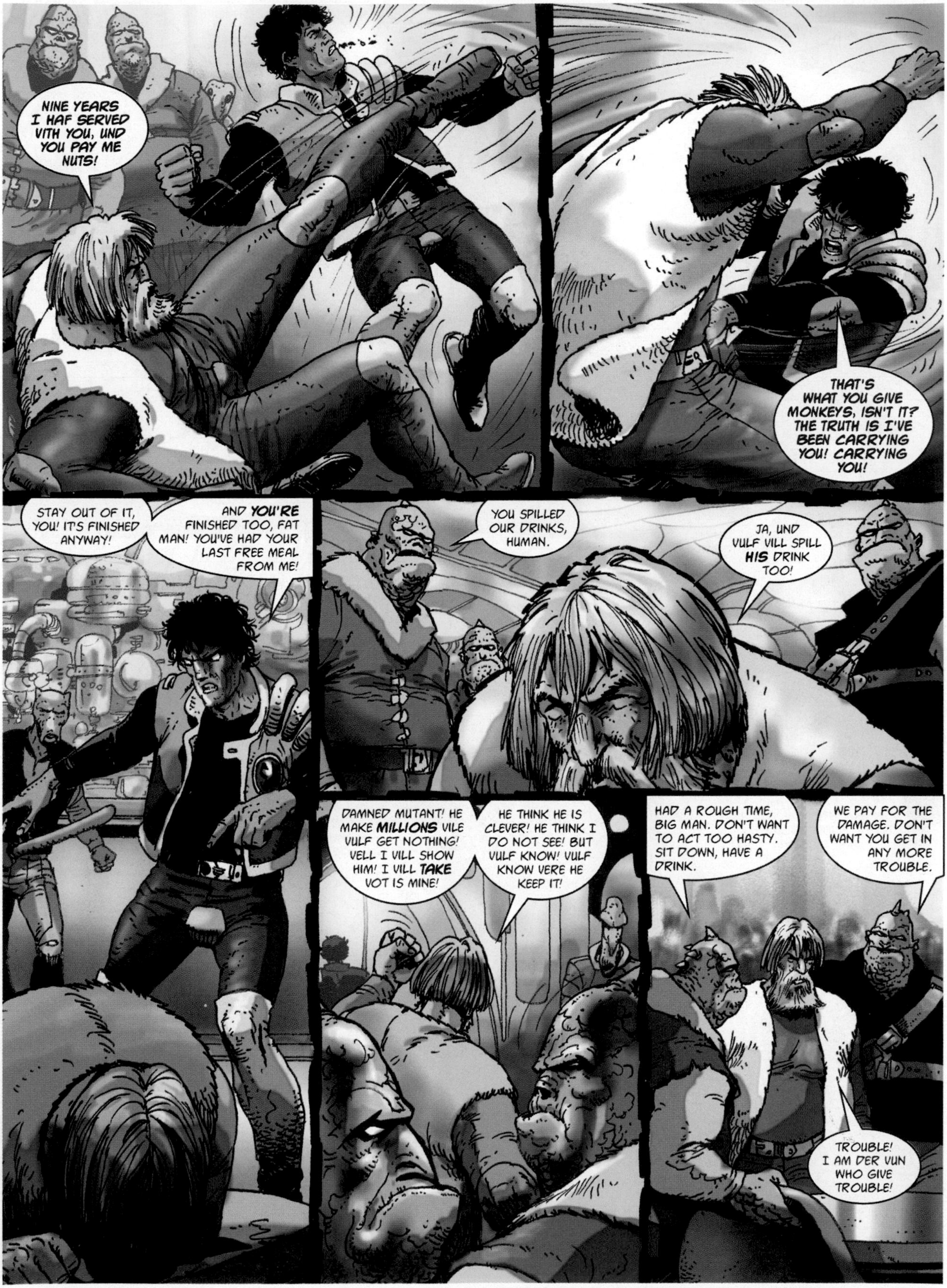
NINE YEARS I HAF SERVED VITH YOU, UND YOU PAY ME NUTS!
THAT'S WHAT YOU GIVE MONKEYS, ISN'T IT? THE TRUTH IS I'VE BEEN CARRYING YOU! CARRYING YOU!
STAY OUT OF IT, YOU! IT'S FINISHED ANYWAY!
AND YOU'RE FINISHED TOO, FAT MAN! YOU'VE HAD YOUR LAST FREE MEAL FROM ME!
YOU SPILLED OUR DRINKS, HUMAN.
JA, UND VULF VILL SPILL HIS DRINK TOO!
DAMNED MUTANT! HE MAKE MILLIONS VILE VULF GET NOTHING! VELL I VILL SHOW HIM! I VILL TAKE VOT IS MINE!
HE THINK HE IS CLEVER! HE THINK I DO NOT SEE! BUT VULF KNOW! VULF KNOW VERE HE KEEP IT!
HAD A ROUGH TIME, BIG MAN. DON'T WANT TO ACT TOO HASTY. SIT DOWN, HAVE A DRINK.
WE PAY FOR THE DAMAGE. DON'T WANT YOU GET IN ANY MORE TROUBLE.
TROUBLE! I AM DER VUN WHO GIVE TROUBLE!

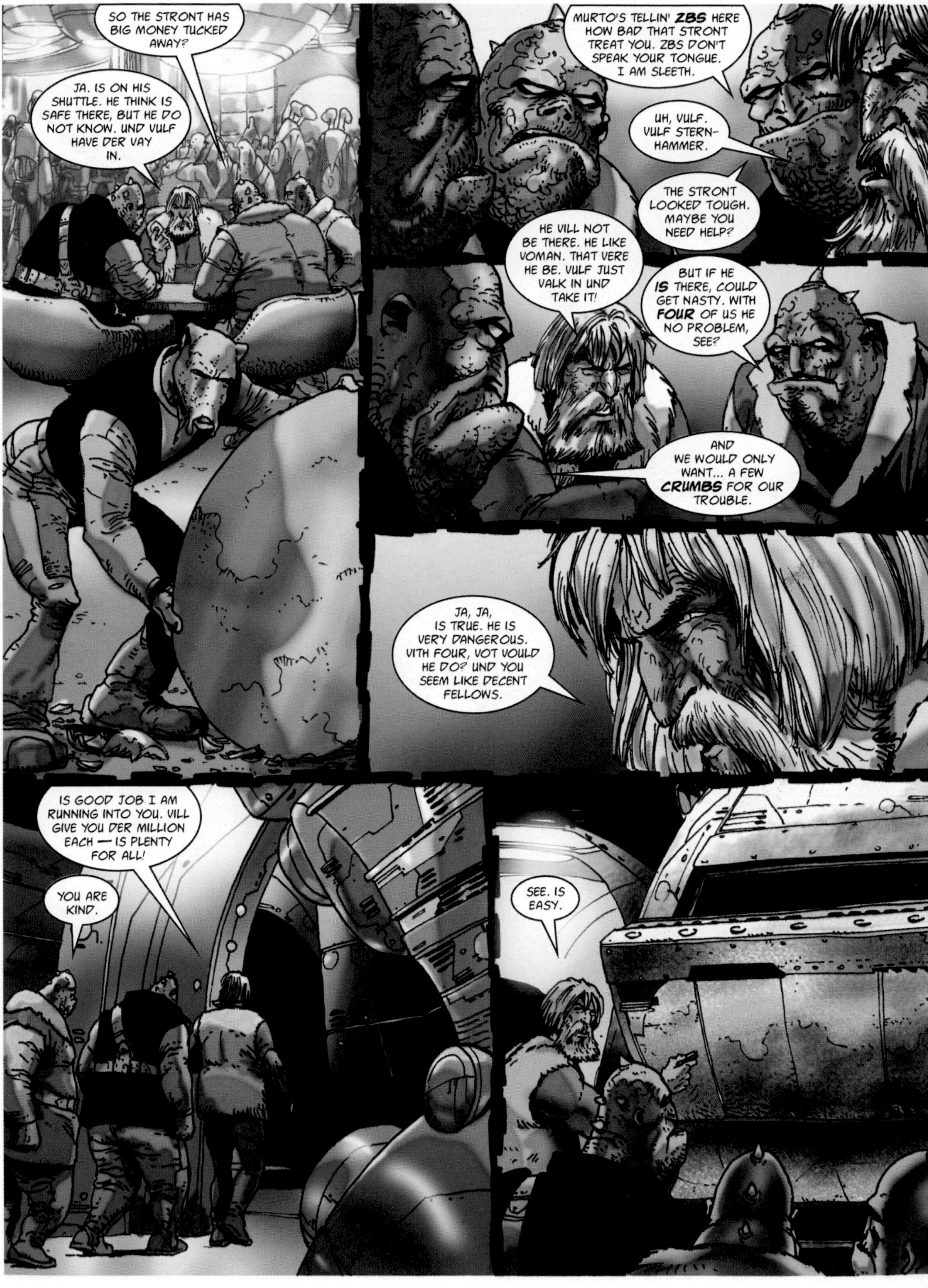
SO THE STRONT HAS BIG MONEY TUCKED AWAY?
JA. IS ON HIS SHUTTLE. HE THINK IS SAFE THERE, BUT HE DO NOT KNOW. UND VULF HAVE DER VAY IN.
MURTO'S TELLIN' ZBS HERE HOW BAD THAT STRONT TREAT YOU. ZBS DON'T SPEAK YOUR TONGUE. I AM SLEETH.
UH, VULF. VULF STERN-HAMMER.
THE STRONT LOOKED TOUGH. MAYBE YOU NEED HELP?
HE VILL NOT BE THERE. HE LIKE VOMAN. THAT VERE HE BE. VULF JUST VALK IN UND TAKE IT!
BUT IF HE IS THERE, COULD GET NASTY. WITH FOUR OF US HE NO PROBLEM, SEE?
AND WE WOULD ONLY WANT... A FEW CRUMBS FOR OUR TROUBLE.
JA, JA, IS TRUE. HE IS VERY DANGEROUS. VITH FOUR, VOT VOULD HE DO? UND YOU SEEM LIKE DECENT FELLOWS.
IS GOOD JOB I AM RUNNING INTO YOU. VILL GIVE YOU DER MILLION EACH — IS PLENTY FOR ALL!
YOU ARE KIND.
SEE. IS EASY.

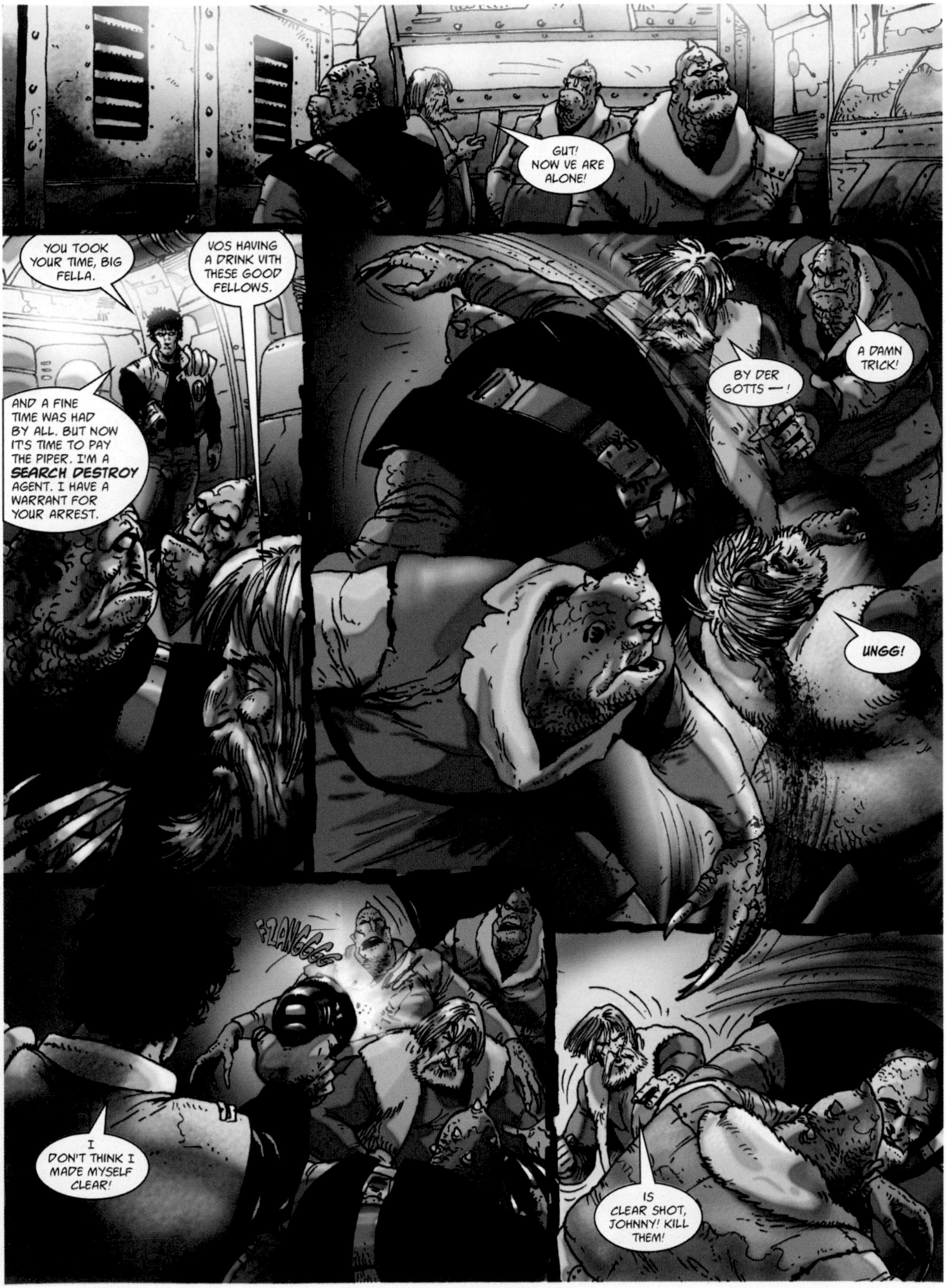
GUT! NOW VE ARE ALONE!
YOU TOOK YOUR TIME, BIG FELLA.
VOS HAVING A DRINK VITH THESE GOOD FELLOWS.
AND A FINE TIME WAS HAD BY ALL. BUT NOW IT'S TIME TO PAY THE PIPER. I'M A **SEARCH DESTROY** AGENT. I HAVE A WARRANT FOR YOUR ARREST.
BY DER GOTTS —!
A DAMN TRICK!
UNGG!
FZANGGGG
I DON'T THINK I MADE MYSELF CLEAR!
IS CLEAR SHOT, JOHNNY! KILL THEM!

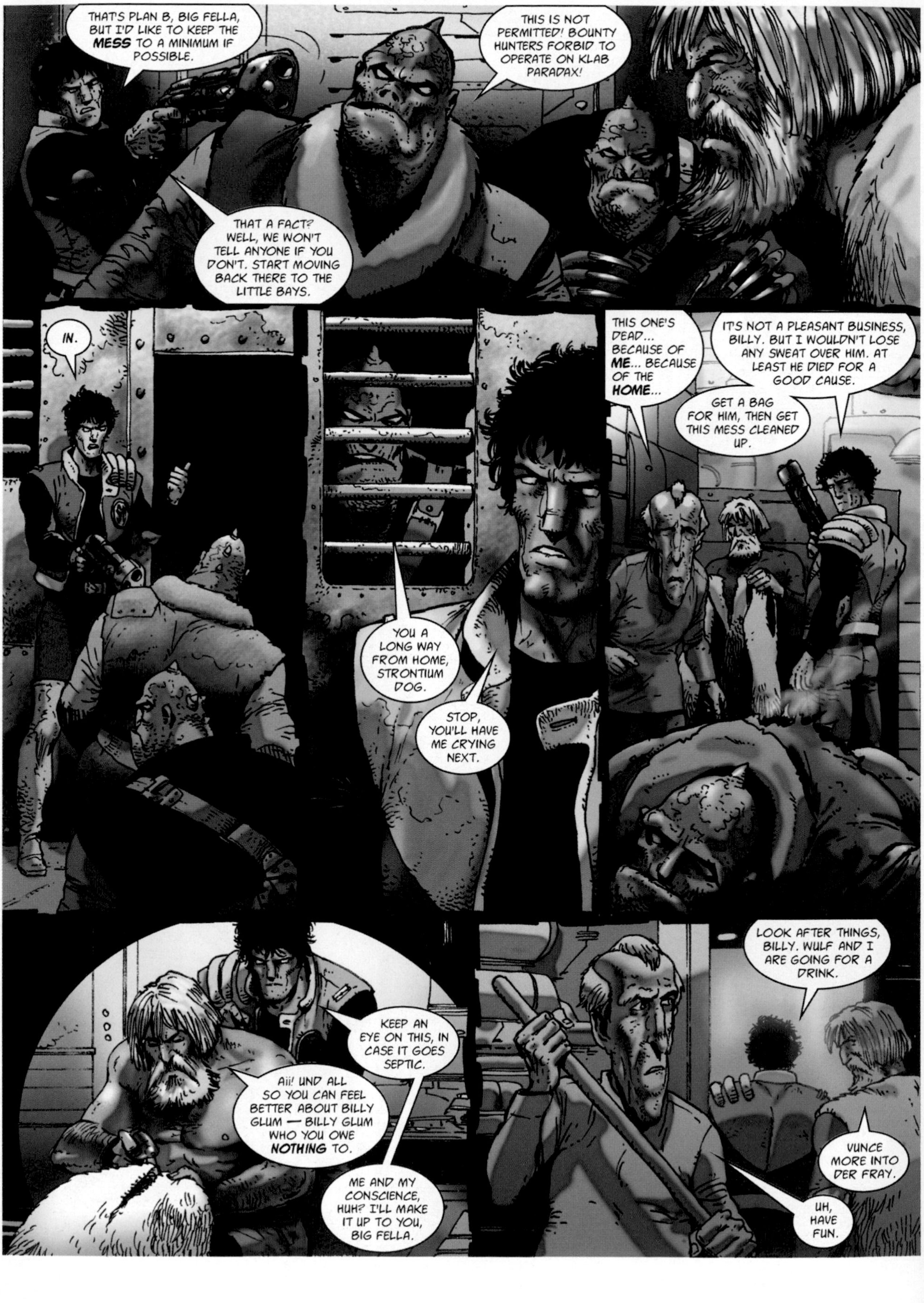

THAT'S PLAN B, BIG FELLA, BUT I'D LIKE TO KEEP THE **MESS** TO A MINIMUM IF POSSIBLE.
THIS IS NOT PERMITTED! BOUNTY HUNTERS FORBID TO OPERATE ON KLAB PARADAX!
THAT A FACT? WELL, WE WON'T TELL ANYONE IF YOU DON'T. START MOVING BACK THERE TO THE LITTLE BAYS.
IN.
YOU A LONG WAY FROM HOME, STRONTIUM DOG.
STOP, YOU'LL HAVE ME CRYING NEXT.
THIS ONE'S DEAD... BECAUSE OF **ME**... BECAUSE OF THE **HOME**...
IT'S NOT A PLEASANT BUSINESS, BILLY. BUT I WOULDN'T LOSE ANY SWEAT OVER HIM. AT LEAST HE DIED FOR A GOOD CAUSE.
GET A BAG FOR HIM, THEN GET THIS MESS CLEANED UP.
KEEP AN EYE ON THIS, IN CASE IT GOES SEPTIC.
Aii! UND ALL SO YOU CAN FEEL BETTER ABOUT BILLY GLUM — BILLY GLUM WHO YOU OWE **NOTHING** TO.
ME AND MY CONSCIENCE, HUH? I'LL MAKE IT UP TO YOU, BIG FELLA.
LOOK AFTER THINGS, BILLY. WULF AND I ARE GOING FOR A DRINK.
VUNCE MORE INTO DER FRAY.
UH, HAVE FUN.

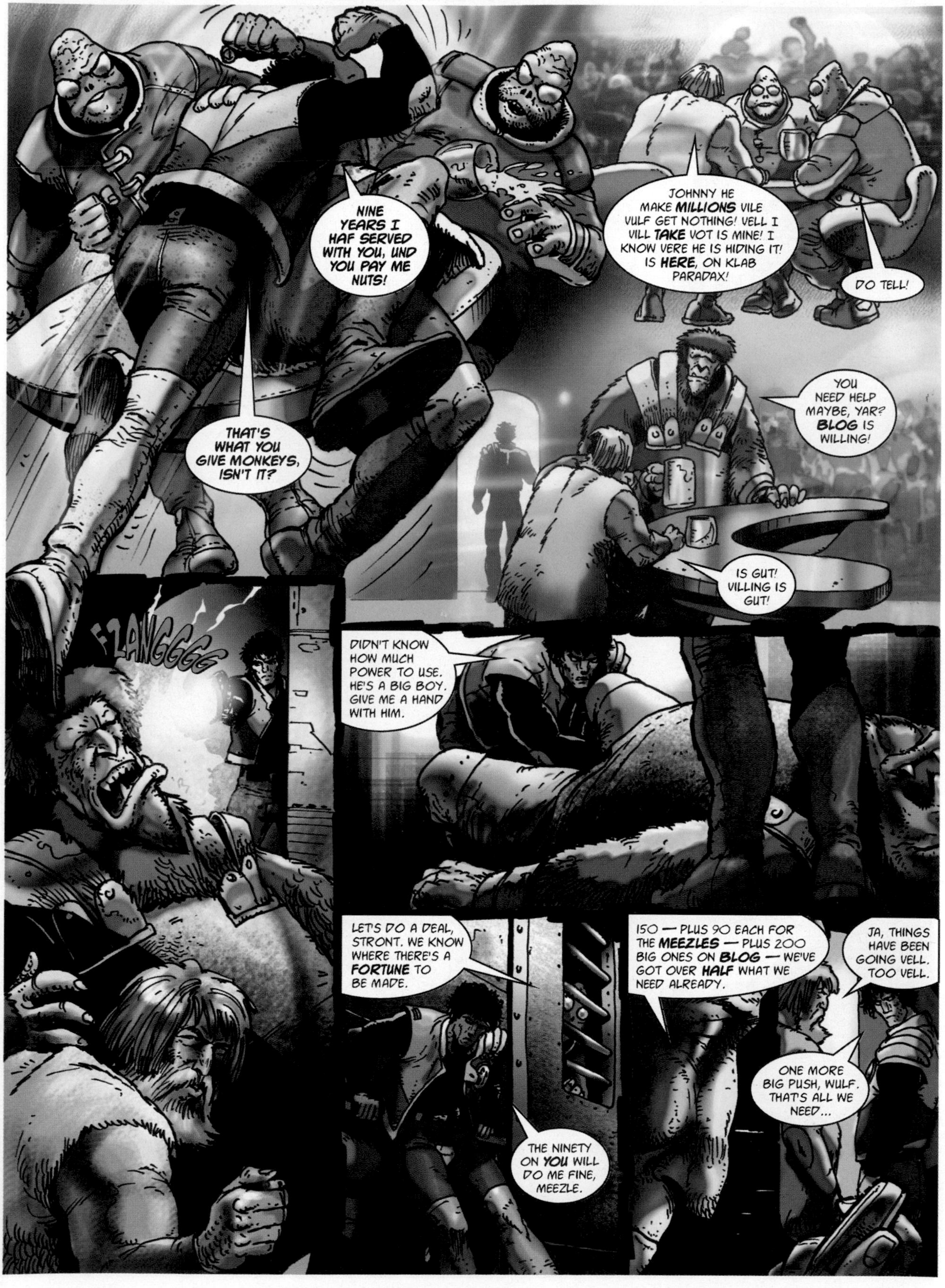
NINE YEARS I HAF SERVED WITH YOU, UND YOU PAY ME NUTS!
THAT'S WHAT YOU GIVE MONKEYS, ISN'T IT?
JOHNNY HE MAKE MILLIONS VILE VULF GET NOTHING! VELL I VILL TAKE VOT IS MINE! I KNOW VERE HE IS HIDING IT! IS HERE, ON KLAB PARADAX!
DO TELL!
YOU NEED HELP MAYBE, YAR? BLOG IS WILLING!
IS GUT! VILLING IS GUT!
FZZANGGGG
DIDN'T KNOW HOW MUCH POWER TO USE. HE'S A BIG BOY. GIVE ME A HAND WITH HIM.
LET'S DO A DEAL, STRONT. WE KNOW WHERE THERE'S A FORTUNE TO BE MADE.
THE NINETY ON YOU WILL DO ME FINE, MEEZLE.
150 — PLUS 90 EACH FOR THE MEEZLES — PLUS 200 BIG ONES ON BLOG — WE'VE GOT OVER HALF WHAT WE NEED ALREADY.
JA, THINGS HAVE BEEN GOING VELL. TOO VELL.
ONE MORE BIG PUSH, WULF. THAT'S ALL WE NEED...

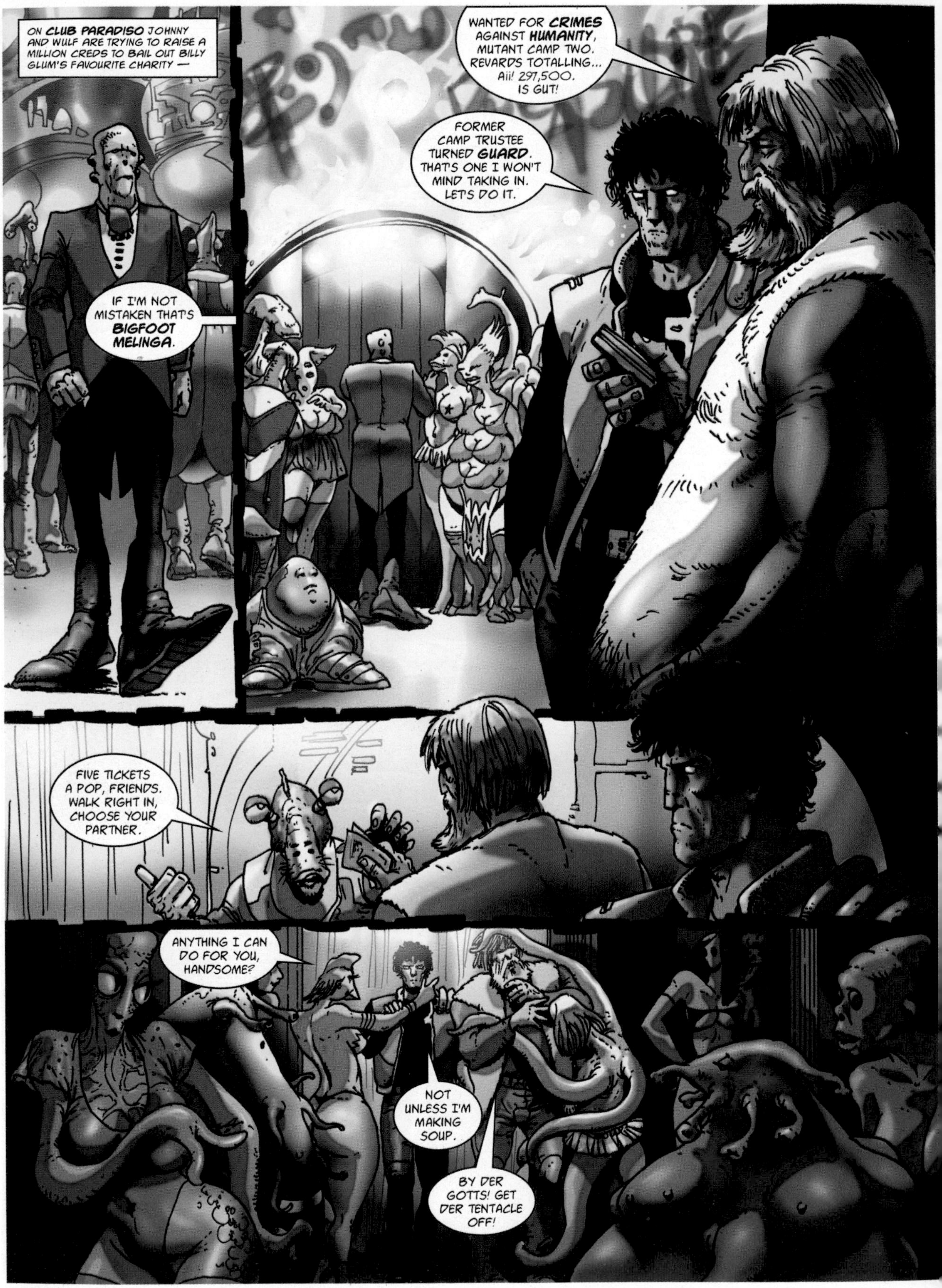
ON **CLUB PARADISO** JOHNNY AND WULF ARE TRYING TO RAISE A MILLION CREDS TO BAIL OUT BILLY GLUM'S FAVOURITE CHARITY —
IF I'M NOT MISTAKEN THAT'S **BIGFOOT MELINGA**.
WANTED FOR **CRIMES** AGAINST **HUMANITY**, MUTANT CAMP TWO. REVARDS TOTALLING... Aii! 297,500. IS GUT!
FORMER CAMP TRUSTEE TURNED **GUARD**. THAT'S ONE I WON'T MIND TAKING IN. LET'S DO IT.
FIVE TICKETS A POP, FRIENDS. WALK RIGHT IN, CHOOSE YOUR PARTNER.
ANYTHING I CAN DO FOR YOU, HANDSOME?
NOT UNLESS I'M MAKING SOUP.
BY DER GOTTS! GET DER TENTACLE OFF!

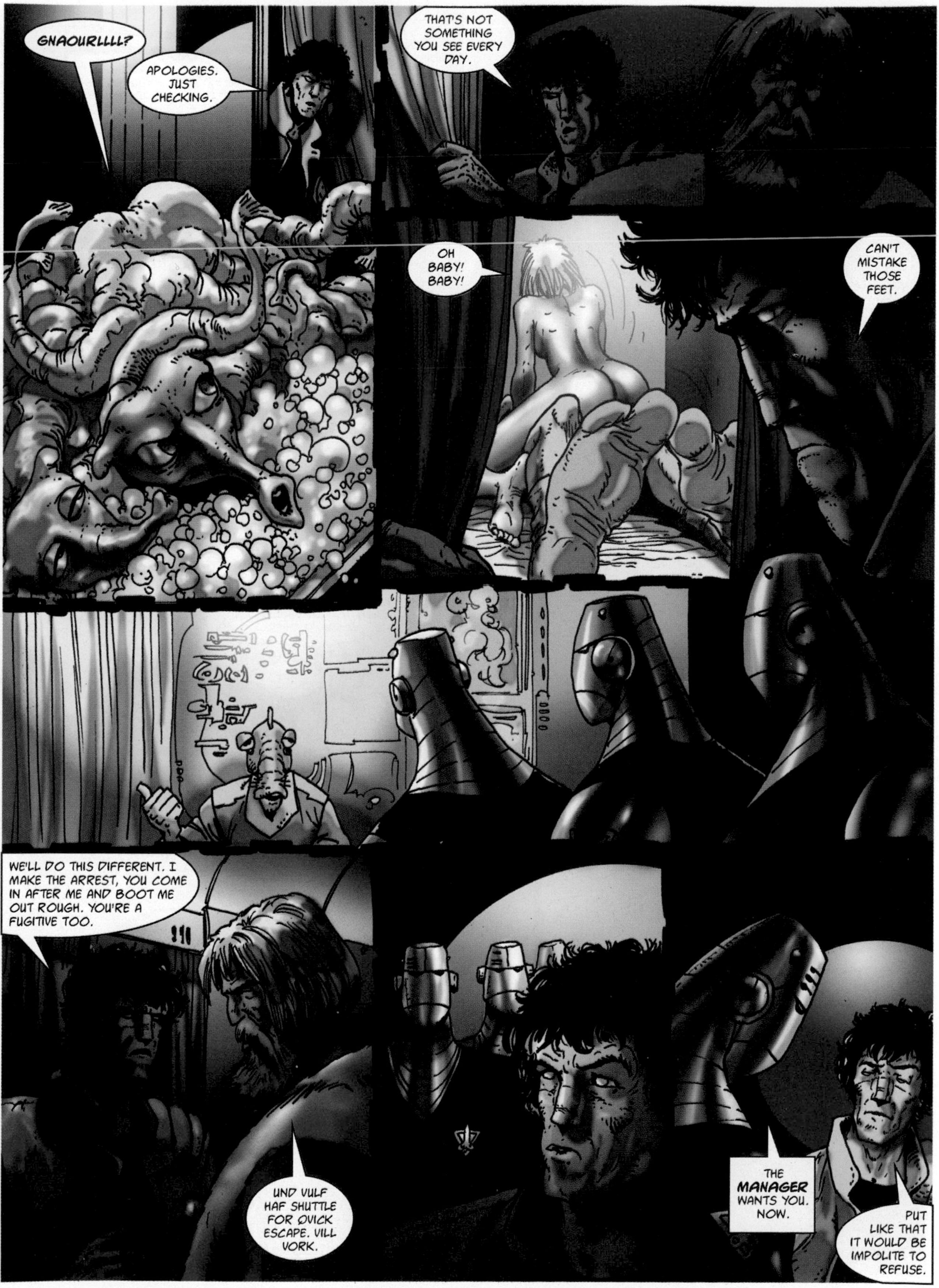
GNAOURLLLL?
APOLOGIES. JUST CHECKING.
THAT'S NOT SOMETHING YOU SEE EVERY DAY.
OH BABY! BABY!
CAN'T MISTAKE THOSE FEET.
WE'LL DO THIS DIFFERENT. I MAKE THE ARREST, YOU COME IN AFTER ME AND BOOT ME OUT ROUGH. YOU'RE A FUGITIVE TOO.
UND VULF HAF SHUTTLE FOR QVICK ESCAPE. VILL VORK.
THE MANAGER WANTS YOU. NOW.
PUT LIKE THAT IT WOULD BE IMPOLITE TO REFUSE.

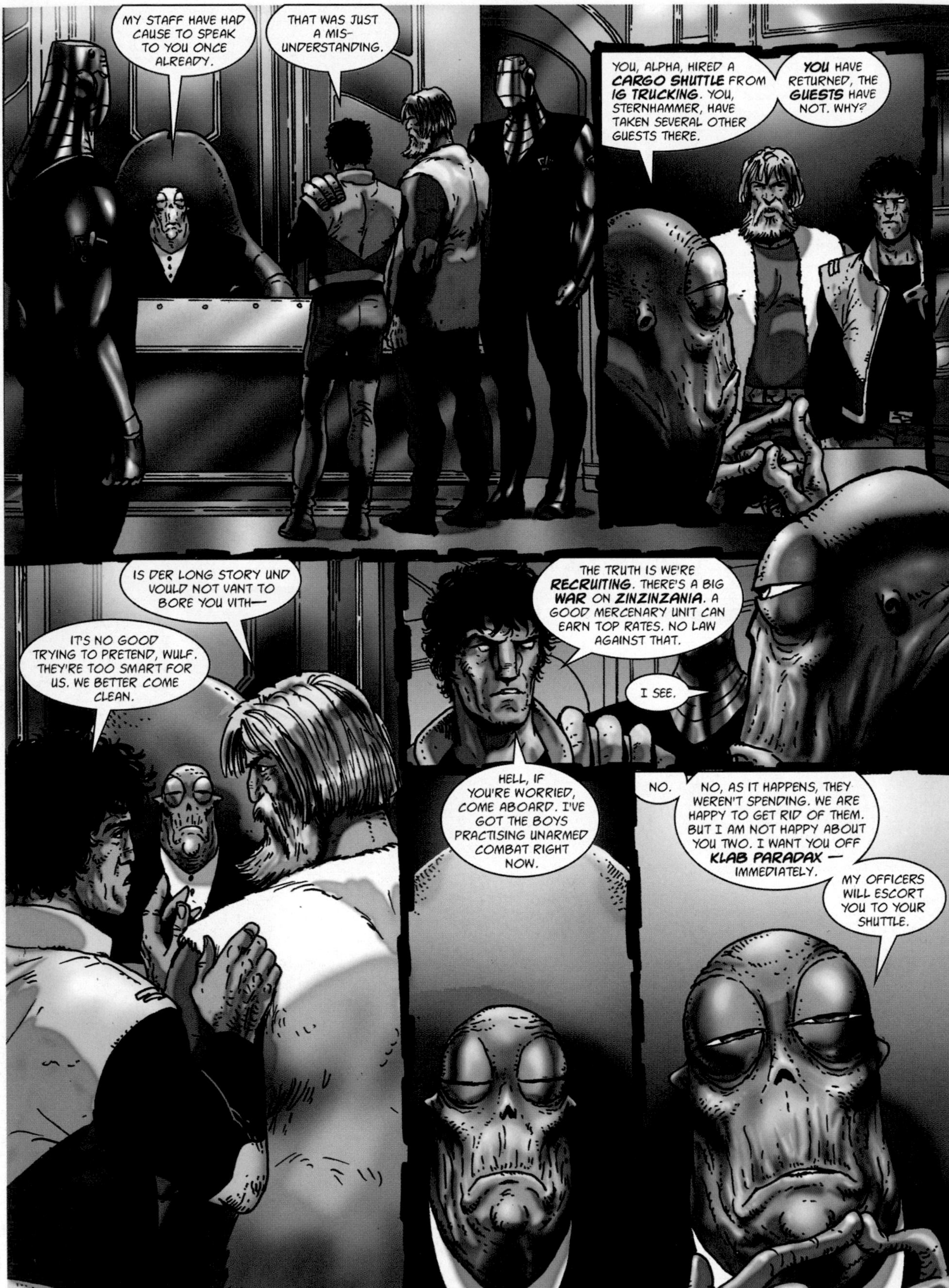
MY STAFF HAVE HAD CAUSE TO SPEAK TO YOU ONCE ALREADY.
THAT WAS JUST A MIS-UNDERSTANDING.
YOU, ALPHA, HIRED A CARGO SHUTTLE FROM IG TRUCKING. YOU, STERNHAMMER, HAVE TAKEN SEVERAL OTHER GUESTS THERE.
YOU HAVE RETURNED, THE GUESTS HAVE NOT. WHY?
IS DER LONG STORY UND VOULD NOT VANT TO BORE YOU VITH—
IT'S NO GOOD TRYING TO PRETEND, WULF. THEY'RE TOO SMART FOR US. WE BETTER COME CLEAN.
THE TRUTH IS WE'RE RECRUITING. THERE'S A BIG WAR ON ZINZINZANIA. A GOOD MERCENARY UNIT CAN EARN TOP RATES. NO LAW AGAINST THAT.
I SEE.
HELL, IF YOU'RE WORRIED, COME ABOARD. I'VE GOT THE BOYS PRACTISING UNARMED COMBAT RIGHT NOW.
NO.
NO, AS IT HAPPENS, THEY WEREN'T SPENDING. WE ARE HAPPY TO GET RID OF THEM. BUT I AM NOT HAPPY ABOUT YOU TWO. I WANT YOU OFF KLAB PARADAX — IMMEDIATELY.
MY OFFICERS WILL ESCORT YOU TO YOUR SHUTTLE.

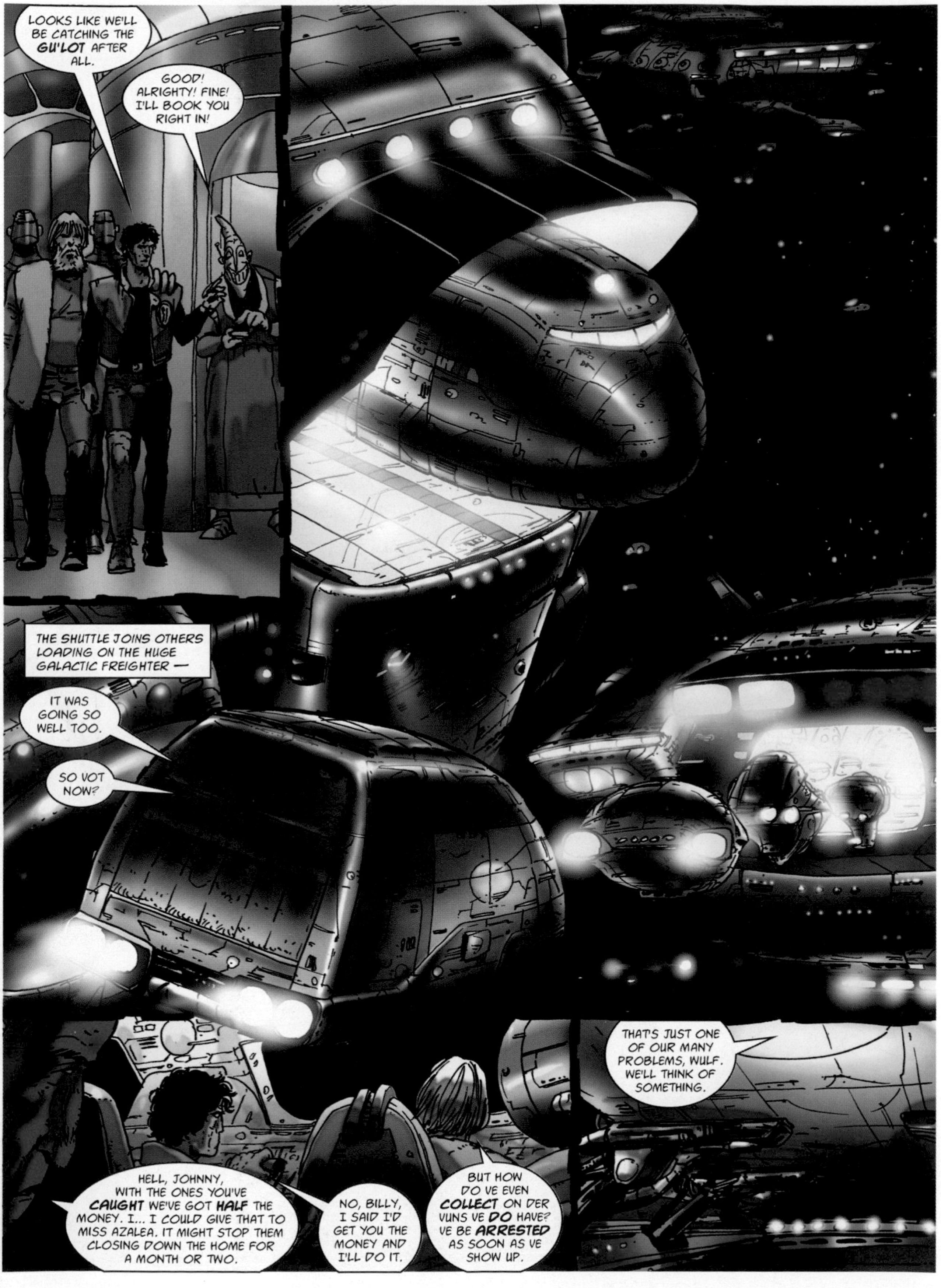
LOOKS LIKE WE'LL BE CATCHING THE **GU'LOT** AFTER ALL.
GOOD! ALRIGHTY! FINE! I'LL BOOK YOU RIGHT IN!
THE SHUTTLE JOINS OTHERS LOADING ON THE HUGE GALACTIC FREIGHTER —
IT WAS GOING SO WELL TOO.
SO VOT NOW?
HELL, JOHNNY, WITH THE ONES YOU'VE **CAUGHT** WE'VE GOT **HALF** THE MONEY. I... I COULD GIVE THAT TO MISS AZALEA. IT MIGHT STOP THEM CLOSING DOWN THE HOME FOR A MONTH OR TWO.
NO, BILLY, I SAID I'D GET YOU THE MONEY AND I'LL DO IT.
BUT HOW DO VE EVEN **COLLECT** ON DER VUNS VE **DO** HAVE? VE BE **ARRESTED** AS SOON AS VE SHOW UP.
THAT'S JUST ONE OF OUR MANY PROBLEMS, WULF. WE'LL THINK OF SOMETHING.

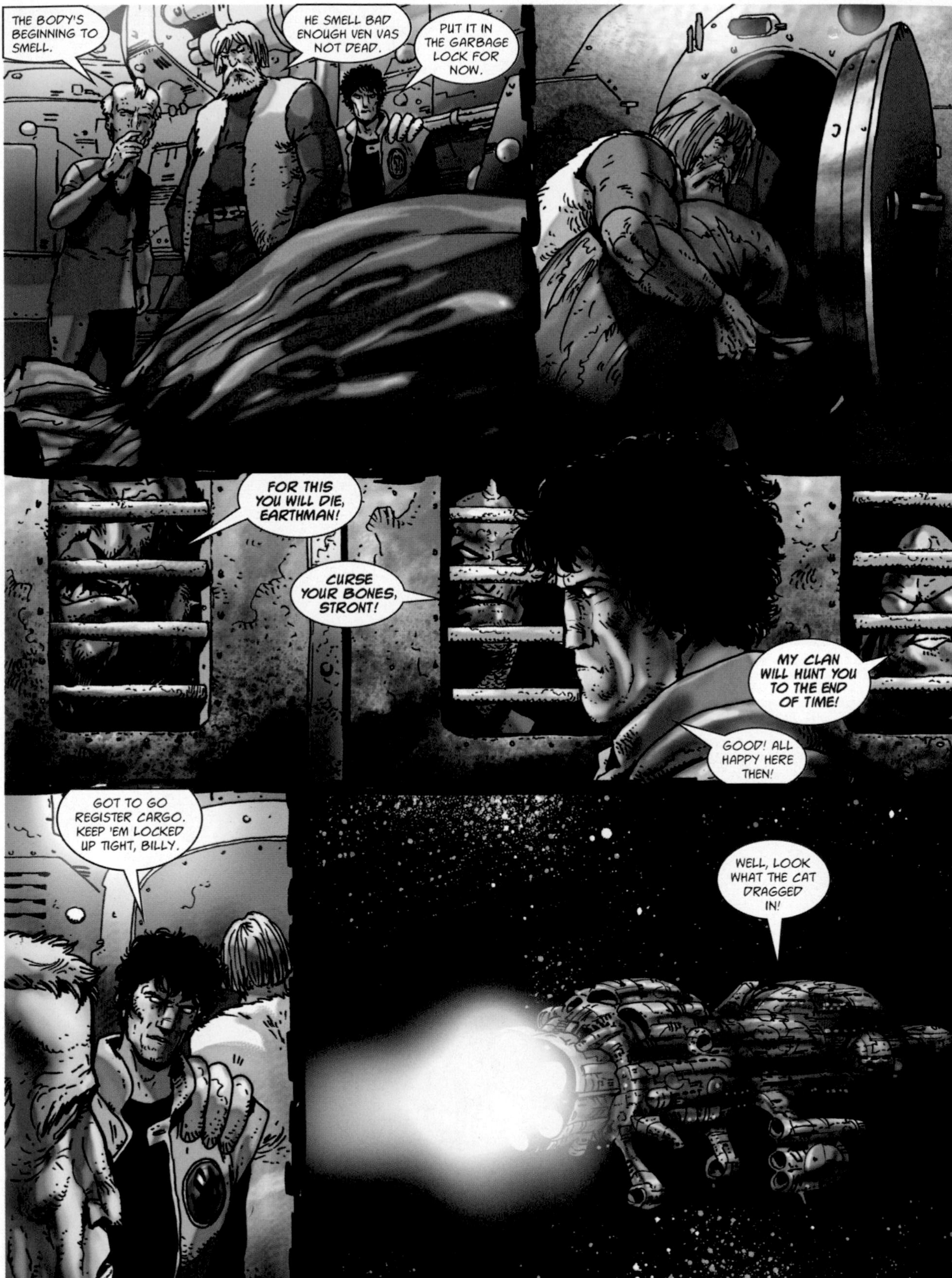
THE BODY'S BEGINNING TO SMELL.
HE SMELL BAD ENOUGH VEN VAS NOT DEAD.
PUT IT IN THE GARBAGE LOCK FOR NOW.
FOR THIS YOU WILL DIE, EARTHMAN!
CURSE YOUR BONES, STRONT!
MY CLAN WILL HUNT YOU TO THE END OF TIME!
GOOD! ALL HAPPY HERE THEN!
GOT TO GO REGISTER CARGO. KEEP 'EM LOCKED UP TIGHT, BILLY.
WELL, LOOK WHAT THE CAT DRAGGED IN!

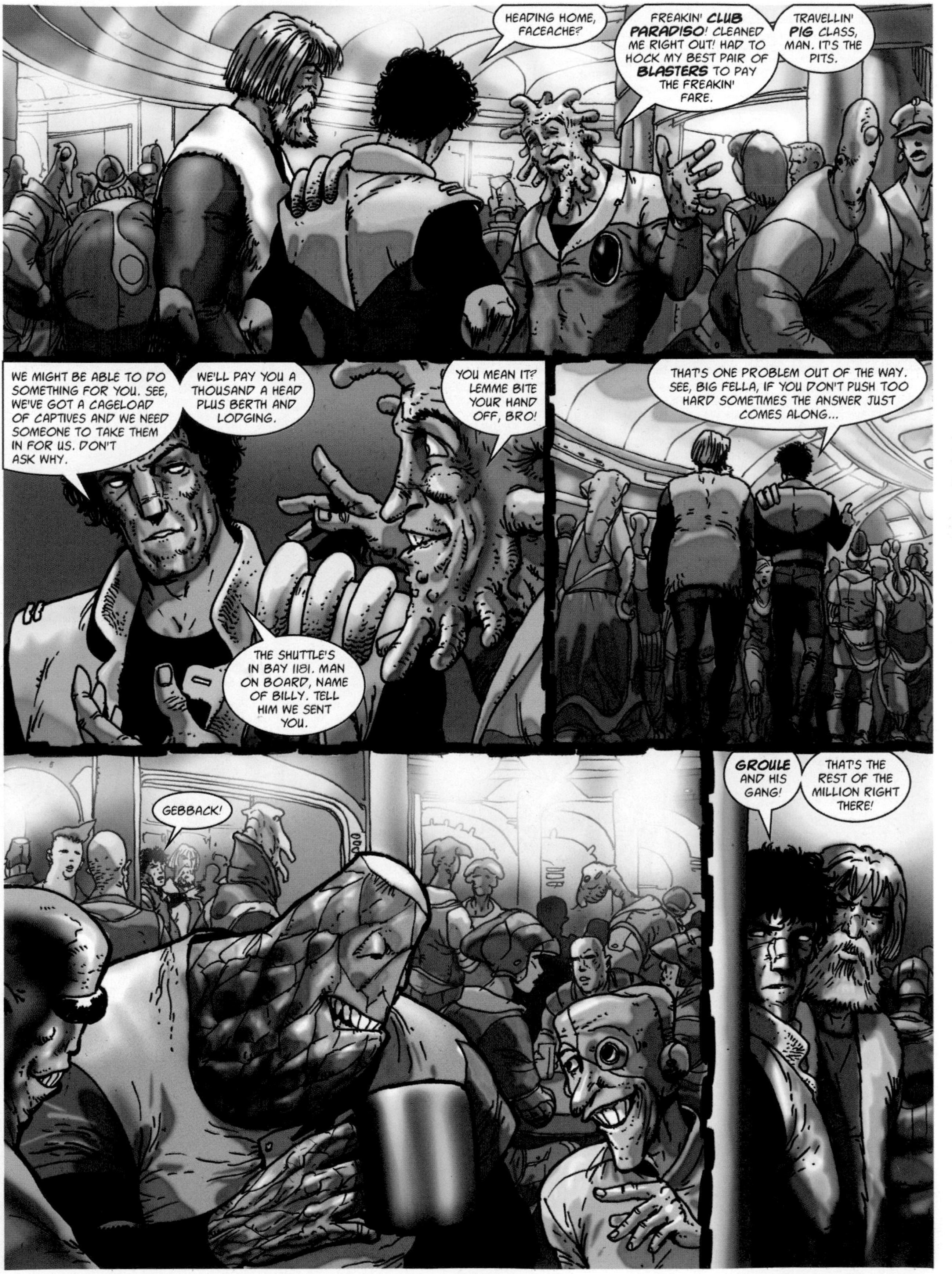
HEADING HOME, FACEACHE?
FREAKIN' **CLUB PARADISO**! CLEANED ME RIGHT OUT! HAD TO HOCK MY BEST PAIR OF **BLASTERS** TO PAY THE FREAKIN' FARE.
TRAVELLIN' **PIG** CLASS, MAN. IT'S THE PITS.
WE MIGHT BE ABLE TO DO SOMETHING FOR YOU. SEE, WE'VE GOT A CAGELOAD OF CAPTIVES AND WE NEED SOMEONE TO TAKE THEM IN FOR US. DON'T ASK WHY.
WE'LL PAY YOU A THOUSAND A HEAD PLUS BERTH AND LODGING.
YOU MEAN IT? LEMME BITE YOUR HAND OFF, BRO!
THE SHUTTLE'S IN BAY 1181. MAN ON BOARD, NAME OF BILLY. TELL HIM WE SENT YOU.
THAT'S ONE PROBLEM OUT OF THE WAY. SEE, BIG FELLA, IF YOU DON'T PUSH TOO HARD SOMETIMES THE ANSWER JUST COMES ALONG...
GEBBACK!
GROULE AND HIS GANG!
THAT'S THE REST OF THE MILLION RIGHT THERE!

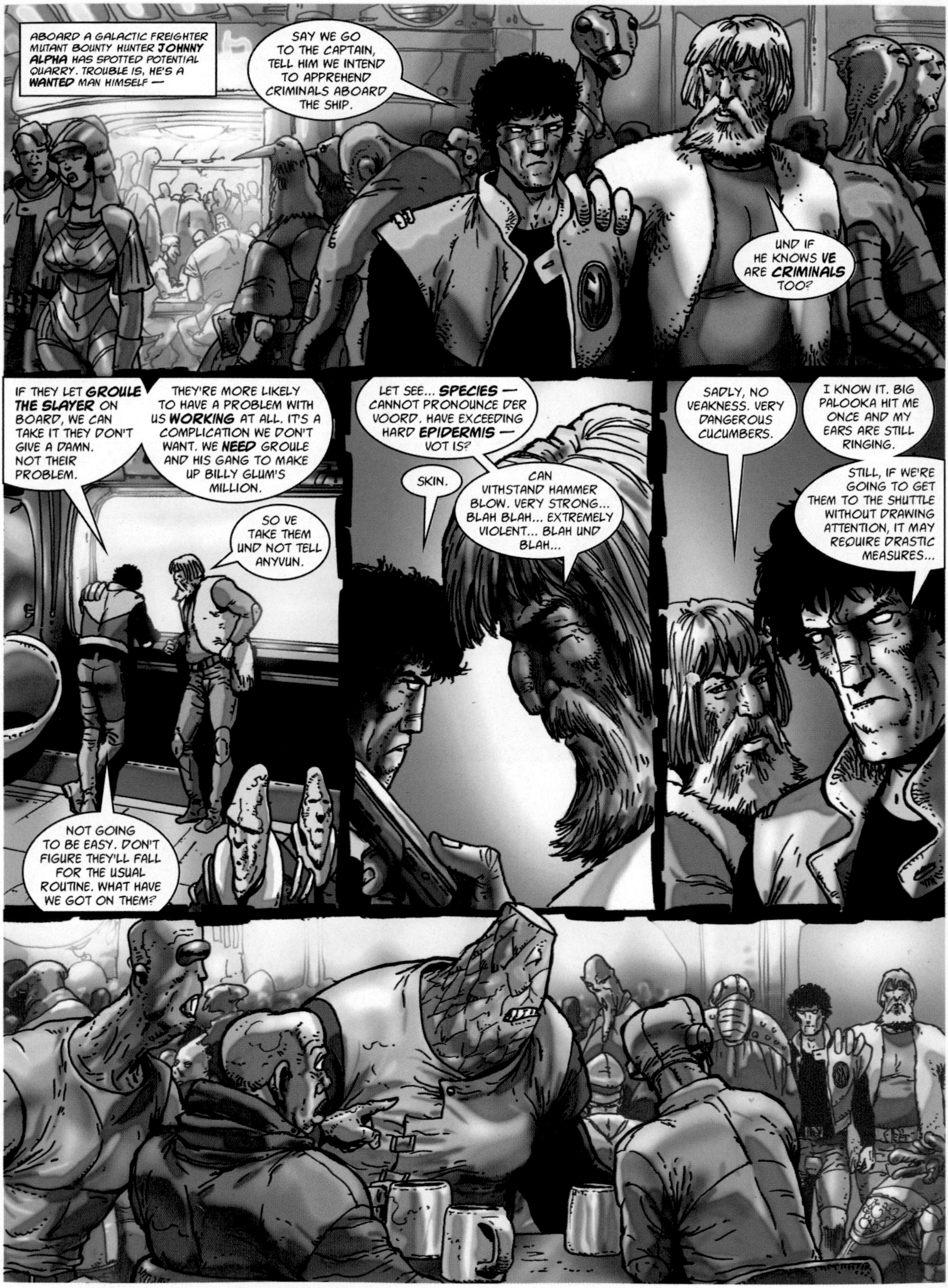
ABOARD A GALACTIC FREIGHTER MUTANT BOUNTY HUNTER JOHNNY ALPHA HAS SPOTTED POTENTIAL QUARRY. TROUBLE IS, HE'S A WANTED MAN HIMSELF —
SAY WE GO TO THE CAPTAIN, TELL HIM WE INTEND TO APPREHEND CRIMINALS ABOARD THE SHIP.
UND IF HE KNOWS VE ARE CRIMINALS TOO?
IF THEY LET GROULE THE SLAYER ON BOARD, WE CAN TAKE IT THEY DON'T GIVE A DAMN. NOT THEIR PROBLEM.
THEY'RE MORE LIKELY TO HAVE A PROBLEM WITH US WORKING AT ALL. IT'S A COMPLICATION WE DON'T WANT. WE NEED GROULE AND HIS GANG TO MAKE UP BILLY GLUM'S MILLION.
SO VE TAKE THEM UND NOT TELL ANYVUN.
NOT GOING TO BE EASY. DON'T FIGURE THEY'LL FALL FOR THE USUAL ROUTINE. WHAT HAVE WE GOT ON THEM?
LET SEE... SPECIES — CANNOT PRONOUNCE DER VOORD. HAVE EXCEEDING HARD EPIDERMIS — VOT IS?
SKIN.
CAN VITHSTAND HAMMER BLOW. VERY STRONG... BLAH BLAH... EXTREMELY VIOLENT... BLAH UND BLAH...
SADLY, NO VEAKNESS. VERY DANGEROUS CUCUMBERS.
I KNOW IT. BIG PALOOKA HIT ME ONCE AND MY EARS ARE STILL RINGING.
STILL, IF WE'RE GOING TO GET THEM TO THE SHUTTLE WITHOUT DRAWING ATTENTION, IT MAY REQUIRE DRASTIC MEASURES...

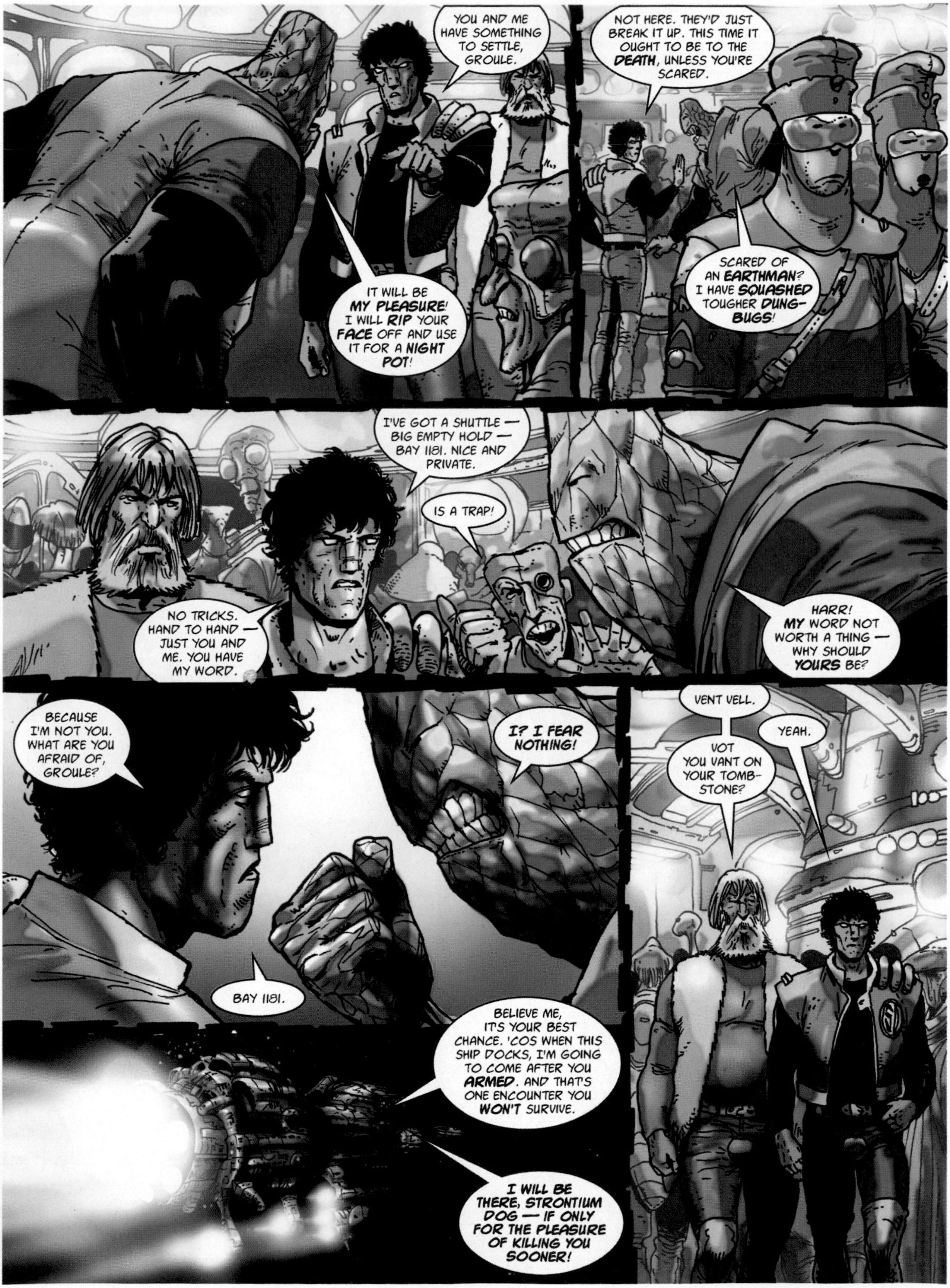
YOU AND ME HAVE SOMETHING TO SETTLE, GROULE.
IT WILL BE MY PLEASURE! I WILL RIP YOUR FACE OFF AND USE IT FOR A NIGHT POT!
NOT HERE. THEY'D JUST BREAK IT UP. THIS TIME IT OUGHT TO BE TO THE DEATH, UNLESS YOU'RE SCARED.
SCARED OF AN EARTHMAN? I HAVE SQUASHED TOUGHER DUNG-BUGS!
I'VE GOT A SHUTTLE — BIG EMPTY HOLD — BAY 1181. NICE AND PRIVATE.
IS A TRAP!
NO TRICKS. HAND TO HAND — JUST YOU AND ME. YOU HAVE MY WORD.
HARR! MY WORD NOT WORTH A THING — WHY SHOULD YOURS BE?
BECAUSE I'M NOT YOU. WHAT ARE YOU AFRAID OF, GROULE?
I? I FEAR NOTHING!
BAY 1181.
VENT VELL.
VOT YOU VANT ON YOUR TOMB-STONE?
YEAH.
BELIEVE ME, IT'S YOUR BEST CHANCE. 'COS WHEN THIS SHIP DOCKS, I'M GOING TO COME AFTER YOU ARMED. AND THAT'S ONE ENCOUNTER YOU WON'T SURVIVE.
I WILL BE THERE, STRONTIUM DOG — IF ONLY FOR THE PLEASURE OF KILLING YOU SOONER!

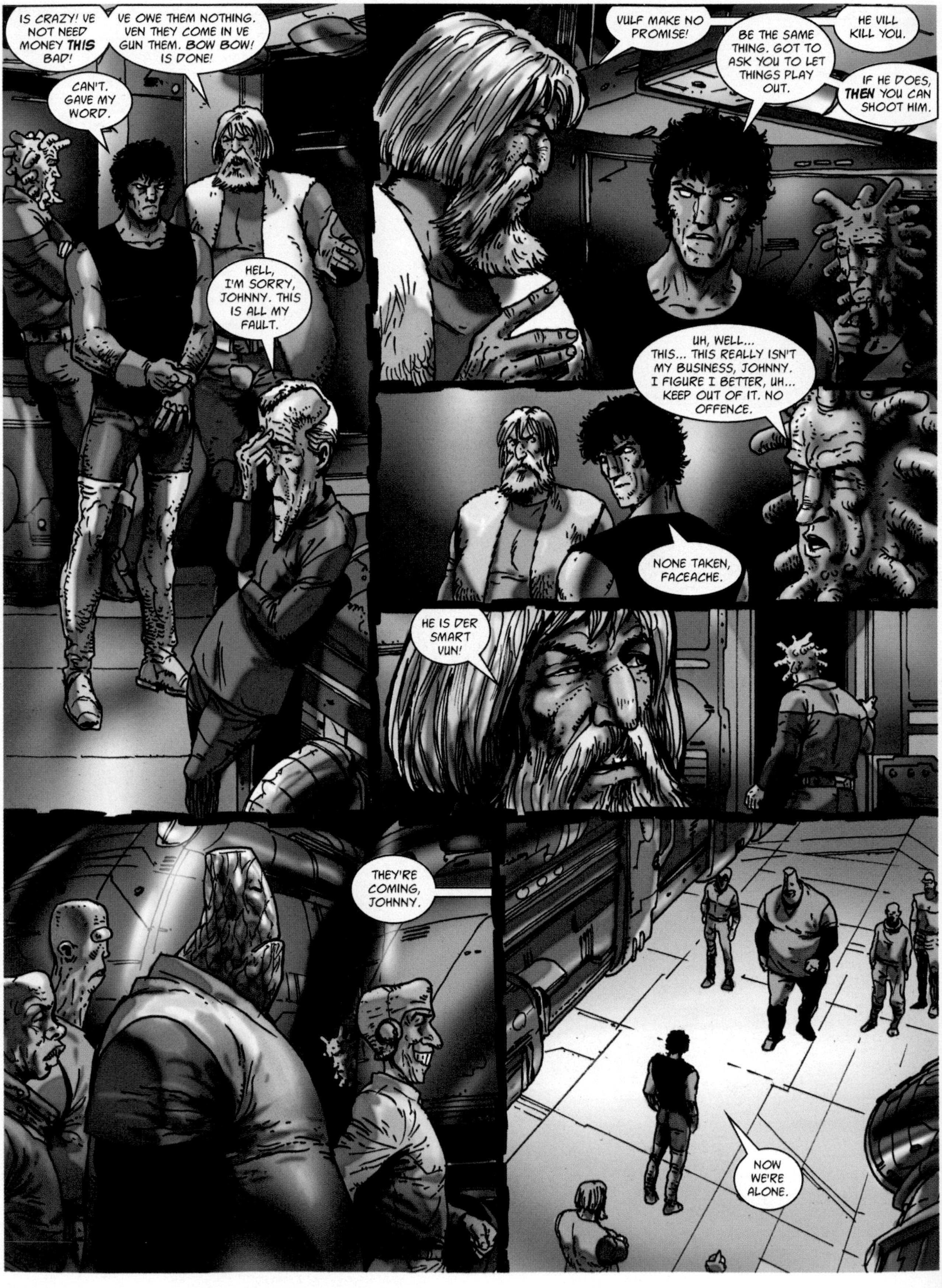
IS CRAZY! VE NOT NEED MONEY **THIS** BAD!
VE OWE THEM NOTHING. VEN THEY COME IN VE GUN THEM. BOW BOW! IS DONE!
CAN'T. GAVE MY WORD.
HELL, I'M SORRY, JOHNNY. THIS IS ALL MY FAULT.
VULF MAKE NO PROMISE!
BE THE SAME THING. GOT TO ASK YOU TO LET THINGS PLAY OUT.
HE VILL KILL YOU.
IF HE DOES, **THEN** YOU CAN SHOOT HIM.
UH, WELL... THIS... THIS REALLY ISN'T MY BUSINESS, JOHNNY. I FIGURE I BETTER, UH... KEEP OUT OF IT. NO OFFENCE.
NONE TAKEN, FACEACHE.
HE IS DER SMART VUN!
THEY'RE COMING, JOHNNY.
NOW WE'RE ALONE.

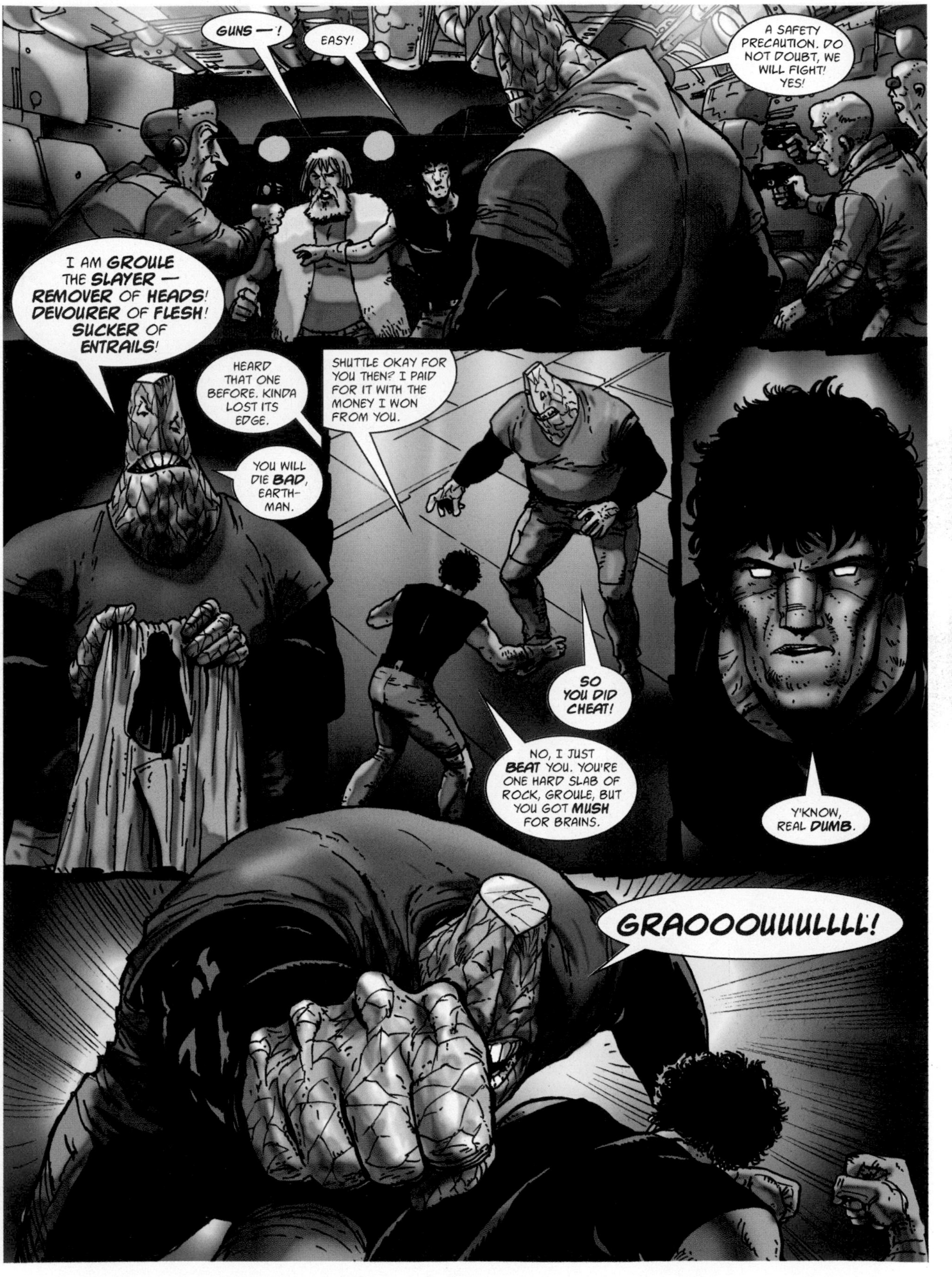

GUNS —!
EASY!
A SAFETY PRECAUTION. DO NOT DOUBT, WE WILL FIGHT! YES!
I AM GROULE THE SLAYER — REMOVER OF HEADS! DEVOURER OF FLESH! SUCKER OF ENTRAILS!
HEARD THAT ONE BEFORE. KINDA LOST ITS EDGE.
YOU WILL DIE BAD, EARTH-MAN.
SHUTTLE OKAY FOR YOU THEN? I PAID FOR IT WITH THE MONEY I WON FROM YOU.
SO YOU DID CHEAT!
NO, I JUST BEAT YOU. YOU'RE ONE HARD SLAB OF ROCK, GROULE, BUT YOU GOT MUSH FOR BRAINS.
Y'KNOW, REAL DUMB.
GRAOOOUUULLLL!

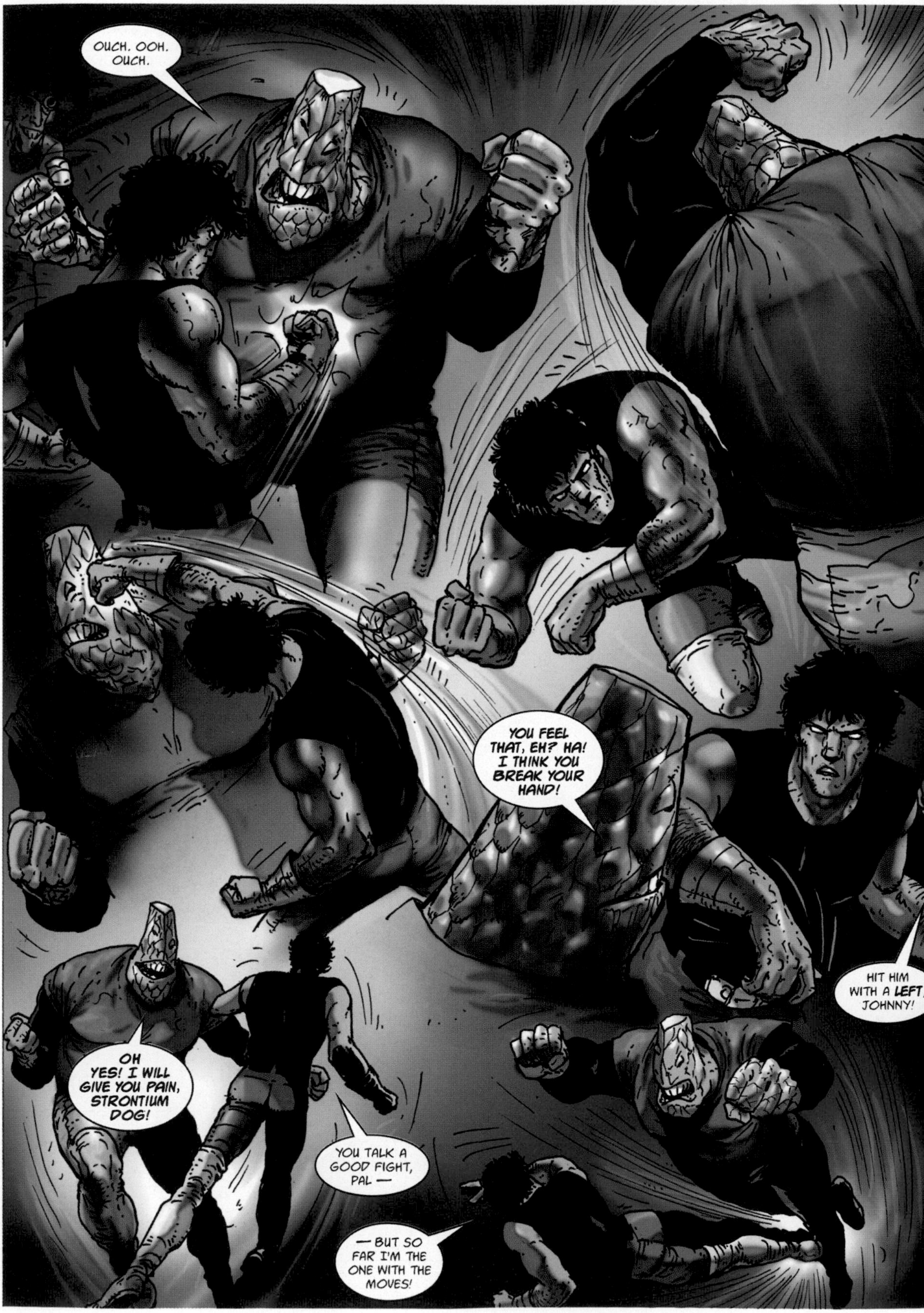
OUCH. OOH. OUCH.
YOU FEEL THAT, EH? HA! I THINK YOU BREAK YOUR HAND!
HIT HIM WITH A **LEFT**, JOHNNY!
OH YES! I WILL GIVE YOU PAIN, STRONTIUM DOG!
YOU TALK A GOOD FIGHT, PAL —
— BUT SO FAR I'M THE ONE WITH THE MOVES!

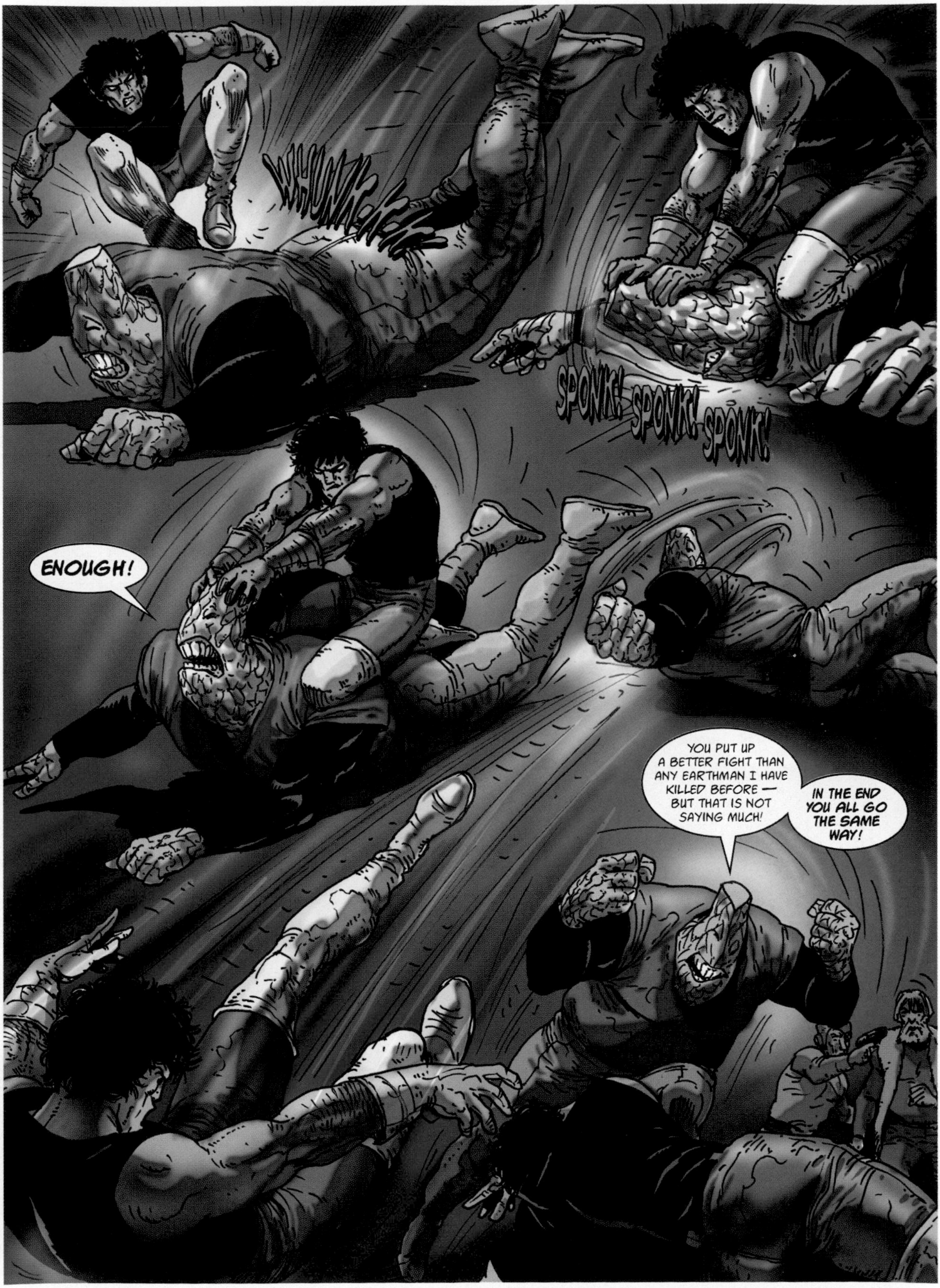
WHUNK-K-K
SPONK! SPONK! SPONK!
ENOUGH!
YOU PUT UP A BETTER FIGHT THAN ANY EARTHMAN I HAVE KILLED BEFORE — BUT THAT IS NOT SAYING MUCH!
IN THE END YOU ALL GO THE SAME WAY!

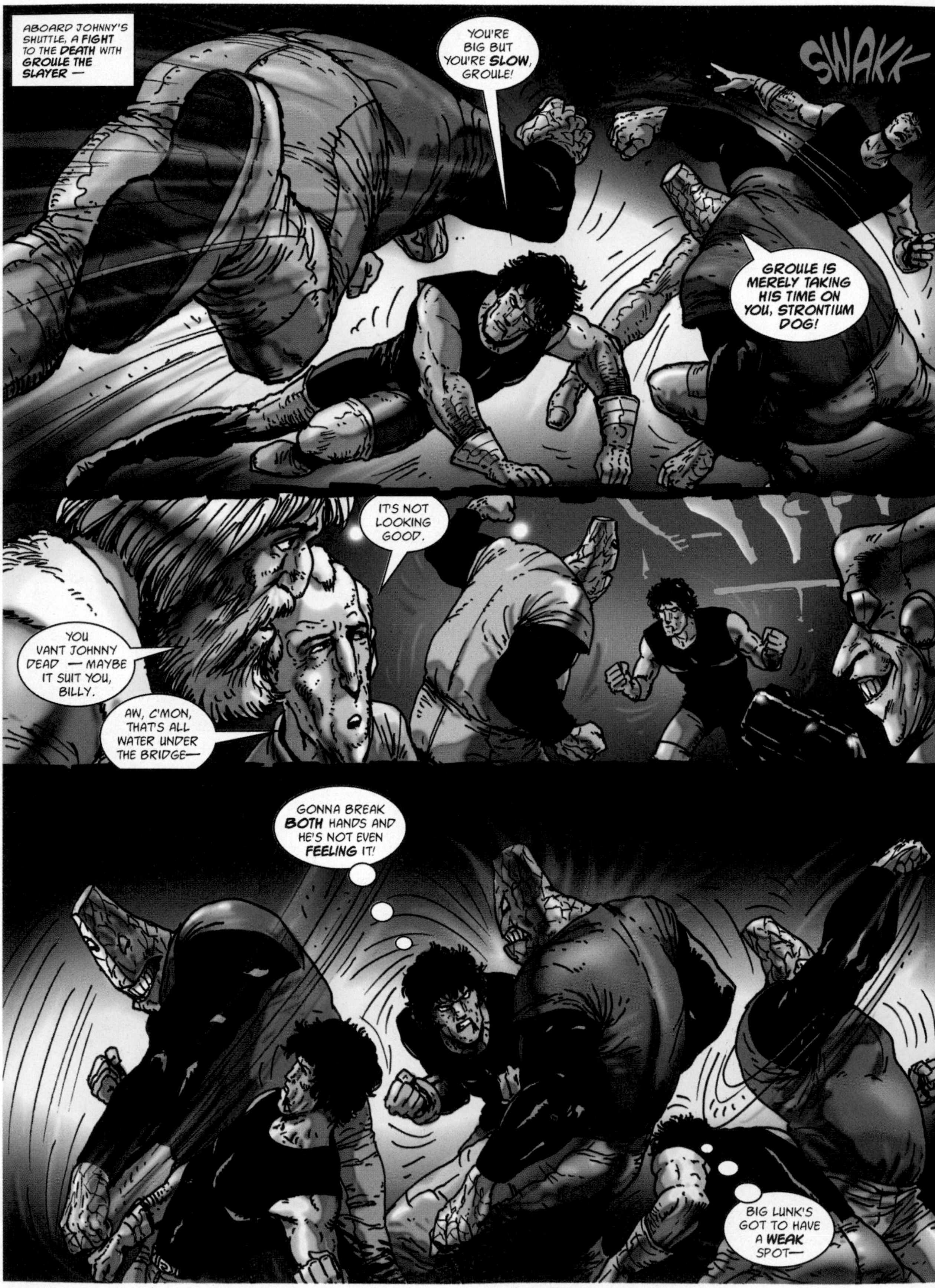

ABOARD JOHNNY'S SHUTTLE, A **FIGHT** TO THE **DEATH** WITH **GROULE THE SLAYER** —
YOU'RE BIG BUT YOU'RE **SLOW**, GROULE!
SWAKK
GROULE IS MERELY TAKING HIS TIME ON YOU, STRONTIUM DOG!
IT'S NOT LOOKING GOOD.
YOU VANT JOHNNY DEAD — MAYBE IT SUIT YOU, BILLY.
AW, C'MON, THAT'S ALL WATER UNDER THE BRIDGE—
GONNA BREAK **BOTH** HANDS AND HE'S NOT EVEN **FEELING** IT!
BIG LUNK'S GOT TO HAVE A **WEAK** SPOT—

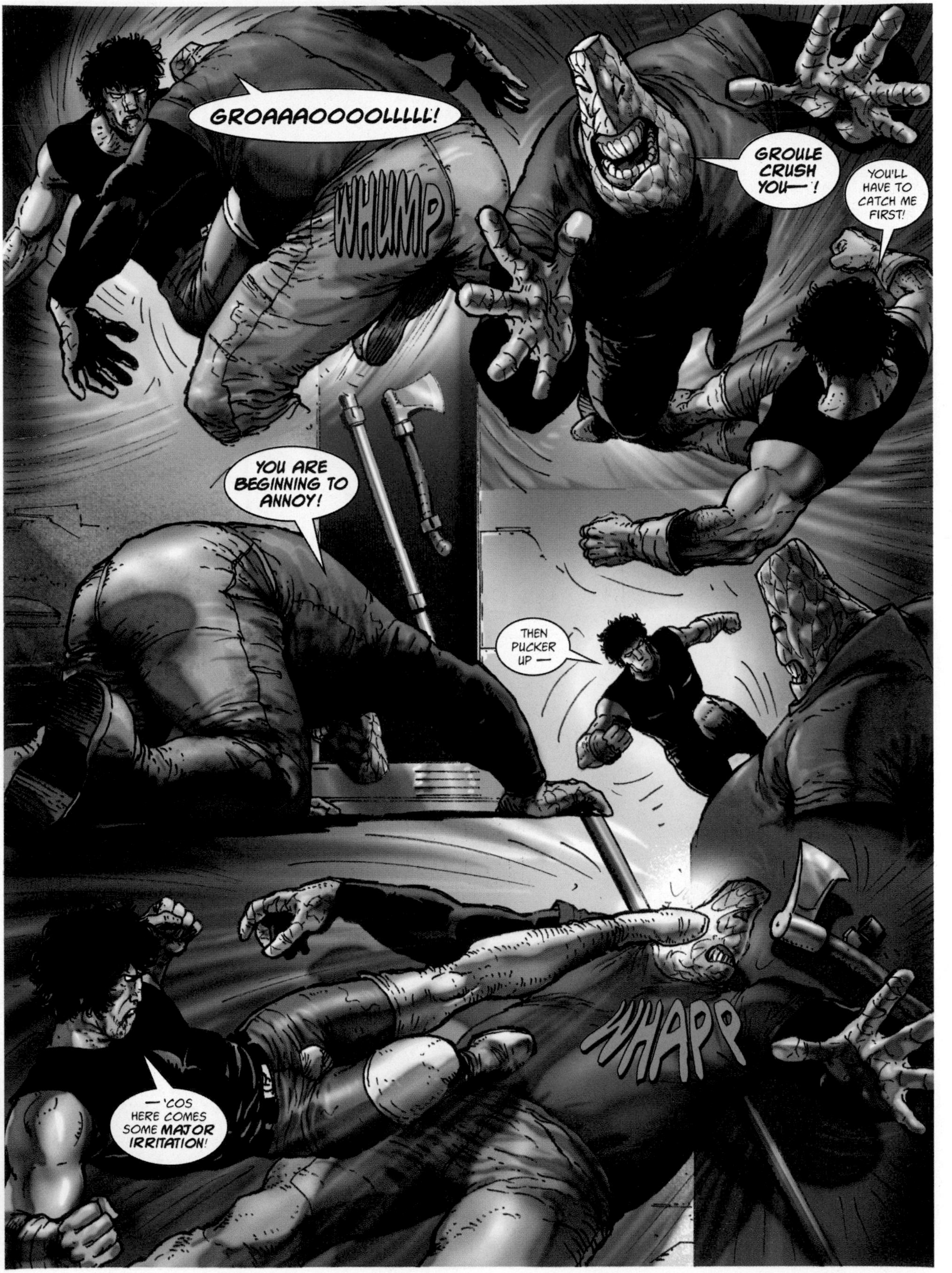

GROAAAOOOOLLLLLL!
WHUMP
GROULE CRUSH YOU—!
YOU'LL HAVE TO CATCH ME FIRST!
YOU ARE BEGINNING TO ANNOY!
THEN PUCKER UP —
—'COS HERE COMES SOME MAJOR IRRITATION!
WHAPP

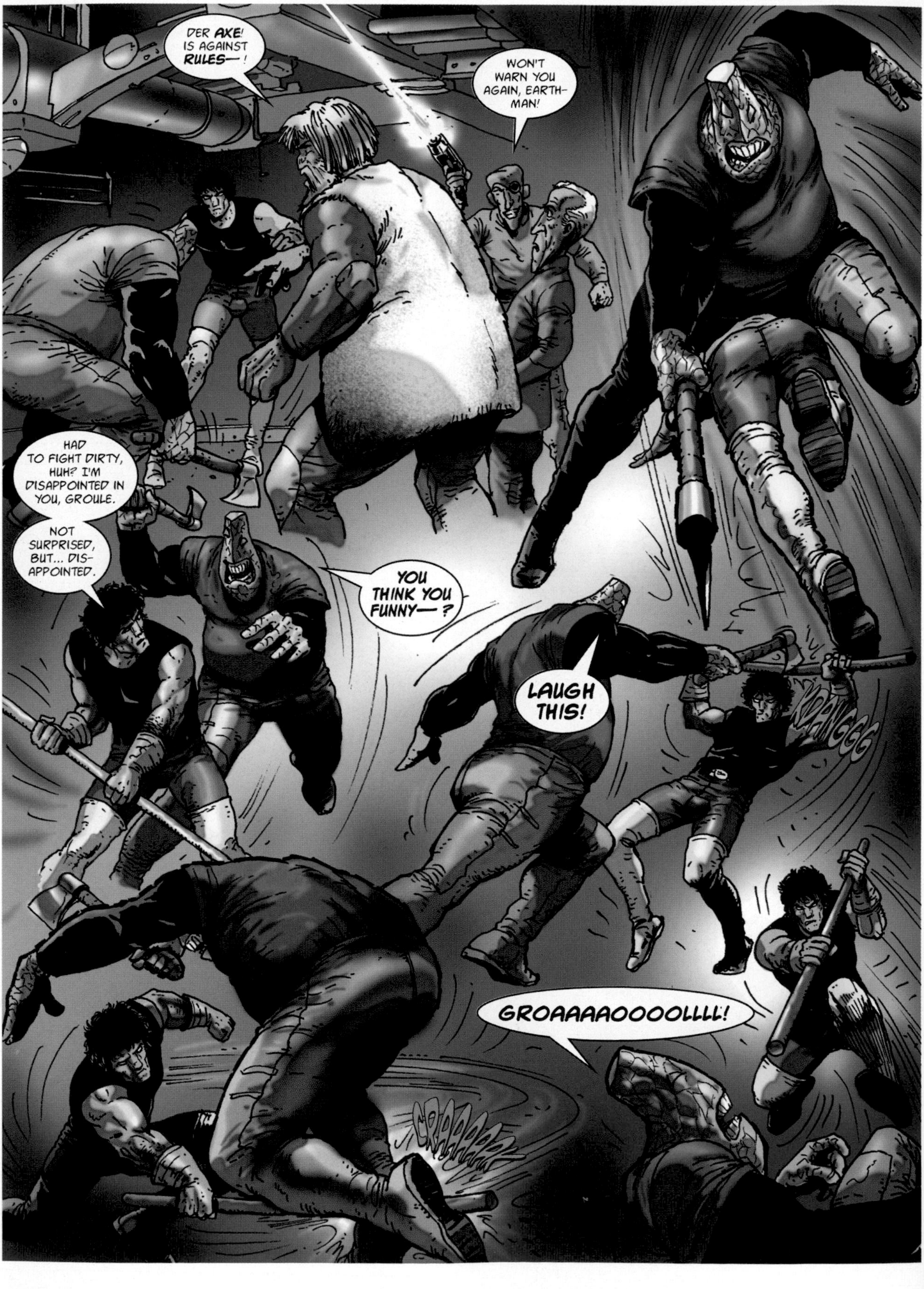
DER AXE! IS AGAINST RULES—!
WON'T WARN YOU AGAIN, EARTH-MAN!
HAD TO FIGHT DIRTY, HUH? I'M DISAPPOINTED IN YOU, GROULE.
NOT SURPRISED, BUT... DIS-APPOINTED.
YOU THINK YOU FUNNY—?
LAUGH THIS!
KRANGGG
GROAAAAOOOOLLLLL!
CRAAAKKK

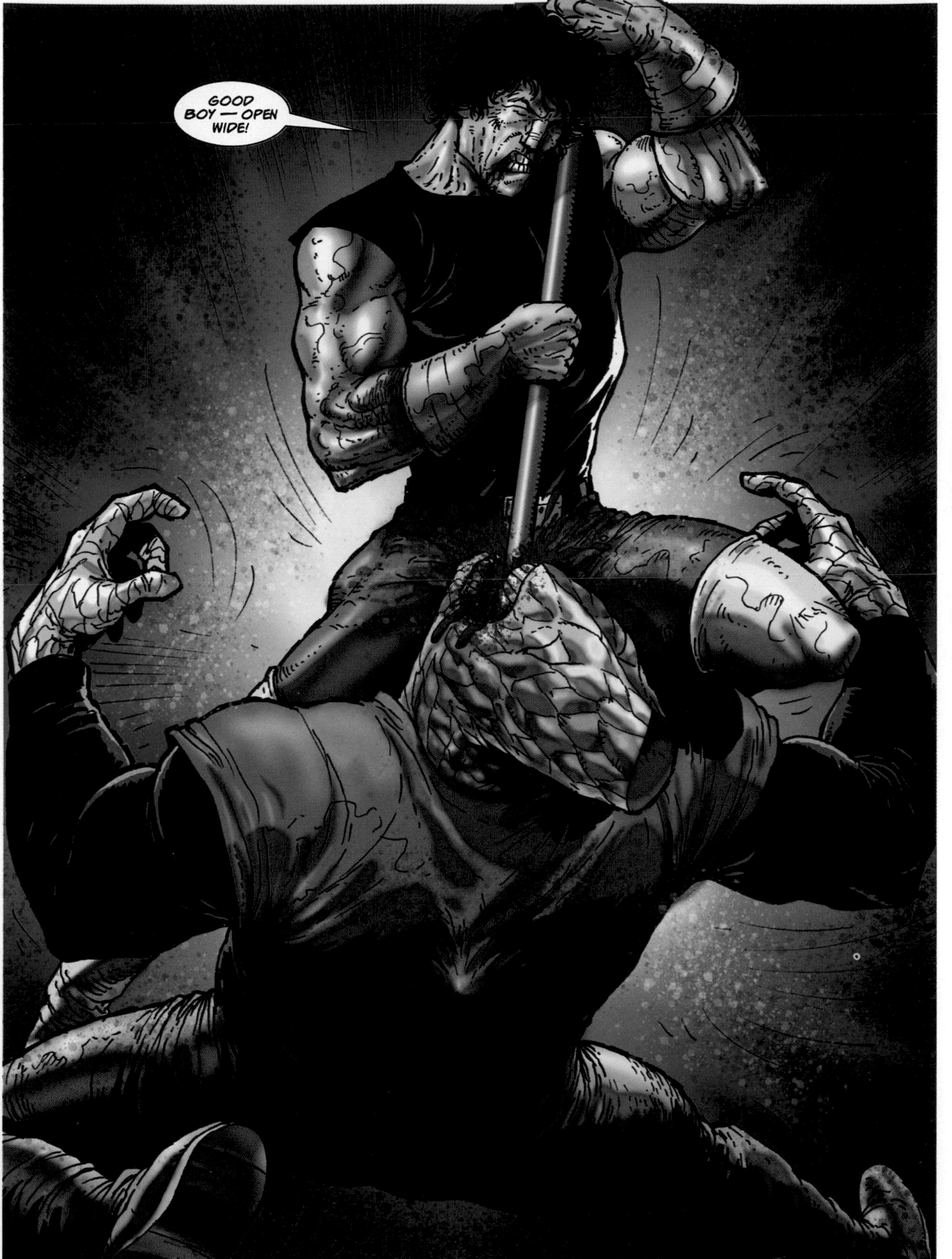
GOOD BOY — OPEN WIDE!

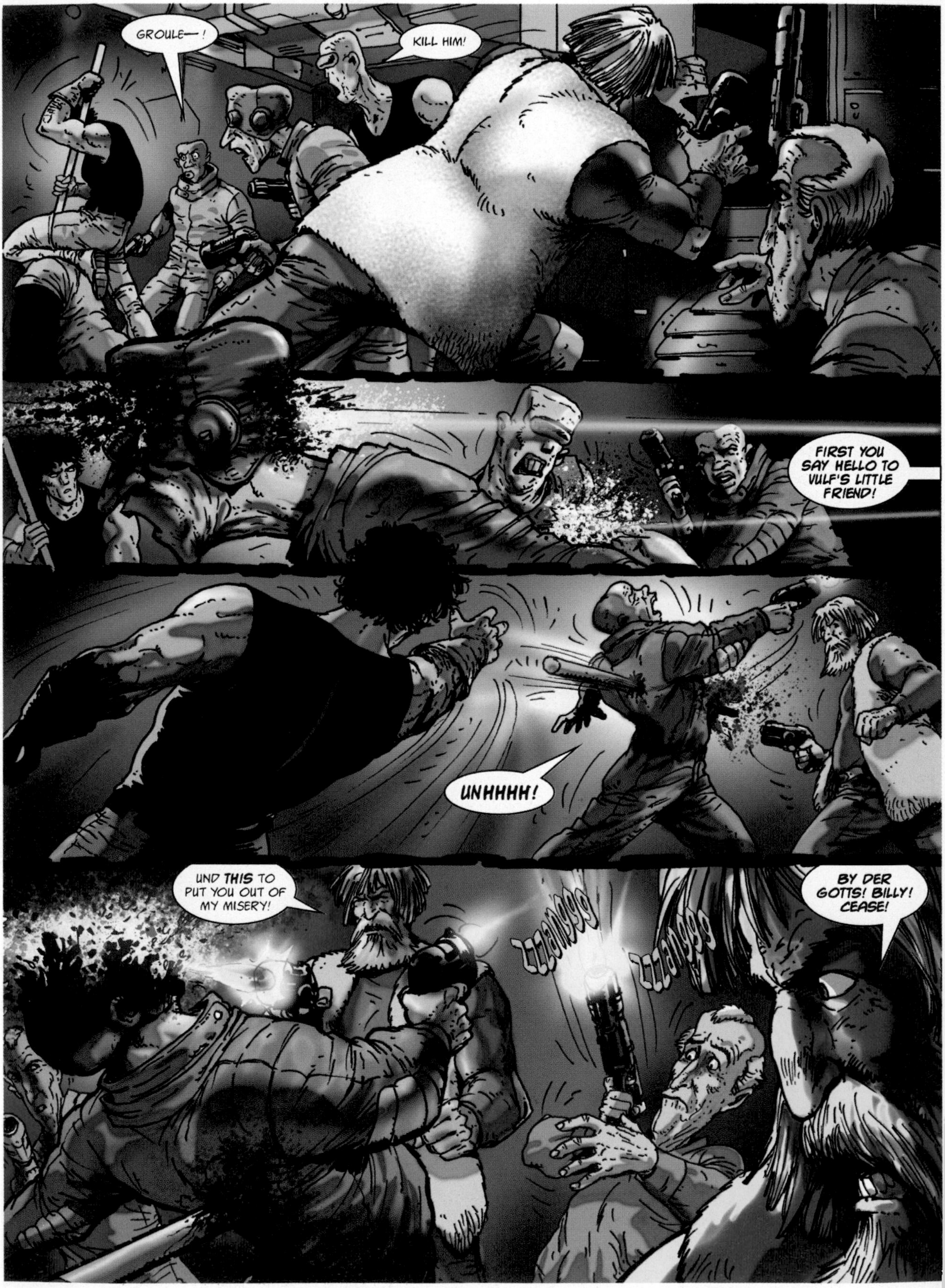
GROULE—!
KILL HIM!
FIRST YOU SAY HELLO TO VULF'S LITTLE FRIEND!
UNHHHH!
UND THIS TO PUT YOU OUT OF MY MISERY!
BY DER GOTTS! BILLY! CEASE!

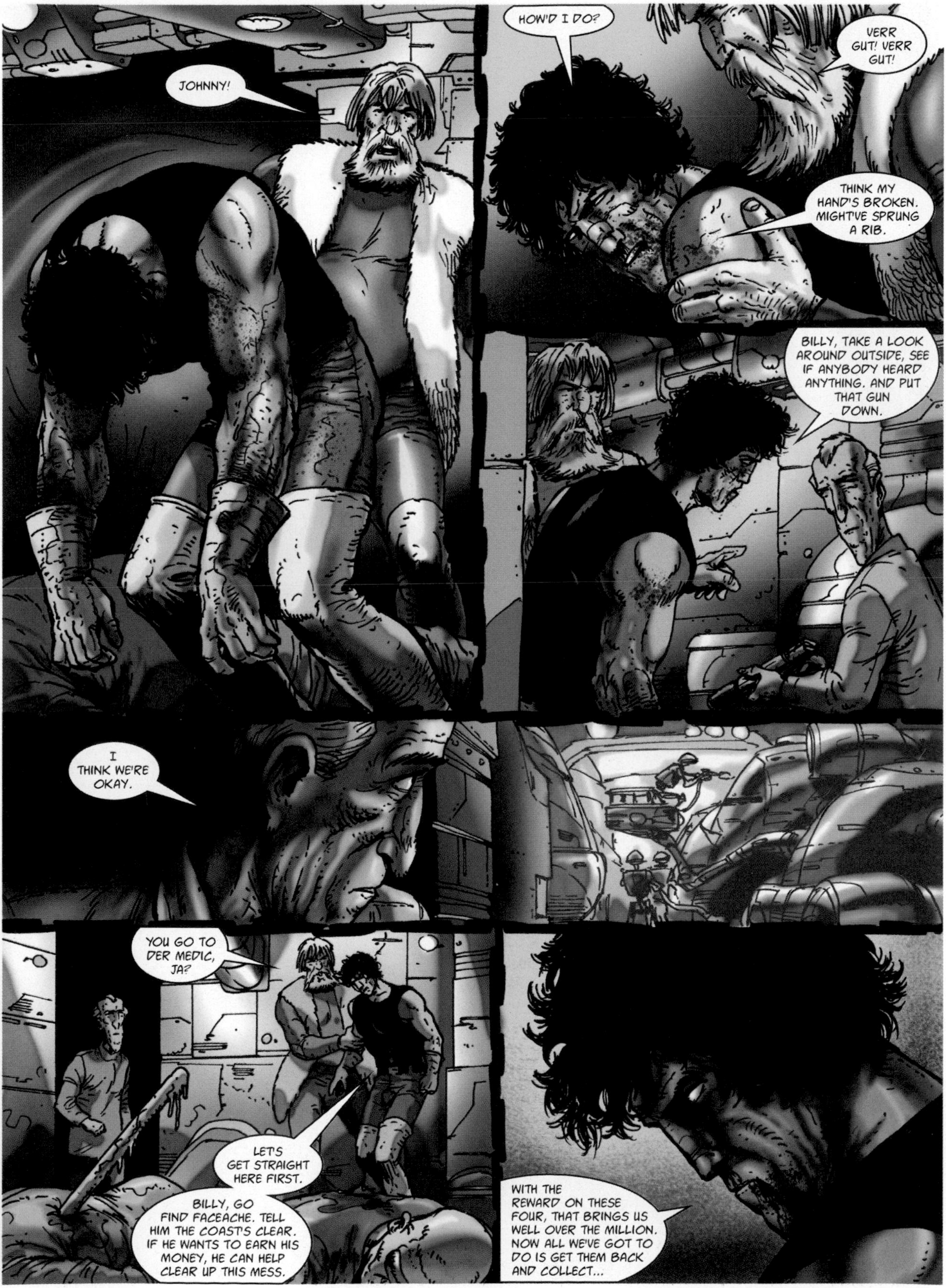
JOHNNY!
HOW'D I DO?
VERR GUT! VERR GUT!
THINK MY HAND'S BROKEN. MIGHT'VE SPRUNG A RIB.
BILLY, TAKE A LOOK AROUND OUTSIDE, SEE IF ANYBODY HEARD ANYTHING. AND PUT THAT GUN DOWN.
I THINK WE'RE OKAY.
YOU GO TO DER MEDIC, JA?
LET'S GET STRAIGHT HERE FIRST.
BILLY, GO FIND FACEACHE. TELL HIM THE COAST'S CLEAR. IF HE WANTS TO EARN HIS MONEY, HE CAN HELP CLEAR UP THIS MESS.
WITH THE REWARD ON THESE FOUR, THAT BRINGS US WELL OVER THE MILLION. NOW ALL WE'VE GOT TO DO IS GET THEM BACK AND COLLECT...

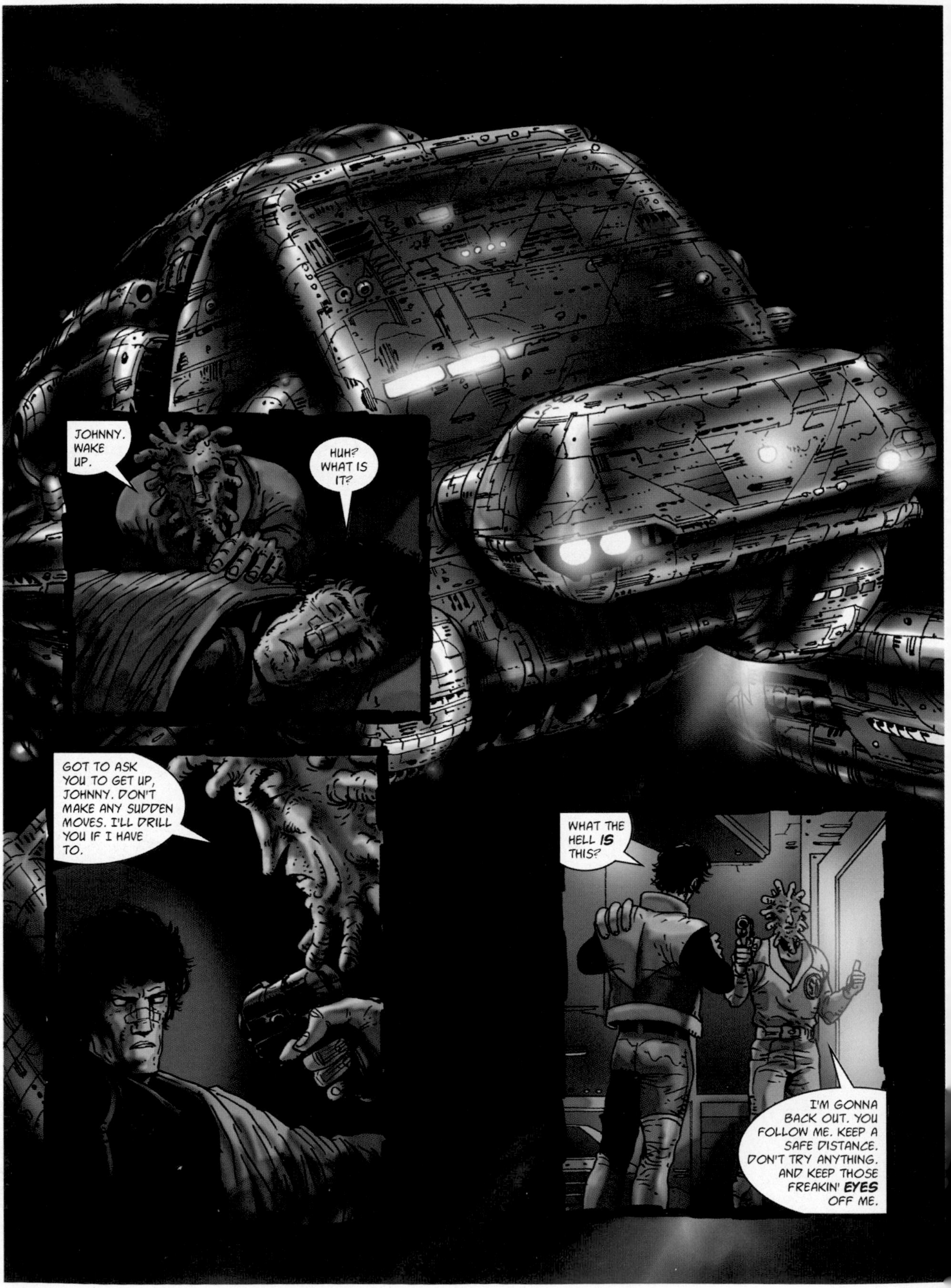
JOHNNY. WAKE UP.
HUH? WHAT IS IT?
GOT TO ASK YOU TO GET UP, JOHNNY. DON'T MAKE ANY SUDDEN MOVES. I'LL DRILL YOU IF I HAVE TO.
WHAT THE HELL IS THIS?
I'M GONNA BACK OUT. YOU FOLLOW ME. KEEP A SAFE DISTANCE. DON'T TRY ANYTHING. AND KEEP THOSE FREAKIN' EYES OFF ME.

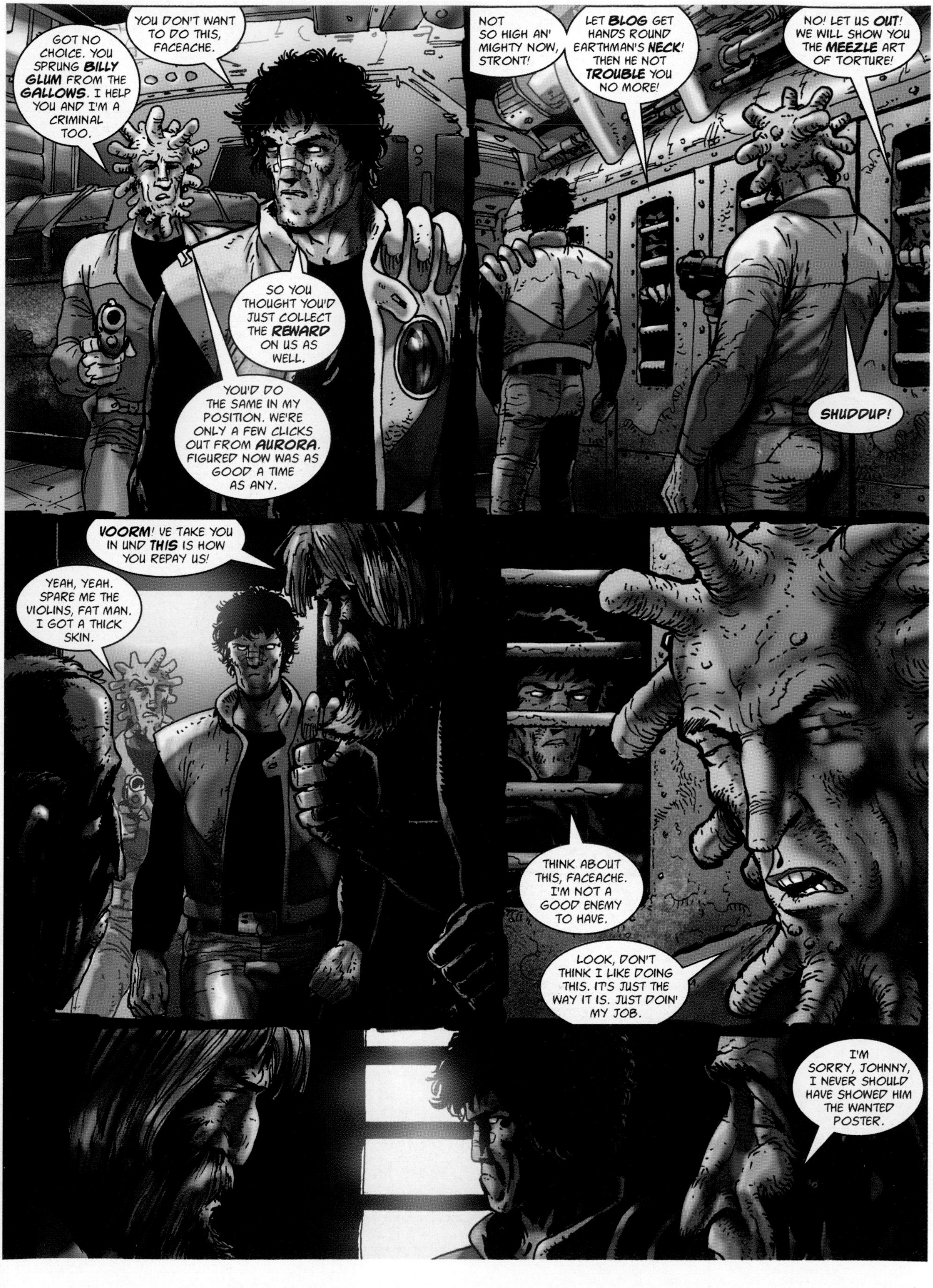
YOU DON'T WANT TO DO THIS, FACEACHE.
GOT NO CHOICE. YOU SPRUNG BILLY GLUM FROM THE GALLOWS. I HELP YOU AND I'M A CRIMINAL TOO.
SO YOU THOUGHT YOU'D JUST COLLECT THE REWARD ON US AS WELL.
YOU'D DO THE SAME IN MY POSITION. WE'RE ONLY A FEW CLICKS OUT FROM AURORA. FIGURED NOW WAS AS GOOD A TIME AS ANY.
NOT SO HIGH AN' MIGHTY NOW, STRONT!
LET BLOG GET HANDS ROUND EARTHMAN'S NECK! THEN HE NOT TROUBLE YOU NO MORE!
NO! LET US OUT! WE WILL SHOW YOU THE MEEZLE ART OF TORTURE!
SHUDDUP!
VOORM! VE TAKE YOU IN UND THIS IS HOW YOU REPAY US!
YEAH, YEAH. SPARE ME THE VIOLINS, FAT MAN. I GOT A THICK SKIN.
THINK ABOUT THIS, FACEACHE. I'M NOT A GOOD ENEMY TO HAVE.
LOOK, DON'T THINK I LIKE DOING THIS. IT'S JUST THE WAY IT IS. JUST DOIN' MY JOB.
I'M SORRY, JOHNNY, I NEVER SHOULD HAVE SHOWED HIM THE WANTED POSTER.

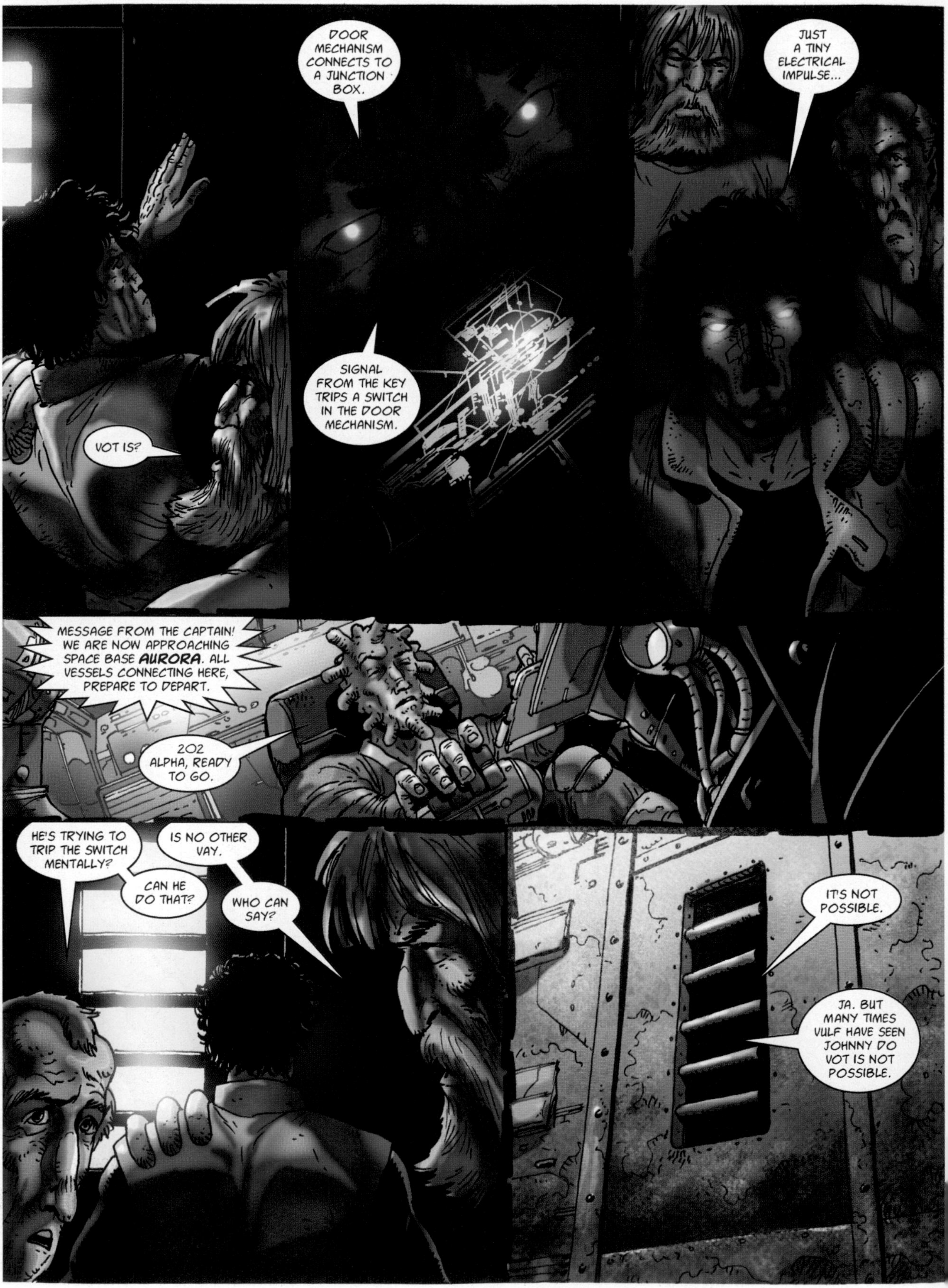
DOOR MECHANISM CONNECTS TO A JUNCTION BOX.
SIGNAL FROM THE KEY TRIPS A SWITCH IN THE DOOR MECHANISM.
VOT IS?
JUST A TINY ELECTRICAL IMPULSE...
MESSAGE FROM THE CAPTAIN! WE ARE NOW APPROACHING SPACE BASE AURORA. ALL VESSELS CONNECTING HERE, PREPARE TO DEPART.
202 ALPHA, READY TO GO.
HE'S TRYING TO TRIP THE SWITCH MENTALLY?
IS NO OTHER VAY.
CAN HE DO THAT?
WHO CAN SAY?
IT'S NOT POSSIBLE.
JA. BUT MANY TIMES VULF HAVE SEEN JOHNNY DO VOT IS NOT POSSIBLE.

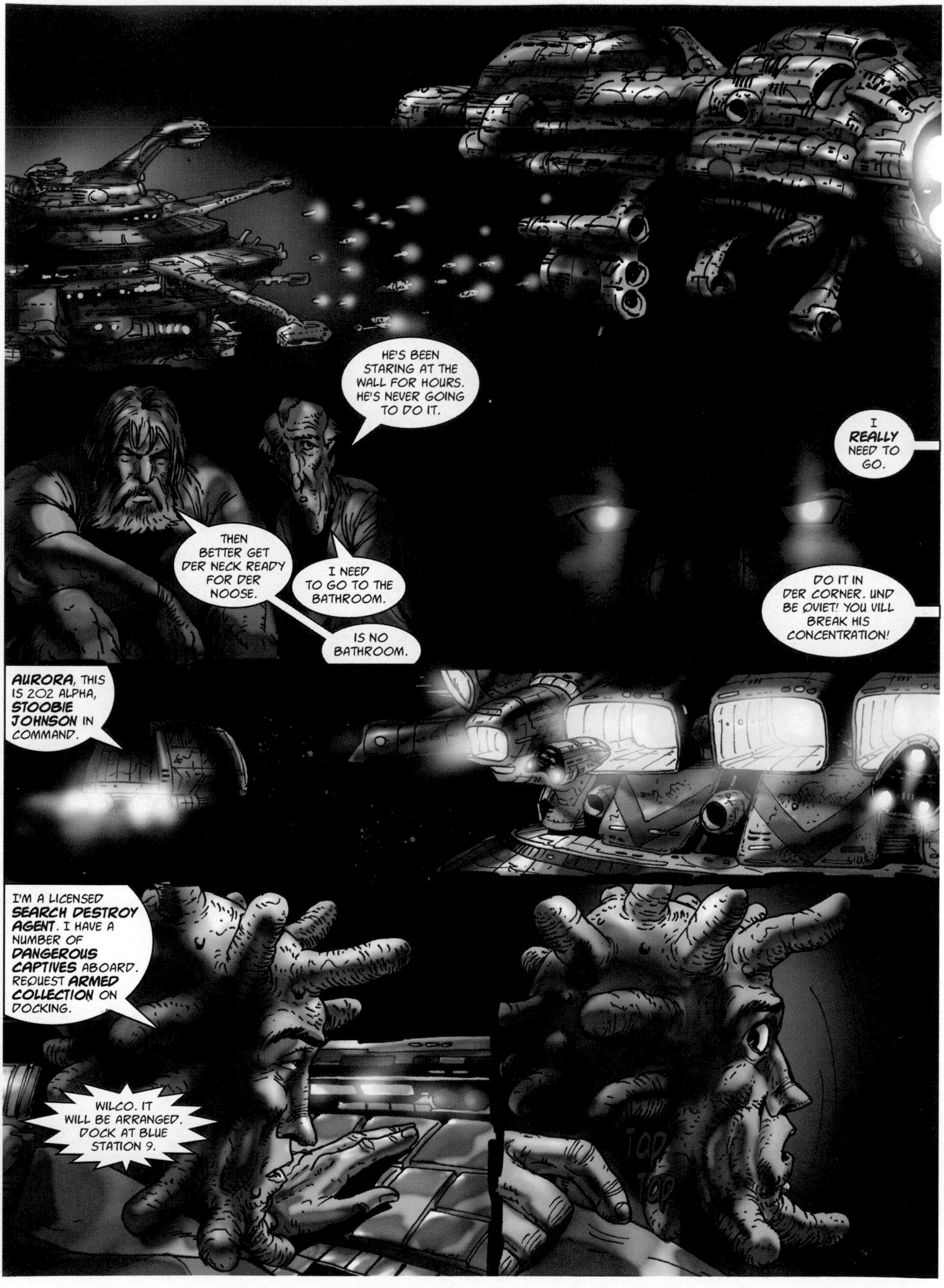
HE'S BEEN STARING AT THE WALL FOR HOURS. HE'S NEVER GOING TO DO IT.
THEN BETTER GET DER NECK READY FOR DER NOOSE.
I NEED TO GO TO THE BATHROOM.
IS NO BATHROOM.
I REALLY NEED TO GO.
DO IT IN DER CORNER. UND BE QUIET! YOU VILL BREAK HIS CONCENTRATION!
AURORA, THIS IS 202 ALPHA, STOOBIE JOHNSON IN COMMAND.
I'M A LICENSED SEARCH DESTROY AGENT. I HAVE A NUMBER OF DANGEROUS CAPTIVES ABOARD. REQUEST ARMED COLLECTION ON DOCKING.
WILCO. IT WILL BE ARRANGED. DOCK AT BLUE STATION 9.

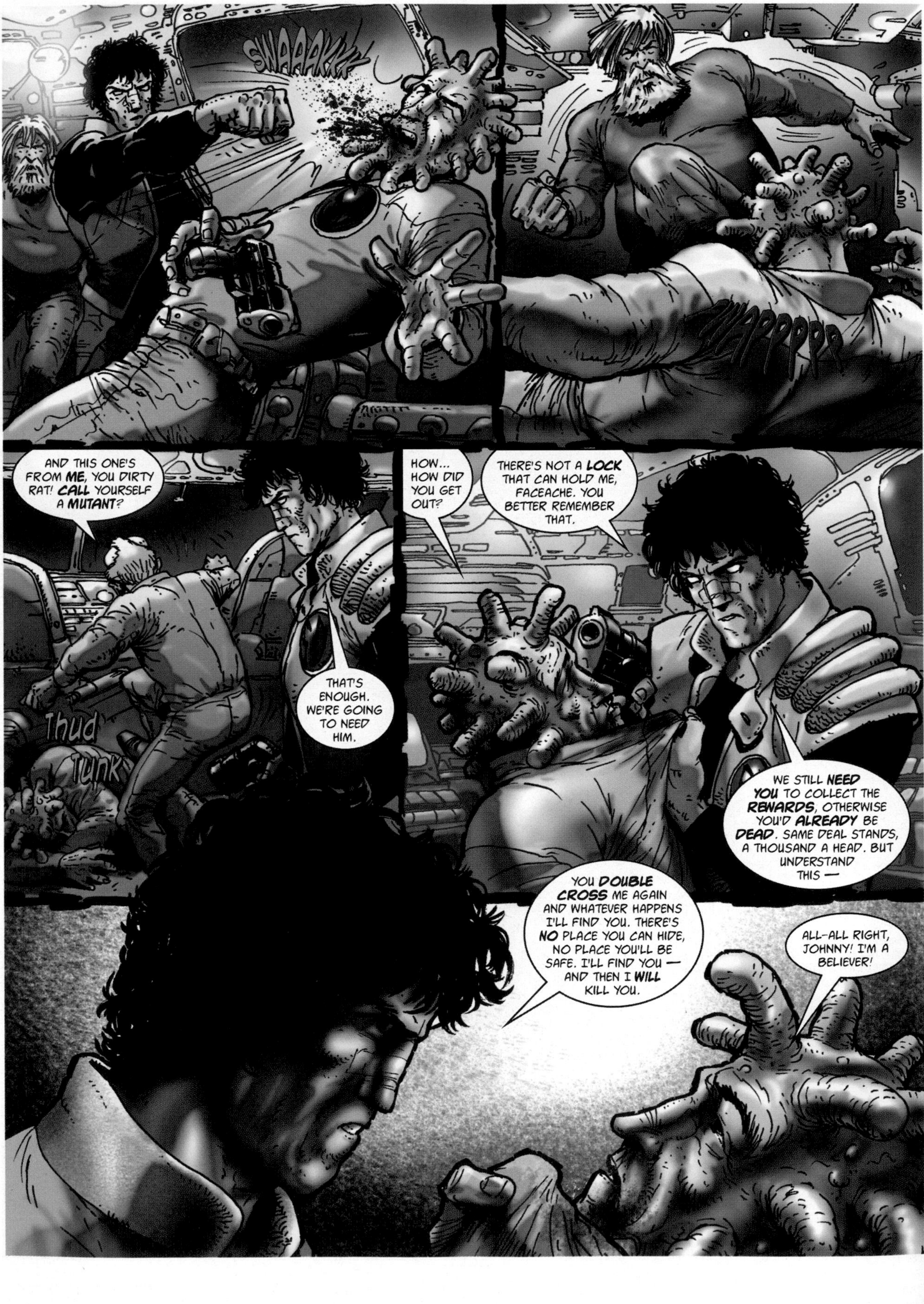

SNAAAKKK
SWAPPPPP
AND THIS ONE'S FROM ME, YOU DIRTY RAT! CALL YOURSELF A MUTANT?
THAT'S ENOUGH. WE'RE GOING TO NEED HIM.
Thud
Tunk
HOW... HOW DID YOU GET OUT?
THERE'S NOT A LOCK THAT CAN HOLD ME, FACEACHE. YOU BETTER REMEMBER THAT.
WE STILL NEED YOU TO COLLECT THE REWARDS, OTHERWISE YOU'D ALREADY BE DEAD. SAME DEAL STANDS, A THOUSAND A HEAD. BUT UNDERSTAND THIS —
YOU DOUBLE CROSS ME AGAIN AND WHATEVER HAPPENS I'LL FIND YOU. THERE'S NO PLACE YOU CAN HIDE, NO PLACE YOU'LL BE SAFE. I'LL FIND YOU — AND THEN I WILL KILL YOU.
ALL-ALL RIGHT, JOHNNY! I'M A BELIEVER!

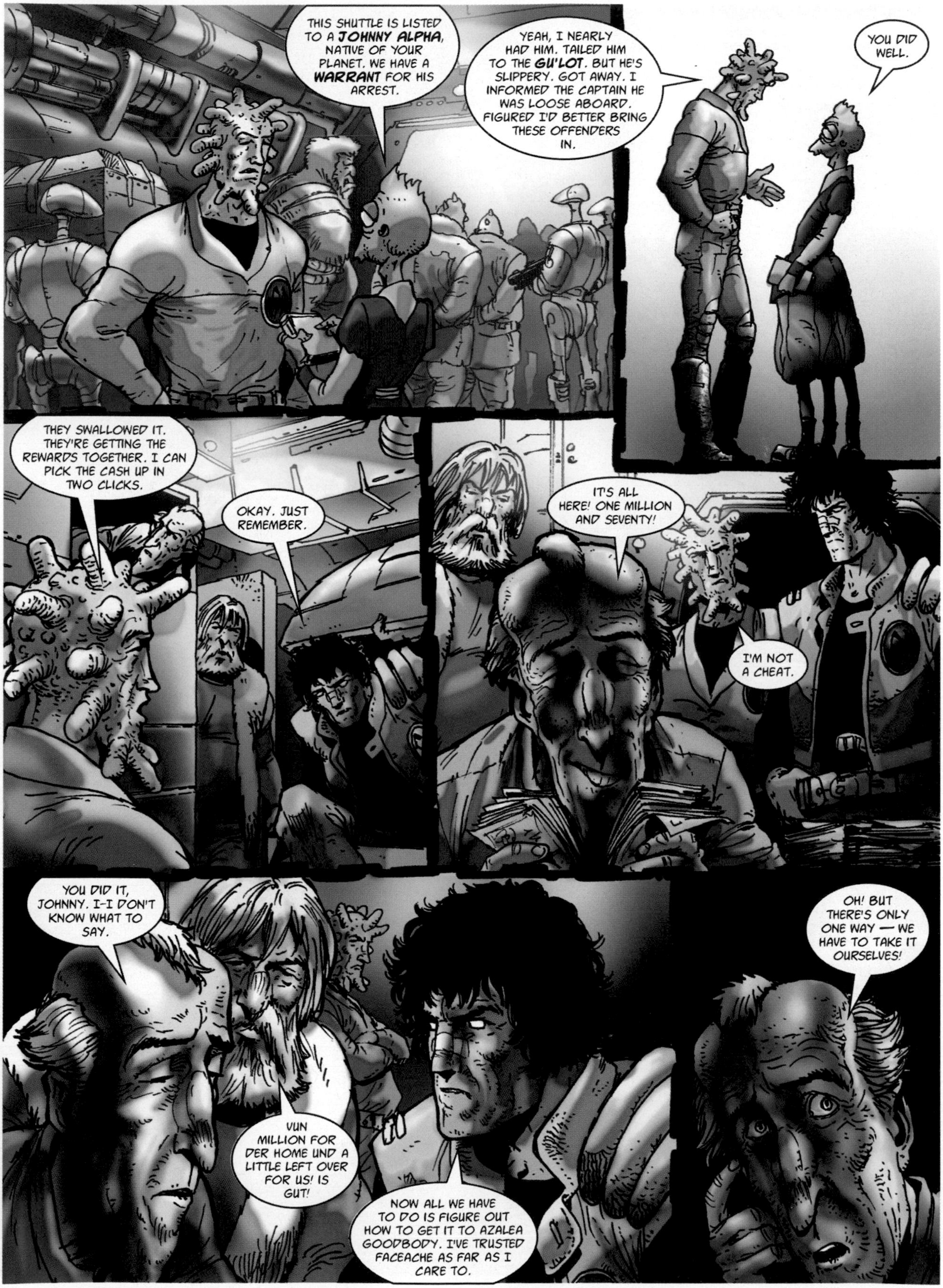
THIS SHUTTLE IS LISTED TO A JOHNNY ALPHA, NATIVE OF YOUR PLANET. WE HAVE A WARRANT FOR HIS ARREST.
YEAH, I NEARLY HAD HIM. TAILED HIM TO THE GU'LOT. BUT HE'S SLIPPERY. GOT AWAY. I INFORMED THE CAPTAIN HE WAS LOOSE ABOARD. FIGURED I'D BETTER BRING THESE OFFENDERS IN.
YOU DID WELL.
THEY SWALLOWED IT. THEY'RE GETTING THE REWARDS TOGETHER. I CAN PICK THE CASH UP IN TWO CLICKS.
OKAY. JUST REMEMBER.
IT'S ALL HERE! ONE MILLION AND SEVENTY!
I'M NOT A CHEAT.
YOU DID IT, JOHNNY. I-I DON'T KNOW WHAT TO SAY.
VUN MILLION FOR DER HOME UND A LITTLE LEFT OVER FOR US! IS GUT!
NOW ALL WE HAVE TO DO IS FIGURE OUT HOW TO GET IT TO AZALEA GOODBODY. I'VE TRUSTED FACEACHE AS FAR AS I CARE TO.
OH! BUT THERE'S ONLY ONE WAY — WE HAVE TO TAKE IT OURSELVES!

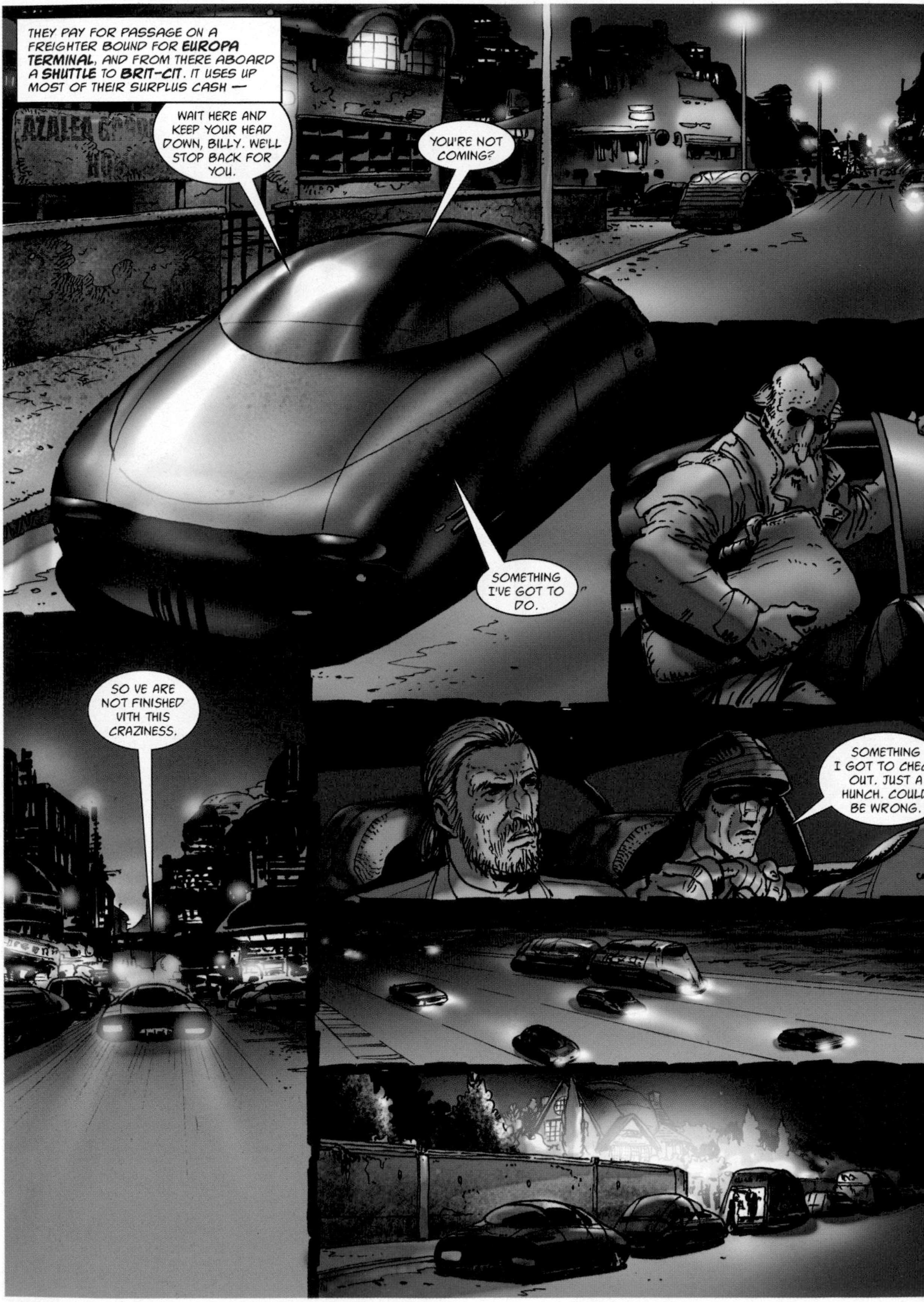
THEY PAY FOR PASSAGE ON A FREIGHTER BOUND FOR EUROPA TERMINAL, AND FROM THERE ABOARD A SHUTTLE TO BRIT-CIT. IT USES UP MOST OF THEIR SURPLUS CASH —
WAIT HERE AND KEEP YOUR HEAD DOWN, BILLY. WE'LL STOP BACK FOR YOU.
YOU'RE NOT COMING?
SOMETHING I'VE GOT TO DO.
SO VE ARE NOT FINISHED VITH THIS CRAZINESS.
SOMETHING I GOT TO CHECK OUT. JUST A HUNCH. COULD BE WRONG.

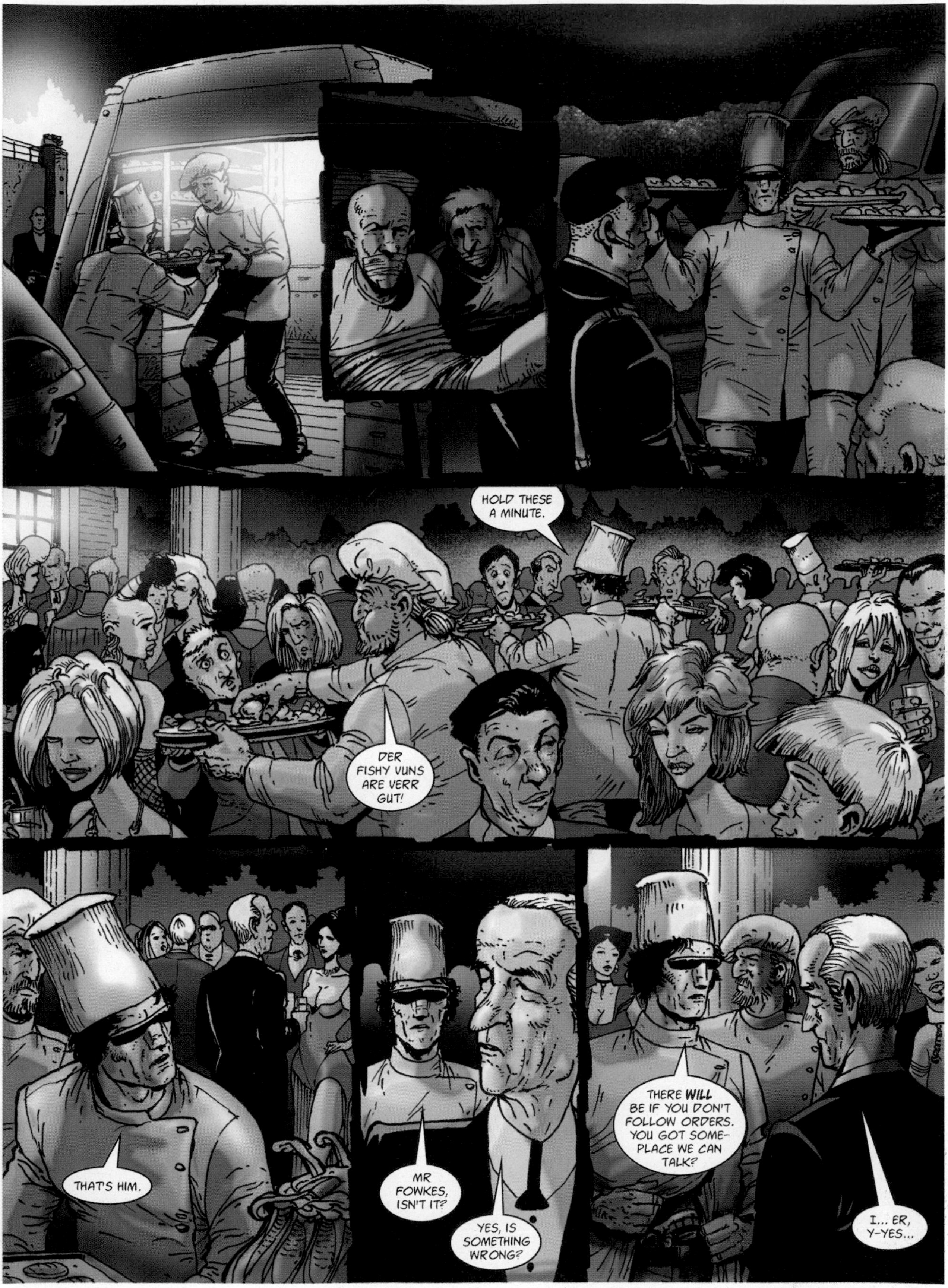
HOLD THESE A MINUTE.
DER FISHY VUNS ARE VERR GUT!
THAT'S HIM.
MR FOWKES, ISN'T IT?
YES, IS SOMETHING WRONG?
THERE WILL BE IF YOU DON'T FOLLOW ORDERS. YOU GOT SOME-PLACE WE CAN TALK?
I... ER, Y-YES...

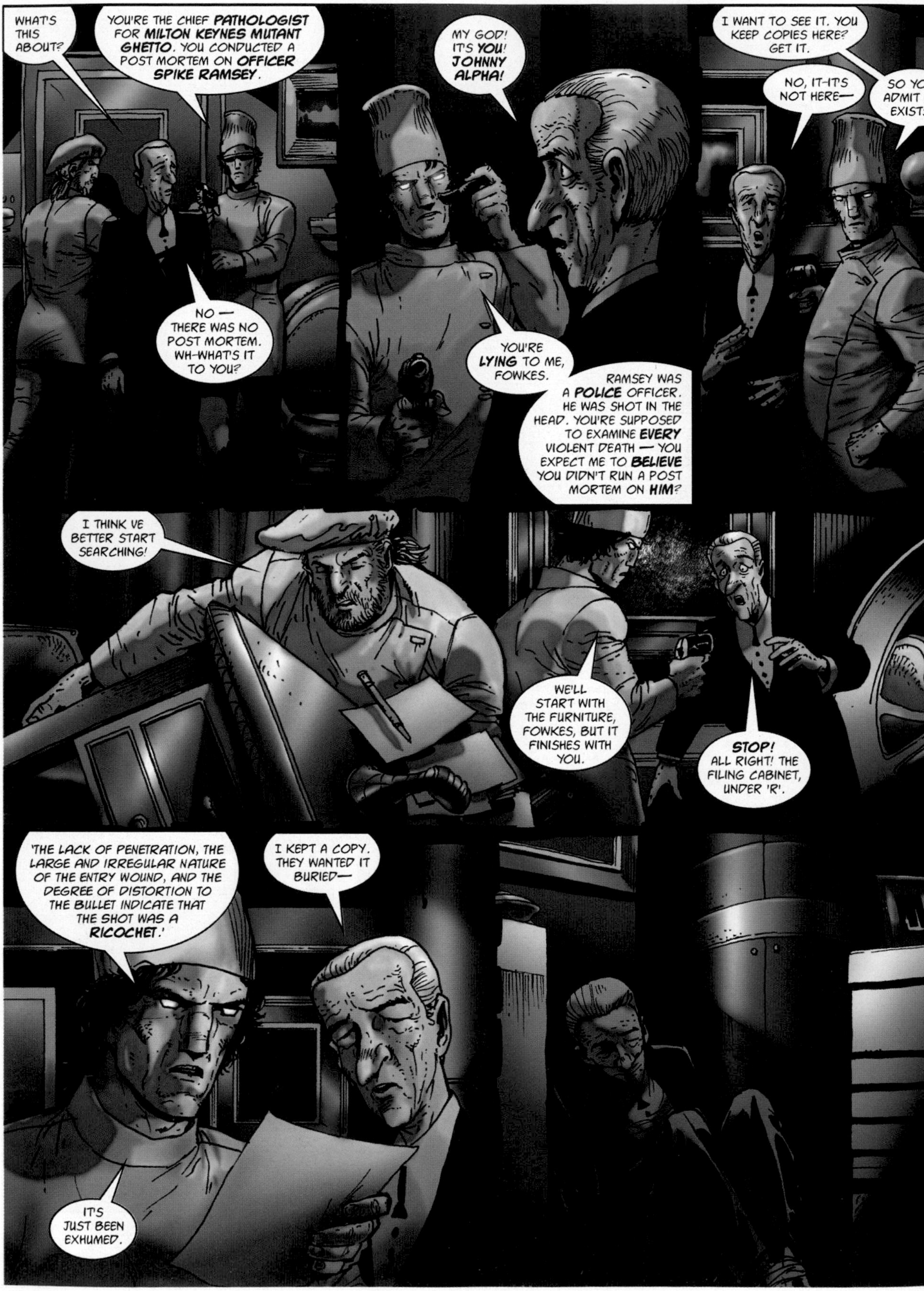

WHAT'S THIS ABOUT?
YOU'RE THE CHIEF PATHOLOGIST FOR MILTON KEYNES MUTANT GHETTO. YOU CONDUCTED A POST MORTEM ON OFFICER SPIKE RAMSEY.
NO — THERE WAS NO POST MORTEM. WH-WHAT'S IT TO YOU?
MY GOD! IT'S YOU! JOHNNY ALPHA!
YOU'RE LYING TO ME, FOWKES.
RAMSEY WAS A POLICE OFFICER. HE WAS SHOT IN THE HEAD. YOU'RE SUPPOSED TO EXAMINE EVERY VIOLENT DEATH — YOU EXPECT ME TO BELIEVE YOU DIDN'T RUN A POST MORTEM ON HIM?
I WANT TO SEE IT. YOU KEEP COPIES HERE? GET IT.
NO, IT-IT'S NOT HERE—
SO YOU ADMIT IT EXISTS.
I THINK VE BETTER START SEARCHING!
WE'LL START WITH THE FURNITURE, FOWKES, BUT IT FINISHES WITH YOU.
STOP! ALL RIGHT! THE FILING CABINET, UNDER 'R'.
'THE LACK OF PENETRATION, THE LARGE AND IRREGULAR NATURE OF THE ENTRY WOUND, AND THE DEGREE OF DISTORTION TO THE BULLET INDICATE THAT THE SHOT WAS A RICOCHET.'
I KEPT A COPY. THEY WANTED IT BURIED—
IT'S JUST BEEN EXHUMED.

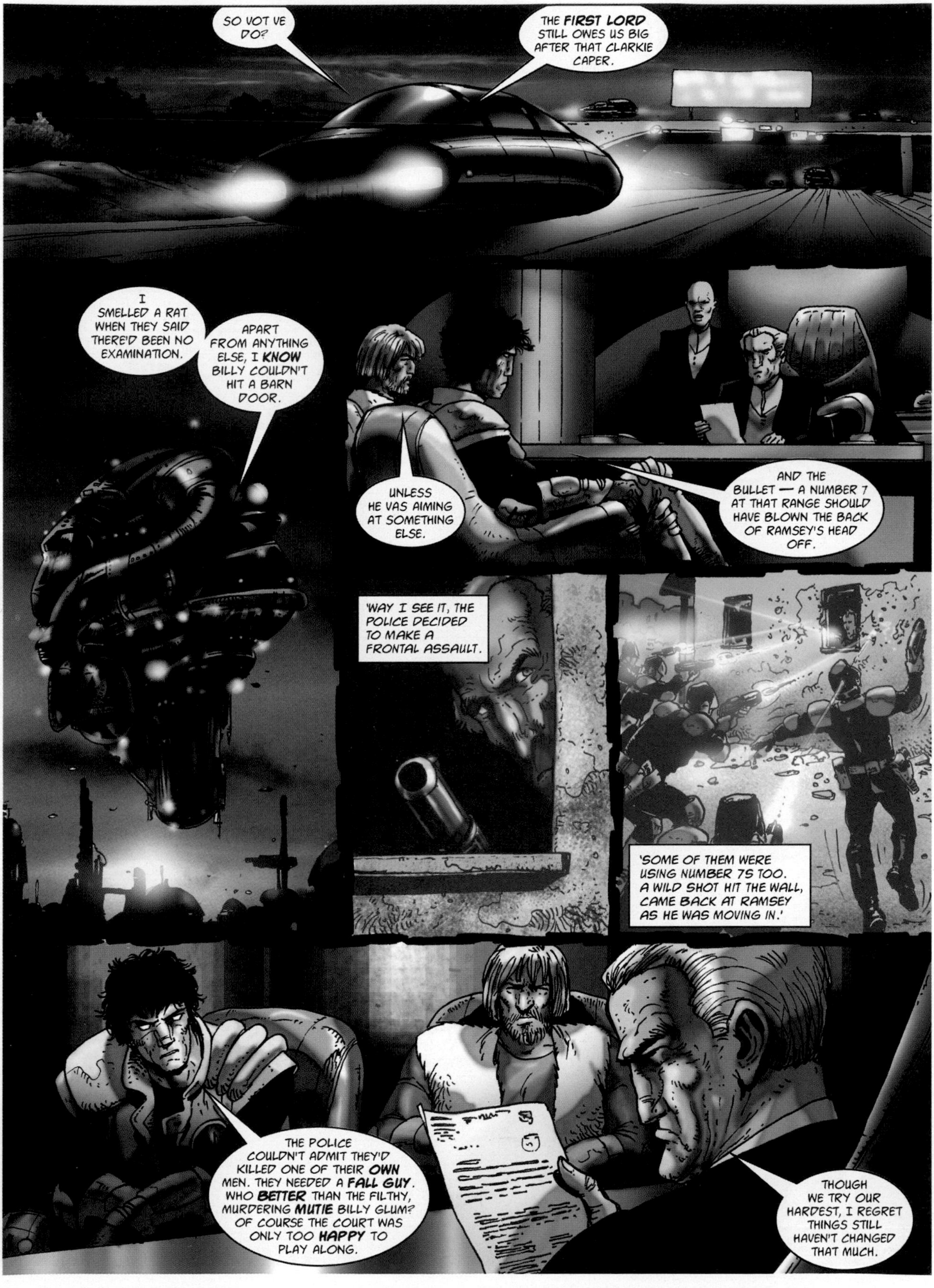
SO VOT VE DO?
THE FIRST LORD STILL OWES US BIG AFTER THAT CLARKIE CAPER.
I SMELLED A RAT WHEN THEY SAID THERE'D BEEN NO EXAMINATION.
APART FROM ANYTHING ELSE, I KNOW BILLY COULDN'T HIT A BARN DOOR.
UNLESS HE VAS AIMING AT SOMETHING ELSE.
AND THE BULLET — A NUMBER 7 AT THAT RANGE SHOULD HAVE BLOWN THE BACK OF RAMSEY'S HEAD OFF.
'WAY I SEE IT, THE POLICE DECIDED TO MAKE A FRONTAL ASSAULT.
'SOME OF THEM WERE USING NUMBER 7S TOO. A WILD SHOT HIT THE WALL, CAME BACK AT RAMSEY AS HE WAS MOVING IN.'
THE POLICE COULDN'T ADMIT THEY'D KILLED ONE OF THEIR OWN MEN. THEY NEEDED A FALL GUY. WHO BETTER THAN THE FILTHY, MURDERING MUTIE BILLY GLUM? OF COURSE THE COURT WAS ONLY TOO HAPPY TO PLAY ALONG.
THOUGH WE TRY OUR HARDEST, I REGRET THINGS STILL HAVEN'T CHANGED THAT MUCH.

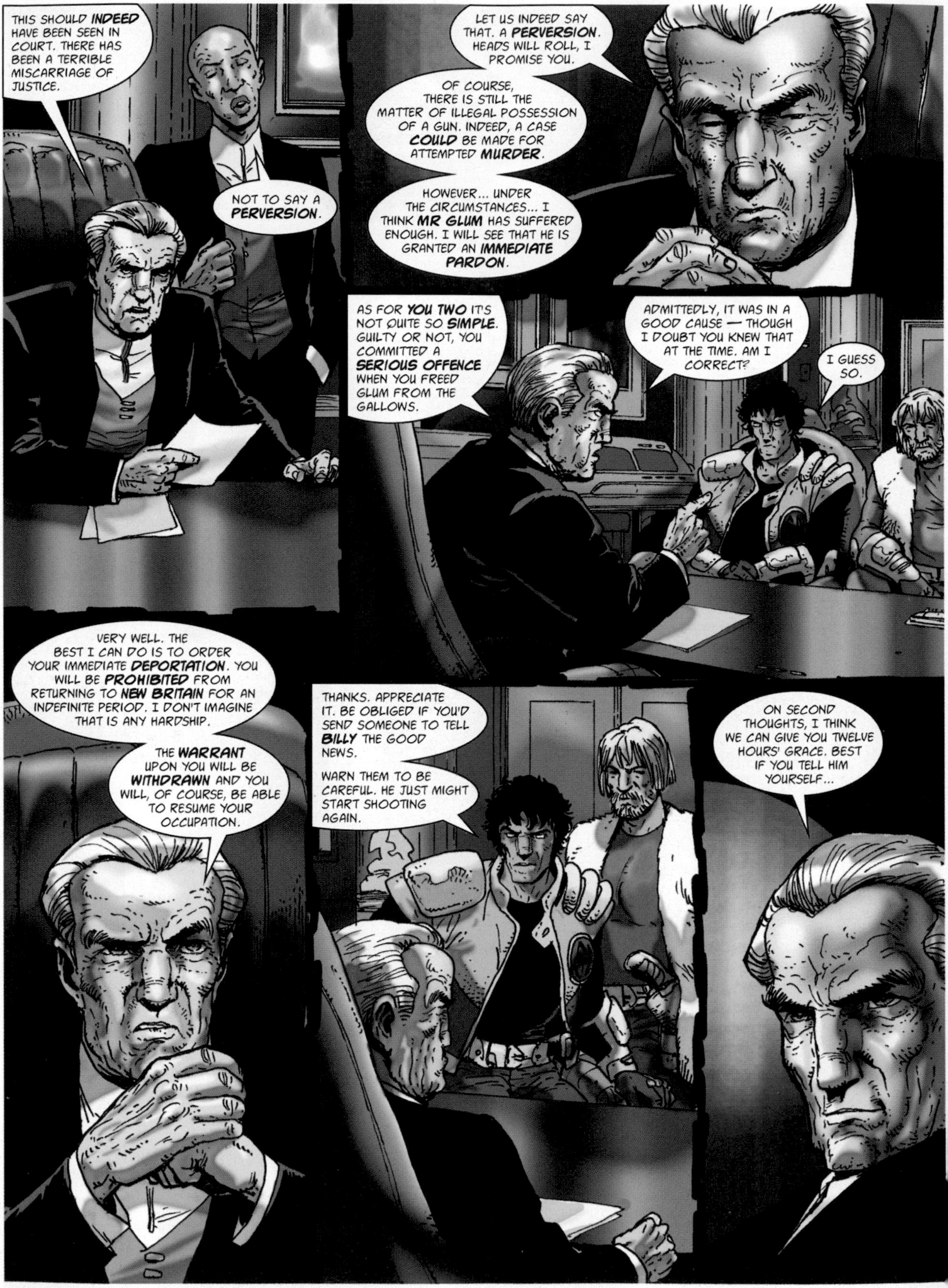

THIS SHOULD INDEED HAVE BEEN SEEN IN COURT. THERE HAS BEEN A TERRIBLE MISCARRIAGE OF JUSTICE.
NOT TO SAY A PERVERSION.
LET US INDEED SAY THAT. A PERVERSION. HEADS WILL ROLL, I PROMISE YOU.
OF COURSE, THERE IS STILL THE MATTER OF ILLEGAL POSSESSION OF A GUN. INDEED, A CASE COULD BE MADE FOR ATTEMPTED MURDER.
HOWEVER... UNDER THE CIRCUMSTANCES... I THINK MR GLUM HAS SUFFERED ENOUGH. I WILL SEE THAT HE IS GRANTED AN IMMEDIATE PARDON.
AS FOR YOU TWO IT'S NOT QUITE SO SIMPLE. GUILTY OR NOT, YOU COMMITTED A SERIOUS OFFENCE WHEN YOU FREED GLUM FROM THE GALLOWS.
ADMITTEDLY, IT WAS IN A GOOD CAUSE — THOUGH I DOUBT YOU KNEW THAT AT THE TIME. AM I CORRECT?
I GUESS SO.
VERY WELL. THE BEST I CAN DO IS TO ORDER YOUR IMMEDIATE DEPORTATION. YOU WILL BE PROHIBITED FROM RETURNING TO NEW BRITAIN FOR AN INDEFINITE PERIOD. I DON'T IMAGINE THAT IS ANY HARDSHIP.
THE WARRANT UPON YOU WILL BE WITHDRAWN AND YOU WILL, OF COURSE, BE ABLE TO RESUME YOUR OCCUPATION.
THANKS. APPRECIATE IT. BE OBLIGED IF YOU'D SEND SOMEONE TO TELL BILLY THE GOOD NEWS.
WARN THEM TO BE CAREFUL. HE JUST MIGHT START SHOOTING AGAIN.
ON SECOND THOUGHTS, I THINK WE CAN GIVE YOU TWELVE HOURS' GRACE. BEST IF YOU TELL HIM YOURSELF...

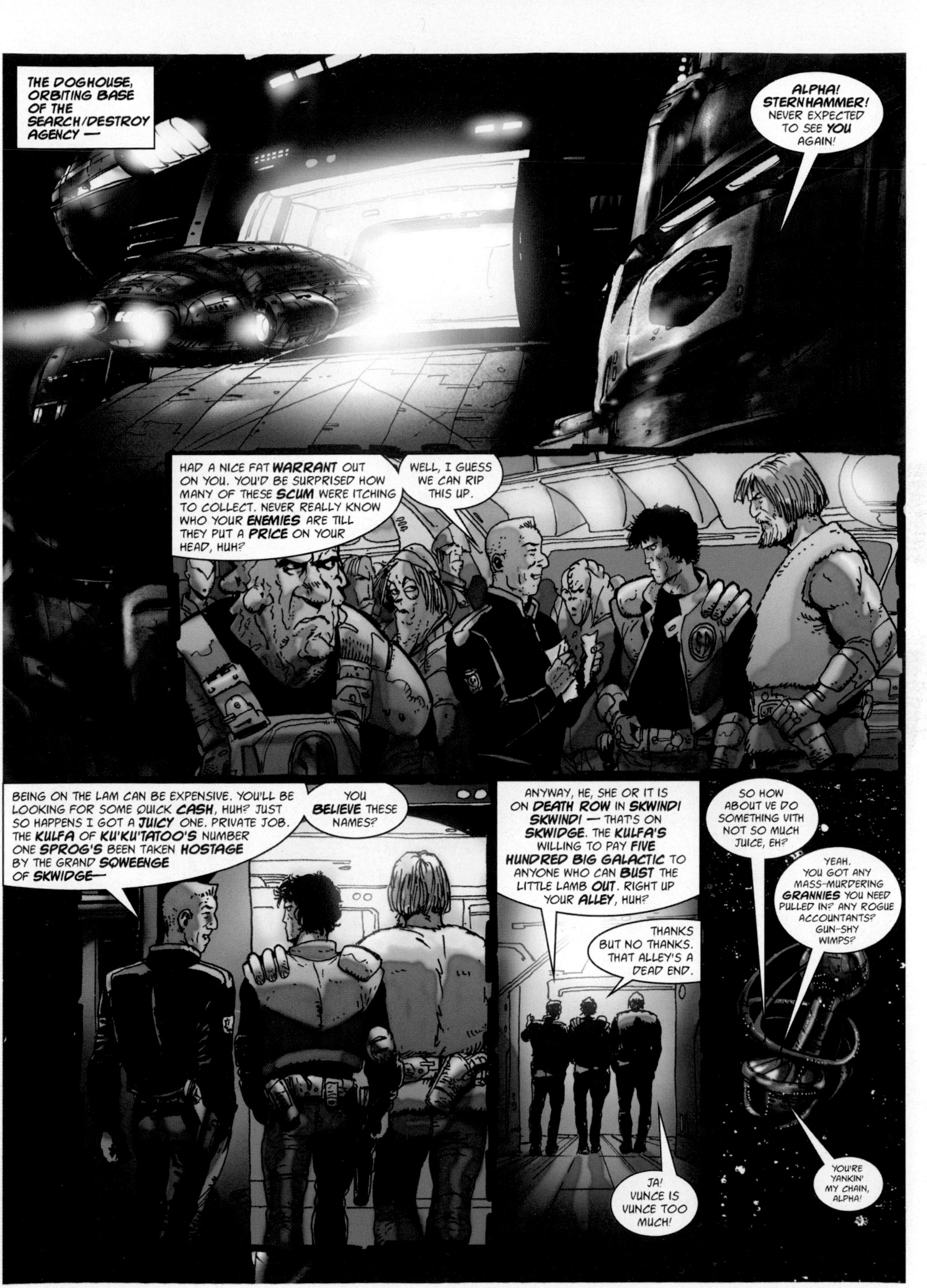

THE DOGHOUSE, ORBITING BASE OF THE SEARCH/DESTROY AGENCY —
ALPHA! STERNHAMMER! NEVER EXPECTED TO SEE YOU AGAIN!
HAD A NICE FAT WARRANT OUT ON YOU. YOU'D BE SURPRISED HOW MANY OF THESE SCUM WERE ITCHING TO COLLECT. NEVER REALLY KNOW WHO YOUR ENEMIES ARE TILL THEY PUT A PRICE ON YOUR HEAD, HUH?
WELL, I GUESS WE CAN RIP THIS UP.
BEING ON THE LAM CAN BE EXPENSIVE. YOU'LL BE LOOKING FOR SOME QUICK CASH, HUH? JUST SO HAPPENS I GOT A JUICY ONE. PRIVATE JOB. THE KULFA OF KU'KU'TATOO'S NUMBER ONE SPROG'S BEEN TAKEN HOSTAGE BY THE GRAND SQWEENGE OF SKWIDGE—
YOU BELIEVE THESE NAMES?
ANYWAY, HE, SHE OR IT IS ON DEATH ROW IN SKWINDI SKWINDI — THAT'S ON SKWIDGE. THE KULFA'S WILLING TO PAY FIVE HUNDRED BIG GALACTIC TO ANYONE WHO CAN BUST THE LITTLE LAMB OUT. RIGHT UP YOUR ALLEY, HUH?
THANKS BUT NO THANKS. THAT ALLEY'S A DEAD END.
JA! VUNCE IS VUNCE TOO MUCH!
SO HOW ABOUT VE DO SOMETHING VITH NOT SO MUCH JUICE, EH?
YEAH. YOU GOT ANY MASS-MURDERING GRANNIES YOU NEED PULLED IN? ANY ROGUE ACCOUNTANTS? GUN-SHY WIMPS?
YOU'RE YANKIN' MY CHAIN, ALPHA!

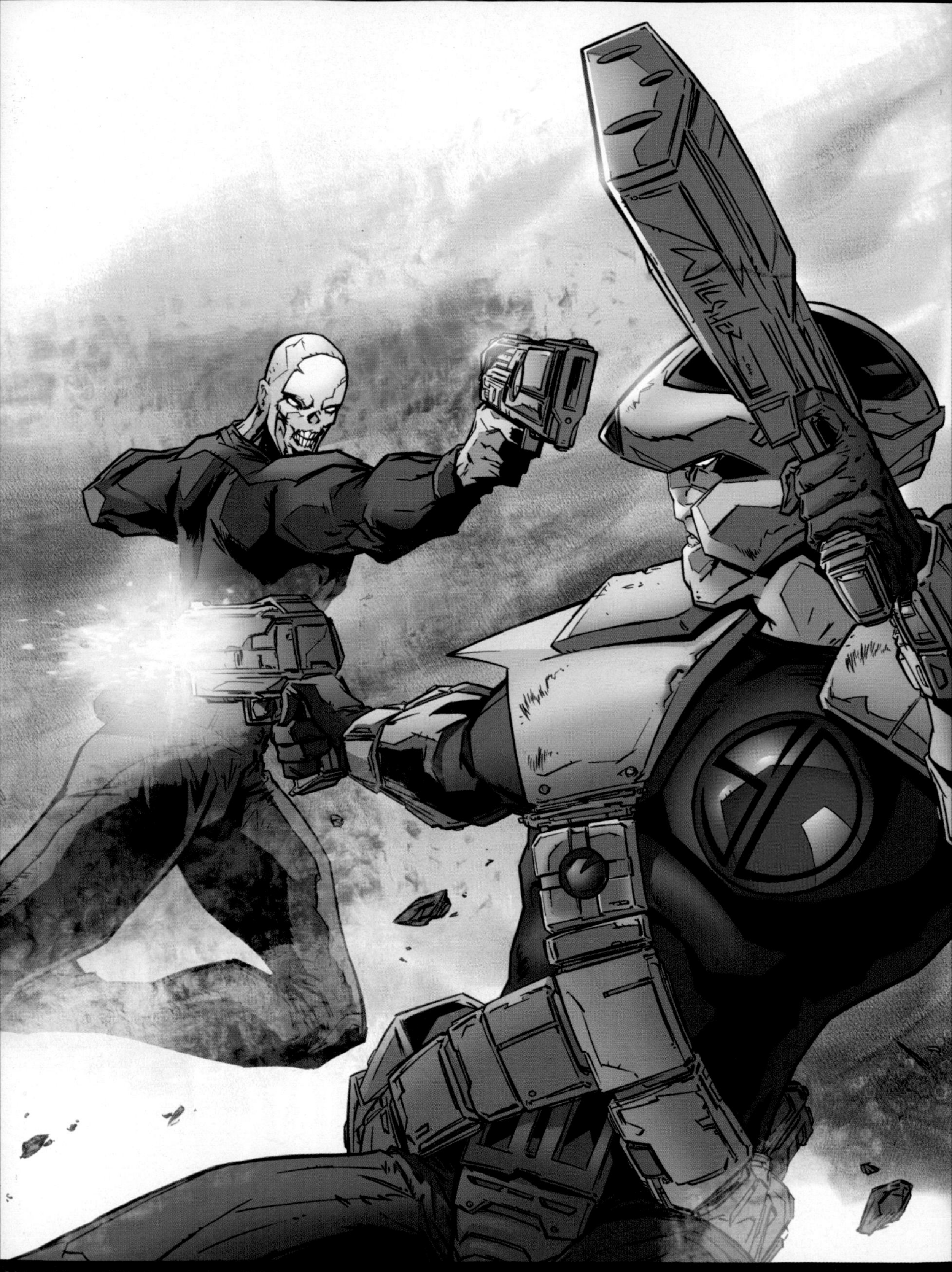
WILLSHER

2000 AD Prog 1408: Cover by **Ben Willsher**

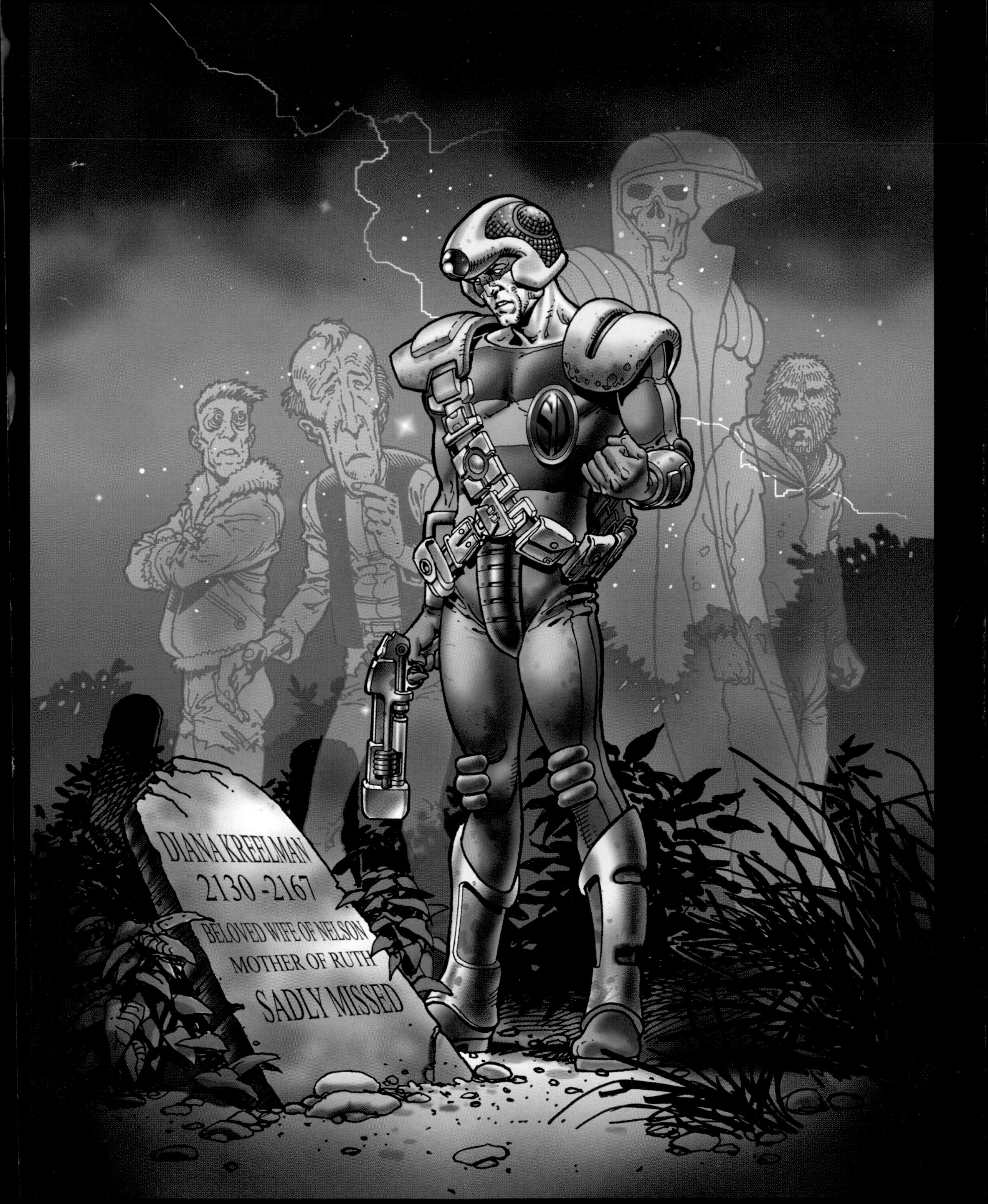
DIANA KREELMAN
2130 -2167
BELOVED WIFE OF NELSON
MOTHER OF RUTH
SADLY MISSED

2000 AD Prog 1415: Cover by **Cliff Robinson**

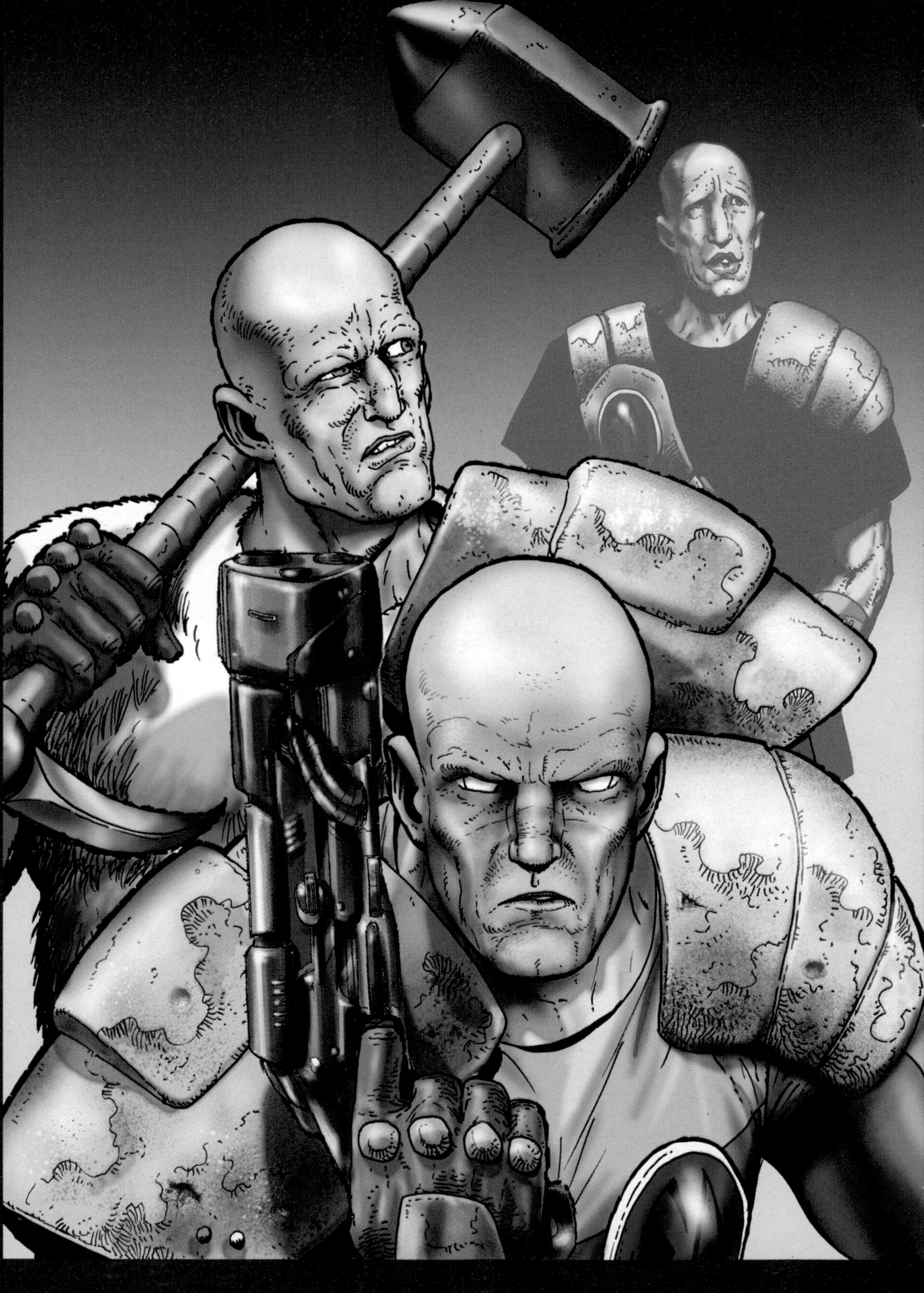

2000 AD Prog 1469: Cover by **Carlos Ezquerra**

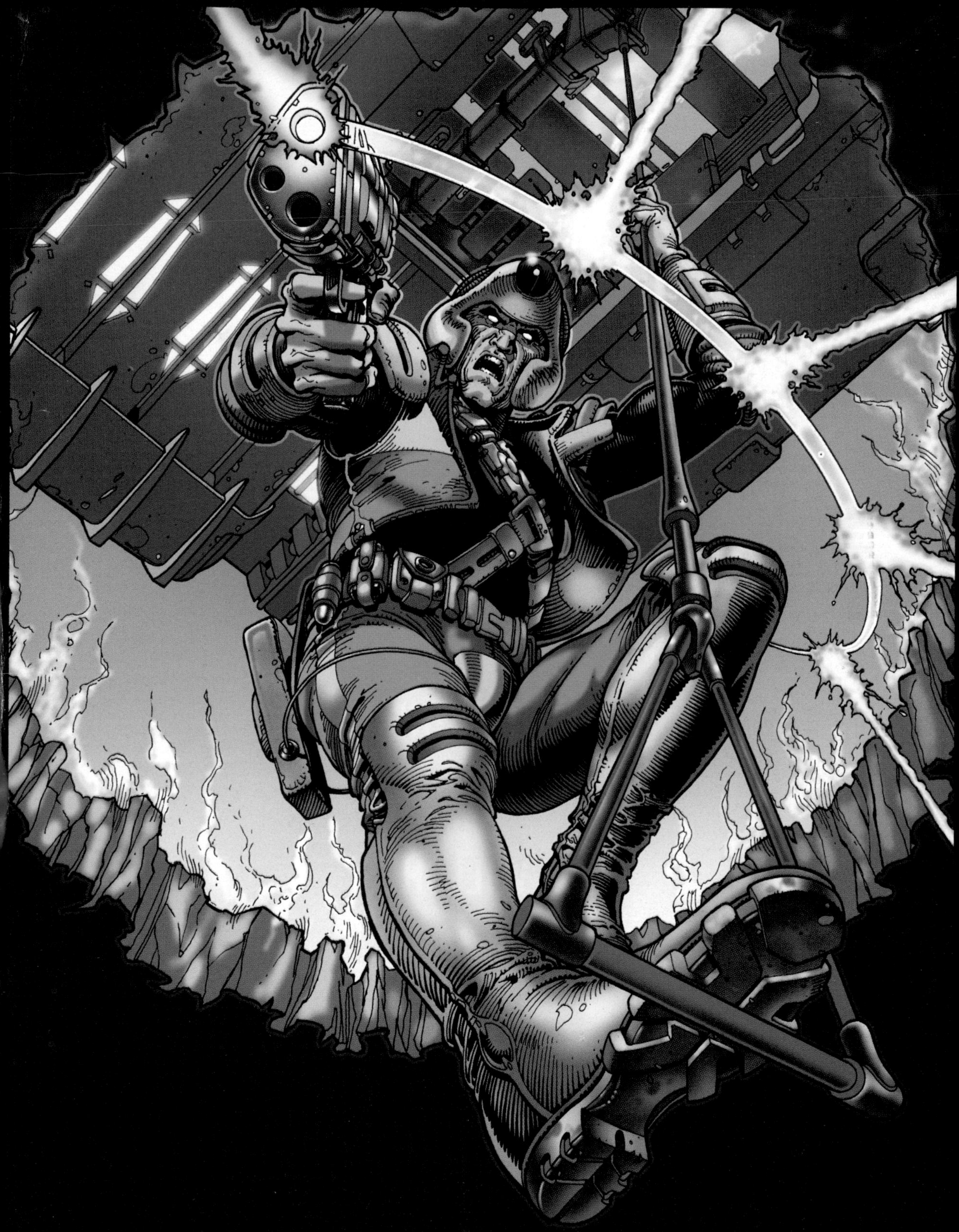

2000 AD Prog 1567: Cover by **Cliff Robinson**

JOHN WAGNER

John Wagner has been scripting for *2000 AD* for more years than he cares to remember. His creations include *Judge Dredd, Strontium Dog, Ace Trucking, Al's Baby, Button Man* and *Mean Machine*. Outside of *2000 AD* his credits include *Star Wars, Lobo, The Punisher* and the critically acclaimed *A History of Violence*.

CARLOS EZQUERRA

As co-creator of *Judge Dredd* **Carlos Ezquerra** designed the classic original costume as well as visually conceptualising Mega-City One. He also co-created *Strontium Dog*. He has also illustrated *A.B.C. Warriors, Judge Anderson, Tharg the Mighty, Al's Baby* and *Cursed Earth Koburn* amongst many others. Outside of the Galaxy's Greatest Comic, Ezquerra first illustrated *Third World War* in *Crisis* magazine, and has since become a regular collaborator with Garth Ennis, working on *Adventures in the Rifle Brigade, Bloody Mary, Just a Pilgrim, Condors* and *The Magnificent Kevin*. He also pencilled two special *Preacher* episodes.

CLIFF ROBINSON

Cliff Robinson is one of *2000 AD*'s longest-serving artists, having made his debut with a *Future Shock* way back in Prog 362! Since then, he has co-created *Mother Earth*, and illustrated numerous *Judge Dredd* strips, as well as *Future Shocks, Judge Anderson* and *Venus Bluegenes*.

BEN WILLSHER

Ben Willsher has provided the art for several *2000 AD* strips, including *Judge Dredd* and *Sinister Dexter*.